*Yale Historical Publications, Miscellany, 135*

# South Africa's City of Diamonds

*Mine Workers and Monopoly Capitalism in Kimberley, 1867–1895*

William H. Worger

*Yale University Press*
*New Haven and London*

Published under the direction of the Department of
History of Yale University with assistance from the
income of the Frederick John Kingsbury Memorial
Fund.

Designed by James J. Johnson
and set in Aster Roman type.
Printed in the United States of America by
Thomson-Shore, Inc., Dexter, Michigan

*Library of Congress Cataloging-in-Publication Data*

Worger, William H.
    South Africa's city of diamonds.

    (Yale historical publications, Miscellany, 135)
    Bibliography: p.
    Includes index.
    1. Diamond industry and trade—South Africa—
Kimberley—History—19th century. 2. Diamond
miners—South Africa—Kimberley—History—19th
century. 3. Blacks—Employment—South Africa—
Kimberley—History—19th century. 4. Rural-
urban migration—South Africa—History—19th
century. 5. Kimberley (South Africa)—
Industries—History—19th century. I. Title.
II. Series.
HD9677.S63K568  1987    331.7′622382′0968711    86–24724
ISBN 0–300–03716–3

10  9  8  7  6  5  4  3  2  1

*To the memory of my parents,*
*Richard and Stella Worger*

# Contents

# Plates, Figures, Maps, and Tables

MAPS

TABLES

# *Preface*

The rise of the Kimberley diamond industry in the last three decades of the nineteenth century transformed southern Africa. Prior to the discovery of diamonds in the late 1860s, the societies of the subcontinent had been agricultural, often semisubsistent, with few links among the major black states—ruled by Cetshwayo, Lobengula, Moshoeshoe, and Sekhukhune—the coastal British possessions of the Cape Colony and Natal, and the interior Boer polities of the Orange Free State and the South African Republic. Diamonds encouraged British imperialism to move back into the interior to secure the newfound wealth for the Crown, established a huge urban community in the middle of the subcontinent, brought tens of thousands of blacks and whites into daily contact in the industrial workplace, and attracted millions of pounds of capital from foreign investors. The ensuing struggles between workers and employers, producers and merchants, locals and foreigners, yielded the most distinctive features of South African society: a huge black migrant labor force moving between impoverished rural homes and the urban workplace; racially discriminatory legal practices which subjected blacks to a constant round of pass-law arrests and to incarceration in closed compounds, locations (or ghettos), convict stations and prisons; the splitting of the industrial work force along racial lines between constrained blacks and relatively privileged whites; and the domination of the mining industry by a few magnates repatriating the bulk of profits to foreign shareholders. Indeed, the diamond industry, within a decade of its establishment, had laid the foundations for a single regional economy stretching from the Cape in the south to the Zambezi in the north and changing forever the relations between black and white, Boer and Briton, Africa and Europe.

This book examines the history of Kimberley and the mining industry from the discovery of diamonds (and the subsequent rush by thousands of prospectors) in the late 1860s to the construction of a monopoly enterprise by Cecil Rhodes and De Beers Consolidated Mines in the 1880s and 1890s. The book has two parts. The first examines the period 1867–85 through a series of chronologically parallel thematic chapters on the transition from individual to large-scale organization of diamond mining, the subjugation of rural black societies to the demands of the industry, the use of law to build an urban community for blacks most resembling a prison, and the crushing and cooptation of white labor. The second part comprises two consecutive narrative chapters that show how a series of crises in the industry led to the establishment of a monopoly enterprise and the creation of a company town. Unlike previous work on this subject, which concentrated ad nauseum on the "Randlords" (Cecil Rhodes, Barney Barnato, and so forth)—usually in a parasitically biographical way, with authors plagiarizing one another freely—this study constructs a new history of the diamond industry based on research done in the company archives of De Beers Consolidated Mines, the archives of the Standard Bank, government records, manuscript collections, and newspapers.

This research could not have been completed without the generous financial support of four organizations: the New Zealand Universities Grants Committee, the Concilium on International and Area Studies and the Council on African Studies, both of Yale University, and the Killam Trust, Dalhousie University.

Numerous librarians and archivists assisted me in my research, and I am grateful to them all. In particular, I would like to thank Mrs. Muriel Macey of the Kimberley Public Library, Mr. Moore Crossey of the Sterling Memorial Library, Mrs. Maryna Fraser of Barlow Rand, Mrs. Gwynneth Crothall and Dr. Moonyean Buys of De Beers Consolidated Mines, Ms. H. Norton of the Alexander MacGregor Museum, and, above all, Ms. Barbara Conradie, formerly of the Cape Archives and now at the Standard Bank.

In writing this book I have benefited from the comments of many people. Frederick Cooper and Charles van Onselen subjected chapter 3 to searching criticism. Members of the Southern Africa Research Program at Yale University submitted themselves to reading voluminous drafts of the dissertation version for more years than they or I care to remember. I thank all of them for their perceptive criticism and their helpful advice.

My teachers and friends have been my most conscientious critics. Keith Sorrenson introduced me to African history. Leonard Thompson supervised the dissertation on which this book is based. David Robinson made detailed comments on the early chapters, and Robert Harms read drafts of the entire manuscript. Conrad Russell provided the insights of an outside reader. Charles Ambler and Robert Baum, in countless conversations about our respective historical enterprises, clarified my conception of what it was I was doing. Paul Clark provided that rare combination of generous support and harsh criticism that only a close friend can. Nancy Clark, my wife, read and reread innumerable drafts of dissertation and book until finally even she said, "Enough!"

# Abbreviations

| | |
|---|---|
| 1/KIM | Kimberley Magistrates' Archives, CA |
| 3/KIM | Kimberley Municipal Archives, CA |
| AG | Attorney General's Archives, CA |
| ATC | Administrator of Transvaal Colony Archives, TA |
| BMB | Bultfontein Mining Board Archives, DBA |
| *BPP* | *British Parliamentary Papers* |
| BRA | Barlow Rand Archives |
| BSA | British South Africa Company |
| CA | Cape Archives Depot |
| *CGHPP* | *Cape of Good Hope Parliamentary Papers* |
| CO | Colonial Office Archives, CA |
| COSC | Colonial Office Sundry Committees Archives, CA |
| CR | Company Records, CA |
| CSO | Colonial Secretary's Archives, NAD |
| DBA | De Beers Consolidated Mines Archives |
| DB Reel | Microfilmed Records of De Beers Consolidated Mines' Secretary, DBA |
| DOK | Deeds Office Kimberley Archives, CA |
| DTMB | Dutoitspan Mining Board Archives, DBA |
| EC | Executive Committee Archives, CA |
| GH | Government House Archives, CA |
| GLW | Griqualand West Archives, CA |
| GM/LO | Extracts from the Standard Bank's Records, Henry Papers |
| GMO | General Manager's Archives, SBA |
| HA | House of Assembly Archives, CA |
| HE | H. E. Eckstein Archives, BRA |

| | |
|---|---|
| IDB | Illicit Diamond Buying |
| INSP | Inspector's Archives, SBA |
| JPL | Johannesburg Public Library |
| KCDM | Kimberley Central Diamond Mining Company Archives, DBA |
| KDM | Kimberley Diamond Mining Company Archives, DBA |
| KMB | Kimberley Mining Board Archives, DBA |
| KMBS | Kimberley Mine Benefit Society Archives, DBA |
| KPL | Kimberley Public Library |
| LC | Limited Liability Company Archives, CA |
| LND | Lands Department Archives, CA |
| LSAE | London and South Africa Exploration Company Archives, DBA |
| NA | Native Affairs Archives, CA |
| *NABB* | *Native Affairs Blue Book* |
| NAD | Natal Archives Depot |
| PMO | Prime Minister's Office Archives, CA |
| PWD | Public Works Department Archives, CA |
| SAL | South African Library |
| SBA | Standard Bank Archives |
| SGGLW | Surveyor General Griqualand West Archives, CA |
| SN | Superintendent of Native Affairs Archives, TA |
| SNA | Secretary of Native Affairs Archives, NAD |
| TA | Transvaal Archives Depot |
| Theal | Theal Papers, CA |
| UCT | University of Cape Town Library |
| USPG | United Society for the Propagation of the Gospel Archives |

# Prologue: 1867

In 1867 Wilkie Collins began writing *The Moonstone*, the first detective story to appear in the English language. The novel recounts the fictional travels of an enormous yellow diamond—"growing and lessening in lustre with the waxing and waning of the moon"—from the time of its theft by Muslims from the forehead of a Hindu deity in 1026, through its subsequent looting by the British from the sultan of Mysore in 1799 and its possession by various unfortunate owners in Britain, up to its return in 1850 to the sacred city and the statue from which it had originally been taken. At once cursed and mysterious, at least to the unbeliever, the moonstone is also quite prosaic:

> As large, or nearly, as a plover's egg! The light that streamed from it was the light of the harvest moon. When you looked down into the stone, you looked into a yellow deep that drew your eyes into it so that they saw nothing else. It seemed unfathomable; this jewel, that you could hold between your finger and thumb, seemed unfathomable as the heavens themselves. We set it in the sun, and then shut the light out of the room, and it shone awfully out of the depths of its own brightness, with a moony gleam, in the dark. No wonder Miss Rachel was fascinated; no wonder her cousins screamed. The Diamond laid such a hold on *me* that I burst out with as large an "O" as the Bouncers [the cousins] themselves. The only one of us who kept his senses was Mr Godfrey. He put an arm around each of his sisters' waists, and, looking compassionately backwards

1

and forwards between the Diamond and me, said, "Carbon, Betteridge! mere carbon, my good friend, after all!"[1]

Collins' fictional moonstone was a combination of two renowned gems, the Koh-i-nur ("mountain of light") and the Orloff. The former, originally weighing 787.5 carats, was found in the mid-seventeenth century and presented to the mogul emperor Shah Jahan, builder of the Taj Mahal. Subsequently this white diamond, ever declining in size as it was cut, fractured, and recut, passed by means of patricide, fratricide, theft, and other treacheries through a number of hands, finally ending up in the early 1850s as a rather thin dullish stone of 106 carats in the British Crown jewels (a gift of the East India Company). The Orloff, a yellow diamond of 194.75 carats, was also once owned by the mogul emperor. A story current in the nineteenth century had it that the stone was later gouged from the eye of a Hindu statue by a French soldier who then sold his prize to an English sea captain. In a series of mysterious transactions the diamond passed through the hands of Jewish, Greek, Armenian, and Persian merchants before coming into the possession of a Russian prince (Orloff), who presented it to his mistress Catherine the Great in 1772. Thereafter the stone remained part of the Russian Crown jewels.[2]

The Koh-i-nur and the Orloff, like almost all the diamonds known from antiquity to the eighteenth century, came from India, dug from the alluvial mines of the kings of Golconda. Diamonds are, as Mr. Godfrey pointed out, pure carbon gases that have fused deep in the earth under the exceedingly high temperatures reached in volcanic activity. Originally embedded in volcanic rock, most of the diamonds discovered up to the late nineteenth century were alluvial stones carried far from their original source during the weathering of the earth. A few of the diamonds found in India were mined from rock conglomerates rather than washed from alluvial

1. Wilkie Collins, *The Moonstone* (Oxford, 1982 [1st ed. 1868], pp. 68–69.
2. The histories of these stones are far more convoluted and contradictory than briefly described here. For a taste of the complexities, see, e.g., C. W. King, *The Natural History of Precious Stones and of the Precious Metals* (London, 1870 [1st ed. 1867]), pp. 76–83, 86–87, which Wilkie Collins relied upon for his source material; E. W. Streeter, *The Great Diamonds of the World* (London, 1882), pp. 63–78, 103–35; and Jean B. Tavernier, *Travels in India by Jean Baptiste Tavernier*, trans. from the French ed. of 1676 by V. Ball (London, 1889), II, app. 1, pp. 431–46.

deposits, but these seem to have been rare.[3] At the height of their development in the mid to late seventeenth century—when demand from competing Portuguese, Dutch, French, and British purchasers pushed carat prices ever higher—the Golconda mines, most of them shallow diggings in areas where diamonds had been carried by alluvial action, were worked intensively. One mine alone, run by merchants who in return for paying a premium to the king each received an area two hundred paces in circumference to dig, employed "close upon 60,000 persons . . . the men . . . digging [to a maximum depth of perhaps fourteen feet, at which point diamond finds petered out] . . . the women and children . . . carrying earth [to be softened by mixing with water, then dried, winnowed and searched]." Each worker received less than the equivalent of a British penny a day for his or her labor.[4] Such activities soon exhausted the alluvial deposits, so that most of the mines had been largely worked out between the end of the seventeenth century and the middle of the eighteenth. Indeed, by 1867 Indian diamond production was insignificant, amounting to no more than one or two thousand carats annually, less than 1 percent of world output.[5]

Long before, from the 1720s onward, Brazil had far surpassed India as a producer of diamonds. Gold miners working along rivers in the province of Minas Gerais discovered the first stone by chance in 1725. Within a decade of this discovery Brazil's output exceeded that of India, the Portuguese Crown had declared diamond mining a state monopoly, and carat prices had fallen by half or two-thirds. During the following one hundred years the Portuguese, in various attempts to secure more revenue and to achieve a more profitable balance of supply and demand, experimented with various forms of government regulation, ranging from the licensing of monopoly contractors to direct state control of production, all of which proved

3. On the formation of diamonds see Gardner Williams, *The Diamond Mines of South Africa* (New York, 1905), II, chapt. 16; and Alpheus Williams, *The Genesis of the Diamond* (London, 1932). On rock mining in India see Godehard Lenzen, *The History of Diamond Production and the Diamond Trade* (London, 1970), pp. 33–34; and Williams, *The Diamond Mines*, I, pp. 16–19.

4. On the Indian mines see Tavernier, *Travels in India*, II, chapts. 15–18 in general and pp. 59, 75–78, 84–86, app. 2, pp. 450–56, app. 3, pp. 457–61 in particular. The only area besides India that produced a noticeable number of diamonds was Borneo.

5. Lenzen, *The History of Diamond Production*, p. 122.

unwieldy and only encouraged the growth of illicit mining. In the mid-1830s, with Brazil having won its independence, diamond mining was finally thrown open to the public. Any person able to pay an annual license fee to the republican government could work one or more claims, each two hundred square meters in size. From these plots located along river banks or in the beds of dried-up water courses the Brazilian miners produced an increasing flow of stones, particularly after the discovery of new diamondiferous areas in the 1840s. Whereas diamond output had averaged close to twelve thousand carats annually during the first three decades of the nineteenth century, it hovered around two hundred thousand carats each year in the forties, fifties, and sixties. Moreover, despite the huge increase in supply, carat prices rose rather than fell in mid-century—a trend accounted for largely by the impact on Europe and America of the industrial revolution, which had led to the growth of large new wealthy classes eager to acquire the gems that were formerly the prerogative of potentates and princes.[6]

By the time Richard Burton visited the capital of Brazil's diamond-mining region in 1867, he found the industry transformed into a complex yet unstable enterprise. In Diamantina and its environs he met some miners—two Cornishmen resident in the area for several decades, a German, and a Brazilian—and inspected a number of diamond diggings. The miners he deemed capitalists, since the days of small diggers were long since past. The Brazilian, for example, had initially invested £6,000 in his properties and employed three hundred black slaves, worth £120 to £150 each, together with a considerable number of overseers. The slaves built dikes in the rivers, dug with pick and shovel to a depth of eighty feet or so, and removed (in "cedar-wood platters, about twice the size of soup-plates," carried on their heads) the diamondiferous sand and gravel to the side of the river, where it was sorted by hand in much the same fashion as it had been done at the turn of the century. Such operations had a number of drawbacks. The onset of the rainy season regularly swept away the dikes, so that the claims could be worked for only six months of the year. Moreover, all work was done by hand: Burton "found . . . no trace of kibble, crane and

6. On the history of the Brazilian mines see John Mawe, *Travels in the Interior of Brazil* (Boston, 1816), chapts. 13–15 and pp. 363–66; Richard Burton, *Explorations of the Highlands of the Brazil* (London, 1869), II, pp. 106–08, 149, and in general chapts. 7–10; and Lenzen, *The History of Diamond Production*, pp. 116–37.

pulley, or rail, no knowledge of that simplest contrivance a tackle; the negro was the only implement. . . ." Yet this "implement" was considered by the Brazilian miner and his peers to be far too expensive and far too few in number for the industry's needs. Worst of all, the slaves (according to their masters) stole, if not a majority of the diamonds, at least the finest.[7]

Despite these problems, Burton was very optimistic about the future of the Brazilian industry. With carat prices rising "prodigiously" in the 1850s and 1860s, largely because of increased demand in the United States, where "even hotel waiters and nigger minstrels wear diamonds in rings and shirt fronts," he thought production could be greatly increased without causing a downturn in market values. Furthermore, Burton believed that Brazil's deposits "had been barely scratched" and that the "next generation" of miners would become far more successful by working "with thousands of arms directed by men whose experience in mechanics and hydraulics will enable them to economize labour. . . ."[8]

But before the new generation could initiate such changes the Brazilian industry was overtaken by far-distant developments. Upon returning home to London Burton read in the *Colesberg Advertiser,* a South African newspaper, of the discovery of a diamond supposedly worth £500 in the Cape Colony. He found the news interesting but of no greater moment than similar reports of small diamond finds in Australia and California.[9] In that judgment Burton was quite mistaken, for in South Africa, unlike any other part of the world, miners were to find the volcanic pipes in which diamonds were formed. Within a few years the South African mines, reaching hundreds of feet into the earth and worked to an ever-greater extent by a combination of servile labor and powerful machinery, had supplanted the alluvial diggings of Brazil as the world's primary diamond producer just as surely as Brazil's mines had supplanted those of India a century-and-a-half before.

7. Burton, *Explorations of Brazil,* II, pp. 98–99, 104, 113–22. On the lack of machinery see also Williams, *The Diamond Mines,* I, p. 145.
8. Burton, *Explorations of Brazil,* II, pp. 149–50, 154.
9. *Ibid.,* pp. 81–82, 104–05.

# Part One: 1867–85

CHAPTER ONE

# The Industrialization of
# Diamond Digging, 1867–85

In 1867, a mineralogist in the Cape Colony determined that a stone sent to him by a Boer from the interior was indeed a diamond. It had been found on the Boer's farm near the confluence of the Vaal and Orange rivers, north of the Colony and west of the Orange Free State—a region claimed by local blacks and as yet unappropriated by either Boer or Briton, making its political status unclear. The mineralogist's conclusion, however, met with suspicion and hostility. European diamond merchants, dealing in a commodity made valuable solely by its scarcity, saw no benefit in new finds and denied that any diamond mines could exist other than those of Brazil (much as their predecessors a century-and-a-half before had ridiculed claims of diamond finds in Brazil and had asserted that all genuine stones could come only from the mines of India). A geologist sent by one London merchant to investigate the site of the Boer's discovery reported back that the countryside was not diamondiferous and that any stones found there, if not planted by hoaxers or land speculators, were no doubt deposited by ostriches migrating from farther north. Although numerous small diamonds were found during 1868, the geologist's claims prevailed until the discovery in March 1869 of a huge 83.5-carat stone—too valuable to be a plant, too large for an ostrich to swallow.[1]

1. The story of the South African diamond discoveries is told in innumerable books. The fullest discussion is that of Marian Robertson, *Diamond Fever: South African Diamond History, 1866–9, from Primary Sources* (Cape Town, 1974). On the merchants' claims about Brazil see Richard Burton, *Explorations of Brazil*, II, p. 108; and on the ostrich claims see George Weakley, *The Diamond Discovery in South Africa* (Colesberg, 1869).

Local landholders in the area of the first finds did not welcome the increasing number of prospectors attracted by this discovery. Blacks, who had found most of the diamonds and who claimed sovereignty over the land, at first attempted to steer white prospectors away from the known diamondiferous areas.[2] Boers resident in the locality likewise objected to the newcomers digging up their farms. Sheer force of numbers, however, made such objections futile. Hundreds of diamond seekers arrived in the final quarter of 1869 and staked out claims in the two areas where finds were most plentiful; the Boer farms of Dorstfontein and Bultfontein. Only the discovery toward the end of the year of greater numbers of diamonds on the banks of the Vaal River thirty miles to the northwest, on lands claimed by the Berlin Missionary Society, saved the white farmers from being totally overrun. At that stage, with most of the diggers gone to the river, the proprietor of Bultfontein sold his property to a group of Port Elizabeth–based merchants. The new owners, who planned to set up a company to work their property, then set about ejecting the few men who remained prospecting on the farm, thereby prefiguring the future pattern of dispossession and consolidation of mine ownership.[3]

THE RIVER DIGGINGS

While several hundred people came to the Vaal River diggings in 1869, all disregarding the German missionaries' claims to ownership, thousands flocked there in 1870 as reports of good diamond finds spread throughout the subcontinent and beyond. There were over five thousand people living in the area by September 1870, many of them Boers from the Orange Free State and the South African Republic encamped along with their families and their black farm servants. Indeed, the river banks were crowded with people dig-

2. For the experiences of one of the first groups of prospectors see "RJD on the Diamond Fields," 1869, ZC 1/1.
3. Robertson, *Diamond Fever,* pp. 220–22, 225–30. On the Berlin Missionary Society's much-disputed claims see Dr. G. Wangemann and J. Kampfmeyer (missionaries) to Sir Henry Barkly (governor of the Cape), 12 September 1872, SGGLW 23.

ging, washing, and sorting the ground, often within a few steps of one another.[4]

The river diggers adopted a simple mining technology that had only limited labor requirements. In general, they excavated their twenty-foot-square claims with pick and shovel to a depth of about five feet, at which point the ground gave way to what was considered non-diamond-bearing soil, loaded the dirt in wheelbarrows or carts and deposited it away from the side of the river. At the depositing sites they washed the material through a series of meshed screens until only a diamondiferous residue remained to be laid out on a table and sorted by hand. The heavy work of digging and washing was done by the diggers or, whenever they could obtain them, by black employees; the sorting of the residue was done by the diggers themselves or, in the case of many of the Boers, by their wives and children, the only people whom they felt they could trust.[5]

With diamond-bearing ground soon becoming scarce as more and more people arrived to try their luck, the diggers limited the scale of production so that as many people as possible could participate in mining. Rules drawn up by the diggers in 1870 stated that no person was to have more than one claim, to be absent from his or her property for more than three working days without risk of forfeit of the claim, or, whether alone or working in combination with partners, to employ more than five black laborers.[6]

The marketing of diamonds was as simple and small-scale as that of production. Most diggers sold their finds direct to the local representatives of European diamond merchants, although some hoarded their diamonds until they had collected enough to make a trip to the Cape or elsewhere worthwhile. One local buyer, for ex-

4. See, for example, C. Hay (lieutenant-governor of the Cape) to Earl Granville (secretary of state for colonies), 4 August 1870, and Hay to the earl of Kimberley, 19 September 1870, GH 1/330; J. G. Steytler, *The Diamond-Fields of South Africa . . . the Immigrant's Guide* (Cape Town, 1870), pp. 8, 14; Anon., *The South African Diamond Fields . . . by a Colonist* (London, 1870), p. 28; Anon., "Two Days at the Diamond-fields: A Social Portrait," *Cape Monthly Magazine*, 2d series 1 (July–Dec. 1870): 243; Anon., "Among the Diamonds: By One Who Has Visited the Fields," *ibid.*, 2d series 2 (Jan.–June 1871): 118–19.

5. Anon., *The South African Diamond Fields*, pp. 26, 31; J. L. Babe, *The South African Diamond Fields* (New York, 1872 [facsimile repr. Kimberley, 1976]), p. 69; Charles Chapman, *A Voyage from Southhampton to Cape Town* (London, 1872), pp. 135–37; C. A. Payton, *The Diamond Diggings of South Africa* (London, 1872), pp. 7–12.

6. "Rules and Regulations for the Vaal-river Diamond-fields," 1870, SAL.

ample, purchased a total of twelve diamonds in just three days in
July 1870, paying £765 to one man, £395 to another, and smaller
sums to several others. At much the same time two parties of successful prospectors chose to avoid the local middlemen and left to
sell their finds, reputedly worth £20,000, in Natal and the Cape.[7]

Attracted by the wealth of the river diggings and the fact that
no one appeared to have clear title to the land, since no political
authority, whether white or black, exercised unquestioned jurisdiction over the area, a number of people cast covetous glances on the
new enterprise. Local blacks, particularly the Griqua, along with
Transvaal and Free State Boers actively contested sovereignty. The
Transvaalers attempted to assert their claims by force with the dis-
patch of a commando, but this was driven off by the river diggers.
The Free State, learning from this failure, took a more moderate
course, sending a magistrate in August 1870 to adjudicate relations
in the digging community. Cape of Good Hope authorities, not wish-
ing to be excluded from possible fortune, sent their own magistrate
in December 1870.[8] While the diggers found these magistrates useful in bringing order to the mining camp, they attempted to forestall any further attempt by outside authorities to lay claim to the
area by establishing their own government, the Diggers' Mutual
Protection Association, and declared themselves a free republic.[9]

By the end of 1870, the main features of the initial phase of
diamond digging were readily apparent. Production was carried
out on a small scale, generally in units consisting of a digger with
perhaps one partner and no more than three or four black laborers;
the technology utilized was very simple, consisting of little more
than a pick and shovel and a series of sieves; and marketing relations were usually personal and limited. Although the competing
claims to sovereignty of blacks, Boers, and English raised fears of
future conflict, the Protection Association, through the strict regulation of the digging camps, ensured that the administration of the
community remained in the diggers' hands. Yet this initial phase
of digging had nearly exhausted itself, though scarcely one year old
and in operation for only three to four months for the 90 percent of

7. See Hay to Granville, 4 August 1870, annexures, GH 1/330; and Anon., *The
South African Diamond Fields*, pp. 28, 29–30, 33, 41–42, 43.
8. On the history of this period see C. W. de Kiewiet, *British Colonial Policy
and the South African Republics, 1848–1872* (London, 1929), pp. 280–301.
9. See the annexures to Hay to Granville, 4 August 1870, GH 1/330; and the
"Rules of the Diamond-diggers' Mutual Protection Association," 1870, SAL.

the diggers who had arrived in the latter half of 1870. There were too many people competing for too few diamonds. All the stones that could be picked up from the surface of the land were long gone, as were those in the river gravel, and all the diamonds of one carat or greater—the only stones for which there was a market—had been won. Boers returned to their farms, other white diggers went back to their homes in the Cape and Natal. The diamond rush appeared to be at an end almost as soon as it had started.

## THE KIMBERLEY DRY DIGGINGS AND
## THE DECLINE OF SMALL HOLDING, 1871–76

As finds at the river diggings declined, many of the diamond seekers turned their attention back to the dry diggings (so named because of the lack of sources of water) that they had previously abandoned. In fact, work had never totally ceased on the farms of Dorstfontein and Bultfontein, which clearly had diamonds on them. Such work, however, had been quite limited. Since most people believed that the diamonds were alluvial deposits, they concentrated their efforts as close as possible to the river; only those who could not make a living at the Vaal had shifted back to the farms before the final quar-

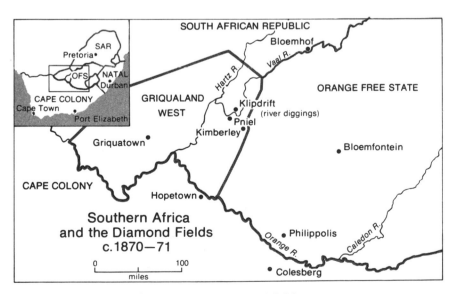

MAP 1.1    Southern Africa and the diamond fields, c. 1870–71

ter of 1870. And even those who moved back faced considerable constraints on their actions: the Boer owner of Dorstfontein demanded a monthly license fee from each digger, while the merchant owners of Bultfontein continued to prohibit access to their property.[10] By the end of 1870, however, Dorstfontein and Bultfontein were at the center of diggers' attention, as reports of considerable diamond finds on the farms in August and September attracted hundreds of men from the river.

This new rush brought to a head the conflict between diggers and proprietors. While the diggers at first limited their attentions to Dorstfontein, they soon forced their way onto Bultfontein and staked out claims, asserting their right to prospect wherever they wished; the proprietors on the other hand argued for the sanctity of private property. In large part, this conflict reflected differing views as to the legal title under which the farms were held. The farmers had Orange Free State titles which permitted each adult male to farm three thousand morgen (approximately six thousand acres) of land and to retain ownership to all minerals. Yet the Free State had never actually ruled the area, claiming only that sovereignty passed to it—if not in practice, certainly in theory—whenever Boers purchased land from blacks. The matter of ownership was further complicated by land claims left over from the period in the late 1840s and early 1850s when the British had claimed jurisdiction over the area as part of the Orange River Sovereignty. To the diggers, claims to such titles, whether Free State or British, in the absence of any constituted authority seemed a legal fiction no more applicable, and in their eyes much less so, than British and Cape law, which reserved the ownership of minerals to the state and thus to the public.[11]

10. Anon., "Among the Diamonds," pp. 120–23; Robertson, *Diamond Fever,* pp. 229–30.

11. On the complicated question of land ownership and mineral rights see David Arnot and F. H. S. Orpen, *The Land Question of Griqualand West* (Cape Town, 1875); *Pamphlet Relative to the Concession of the Government of the South African Republic in Favour of Messrs Munnick, Posno & Webb for the Exclusive Right of Mining for Diamonds and Other Minerals, between the Hart and Vaal Rivers* (Kimberley, January 1875); "Report on the Land Question in Griqualand West by Lieut-Colonel Charles Warren, R.E., C.M.G.," Colonial Office, June 1880; "Copy of Proposed Title Deed to the Farm Bultfontein in Favour of the London and South Africa Exploration Company," 11 September 1881, SGGLW 29; and the "Statement Shewing the Position of the London and South Africa Exploration Company Limited in Respect of Their Property . . . Years 1871 and 1890 Inclusive" (Cape Town, 1890).

The struggle intensified as merchants extended their control over the diamond diggings. To expel the diggers, the owners of the two farms enlisted the aid in January 1871 of a Boer commando, composed of property owners equally fearful that their farms might soon get staked out. One month later a group of London diamond merchants, having floated a company to acquire the new diamond finds, purchased Bultfontein from its Port Elizabeth owners and soon bought Dorstfontein as well. The new absentee owners then proceeded to order, through their local agent, all the diggers still on the farms (for many had returned once the commando dispersed) to leave. On 15 May 1871, however, the day the new proprietors' ultimatum expired, the diggers massed two thousand strong and demanded the right to hold claims. In the face of such unity, and this time lacking the support of a commando (for Boers were unlikely to come to the aid of English merchants) or recourse to any other form of authority to back up their position, the proprietors capitulated and agreed to throw the farms open to diggers who would pay a monthly license fee. In the absence of any authority other than their own, diggers could assert their dominance over landowners and ensure that merchants did not get control of the diamond fields.[12]

With the dispute over access to the land and mineral rights settled for the moment, and plenty of diamonds being found, tens of thousands of people came to try their luck. Whereas in 1870 there had been at most five thousand people at the river diggings, by the end of 1871 there were nearly fifty thousand (approximately twenty thousand of whom were white, the rest black) encamped on Dorstfontein and Bultfontein, as well on the adjacent farm Vooruitzigt, where two new diamondiferous areas had been located in April and July. Though most of these people came from southern Africa, where depressed conditions in rural and urban areas afflicted blacks and whites alike, thousands came also from England, Europe, America, and the gold fields of Australia, driven to seek a living, and perhaps

12. The rules and regulations agreed on by diggers and proprietors in May 1871 are reprinted in Frederick Boyle, *To the Cape for Diamonds: A Story of Digging Experiences in South Africa* (London, 1873), pp. 402–03. For the complaint of the proprietors that they only agreed to these regulations under duress see the letter of C. J. Posno (chairman of the London and South Africa Exploration Company, which owned Dutoitspan and Bultfontein) to the earl of Kimberley, 31 July 1871, GH 1/333.

a fortune, by a combination of economic need and the end of the gold rushes.[13]

Faced with the growth of a huge new population center, larger than Cape Town (the major city in southern Africa) and having as many people as each of the Boer republics, the British decided to extend imperial rule northward. The Colonial Office had already concluded in May 1871 that British rule should be imposed on the diamond fields but hesitated to move for fear of acquiring a financial liability (since the long-term value of the diamond finds had still to be demonstrated) and of antagonizing the Boers to no purpose. After the conflicting land claims of Griquas, Transvaalers, and Free Staters had been adjudicated by a British official, however, and an award (much protested by the Boers) made in September in favor of the Griqua, the governor of the Cape, Sir Henry Barkly, readily accepted the request of Andries Waterboer, the Griqua leader, for imperial protection and in October annexed not only the diamond fields but a considerable area besides as the colony of Griqualand West. Thereafter the diamond fields were administered first by three commissioners and then by a lieutenant-governor, Richard Southey, who were answerable for their actions to the governor of the Cape and ultimately to the British Colonial Office. Although some of the diggers opposed this move, preferring to remain independent, there was little that they could do. Indeed, within eighteen months most had come to terms with colonial rule, for they renamed their community Kimberley in honor of the British secretary of state for colonies responsible for their annexation.[14]

Although far greater numbers of people worked at the dry diggings than had at the river diggings, they retained the same small-scale organization of production. While the four thousand or so claims that the diggers staked out on the approximately fifty to sixty acres considered diamondiferous were each half as large again as

13. For descriptions of the diggers see, e.g., F. Algar, *The Diamond Fields with Notes on the Cape Colony and Natal* (London, 1872), pp. 46, 52; John Angove, *In the Early Days: The Reminiscences of Pioneer Life on the South African Diamond Fields* (Kimberley, 1910), p. 57; Anon., "The Diamond-fields from a Commercial Point of View," *Cape Monthly Magazine*, 2d series 3 (July–Dec. 1871): 309; Anon. ["An Officer of the Royal Engineers"], *A Story of a Four-months Sojourn in the Diamond Fields of South Africa* (Rangoon, n. d. [1871]), p. 47; Boyle, *To the Cape for Diamonds*, pp. 155, 285, 315.

14. The earl of Kimberley to Barkly, 18 May 1871, GH 1/331; proclamations nos. 67, 68, and 70 of Barkly, 27 October 1871, repr. in Boyle, *To the Cape for Diamonds*, pp. 378–89; de Kiewiet, *British Colonial Policy*, pp. 280–301.

those at the river—thirty-one feet square rather than twenty feet—restrictions were placed on the size of claim holdings. No digger could have more than two claims, and his property would be forfeit if he failed to work it for eight consecutive days. There was, however, no limitation placed on the number of black workers who could be employed. And blacks were now prohibited, at least by the regulations that the white diggers drew up, from holding claims.[15] There was also a difference at the dry diggings between the organization of operations in the two diamondiferous areas on Vooruitzigt (Kimberley and De Beers, purchased in late 1871 by another group of Port Elizabeth merchants) and the two on Dorstfontein and Bultfontein (Dutoitspan and Bultfontein). Whereas the claims in the latter areas were laid out in a haphazard fashion, much as they had been staked out in the original rush, those in Kimberley and De Beers were much more carefully organized. There an inspector of mines from the Orange Free State had managed to survey the land before it was fully rushed and had laid out roadways to provide access from the edge of excavations to the claims in the very center of operations. In Bultfontein and Dutoitspan, by contrast, those who held claims in the middle of the diggings had to cross the properties of fellow diggers to get to work and to remove excavated ground.[16]

The mining technology adopted at the dry diggings was much the same, and equally simple, as that of the river diggings. Using picks, shovels, and buckets, the average claim holder, perhaps assisted by a white partner and employing four or more black laborers to do the heavy work, excavated his claim, separated the diamond-bearing from the non-diamond-bearing ground through a series of sieves, and sorted through the residue himself at a sorting table. The only major difference was the limited use of water; the dry diggings were quite literally dry, and all the water used had to be carted there from the Vaal River. In Kimberley and De Beers, be-

15. Boyle, *To the Cape for Diamonds*, pp. 123–25; "Rules and Regulations Framed by the Committee of Dorstfontein, or du Toit's Pan Diggings," July 1871, and "Rules and Regulations . . . on the Farms Vooruitzigt and Bultfontein," GLW 23; proclamation no. 71 of Barkly, 27 October 1871, repr. in Boyle, *To the Cape for Diamonds*, pp. 389–95. The British government refused to sanction the prohibition of black license holders, and thus some claims continued to be worked by black proprietors. See J. M. Smalberger, "The Role of the Diamond-mining Industry in the Development of the Pass-law System in South Africa," *International Journal of African Historical Studies*, 9:3 (1976): 420–21.

16. Boyle, *To the Cape for Diamonds*, p. 120; Williams, *The Diamond Mines*, I, pp. 196–97.

cause of the ease of egress provided by the roads, the worked-over ground was removed from the area of excavations; in Dutoitspan and Bultfontein it had to be heaped up on the claims.

The dry diggers produced far greater amounts of diamonds than had their counterparts at the river. Whereas river diggers exported £153,460 worth of diamonds in their most productive year (1870), the dry diggers produced over twice that figure in 1871 and ten times as much in 1872.[17] These diamonds were marketed in much the same way as they had been at the river—sold direct by claim holders to independent diamond dealers or to the representatives of European merchants.

Despite the initial similarities between river and dry digging, considerable changes soon took place in the forms of organization and production in the latter. The extremely limited area in which diamonds were found at Kimberley made the competition for claims intense. As more and more people dug, they found the diamonds concentrated in relatively small areas: no more than thirty-two acres at Kimberley and De Beers, fifteen at Dutoitspan, and eight at Bultfontein in 1872. And even then the diggers did not find diamonds in equal quantities in each of these areas. Kimberley was easily the richest, while finds at Bultfontein were so scanty and unprofitable that it was soon known as "the poor man's digging."[18] Consequently, most people sought to dig at Kimberley, with the result that claim prices skyrocketed at the same time that the diggings were divided into ever-smaller units. In 1872, for example, one portion of a claim measuring no more than four by seven feet sold for £900, whereas another part-claim measuring seven by thirty feet went for £1,500.[19] Indeed, so rapid was this process of fragmentation that within a few months of the first discovery of diamonds at the Kimberley digging the 450 or so claims laid out by the Orange Free State inspector of mines in July 1871 had been subdivided into 1,600 to 1,800 separate properties, nearly all of which were worked by whites who had paid hundreds, sometimes thousands, of pounds for the privilege.[20]

17. The value of diamonds produced between 1867 and 1872 was as follows: 1867, £500; 1868, £450; 1869, £24,813; 1870, £153,460; 1871, £403,349; 1872, £1,618,076. See the table in S. W. Silver & Co., *Handbook to South Africa* (Cape Town, 4th ed. 1891), p. 108.

18. Boyle, *To the Cape for Diamonds*, pp. 120–21.

19. *Ibid.*, pp. 175, 176, 369–70.

20. Anthony Trollope, *South Africa* (London, 1878), II, pp. 171, 174; M. A. Moulle, *Mémoir sur la géologie générale et sur les mines de diamants de l'Afrique du Sud* (Paris, 1886), p. 103; Theodore Reunert, *Diamonds and Gold in South Africa* (London, 1893), p. 25; Williams, *The Diamond Mines*, I, p. 197.

Such high prices put claim ownership beyond the reach of most people at the diamond fields and encouraged the growth of share working. While many of those who came to the diamond fields brought with them considerable amounts of capital, particularly the large numbers described at the time as the younger sons of aristocrats or other well-to-do men of England, most of those from southern Africa, especially the Boers, had no such resources—certainly not enough to pay for an expensive claim and be able to afford the high cost of living at the fields.[21] People who visited the area in 1871 reported that anyone contemplating trying his luck should have at least £200 to £500 put aside to see himself through the first six months of digging.[22] Those people without such sums who did not congregate on the relatively poor Dutoitspan, Bultfontein, and De Beers diggings sought to work on shares in the Kimberley digging. In exchange for a proportion, perhaps as much as half, of the diamonds found, they worked the property for the claim holder, supplying not only their own labor but also that of the black workers they contracted to their service. So popular was share working that claim holders could pick and choose with whom they did business. The result was that only those able to prove that they had a plentiful supply of black workers could find a claim holder willing to take them on.[23]

As excavations deepened, problems increased. Claim holders could work down by sinking shafts or by cutting steps into the sides of their claims, but at some point both methods were sure to fail; the sides of the shafts caved in or the bottom step covered the entire floor of the digging. With regard to the four-by-seven-foot claim mentioned above, barely the size of a grave, the limit of excavations must have been reached very quickly. Men did not stop digging, however. Rather, they kept on working as the sides of their claims, their neighbors' claims, and, in Kimberley and De Beers, even the roadways collapsed on them. At the beginning of 1872, for example, some claims in the Kimberley diggings were already eighty feet deep; by the end of the year all the roadways had collapsed into the excavations. Thereafter, the task of digging became doubly difficult

21. Boyle, *To the Cape for Diamonds*, pp. 368–69. Boyle estimated that three-quarters of the diggers were colonial born, with one-third of that proportion Boers.

22. John Robinson (ed.), *Notes on Natal: An Old Colonist's Book for New Settlers* (London, 1872), p. 209; Payton, *The Diamond Diggings*, pp. 44–45; Babe, *The South African Diamond Fields*, p. 71.

23. On share working in general see Boyle, *To the Cape for Diamonds*, p. 149; Payton, *The Diamond Diggings*, p. 111; and Robinson, *Notes on Natal*, p. 212.

because all the fallen ground had to be removed before the claims could be sunk deeper, and this digging in turn set off further slips in a never-ending process.[24]

The demanding nature of this method of working explains why claim holders and share workers alike put such a premium on black labor. Indeed, as the excavations went deeper, the dry diggers employed more and more black laborers, generally twenty men each (four times as many as a river digger).[25] Yet a common complaint of dry diggers was that there were never enough black workers available. In large part this was really a complaint about the cost of labor, for in 1872 there were at least twenty thousand blacks on the diamond fields, enough at first glance to supply the needs of the diggers. The black laborers, however, rather than accept the relatively low wages that the diggers first offered, took advantage of the great demand for their services to bargain their wage rates upward. During 1872 alone they doubled the ruling rate by continually changing employers in search of higher wages and by this form of circulation creating a constant shortage of labor.[26] The white diggers' complaints about the cost of labor (almost as frequent as those about supply) reflected the high proportion that wages comprised of their total production and living costs. One early commentator estimated that black wages accounted for approximately 86 percent of the average digger's working costs and 56 percent of his combined working and living expenses.[27]

Adding to the diggers' problems with the methods of working and the supply and cost of labor, the price of diamonds fell as the new finds flooded the European market. For half a century prior to 1870, the price of diamonds had been on the rise while production in the Brazilian mines continued to fall.[28] Throughout the 1870s, the average annual production of Brazil was no more than two hundred thousand carats. That output was more than equaled by the dry diggings in 1871, while in 1872 the Griqualand West mines

24. Boyle, *To the Cape for Diamonds*, pp. 134–35, 288; John X. Merriman to J. B. Currey (government secretary), 15 February 1872, Merriman Papers, Letters to J. B. Currey; *Diamond Field*, 23 May, 6 June 1872; Williams, *The Diamond Mines*, I, pp. 198–204, 221–23.

25. Boyle, *To the Cape for Diamonds*, p. 370; W. J. Morton, *South African Diamond Fields and the Journey to the Mines* (New York, 1877), pp. 20–21.

26. See chapt. 3 on the conflict over wages.

27. Payton, *The Diamond Diggings*, pp. 44–45; and also A. H. Hornsby, *The South African Diamond Fields* (Chicago, 1874), p. 66.

28. Lenzen, *The History of Diamond Production*, pp. 134–35.

exported over a million carats.[29] The diamond monopoly that controlled the European market had at first attempted to exclude Kimberley's output, partly on the basis that most of the diamonds were
of inferior quality, but this measure soon failed as the stones flooded
in. In consequence, the price of diamonds, particularly of the largest stones, dropped dramatically. For example, a diamond that
might have fetched £5,000 at the time of the first discoveries was
worth only £200 or so by 1872 as prices continued to decline.[30]

Quite apart from the effect of this fall in prices on profits, there
was no guarantee that all diggers would find diamonds. Frederick
Boyle's experiences were typical of those of many diggers. Boyle,
an Englishman of some means, arrived at the diamond fields in 1871,
purchased a quarter portion of a claim for £365, and got three partners to work the property on shares with all finds to be split evenly.
It was not a good investment. On the first day of work the adjoining
roadway collapsed into the claim. Thereafter in quick succession
the two mules used to haul the excavated dirt out of the mine fell
into a claim and one of them died. Three days later the haulage
cart was destroyed in a collision with an oxwagon. Five days after
that the two donkeys bought to replace the mules bolted at much
the same time that the black laborers, having received their wages,
left in search of better paying employers. After two months of work
Boyle's partners had only found £42 worth of diamonds. When Boyle
finally reckoned up his investment he found that he had made a working profit of £5, but he had essentially lost the purchase price of the
claim since, the finds being so minimal, the property had been
proven valueless. Boyle had also tried to make some money dab-
bling in diamond buying, with equally disastrous results. A stone
which a partner purchased for him for £250 split before he could
sell it. Boyle left the diamond fields soon after, convinced (as were
most of the people who remained behind) that diamond digging
was a lottery in which there were very few winners.[31]

These factors—high claim prices, inefficient methods of working,
costly labor, falling diamond prices, and limited finds for the majority of diggers—cumulatively produced widespread hardship and

29. "Memorandum Showing the Weight and Value of Diamonds Despatched
through the General Post Office, Kimberley, from 1872 to 30 June 1881," CO 3357.
30. Boyle, *To the Cape for Diamonds*, pp. 228–34, 371; *Diamond Field*, 23 May,
18 July 1872. On the European monopoly see Lenzen, *The History of Diamond Production*, pp. 131–36.
31. Boyle, *To the Cape for Diamonds*, pp. 176, 235, 237, 279, 369–70.

often poverty. The proportion of diggers estimated to make at least a subsistence living from diamond digging ranged from 10 to 50 percent, with most commentators settling on the lower figure.[32] One local newspaper summed up the state of affairs reached by the middle of 1872 in the following way: "The average digger is getting impoverished, the lately successful one is barely paying expenses, while only the few happy possessors of exceptionally rich claims are coining money."[33]

That a few people *were* making money does, however, point to the quite different fates of the river diggings and the dry diggings. Developments in both had appeared to run a somewhat similar course of too many people competing for too few diamonds, so that in both cases the initial hopes of fortune had turned to broken dreams and depression within twelve months. And people made similar predictions that dry digging was at an end in 1872 and that everyone would have to move on in search of new finds.[34] But, unlike the river diggings where diamonds had largely run out after the first few months of intensive work, claim holders at the dry diggings continued to find diamonds no matter how deep they dug. Indeed, it had become obvious that the Kimberley diamonds were not alluvial deposits but reached deep into the earth. Those who made these finds were generally the people who had, through luck, acquired particularly rich claims in the first rush or, more often, had arrived with capital and purchased proven claims. Boyle, a man of no small means himself, believed that most of the claims in the Kimberley mine were owned by "bankers, tradesmen, rich farmers and successful diggers" who, apart from the last, had probably never seen their properties.[35] Already wealthier than their fellows, the holders of the more productive claims could afford to pay more to their employees, hire more black workers, and thus dig faster and deeper than many of their neighbors, whose claims they often undercut, working that material as well. The process, as contemporary observers noted, was the familiar one of the rich getting richer and the poor poorer.[36]

32. Algar, *The Diamond Fields*, pp. 54, 58; Boyle, *To the Cape for Diamonds*, pp. 367, 376.

33. *Diamond Field*, 6 June 1872.

34. Boyle, in leaving Kimberley in February 1872, considered the diggings nearly exhausted. See *To the Cape for Diamonds*, pp. 365–77.

35. *Ibid.*, p. 366.

36. *Ibid.*, p. 377; Payton, *The Diamond Diggings*, pp. 109–10.

Yet even the most successful diggers could not escape the constraints on production that drove so many of their peers to ruin, for the technological and organizational problems of mining became increasingly difficult during the next three years, 1873–75. Such problems resulted from the greater depth of excavations, particularly in the Kimberley mine and to a lesser extent in the De Beers mine, and from the continuance of a mode of working in the Dutoitspan and Bultfontein mines that had already proved profitless by the end of 1872. In the case of all four mines, the retention of the single claim or portion thereof as the common unit of production exacerbated the difficulties of digging.

The case of the Kimberley mine exemplifies the problems of digging at ever-greater depths. The collapse of all the roadways into the mine at the end of 1872 (when excavations had reached a depth of one hundred feet) left the central claims largely inaccessible. To overcome this problem, the diggers erected an elaborate haulage system with pulleys and wooden staging around the rim of the mine. Wires stretched from the staging to each of the claims and along these were hauled up buckets of excavated ground, a system whose operation is shown clearly in plates 1.4, 1.5, and 1.6.[37] Although this haulage system, run in conjunction with a private steam tramway that reached into part of the mine, permitted work to continue in the central claims, it lacked the capacity to remove the growing amounts of ground that slipped into the mine as digging reached greater depths and progressively undercut the sides of the excavations. Moreover, flooding became an increasingly difficult problem as diggings neared the water table. A huge fall of rain in January 1874 completely flooded the mine, and the deepest diggings (then at two hundred feet) remained under water until November because of the inadequacy of the available pumping equipment. At that point the north side of the mine, weakened by the flooding, collapsed into the central claims. By the end of the year, the combination of flooding and slips had left at least half the mine unworkable.[38]

37. See Williams, *The Diamond Mines*, I, pp. 224–31.
38. *Diamond Field*, 24 June 1874; Henry Tucker (secretary, Kimberley Mining Board) to Richard Southey, 10 July 1874, GLW 64; *Diamond News*, 11, 16 July, 8 September 1874; *Mining Gazette*, 30 March 1875; reports of the mining engineer, Francis Oats, repr. in the "Report of Lieut-Colonel Crossman, R.E., on the Affairs of Griqua-Land West," June 1876, Colonial Office Confidential Print African No. 96, pp. 76–81.

Conditions were even worse in the De Beers, Dutoitspan, and Bultfontein mines. At De Beers excavations had reached no deeper than sixty feet by the end of 1874, so falling reef was not yet a severe problem. Flooding, however, had almost crippled production in the mine, with no less than two-thirds of the claims abandoned by the beginning of 1875. Dutoitspan and Bultfontein were in an even greater mess. One newspaper described operations in the former mine in 1874 as a "spectacle of unintelligent grubbing," as each claim holder dug in one corner of his property, sorted in another, and piled huge heaps of debris either in yet another corner or on adjoining abandoned claims. The description of the central part of the mine as a "wilderness of rubbish heaps" applied equally to the Bultfontein mine. By the beginning of 1875, diggers in each of the two mines worked less than one-third of the claims available.[39]

These problems with the technology and organization of mining increased the dependence of diggers on their black laborers. Both the haulage system adopted in the Kimberley mine and the excavation methods used in the other three mines relied almost totally on black labor to do the digging, remove the ground from the mines where that was possible, cart it to depositing areas and there break up the diamondiferous material until it was small enough to be sorted by the white claim holder. While the expansion of working in the Kimberley mine in 1873, thanks to the development of the new haulage system, had increased the demand for laborers, the problems encountered in 1874 made the services of such men hardly less essential, since the fallen reef had to be removed if most properties were to be made workable. But although the number of jobs in the mine fell with half the claims under water, this did not necessarily mean an increased supply of cheaper workers for those diggers who continued operations. Rather than accept the lowered wages that most employers offered, many blacks left the diamond fields for their rural homes. There was a temporary surplus of labor at the end of the year when the huge slip on the north side of the mine stopped most operations, but as soon as work began again in earnest in early 1875 the diggers had to compete amongst themselves even more intensively for the services of the available laborers. Because of this competition wages rose, causing

39. See Oats' report in Crossman, pp. 81–84; and also in the *Diamond Field*, 24 August, 14 October, 4 November 1874, 16 January 1875.

production costs to rise at the same time that digging was becoming increasingly difficult and generally profitless.

Neither share workers nor claim holders could count on loans to see them through the hard times. The former, whose net worth consisted of their own labor and that of their black employees, had no collateral to offer banks and other money lenders. Claim holders could mortgage their properties, but only at ruinously high rates of interest. In 1873–74 the ruling rate of interest offered by private money lenders ranged from 10 to 20 percent per month. Any claim holder who accepted such terms had to be very desperate indeed.[40]

Despite such usurious rates many claim holders were forced to gamble their future with the private money lenders—who included lawyers, merchants, and the more successful diggers—since the local banks refused to accept claims as collateral. The merchant proprietors of the farms (Dorstfontein, Bultfontein, and Vooruitzigt) were pursuing court action to obtain clear title to both the land and the minerals. Therefore, the banks did not dare risk money on securities that might soon become worthless. Moreover, while the issue of ownership awaited final decision, the farm proprietors decided in February 1874 to raise the rents that they charged for house and business properties in the town. Because everyone in Kimberley dwelt on land owned by one or other of these proprietors, the increase in rents added yet another problem to those already burdening the diamond fields' population.[41]

The combination of these various constraints on production—technological and organizational, the supply and cost of labor and capital, and the conflict over proprietary rights—caused widespread hardship, effectively reduced Kimberley's population, and made those people who remained fear for their future. By the end of 1874, the total white population of the diamond fields amounted to seven thousand men, women, and children, less than half the number who had been there in 1872, while the black population had dropped to approximately ten thousand, one-third its earlier size.[42] Poverty among the white population was widespread, and starvation among

40. *Diamond Field*, 7 January 1873; *Diamond News*, 20 January 1874; Southey to Barkly, 27 August 1874, GLW 184.

41. Southey to Barkly, 26 April, 4 May 1874, GLW 183; *idem*, 27 August 1874, GLW 184. For background see *idem*, 12 January, 21 March, 1873, GLW 180; and *idem*, 6 November 1873, GLW 182.

42. *Diamond News*, 18 August, 19 September 1874; *Diamond Field*, 7, 28 November 1874.

the black common. And the future held out little prospect of recovery. As at the end of the first year of river digging, and of dry digging, ruin seemed near.[43]

Faced with such a dire prospect, Kimberley's residents contemplated the state's role in the economy. With several thousand people beset by production problems, competing ferociously against one another, and the price of diamonds falling, there seemed to be a need for some outside force to intervene and rationalize the working of the mines. Yet share workers, claim holders, speculators, landed proprietors, and merchants did not necessarily share the same vision of the future or of what the role of the state should be, and therein lay the seeds of conflict.

Share workers and the majority of claim holders looked to the state to protect their interests. As conditions worsened at the end of 1874, they demanded that the lieutenant-governor, Richard Southey, extend greater official controls over blacks and thereby increase the regularity and reduce the cost of black labor. At the same time, they called for continued restrictions on the maximum size of claim holdings in order to keep out absentee speculators and retain the mines in the hands of small diggers.[44]

Though the more successful claim holders supported the demands for stricter controls over black labor, they took quite a different tack on the matter of claim ownership. They contended that there should be no state-enforced limitation but that market forces alone should determine the scale of production. From their point of view, the future of mining lay with large capitalists, financed by European investors, working the mines in large blocks of claims, and with machinery replacing much of the black labor contingent. Indeed, some of the claim holders had already formed a number of small private companies late in 1873 and early in 1874 to carry out operations on a larger scale than then practiced. Moreover, the largest claim holder in the Kimberley mine had a scheme well under-

43. *Diamond News*, 27 October 1874; W. Grimmer (medical inspector) to Currey, 8 November 1874, GLW 52; *idem*, 16 November 1874, GLW 70; *Diamond Field*, 28 November, 9, 10 December 1874, 13 January 1875.

44. See, e.g., the *Diamond News*, 18 August, 10, 27 October, 10, 12, 21 November 1874; *Diamond Field*, 20 August, 5, 16 September, 7, 10, 14, 28 October, 4, 7, 11, 14, 25 November 1874; Southey to Barkly, 20 August, 21 November 1874, GLW 184; *idem*, 26 November 1874, enclosure 1 in no. 1, "Correspondence Relating to the Colonies and States of South Africa: Part 1. Cape of Good Hope and Griqualand West," *BPP*, C1342 (1875), p. 2; George Paton to Merriman, 20 September 1874, Merriman Papers, 1874/47.

way in 1874 to float a company in London that would take over the entire mine and work it as a single unit. Naturally he did not want the state to step in and ruin his plans.[45]

The proprietors of the farms likewise had particular economic interests with regard to the role of the state. They derived their income from rents, paid largely by claim holders, that were collected by state intermediaries. Because of this method of collection, first established at the time the British annexed the diamond fields as a measure to ameliorate the hitherto bitter relations between diggers and landowners and to provide the state with some revenue, the landowners had to secure government approval for any rent increase. Beyond the need for state support in the generation of their income, the proprietors saw economic advantage in both small holding and in company production. The former scale of organization offered considerable income from the great number of people required to pay license fees, the latter from the equally large rates that could be levied on companies.[46]

Merchants, however, had no such ambivalence in their vision of the future. For them small holding offered the greatest benefits, since the extent of their income was more a product of population size than of efficiency of production. Thus, they joined their voices to those who called for state action to prevent the introduction of company production in the mines.[47]

The state's own economic interest in mining lay in the generation of revenue. In 1874, as table 1.1 shows, two-thirds of gov-

45. On the views of the nascent capitalists see in particular the letter of W. J. R. Cotton to Lord Carnarvon, 16 June 1874, enclosed in Carnarvon to Barkly, 23 June 1874, GH 1/348 (55); and those of Maj. H. G. Elliot, and Goodliffe et al. to Carnarvon, 23, 25 June 1874, enclosed in Carnarvon to Barkly, 25 June 1874, GH 1/348 (57). See also Southey to Barkly, 30 July 1874, GLW 183; *idem*, 6, 13, 20, 27 August 1874, 18 February, 18 March 1875, GLW 184; *idem*, 25, 27 March, 3 April 1874, GLW 185; and Paton to Merriman, 20 September 1874, Merriman Papers, 1874/47. On early company formation see Southey to Barkly, 3 July 1873, GLW 180; *Diamond News*, 23, 28 August 1873, 29 January 1874; *Diamond Field*, 31 January, 26 August 1874; "Articles of Association of the Finlason's Claim Company Limited," registered 4 December 1873 with a capital of £3,000, DOK 3/3.

46. On the concerns of the proprietors see in particular John Paterson to Merriman, 13 February, 5 September 1874, 17 March 1875, Merriman Papers, 1874/32, 1874/38, 1875/12; Paton to Merriman, 20 September 1874, Merriman Papers, 1874/47; Southey to Barkly, 1 April 1875, GLW 185.

47. See Southey to Barkly, 18 March 1875, GLW 184; "Petition from Bankers, Professional Men, Merchants, Claimholders, Diggers and Others of Griqualand West," enclosure 2 in no. 4, *BPP*, C1342 (1875), pp. 33–35.

ernment revenue came from sources outside the mining industry, largely from license fees levied on merchants, while the bulk of the third derived from the mining industry came from license fees collected from claim holders. Reduction in either the number of claim holders or merchants would reduce significantly the state's revenue. And this Southey's administration could ill afford: in that year alone it projected a deficit exceeding its income by 50 percent.[48]

Lieutenant-Governor Southey bore the question of revenue in mind when he decided to intervene in the economy to ensure that small holding not only survived but predominated in mining's future. Early in 1874, when the likelihood of deficits was already clear, he enacted measures to rationalize the organization of mining by giving considerable administrative powers to mining boards (one for each mine and composed of representatives of the claim holders) and even greater authority to a government inspector of diamond mines. In the same legislative measure he also introduced regulations to entrench small holding, yet permit some expansion of operations, by limiting the number of claims that any one person or company could have to ten. He increased taxation at the same time and at a later date introduced legislative measures to limit the rents that landowners could charge, establish once and for all the principle of Crown ownership of all minerals, and make it possible

TABLE 1.1   Sources of State Revenue, Griqualand West, 1872–75 (Pounds)

|  | 1872 | 1873 | 1874 | 1875 |
|---|---|---|---|---|
| Revenue derived exclusive of the mines | 41,371 | 51,603 | 43,840 | 56,795 |
| Revenue derived from the mines | 17,309 | 15,371 | 17,127 | 21,298 |

SOURCE: CGHPP, G63 1877.

48. See Ordinance 17, 29 June 1874, proposing an expenditure for 1874–75 of £78,747/11/0, and Ordinance 15, 23 June 1874 proposing to borrow £25,000 to cover the anticipated deficit. See also the "Financial Statement of Griqualand West," CGHPP, A4 1877 and G63 1877; and the tables of "Actual Revenue and Expenditure in the Province of Griqualand West, 1870 to 1879," GH 21/2. On the growing concern of the Colonial Office about the problem of revenue see Carnarvon to Barkly, 9 September 1874, BPP, C1342 (1875), p. 32; and C. W. de Kiewiet, The Imperial Factor in South Africa: A Study in Politics and Economics (London, 1941), pp. 50–51.

for diggers to use their claims as collateral for bank loans.[49] But, ignoring public demand, he refused to introduce or enforce racially discriminatory legislation against black laborers, arguing that in the case of those who were British citizens color should not determine legal rights.[50]

Southey's measures satisfied no one. The share workers and the claim holders objected to the expanded powers of the inspector of mines and to the higher taxes, and they claimed that the lack of racial legislation crippled their operations. Company promoters saw their dreams of future profits dashed. Merchants found little that was encouraging in the measures so long as their immediate economic situation remained depressed. And the landed proprietors used influential London backers to overturn Southey's limitations on their property rights. By the middle of 1875 a crisis loomed, with the mines barely working and the disaffected parading under arms through the streets of Kimberley and raising the black flag of anarchy.

The intervention of the imperial state resolved the crisis. British troops despatched from Cape Town in June 1875 disarmed the "Black Flag rebels" and reinforced Southey's authority. It appeared that the lieutenant-governor would now have the power to implement his ideas on the future of diamond mining. This was not to be the case, however, for the imperial authorities decided that Southey had misconstrued his role and had supported the wrong form of diamond mining. As had been the case with Southey, revenue was the major concern of Lord Carnarvon, the colonial secretary, who, two months after the successful military expedition, dismissed the lieutenant-governor on the grounds of financial mismanagement.[51]

A one-man commission of enquiry into the causes of the unrest, held soon after Southey's dismissal, placed similar emphasis on

49. Ordinance 5, 11 March 1874, and Ordinance 10, 13 May 1874. See also Southey to Barkly, 4 May, 30 July 1874, GLW 183; *idem*, 27, 28 August, 1, 3, 6 September 1874, GLW 184; and Southey to Merriman, 8 September 1874, Merriman Papers, 1874/39.

50. See chapt. 3.

51. Carnarvon to Barkly, 4, 25 August 1875, GH 1/353 (69, 80). For historians' accounts of the events of 1874–75 see de Kiewiet, *The Imperial Factor*, pp. 49–59; I. B. Sutton, "The Diggers' Revolt in Griqualand West, 1875," *International Journal of African Historical Studies*, 12:1 (1979): 40–61; and Robert Turrell, "The 1875 Black Flag Revolt on the Kimberley Diamond Fields," *Journal of Southern African Studies*, 7:2 (1981): 194–235.

financial concerns. Colonel William Crossman concluded in his report that the state's administrative structure at the diamond fields was far too large and expensive for a community of twenty-four thousand collected together in an area of less than six square miles—"no larger than . . . a small English town." Strongly influenced by the findings of a mining engineer that the subdivision of the Kimberley mine into quarters, eighths, and sixteenths of claims made profitable working impossible, Crossman also recommended that there be no state-enforced limitation on the size of claim holdings, since he agreed with the engineer that the future of diamond mining belonged to capitalists and companies. He recommended that "the mines should be looked upon partly as a municipality and partly as a trading corporation, and Government should interfere with them as little as possible." These recommendations—for state retrenchment and increased emphasis on the role of private mining capital—were adopted by the British government.[52]

## THE FIRST PHASE OF COMPANY PRODUCTION, 1877–79

Changes in the Griqualand West administration, however, did not precipitate an immediate transformation from small- to large-scale production, for a number of factors hindered mining throughout much of 1876. First, the new administration did not immediately repeal the claim-limitation law. Colonel Owen Lanyon, Southey's successor, left a decision on this matter, still a source of considerable tension in the community, open to further debate.[53] Therefore, despite the attempts of a few men to get around the law by registering their claims in the names of dummy holders, most work in the mines continued to be performed on the same small scale as in the past, accompanied by all the problems which beset that form of production. As a result, more than half the claims in the De Beers, Dutoitspan, and Bultfontein mines went unworked, and additional slips in the Kimberley mine threatened to close down operations there entirely.[54]

Second, diamond prices fell. In the face of increasing mining difficulties, diggers tried to produce as many diamonds as possible

52. "Report of Lieut-Colonel Crossman," pp. 1–26, 62–65, 76–84.

53. *Diamond News*, 20, 29 July 1876.

54. *Ibid.*, 20 June, 20, 22 July 1876; *Diamond Field*, 27 December 1876; general manager, Standard Bank, to London, 15 August 1876, GM/LO, p. 146, Henry Papers.

PLATE 1.1   At the diamond diggings, 1870–71 (*The Graphic*, 22 June 1872)

THE DIAMOND DIGGINGS, SOUTH AFRICA.

PLATE 1.2   The diamond diggings, 1872 (*Illustrated London News*, 31 August 1872)

PLATE 1.3  Kimberley mine, claims and roadways, 1872 (Williams, *The Diamond Mines of South Africa*, vol. 1, p. 196)

PLATE 1.4  Kimberley mine, 1873 (*The Graphic*, 22 December 1873)

PLATE 1.5   Kimberley mine, hauling gear, 1873–74 (Cape Archives, AG 4185)

PLATE 1.6   Kimberley mine, hauling gear, 1874 (Cape Archives, AG 4201)

PLATE 1.7   Kimberley mine, 1875 (Johannesburg Public Library)

as quickly as possible in order to get enough of a return to make a living and continue operations. Yet the European diamond market could not absorb this output, especially since a severe depression affected the continent at the time. As a result carat prices declined 30 percent in the second quarter of 1876 and continued to fall through to the end of July.[55]

Third, the price of black labor, the largest factor in production costs, rose. Faced with a huge drop in their financial returns on production, diggers sought to alleviate their problems in part by lowering the wages of their black employees. Rather than accept a 50 percent wage cut, however, the workers left the mines altogether and either went home or sought employment in the Cape. Within a couple of months black wage rates were running at least 25 percent higher than they had been before the cut as diggers tried desperately to encourage men to return to the mines.[56]

Fourth, capital was in very short supply. On the one hand, diggers could not borrow more money locally because, in the case of those who held claims in the De Beers, Dutoitspan, and Bultfontein mines, the value of the properties was too low to be accepted as collateral and, in the case of the Kimberley mine, most claim holders had already mortgaged their properties to the hilt.[57] On the other hand, the lack of profits, the continuation of the claim-limitation clause, and, at the Kimberley mine, extremely high claim valuations (assessed for taxation purposes by the Kimberley Mining Board), effectively discouraged investment in the industry from outside Kimberley. People were not prepared to pay high prices for properties that could obviously not provide a sufficient return on capital.[58]

Together these factors caused a depression in the mining in-

55. *Diamond News*, 13 May, 23 November 1876; general manager, Standard Bank, to London, 24 July 1876, GM/LO, p. 144, Henry Papers; Lanyon to his father, 27 July 1876, ZT 1/1/2, vol. 11, Lanyon Papers.

56. *Independent*, 29 June 1876; *Diamond News*, 15, 18, 20, 29 July, 3, 8 August, 5 October 1876; *Diamond Field*, 29 November 1876. See also chapt. 3.

57. General manager, Standard Bank, to London, 17, 24 July, 5, 28 August 1876, GM/LO, pp. 143, 144, 145, 148, Henry Papers; Lanyon to his father, 27 July 1876, ZT 1/1/2, vol. 11, Lanyon Papers; *Independent*, 29 June 1876; *Diamond Field*, 2 August 1876; *Diamond News*, 19 October 1876.

58. The Kimberley mine was valued at £528,700 in 1875 and £1,030,000 in 1876. See the "Plan of Assessment of the Kimberley Mine, 9 March 1875," GLW 130 (106); and the "Plan of Assessment of the Kimberley Mine for the Year 1876," GLW 85.

dustry and brought about a local commercial crisis. The bankers and money lenders called in past loans, foreclosed on many diggers, and in general brought most financial transactions in the community to a halt. Lanyon summed up the situation reached by July 1876 thus: "Merchants are tottering, bank managers' hearts failing them, and money lenders are finding out that they have killed the bird which laid the golden egg."[59] As a result of the combined effects of industrial depression and commercial crisis, population and property values fell, the former by at least 50 percent, the latter by up to 1,000 percent.[60]

Such developments rekindled the debate over the future of mining and the state's role in determining that future. While some people, merchants in particular, argued that future prosperity depended on the retention of a large population of diggers protected in their small-scale operations by the state, others, those who preferred to invest in production rather than commerce, countered that if outside capital were not introduced into the mines and large companies formed then there would be no industry to support anyone. Perhaps the most vigorous exponent of the latter point of view was the editorialist for the *Diamond News* who argued that there should be no legal restraints on economic development, since "the Darwinian law [of] the survival of the fittest" held supreme in "commerce as in nature," and he suggested that that natural law alone should determine the future of mining.[61]

Without necessarily following the editorialist of the *Diamond News* to the extremes of Darwinian logic, Colonel Lanyon did agree that his government should not attempt to determine the future course of mining by limiting the size of claim holdings, a view that had already been given strong support in Crossman's report. Lanyon, much like Southey before him, aimed above all else to make the Griqualand West colony solvent. Indeed, he had so successfully implemented many of Crossman's recommendations for reductions in state activities that his was the first administration in Griqualand West's five-year history not to have a deficit.[62] Past debts remained a huge burden, though, totaling nearly twice the administration's an-

59. Lanyon to his father, 27 July 1876, ZT 1/1/2, vol. 11, Lanyon Papers.
60. *Diamond Field*, 9 August 1876.
61. *Diamond News*, 19 October 1876.
62. "Financial Statement of Griqualand West," *CGHPP,* A4 1877 and G63 1877; Lanyon to his father, 8 January 1877, ZT 1/1/2, vol. 11, Lanyon Papers.

nual income: £100,000 owed to the Orange Free State as recently agreed upon compensation for the latter's disputed claims to the diamond fields; £30,000 to the Cape government for past loans; and £20,000 to the British government for the cost of the 1875 military expedition to deal with the uprising in Kimberley.[63] Because any increase in revenue depended on a return to prosperity in the diamond industry, Lanyon acted in late 1876 to secure both objectives. Accepting that outside capital had to be attracted so that the industry could be put on a secure financial footing, he repealed the claim-limitation law and at the same time reconstituted the mining boards to give greater weight to the interests of large claim holders. To ensure, however, that Darwinian competition not get beyond the control of the state, he required that a majority of the members of the mining boards be government appointees. The state's economic interest, after all, had to be protected.[64]

With the repeal of the claim-limitation law the era of small holding ended and that of capital began. The *Diamond News* editorialized that the mining industry had now moved out of the "narrow belt" by which restrictive legislation had protected the individual digger and "into that wide region where the laws of trade are all powerful; laws of capital and labour and of supply and demand and to them its future development must be committed."[65] Certainly this new era of mining required that diggers have greater capital resources than in the past if they wanted to keep working; one commentator suggested that anyone who hoped to succeed at diamond mining now needed at least £1,000 in initial outlay, while another considered £5,000 a more realistic figure—a far cry from the £200 to £500 deemed sufficient in 1872.[66]

But even a sum of £5,000 was paltry compared to the amounts now invested in the Kimberley mine by one London diamond merchant. In the first four months of 1877, Jules Porges, one of the largest buyers of the diamond fields' output, spent over £70,000 on claim purchases. Through this expenditure, Porges not only acquired a 10 percent interest in the Kimberley mine but also forestalled the

63. On the need to raise a loan to cover these debts see the *Diamond News,* 14 November 1876.
64. See Lanyon to his father, 10 October 1876, ZT 1/1/2, vol. 11, Lanyon Papers; and Ordinance 12 and Government Notice 332, 1876.
65. *Diamond News,* 23 November 1876.
66. *Ibid.,* 6 October 1876; Morton, *South African Diamond Fields,* p. 25.

plans of another London diamond merchant to float a company to take over the entire mine.[67]

Although made on a far larger scale than any that had taken place in the past and introducing a large amount of foreign capital directly into the industry for the first time, Porges' acquisitions mirrored a pattern of concentrating claim ownership that had been going on for some time as the wealthier claim holders, often men who had made their money as diamond dealers rather than as diggers, purchased the properties of their poorer and often bankrupt neighbors. In the Kimberley mine, for example, the diamond merchants, Lewis and Marks, Paddon Brothers, and J. B. Robinson already had considerable claim holdings by late 1876.[68] With the infusion of Porges' cash in early 1877 setting off a flurry of claim transactions, these merchant speculators increased their holdings. Lewis and Marks spent almost £20,000 on purchases in the first quarter of 1877, much of this money being a reinvestment of profits made from selling their previous holdings to Porges.[69] The mine was rapidly falling into fewer and fewer hands. In contrast to the 1,600 claim holders in the Kimberley mine in 1872, there were just 300 in 1877, and of that reduced number fewer than 20 owned more than half the mine. Lewis and Marks, Paddon Brothers, J. B. Robinson, and Jules Porges between them possessed one quarter of the claims. As the *Diamond News* summed up matters: "It is evident that the working of the Kimberley Mine is passing, by the force of circumstances, into the hands of companies and capitalists."[70]

67. For Porges' purchases see the "Return of All Transfers of Claims in Kimberley and De Beers Mines from 1st January to 1st October 1877," GLW 109 (2412); and the report of the Standard Bank's inspector, 20 March 1877, p. 202, INSP 1/1/84, SBA. Porges formed the Griqualand Diamond Mining Company in London in June 1877 with a nominal capital of £400,000. See the "Memorandum of Association of the Griqualand Diamond Mining Company Limited," 20 June 1877, DOK 3/4. On the scheme to take over the mines see the *Diamond News*, 15 April 1876; general manager, Standard Bank, to London, 5 August, 4 September, 1, 29 December 1876, 23 February 1877, GM/LO, pp. 145, 148, 153, 156, 163, Henry Papers. Another scheme to take over the mines, floated in mid-1877, also failed. See the *Diamond News*, 12, 14 June 1877; and the *Diamond Field*, 15 June 1877.

68. "List of Claimholders in Arrears for Licence Payments," 30 April 1876, GLW 95 (3174); Standard Bank's inspector's report, 1 September 1876, pp. 202–03, INSP 1/1/84, SBA; general manager, Standard Bank, to London, 29 December 1876, GM/LO, p. 156, Henry Papers.

69. See the returns of share transfers cited in note 67.

70. *Diamond News*, 24 April 1877. Paddon Brothers and Lewis and Marks combined their holdings in 1877 to form the Kimberley Mining Company, a privately held operation with a capital of £82,000. See the Standard Bank's inspector's report, 31 December 1877, pp. 55–56, INSP 1/1/84, SBA.

This pattern of concentrated claim ownership was repeated in the other mines, but without the assistance of foreign capital. These mines were too unprofitable to attract overseas investment, an assessment reflected in their low valuations compared to that of the Kimberley mine. Whereas the Kimberley mine claims were officially valued at over £1,000,000 in 1877, those of De Beers were considered worth only £200,000, of Dutoitspan £76,000, and of Bultfontein £30,000.[71] Yet despite the lack of investment capital, claim holders in these poorer mines also consolidated their holdings, some by direct purchases, others by forming partnerships. By the end of 1877 a majority of the working properties in these mines consisted of blocks of ten claims or more.[72]

With claim ownership concentrated in fewer hands the scale of

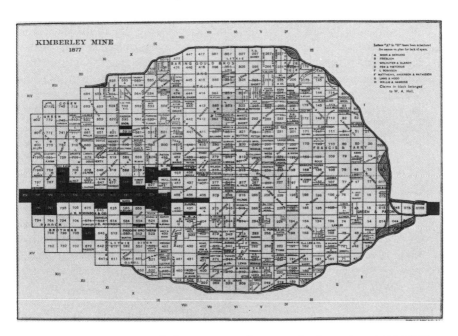

FIGURE 1.1    Diagram of claim ownership, Kimberley mine, 1877 (Williams, *The Diamond Mines of South Africa*, vol. 2, between pp. 276 and 277)

71. "Results of the Census Recently Taken in the Province of Griqualand West," *CGHPP*, A14 1877, p. 3.

72. On the Dutoitspan mine see the list of "Claimholders Who Voted for Members of the Dutoitspan Mining Board," 29 December 1876, GLW 98 (4); on Bultfontein see the "Return of All Transfers of Claims in Bultfontein," January to October 1877, GLW 68 (2420); and on De Beers see the list of transfers in GLW 109 (2412).

production increased dramatically; much greater use was made of machines, and extensive numbers of white wage workers were employed for the first time. One of these new operations, typical of many, was that of E. Solz and Company in the Dutoitspan mine. Solz, who had increased his property holdings from ten claims in 1876 to thirty in 1877, employed a much larger work force than the small claim holders; he had eighty-seven black laborers, approximately five to eight white men to oversee them, and an engineer to run his steam engines. Production was organized in the following manner:

> [S]team is got up, Mr Solz takes his stand on the depositing box [on the margin of his property], the white overseers are with the boys some forty or fifty feet below, the engineer starts the engine, and the tubs begin to move on the wires. The engine house contains one four-horse power vertical engine, which pumps water from the Gully [the deepest part of the mine], and turns two circular washing-machines measuring 6 feet and 6 inches in diameter. The claims are thus kept free of water, and washing operations can be carried on without impediment. The water is received as it comes out of the claims, into a large iron tank, and is then turned on to the washing machines. Placed immediately beside the vertical engine is one of Ransomes and Sims 8-horse-power horizontal engines, used for pulling out ground from the 30 claims belonging to Mr Solz & Co. The average number of tubs of stuff hauled out during the day is 300, though this number will shortly be increased, and indeed on Saturday 180 tubs had been got out by 11 o'clock, or five hours work. Three of the tubs go to a load, and as each consignment of "yellow" [the excavated ground] comes up to the depositing box, it is shovelled into a large cylinder by two or three boys, passes into the "rotaries" [the washing machines], and the majority of it, of course, goes away as "tailings" [debris].[73]

While Solz's organization and integration of machinery and human labor was particularly efficient, this new form of production was by no means exclusive to him. Indeed, steam machinery was introduced on a much larger scale in the Kimberley mine, where the depth of excavations (then at two hundred feet compared with only sixty to seventy feet in the other three mines) and the infusion of Porges' capital permitted greater purchases. By the middle of 1877 all the larger operations in the mine had steam production in full

73. *Diamond News*, 13, 20 March 1877.

force.[74] As the *Diamond News* put matters, "Steam is rampant, and steam engines are *the* investment of the day. . . ."[75]

These changes in the scale and form of ownership and production made mining profitable once again. Even though diamonds fetched only two-thirds of the price they had in the early 1870s, output increased at a rate faster than prices fell. Solz and Company, for example, sold its diamond output for at least twice the cost of production, netting a very handsome profit indeed.[76]

The prospect of obtaining such profits encouraged people to acquire ever-larger properties, engendering considerable bitterness between the smaller claim holders and those who sought their properties. Few claim holders sold their property by choice. More often than not digging problems, particularly falling reef in the Kimberley mine, slips in the De Beers mine, and accumulation of debris in the Dutoitspan and Bultfontein mines, forced people to cease operations and sell their claims for whatever they could get. Human factors exacerbated mining difficulties. In the Kimberley mine, for example, the mining board had responsibility for removing all fallen reef, usually by contracting out the work and levying all claim holders for the costs involved. Despite high expenditures on this work in the late 1870s, generally upward of £10,000 annually, the board never succeeded in completely clearing the mine. Indeed, at least a quarter of the claims were covered by debris in 1878 and more slips threatened. Those whose claims were affected, often for months and sometimes years, not only had to do without any return on their investment but also had to continue paying various rates, taxes, reef-removal levies, and mortgage interest on their unproductive properties. The process of forced sale was often made worse for many by the undue influence that large claim holders exercised on the mining boards. After Lanyon's reconstitution of these bodies the largest claim holders received voting rights disproportionate to their property holdings, won control of the boards, and could therefore determine reef-removal priorities. Not surprisingly, most such work was done on the properties of the large claim holders and the costs paid for by levies collected from all claim holders, including

74. *Ibid.*, 19 June 1877. For a detailed description of work in the mine see Trollope, *South Africa*, pp. 173–79.
75. *Diamond News*, 24 March 1877. Emphasis in the original.
76. *Ibid.*, 13, 20 March 1877. On the general profitability of mining see the Standard Bank's inspector's report, 15 March 1879, INSP 1/1/85, SBA.

those people left with submerged or buried properties. Many of the latter, burdened with debt and seeing little chance of their problems being alleviated, "had to sell to capitalists."[77]

As a result of such practices the process of consolidation speeded up. By 1879, just twelve private companies or partnerships controlled three-quarters of the Kimberley mine.[78] In the other three mines, consolidation was no less pronounced, although there speculators predominated and many of the claims acquired new owners (but often remained unworked). In the De Beers mine in 1870, almost half the mine was held by five claim holders, the remainder being divided among approximately seventy people. That same year half the claims in the Dutoitspan mine and two-thirds of those in Bultfontein were in the hands of, respectively, one-sixth and one-third of the claim holders.[79] As one local bank manager summed up matters at the beginning of 1879, "The claims were in the hands of rich private companies. . . ."[80]

Despite bringing with it a legacy of bitterness, the transition to capitalist production did put the diamond industry on a stronger footing. With regard to output, for example, the new companies produced nearly as many diamonds in the three-year period 1877–79 as had the small-scale producers in the previous six years.[81] In 1879 alone, the diamonds exported sold for nearly £3,000,000, almost twice the sum earned in any one year before 1876.[82] Because of such productivity and the high returns earned from diamond sales, claim values were assessed upward in the later 1870s: by 50 percent in the richest mine, Kimberley, and by even higher rates in the poorer mines (from 400 percent in De Beers to 1,600 percent in Bultfontein). By 1880, the mines were valued at just over £3,000,000

77. F. W. North, "A Valuable and Interesting Paper by Frederick William North, Esq., M.E., F.G.S., on the Diamond Mines of Kimberley," 1878, p. 35, Smalberger Papers.

78. On the growth of these companies see the *Diamond News*, 6 October 1877, 4 May, 15 August 1878, 10 July 1879; N. G. Koefoed (chairman, Kimberley Mining Board) to acting colonial secretary, 28 May 1878, GLW 135 (1178); general manager, Standard Bank, to London, 15 August 1879, GM/LO, p. 233, Henry Papers.

79. See the "Poll for the Election for Members of the De Beers Mining Board . . . 31 December 1878," GLW 130 (2); and the London and South Africa Exploration Company's lists of claim holders in the Dutoitspan and Bultfontein mines in 1878, filed in GLW 12 and 147.

80. General manager, Standard Bank, to London, 28 February 1879, GM/LO, p. 221, Henry Papers.

81. Louis de Launay, *Les diamants du Cap* (Paris, 1897), pp. 4–5.

82. See the statistical returns contained in *CGHPP,* A42 1883.

(the Kimberley mine alone at £1,500,000), compared with £1,300,000 in 1877.[83]

Regardless of the obvious financial benefits of capitalist production, this new mode of working had still not, by 1879, solved the problems of technology, labor, and capital that had led to its introduction. The greater prevalence and increasing severity of these problems at the end of the first decade of diamond mining were assessed in a series of reports commissioned from a Cornish mining engineer, Thomas Kitto.[84]

Kitto argued that production methods in all four mines were very deficient. In the Kimberley mine, then excavated to a depth of three hundred feet, at least one-third of the claims were unworkable at any one time because of the problem of slips. Although the Kimberley Mining Board expended considerable sums of money and much energy on reef removal, it did not deal with the problem at its source by cutting back the sides of the mine. Kitto estimated that £800,000 would have to be spent lowering the angle of the sides and removing reef if the slippages were not to be a recurring problem. He found production problems less severe in the De Beers mine, partly because it was not as deep as Kimberley, but more so because most of the claims were held "for speculative purposes" and were not being worked. The situation was much the same in Dutoitspan and Bultfontein where close to three-quarters of the claims were in the hands of speculators. In fact, Kitto considered the latter two mines barely productive.

With regard to the matter of labor, Kitto felt steps had to be taken to ensure employers of a regular and plentiful supply of cheap black workers. Based on his knowledge of the Brazilian diamond industry, where much slave labor was used, Kitto recommended that Kimberley claim holders adopt somewhat similar means of controlling their workers by housing them in fenced and guarded barracks, providing them with the essentials of daily life, and placing them under the constant supervision of white overseers. Company barracking and white overseeing, Kitto argued, would permit employers to free themselves from dependence on an "uncivilized people" and instead acquire a work force regimented to the demands of mining.

83. Valuations for the four mines are contained in the following files: GLW 146 (3653), 150 (281), 154 (897), and 158 (1668).

84. Kitto's reports were published in the *Griqualand West Government Gazette*, 15 August, 5, 19 September 1879.

While Kitto's views on the organization of production and labor were widely accepted, his further recommendations with regard to capital were regarded as more contentious. Kitto believed that the expenditures that he had proposed could be met within Kimberley, largely through greater levies on all claim holders. In addition, he argued that production could be carried out on a rational basis in the four mines without any further consolidation of claims. He stated that there was no need to form a single company to work each mine, as some had proposed in 1877, but that as many as twenty separate operations could work independently and with profit so long as they did not attempt to undercut one another's property. Indeed, he contended that if his recommendations were adopted the Kimberley mine could still be worked at a profit even if diamond prices fell by half.

Many claim holders, however, and in particular the larger ones, did not appreciate the idea of ploughing back their new-won profits into measures for the general good. Rather, they argued that capital should come from outside Kimberley, and in much greater quantities than the local community could provide, so that machine production could be developed on an even larger scale and claim holdings further consolidated. The *Diamond News* reflected this point of view when it editorialized in 1879 that the supply of outside capital, or the lack of it, would alone determine whether or not Kimberley and the mining industry had any future.[85]


THE SECOND PHASE OF COMPANY PRODUCTION, 1880-85

Claim holders addressed the problem of capital by going public in 1880. They sought to attract investment capital to the industry through the establishment of joint stock companies. On the basis of their own valuations of their property (claims and plant) the claim holders, often in partnerships, set the capital of these new operations, took shares equivalent to what they believed was the value of their own interest, and offered the remainder to the public. Such company promotion promised financial benefits for producers and investors alike. To producers it was a means to realize the cash value of their past investment of money and labor, and to finance expanded production through the purchase of more machinery. To

85. *Diamond News*, 8 May 1879.

investors joint stock companies provided an opportunity for people other than producers or diamond merchants to share in the profits of mining. So promising were these benefits that the transition from private to public mining operations was a matter of months rather than years. The first companies were floated in Kimberley in April 1880. By the end of July one observer reported that there were "no diggers here now in the old sense of the word" and that the mines were "rapidly falling into the hands of [joint stock] companys. . . ."[86]

The expanding role of outside (mainly European) merchants in the control of diamond production provided the impetus for this transformation. At the beginning of 1879 Jules Porges had begun negotiations to acquire the properties of two of the largest claim-holding partnerships in the Kimberley mine and absorb them into his own company. These negotiations bore fruit at the end of the year with Porges' formation in Paris of the Compagnie Française des Mines de Diamants du Cap, a joint stock company which, with a capital of £560,000 and controlling one-quarter of the Kimberley mine, was by far the largest mining operation on the diamond fields.[87] In the same year a group of Port Elizabeth merchants formed another joint stock company, the Cape Diamond Mining Company Limited, with a capital of £100,000, to take over the property of a large private claim holder in the Kimberley mine, while early in 1880 the Hamburg diamond traders, Lippert and Company, bought out the largest claim holder in the De Beers mine.[88] The mines appeared to be falling into the hands of outside capitalists, the most prominent of whom were diamond merchants.

To offset this foreign mercantile challenge, Kimberley's diamond producers formed their own joint stock companies. One of the first and largest of these new operations was the De Beers Mining

86. George Kilgour (Kimberley manager of the London and South Africa Exploration Company) to the London secretary, 29 July 1880, letter book no. 1, 1880–82, no. 927, p. 140, LSAE, DBA.

87. R. M. Roberts to Messrs. J. Lewis and S. W. Paddon, 13 January 1879, R. M. Roberts, private letter book, 5 January–25 November 1879, p. 9, DBA; "Compagnie Française des Mines de Diamants du Cap. . . . Rapport de Messieurs Maurice Schlesinger et Eugène Fontenay, Commissaires," Paris, 31 January 1880, KPL; general manager, Standard Bank, to London, 6 August 1880, GM/LO, p. 264, Henry Papers.

88. "The Cape Diamond Company Limited," registered 22 September 1879, LC 13; general manager, Standard Bank, to London, 6 August 1880, GM/LO, p. 264, Henry Papers.

Company, which Cecil Rhodes (one of the most successful entrepreneurs on the diamond fields) promoted in April 1880. He formed this company in partnership with several of the largest claim holders in the De Beers mine. Having assessed the value of their ninety-odd claims at £200,000, Rhodes and his partners floated the company with a nominal capital of that sum, divided 1,900 of the £100 shares among themselves, and offered the remaining 100 to the public.[89]

Rhodes' was not the only large company floated. At much the same time claim holders in the Kimberley mine promoted several sizable operations—J. B. Robinson floated the Standard Company with a capital of £225,000 and the Rose Innes Company with a capital of £111,000; George Bottomley, the Kimberley Central Company with a capital of £149,000. A considerable number of smaller companies were also formed.[90] So popular were these promotions that over the course of the twelve months between April 1880 and April 1881 claim holders in the four mines established close to seventy joint stock companies with a nominal capital totaling just over £7,000,000.[91]

The floating of these companies initiated a period of massive speculation. Thousands of people applied for the relatively limited number of shares made available to the public. With regard to the Standard Company, for example, the 750 shares of £100 open to public subscription were all taken up within a month of the com-

89. See the Deed of Settlement, De Beers Mining Company Limited, 28 April 1880, DOK 3/2. For the company's prospectus see the *Daily Independent*, 13 May 1880; and the *Prospectuses of the Diamond Mining and Other Companies of Kimberley, Du Toit's Pan, Old De Beers, Bultfontein, Jagersfontein, and Koffyfontein, etc.* (Kimberley, 1881), pp. 56–57. The fullest accounts of Rhodes' early business activities are contained in Lewis Michell, *The Life and Times of the Right Honourable Cecil John Rhodes* (New York, 1910); and Basil Williams, *Cecil Rhodes* (New York, 1921).

90. Robinson also promoted the Griqualand West Company with a capital of £280,000 in the Dutoitspan mine. The Kimberley Central's capital was soon increased to £576,860 as it absorbed numerous smaller operations. See the pamphlet of prospectuses cited in the previous note for descriptions of these various promotions.

91. The exact number of companies, and their total capital, is difficult to determine because this was such a period of boom, with operations appearing and disappearing almost overnight. For some variations in the estimates given, of no more than plus or minus five companies and £500,000 in total capital, see the *Prospectuses of the Diamond Mining Companies*; the *Daily Independent*, 21 February 1882; and J. W. Matthews, *Incwadi Yami; Or, Twenty Years' Personal Experience in South Africa* (London, 1887), pp. 243–56.

pany's formation.[92] That record paled into insignificance as the speculative urge reached fever pitch in the early months of 1881. When the Barnato Company was floated on the share market in March 1881, the £75,000 worth of shares available were subscribed twice over within an hour and were selling at a premium of 25 percent after two days.[93] The competition for shares was so intense that it soon became common for most stock to trade at premiums ranging from 25 percent up to 300 percent and more as investment capital poured into the industry from merchants and bankers in Port Elizabeth and Cape Town.[94] With such premiums available many of the mining-company promoters themselves engaged in speculation rather than investing their profits in production, often by selling the shares of the companies first established in the Kimberley and De Beers mines and reinvesting their profits in new and more speculative ventures floated in Dutoitspan, Bultfontein, and in largely unproven mines in the Orange Free State.[95] In August 1880, the manager of a Kimberley bank summed up the initial effects of company formation and share speculation in the industry and the community as follows: "On the whole I think this province was never in so flourishing a condition as it is at present."[96]

But the foundations of this speculative enterprise were extremely weak. In the first place, claim holders had often floated the companies with an excessively high value placed on their properties. The total nominal capital of the companies—£7,000,000, of which over 90 percent had been fully paid up by the middle of 1881—was over twice the officially assessed value of the mines in 1880. The large premiums at which shares changed hands added to the problem of overvaluation, with the result that the price paid

92. *Daily Independent*, 22 April, 4 June 1880.
93. Matthews, *Incwadi Yami*, p. 253.
94. General manager, Standard Bank, to London, 6 August 1880, GM/LO, p. 264, Henry Papers; *Daily Independent*, 3 February, 12 March 1881. For the sources of capital see the "Returns of Transfers of Shares," Miscellaneous Companies, Jan.–Dec. 1881, and Jan.–June 1882, DOK 2d series 2/1, 2/3; and the share registers of the various companies contained in CR 3/1–10.
95. General manager, Standard Bank, to London, 6 August 1880, GM/LO, p. 264, Henry Papers; the *Griqualand West Investor's Guardian and Commercial Register*, 21 April 1881. On the Orange Free State mines see Douglas McGill, *A History of Koffiefontein: Town and Mine, 1870 to 1902* (privately printed, 1976).
96. Kimberley branch manager, Standard Bank, quoted in general manager to London, 6 August 1880, GM/LO, p. 264, Henry Papers.

for stock bore little relation to the value of the companies in terms of their production capacity.[97]

Second, since most of the companies were floated in Kimberley and the Cape nearly all the stock was taken up locally before foreign investors had a chance to make purchases.[98] Often these local investors applied for shares but delayed paying for them in the hope of selling for a profit as prices rose before they had to put up any cash.[99] Others with capital invested everything they had in a single company to boost its share prices, secure a quick profit, and then reinvest in a new venture. In short, the company promoters and speculators created a vicious cycle: as share prices went higher, foreigners would not buy in because the stock was obviously overvalued; without new capital the current investors could not realize a profit on their speculation; and those who had made paper purchases had no money to pay for the shares for which they had applied when the companies finally called upon them to make good their obligations.

The banks burst this speculative bubble. In April 1881, at the height of the share mania, the Kimberley banks refused to accept diamond mining company scrip as collateral for loans.[100] Since there was no other capital available for speculation, all that of Kimberley and the Cape being already tied up in the industry and that of Europe frightened off, the inflationary cycle was rapidly replaced by spiraling depression. Those who had shares rushed to sell them and as a result pushed prices down. Instead of trading at a premium shares sold below par, often for half their face value or less. Moreover, as prices continued to fall the share market became stagnant; no one wanted to buy because there were no signs of improvement, few wanted to sell because the only price they could get was so low that it would be tantamount to throwing their investment away. By

97. *Ibid.*, 2 June 1881, GM/LO, p. 294, Henry Papers; *Daily Independent*, 7 February, 21 July 1881.

98. Managing director of the Kimberley Share Exchange Company to Messrs. Fairbridge and Pettit, 7 October 1880, letter book, The Kimberley Share Exchange Company Limited, 1880–81, CR 2/6; general manager, Standard Bank, to London, 19 November 1881, GM/LO, p. 320, Henry Papers; "Return of Transfers of Shares," Jan.–June 1882, DOK 2d series 2/3.

99. General manager, Standard Bank, to London, 2 June, 19 November 1881, GM/LO, pp. 294, 320, Henry Papers; *Daily Independent*, 30 March 1881; letter signed Investor, the *Griqualand West Investor's Guardian*, 10 November 1881.

100. General manager, Standard Bank, to London, 2 June 1881, GM/LO, p. 294, Henry Papers; *Daily Independent*, 7 April 1881; the *Griqualand West Investor's Guardian*, 14 April 1881.

the second half of 1881 the economies of Kimberley and the Cape were locked together in recession.[101]

While the speculative fever exhausted local capital resources, it also crippled the production capacity of many of the newly formed companies. First, the claim holders-cum-company promoters recycled most of the subscribed capital into further speculation rather than into production. Of the small proportion of capital that they did retain for such investment—no more than 10 percent of the total capital of the companies floated—they spent nearly all of it immediately on receipt in purchasing machinery.[102] Since these company men fully expected to make quick profits, from speculation and expanded machine production, they seldom put aside reserve funds.[103] Furthermore, because of the general speculative fever, investors demanded a quick return on their money, forced the payment of frequent and large dividends, and thus ensured that whatever surpluses the companies generated were immediately disbursed to shareholders rather than reinvested in production.[104] As a result few companies had any capital resources to fall back on if any difficulties arose in mining. The president of the Cape Town Chamber of Commerce noted in a speech on the state of the diamond industry that by the end of 1881 none of the mining companies had any reserve funds: all monies had been expended either in working costs or in dividend payments.[105]

Second, increased mining difficulties, aggravated by the expanded scale of company operations, made this lack of capital a critical weakness for the industry. As the company men competed against one another to produce as many diamonds as possible as quickly as possible they adopted inefficient and often dangerous methods of working, misused their machinery, and added to the technological problems of mining. With regard to the method of working, company production recreated the problems of small

101. For contemporary discussions of the causes of Kimberley's problems see the *Griqualand West Investor's Guardian*, 5 May, 13 October 1881; and the *Daily Independent*, 12 April, 5, 22 August, 7 October 1881.

102. Matthews, *Incwadi Yami*, p. 251, estimates that £650,700 was spent on machinery. See also the *Griqualand West Investor's Guardian*, 6 August, 1 September 1881, and 6 July 1882.

103. See the *Prospectuses of the Diamond Mining Companies*, for evidence of the minute sums put aside for emergencies.

104. For examples of such high dividends see the *Griqualand West Investor's Guardian*, 5 May 1881; and the *Daily Independent*, 26 May, 7 October 1881.

105. *Daily Independent*, 21 February 1882.

claim holders—only on a much larger scale. There were a considerable number of companies in each mine and all of these carried out independent operations, often undercutting the claims of adjoining properties that were not so extensively excavated or, alternatively, allowing their ground to slip and cover competitors' operations. With regard to machinery, many of the companies lacked skilled men to operate the new machines—few of the men employed as engineers were officially certificated—while in the rush to make profits little attention was given to safe operations. The government inspector of mines noted in a report on the mines that most hauling gear lacked such normally required equipment as brakes and safety valves. The result of such dangerous working and poor management, the inspector argued, was that digging in the Kimberley mine had become a far more dangerous activity than it had ever been in the past, and he expected it to become even more so in the future.[106] Poor digging methods and mismanaged machinery exacerbated the problem of fallen reef in the Kimberley mine. In 1881, only one-third of the claims in the mine were workable, the rest were covered by reef.[107] The lack of capital meant that neither the companies nor the Kimberley Mining Board could raise the money for reef-removal work and thus return the mine to full production.[108]

Third, the competition between companies to produce diamonds and profits raised the price of black labor. Although more blacks came to Kimberley and worked in the mines during 1881–82 than ever before, the complaints of employers at the high rates of wages and the shortage of workers had never been greater. Wages rose from the 10s. to 20s. per week that ruled in the later 1870s to near 40s. by the end of 1881. Moreover, despite the increased supply of men drawn by these wage rates, many companies experienced critical shortages of labor because the workers constantly changed employers in search of higher wages, forcing operations to cease

106. *CGHPP,* G34 1883, p. 59.
107. "Report of the Inspector of Diamond Mines for the Year 1881," *CGHPP,* G27 1882, p. 9.
108. On the financial problems of the Kimberley Mining Board, which had debts of over £300,000 by 1883, see the letter from the secretary of the board to the chairman and members, 3 July 1883, LND 1/139 (59); the "Report by T. P. Watson upon the Excavations at the Diamond Mines of Kimberley and De Beers," *CGHPP,* G101 1883; and the "Report upon the Financial Position of the Kimberley Mining Board by E. A. Judge, Esq.," *CGHPP,* G107 1883.

periodically and preventing the new machinery from being used to its full capacity. Some companies sought to overcome these problems by contracting with recruiting agents in the Transvaal, Natal, and southern Mozambique, but this was an expensive option: the agents charged considerable fees, often as much as £4 per worker; the transportation costs of those recruited had to be borne by employers; and once the men were in Kimberley they had to be paid the ruling wage rate (no matter what lower figure their contracts stated) or else they would "desert" to other employers. Thus, labor costs appeared out of control.[109]

The resulting loss of capital for production, increased technological problems, and much higher labor costs meant the evaporation of the industry's profitability. After a year-and-a-half of intensive company formation, the investment of millions of pounds, the purchase of hundreds of steam engines, and an enormous expansion in digging operations, no more than 10 percent of the mining companies had paid a dividend by the end of 1881.[110] Many of the mining operations were at a standstill and some companies verged on bankruptcy. The editorialist of Kimberley's main business newspaper, the *Griqualand West Investor's Guardian*, knew who was to blame: "There is no use denying that we have botched our own affairs to a very considerable extent."[111]

Having exhausted their own and the Cape's capital, Kimberley's mining men looked to foreign investors for their salvation. They believed that the mining industry could only be put on a sure footing through the infusion of massive amounts of new capital. With the local public no longer interested in risking whatever money they had left, and the banks not ready to advance money to mining companies, the only sources of capital that remained were in England and Europe.[112]

Yet most investors in those countries had initially been shut out of the industry when locals took all the shares and pushed them to absurdly high prices and then been completely deterred when the bottom fell out of the share market. The only foreign investors likely

109. See chaps. 2 and 3 for discussion of labor struggles.
110. The *Griqualand West Investor's Guardian*, 1 September, 6, 13 October 1881; *Daily Independent*, 21 February 1882.
111. The *Griqualand West Investor's Guardian*, 22 December 1881.
112. On more capital as the solution for all ills see the *Griqualand West Investor's Guardian*, 5 May, 7 July, 1, 8, 22 September, 6, 13 October 1881; and the *Daily Independent*, 2 June, 8, 21 July 1881.

to show interest in the industry after the middle of 1881, when their capital was so desperately needed, were those whom Kimberley's company promoters had originally tried to exclude: the diamond merchants and their bankers. Though some in Kimberley saw nothing wrong with overseas investors taking over the diamond industry—the manager of the Standard Bank for one believed that the industry's depressed state could only be alleviated when "foreign capitalists" took "the place of weak Colonial proprietors"—the producers saw little advantage in attracting capital at the cost of their own controlling position.[113]

The producers, however, believed that the introduction of one measure held the key to their retention of control over the industry and to the attraction of foreign capital: the amalgamation of the dozens of separate companies into either four large combinations to work each of the mines or a single giant corporation. Amalgamation as they envisaged it in the latter half of 1881 promised major benefits to the industry. Production could be rationalized with the elimination of competition, the multitude of small hauling engines replaced with much more powerful machinery, and working costs reduced. Furthermore, the concurrent elimination of competition among employers for workers would make the control of black labor much easier. The output of diamonds could be regulated and control over the price of stones taken out of the hands of merchants and put into those of producers. Finally, the combination of these benefits would, by promising considerable future profits, attract foreign investors to the diamond fields.[114]

But amalgamation schemes could be pursued as easily by foreign capitalists as by local producers, and the matter of speed was therefore important. In March 1882, at the same time that rumors were circulating of a European-based scheme to buy out the Kimberley mine, Cecil Rhodes and his partners in the De Beers Mining Company put forward their own plan to amalgamate the De Beers mine.[115] Rhodes and his partners argued that working costs in the mine could be cut by 27 percent and the net yield of production

113. General manager, Standard Bank, to London, 19 November 1881, GM/LO, p. 320, Henry Papers. On the ambivalent attitudes that local mining people had toward foreign capital see the *Griqualand West Investor's Guardian*, 29 December 1881.

114. See, e.g., the *Daily Independent*, 27 October, 27 November 1881.

115. See the *Griqualand West Investor's Guardian*, 6 October 1881; and the *Daily Independent*, 14, 15, 25 March 1882.

increased by 435 percent if the companies and claim holders amalgamated. Such financial benefits would be produced by two key features of the proposed scheme: underground mining would replace open-cast, and black workers would be confined in barracks. The transition to underground mining would permit the replacement of the numerous small machines then in operation by four giant hauling machines, which were both more efficient and economical to operate, and through the consolidation of managements and work forces greatly reduce the required number of costly white workers. Barracking of black workers promised to eliminate all competition for labor, assist the better regulation of supply through the concomitant establishment of recruitment depots in the interior, and provide profits, estimated at a sum equivalent to at least 50 percent of the wages paid, on the sale of goods to the men while locked up.[116]

To put this plan into operation Rhodes and his partners had to juggle the interests of foreign investors and local producers. While underground working promised great profits in the long term, it needed an immediate infusion of capital to pay for its introduction; Rhodes estimated £500,000. Since this amount of money could come only from outside the industry, Rhodes and his partners first took their proposed scheme to the Paris bankers, Baron Erlanger and Company, convinced them of its viability, and secured a promise of financial support. Having valued the various operations in the mine and come up with a total figure of £2,511,500, they next called on other company directors and claim holders to join together to form a single new corporation. Those who agreed to join would receive 50 percent of the estimated value of their property in cash (courtesy of the baron) and the other 50 percent in scrip in the new company.[117]

The scheme foundered, however, on the matter of valuations. Few in the mining industry could come to any common agreement about a mining property's worth, especially since so many different factors had to be taken into account: whether the ground was rich

116. Rhodes estimated a total savings of £206,430, broken down as follows: £61,900 from reduced management and white-labor needs; £31,590 from reduced black-labor needs; and £112,940 from having fewer steam engines, horses, and other equipment. See the "Statement Respecting De Beers Mine," enclosed in the file "De Beers Mine: Letters Regarding the Amalgamation, 1882," KPL.

117. *Ibid.* See also W. Alderson and H. W. H. Dunsmore (Rhodes' partners) to the chairman and directors of the Birbeck Diamond Mining Company Limited, 28 March 1882, CR 6/1; and the *Daily Independent*, 27 March, 4 April 1882.

in diamonds or not; whether the claims were covered in reef or submerged in water; how much ground had been excavated but not yet washed; and so forth. By May, Rhodes and his partners had upped the valuation of the mine properties to £3,000,000 but still could not secure agreement for amalgamation. The baron pulled out, and the scheme collapsed.[118]

Continued production and marketing problems only made the need for fundamental restructuring of the industry more urgent. In the Kimberley mine the depth and intensity of excavations had so exacerbated the problem of slips that most companies had to concentrate their efforts on removing fallen reef rather than on working diamondiferous ground. As a result diamond output fell at the same time that costs increased, a process that the inspector of diamond mines concluded could only be turned around by amalgamation and the introduction of deep-level mining.[119] The most important incentive to amalgamation, however, came not from the problems of production but from those of marketing. In the latter half of 1882 the European diamond market collapsed, largely because of overproduction in Kimberley, and the price of diamonds went into a tailspin. Between September and December carat prices fell by an average of 30 percent and continued to decline during the following year.[120] Receipts from diamond sales plummeted by 16 percent in the De Beers mine, 25 percent in Kimberley, and 36 percent in Dutoitspan and Bultfontein.[121] For many companies already in a weakened state this was the final blow that sent them into bankruptcy; for the remainder the future seemed very bleak indeed.[122]

Amalgamation schemes proliferated. Two in particular were promoted with considerable vigor—one in the Dutoitspan mine by foreign capitalists, the other in the Kimberley mine by local producers. The European merchant bankers N. M. Rothschild and Sons sent a representative to the diamond fields in November 1882 to investigate the possibility of amalgamating the Dutoitspan mine. The

118. Alderson and Dunsmore to the chairman and directors, Birbeck Company, 22 May 1882, CR 6/1; *Daily Independent*, 29 November 1882.

119. *CGHPP,* G34 1883, p. 5.

120. *Daily Independent*, 17, 19 January 1883.

121. Board for the Protection of Mining Interests, *Returns, Showing Imports of Diamonds into and Exports from Kimberley . . . [and] Summary for Period Dating from September 1st, 1882, to December 31st, 1885* (Kimberley, 1886).

122. By 1883–84 over one-third of the companies floated in 1881–82 had gone bankrupt. For a report on these companies and their liabilities see the *Daily Independent*, 13 June 1888.

representative, Albert Gansl, met with the directors of the various mining companies and requested that they estimate the value of their properties, assess their liabilities, and determine how much capital would be needed to bring the mine into full production. Late in January 1883, Gansl informed the companies that Rothschild's had determined that an amalgamated Dutoitspan mine could be a profitable operation and had decided to go ahead with the scheme.[123] In the same month, producers in the Kimberley mine held the first of several meetings to promote their own amalgamation scheme. J. B. Robinson, the director of one of the largest companies in the mine, the Standard, dominated proceedings. Speaking to the various directors gathered, he stated that the time was ripe to consolidate all operations in the mine under the control of a single giant joint stock company. He argued that if the current system of irrational mining continued, the producers would only succeed in rendering their own properties valueless.[124]

Both schemes came to nothing. In the case of Rothschild's, most of the Dutoitspan mining companies, all of them in a perilous financial condition, did settle on a common valuation for their properties and agreed to amalgamate. But Rothschild's kept changing the terms. At one stage they proposed that as the promoters they get a guaranteed preferential dividend on their shares in the amalgamated company. Later they reduced the amount of cash they were prepared to advance to cover the mining companies' liabilities. Finally they decided that the scheme would not be profitable after all, especially with the price of diamonds continuing to plunge, and withdrew altogether.[125] Although the Kimberley companies got as far as agreeing on a common valuation, their scheme failed because they could not attract the interest of any foreign investors.[126] Just as the fall in diamond prices, on top of the production problems of the industry, had made consolidation of operations more and more necessary, this same combination of factors made the diamond fields an unattractive area for investment and thus kept away the capital so necessary for the industry's restructuring.

123. *Ibid.*, 29 November, 6, 7 December 1882, 11, 18, 20 January 1883.
124. *Ibid.*, 18 January 1883.
125. See Francis Oats to the liquidators of the Victoria Diamond Mining Company, 8 August 1883, CR 5/3; and the *Daily Independent*, 12, 14 February, 13, 14 March, 9 April, 18, 23 May, 16 June, 9 August, 31 December 1883, 10 January 1884.
126. *Daily Independent*, 26 February 1883.

With the failure of these schemes to bring about amalgamation through negotiation, the largest companies pursued consolidation policies of their own design. Two companies in particular took the lead in acquiring the properties of smaller competitors: the Kimberley Central Company and the De Beers Mining Company. Each had become the largest operation in its respective mine at the time of company formation in 1880–81. Their very size insulated them to some extent against the problems crippling many of the smaller companies. They had considerable capital resources and could afford more powerful machinery, could pay higher wages, and, with extensive claim holdings, were less likely to have all their property covered by fallen reef or water. Moreover, their dominance increased partly as a matter of attrition, with so many of the smaller companies going to the wall in the aftermath of the collapse of diamond prices in 1882.

The amalgamation process pursued by both companies was more often one of forced takeovers rather than of mutually agreed upon combinations. A crucial factor in this process was the power that the Kimberley Central and the De Beers companies exercised over their respective mining boards. In 1883 Rhodes, a member of the governing ministry at the Cape, secured a change in the legislation that determined the structure of these organizations. Whereas before 1883 no company, no matter what the size of its holdings, could have more than one representative on a mining board, the new legislation eliminated this restriction.[127] As a result the Central and De Beers companies, having the most votes since the franchise was based on a property qualification, took control of the boards. Both companies used this new source of power against their mining competitors in much the same manner that large claim holders had used the boards against small claim holders in the late 1870s. The Kimberley Board, for example, carried out only limited reef-removal work and restricted most of its operations to the property of the Kimberley Central Company while levying all claim holders for the work done. By such means the Central forced a number of companies so close to bankruptcy that they agreed to amalgamate.[128] The De Beers Company adopted similar tactics,

127. Act 19, 23 September 1883, Act for the Establishment, Working and Management of Alluvial Digging and Mining of Precious Stones and Minerals.

128. On the processes by which the Central forced other companies into submission see the *Daily Independent*, 18 August 1884.

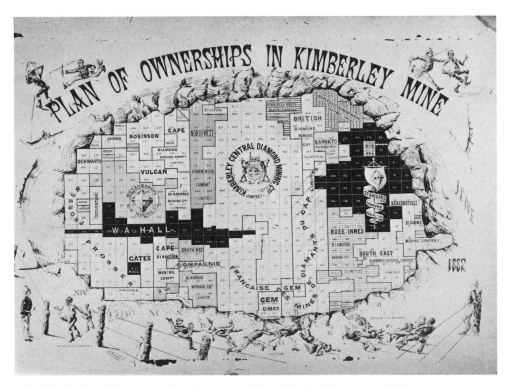

FIGURE 1.2    Diagram of claim ownership, Kimberley mine, 1882
(Johannesburg Public Library)

making use of its control of water and reef removal (through the
De Beers Mining Board) to force several companies into bankruptcy
and then to purchase their properties for very low prices.[129]

Whatever the means used, the result was increasing dominance
for the two companies in their respective mines. In January 1884
the chairman of the Kimberley Central reported to his shareholders
that amalgamations with a number of former competitors had
given his company "such strength in the mine . . . that no combination can take place against us in the Kimberley Mine to-day." In
May the chairman of De Beers likewise announced a string of takeovers, which he claimed had effectively broken all opposition and
ensured that when final amalgamation took place in the De Beers

129. See the "Report of the Directors of the De Beers Mining Company Limited," 5 May 1884, SAL. See also the *Daily Independent*, 14 March and 18 August
1884.

mine it would be carried out on terms dictated by his company. Both men expected that the consolidation of all operations under the control of a single company in each mine would be a relatively straightforward process and only a matter of time.[130]

Expansion, however, produced quite different financial returns for the two companies. The Kimberley Central, for the first time in its history, went into the red at the beginning of 1884 and got further and further into debt as the year progressed.[131] De Beers, on the other hand, did very well, clearing a net profit of £92,976 on total revenues of £209,225 in the year ending 31 March 1884 and posting even better returns in 1884–85.[132]

The difference in returns was largely a product of the much greater mining difficulties faced by the Central and other companies in the Kimberley mine. A reef fall in November 1883 rendered much of the mine unworkable for months afterward. Additional slips in 1884 limited most operations to the removal of debris rather than the excavation of diamond-bearing blue ground. Indeed, no more than 50 out of 460 claims remained workable during the year, with the result that the output of stones in 1884 was only two-thirds of what it had been in 1883.[133] By contrast, open-cast operations in the De Beers mine were relatively unencumbered by such difficulties. An average of 250 claims remained operational during 1884 and diamond output increased 17 percent over the previous year's level.[134] Furthermore, with fewer mining problems De Beers' pro-

130. See the Central's half-yearly report printed in the *Daily Independent*, 11 January 1884; and the "Report of the Directors of the De Beers Mining Company Limited," 5 May 1884, SAL.

131. See the company's reports printed in the *Daily Independent*, 11 January, 15 December 1884. On the generally poor financial returns of companies in the Kimberley mine see also the half-yearly reports of the general manager, Standard Bank, to London, 6 February 1884, pp. 25–26, GMO 3/1/16, and 9 August 1884, pp. 38–39, GMO 3/1/17, SBA.

132. See the "Report of the Directors of the De Beers Mining Company Limited," 5 May 1884, SAL; the company's annual report for 1884–85 printed in the *Daily Independent*, 9 May 1885; and for a tabular listing of dividends, Henry Mitchell, *Diamonds and Gold of South Africa* (London, 1888), p. 8.

133. On the production difficulties of the Kimberley mine see the annual reports of the inspector of diamond mines, *CGHPP*, G30 1884, p. 6, and G28 1885, pp. 3–6. Because of such difficulties the debt of the Kimberley Mining Board, which had amounted to £300,000 in 1883, approached £500,000 in 1884. For diamond returns see the Board for the Protection of Mining Interests, *Returns of Diamonds September 1st, 1882, to December 31st, 1885*, p. 26.

134. See the reports of the inspector of diamond mines, *CGHPP*, G30 1884, p. 8, and G28 1885, pp. 6–9. The De Beers Mining Board, unlike its Kimberley counterpart, had a surplus of funds in 1884.

duction costs per load excavated averaged half or less those of the Kimberley mine, while the decrease in output levels in the latter mine meant that De Beers could market its increased output without weakening demand.[135] In short, De Beers profited from its own strengths and Kimberley's weaknesses.[136]

The directors of the Kimberley Central, faced with the prospect of even more dismal returns if nothing was done, took steps in 1884 to restructure mining operations in an attempt to return the company to profitability. Initially they lowered labor costs by subjecting their employees to greater levels of discipline and by reducing wage rates.[137] More fundamentally, they sought to mechanize the work process further (thereby cutting the cost of production) and overcome the near-crippling problems of open-cast mining by changing to a system of underground operations. Throughout 1884 the Kimberley Central sunk exploratory shafts in the mine. In 1885 the company developed these shafts, along with networks of tunnels, into a full-scale system of deep-level digging. By the beginning of 1886 its competitors had largely followed suit and practically all mining operations were being carried out underground.[138]

The transition to deep-level digging did not immediately return the Kimberley Central to profitability. Development work consumed most of the company's funds and much of its employees' energies. The initial system of underground excavations proved poorly designed, collapsing soon after its installation, and had to be completely redeveloped.[139] With diamond output from the mine even

135. The Central's costs exceeded 20s. per load; De Beers' averaged closer to 8s. See the *Daily Independent*, 30 May 1883, 8 May 1885; and Mitchell, *Diamonds and Gold*, p. 8.

136. On the generally profitable condition of companies in the De Beers mine, and the benefits they derived from Kimberley's problems, see the half-yearly reports of the general manager, Standard Bank, to London, 6 February 1884, p. 25, GMO 3/1/16, 9 August 1884, pp. 38–39, GMO 3/1/17, SBA. On the 1884 rise in diamond prices in De Beers mine see the Board for the Protection of Mining Interests, *Returns of Diamonds September 1st, 1882, to December 31st, 1885*, p. 17.

137. For discussions of the linkage between increased labor control and lowered costs see the *Daily Independent*, 12 August, 23 October 1884. On the fall in wages see the reports of the inspector of diamond mines, CGHPP, G30 1884, p. 7, and G28 1885, p. 6.

138. *Daily Independent*, 25 April, 20 June 1885; reports of the inspector of diamond mines, CGHPP, G28 1885, pp. 5, 24–25, and G40 1886, pp. 3–5.

139. See the reports of the inspector of diamond mines, CGHPP, G28 1885, pp. 3–4; the general manager, Standard Bank, to London, 6 February 1885, p. 38, GMO 3/1/17; and the inspector, Standard Bank, 22 December 1885, pp. 209–10, INSP 1/1/86, SBA.

lower in 1885 than in 1884, receipts fell, and although the Central made a small profit (of less than £10,000) for the twelve months ending 30 April 1885, it went back into the red in the following financial year.[140]

But the Central's long-term prospects were excellent. Kimberley had always had a greater concentration of diamonds than the other mines, and this advantage continued with the move underground; in 1885 each load excavated yielded 1.5 carats compared with 0.9 carats in Beers, 0.3 in Bultfontein, and 0.2 in Dutoitspan.[141] Once amalgamation and deep-level digging reduced working costs to a level more in line with those of the other mines, Kimberley would not only produce more diamonds than its competitors but do so at a higher rate of profit. Rhodes estimated that with similar working costs in the Kimberley and De Beers mines (a stage he expected to be reached in 1886), Kimberley could produce diamonds for a net profit per load one-third larger than could De Beers (and for ten and thirteen times the amount of profit made in Bultfontein and Dutoitspan respectively) and continue to maintain this margin even after the De Beers mine changed to underground operations.[142]

Such potential profits, however, depended on producers balancing supply and demand. Difficulties with open-cast working followed by the problems of underground development kept output low from the Kimberley mine in 1883–85 and ensured that the industry did not suffer greatly from overproduction and falling carat prices during that period.[143] But as soon as the deep-level diggings of the

140. See the company's reports printed in the *Daily Independent*, 16 June 1885, 10 June 1887; and, on diamond receipts, the Board for the Protection of Mining Interests, *Returns of Diamonds September 1st, 1882, to December 31st, 1885*, pp. 21, 26.

141. "Report of the Inspector of Diamond Mines for the Year 1885," *CGHPP*, G40 1886, pp. 6, 10. Rhodes thought the De Beers mine capable of producing 1.25 carats per load, so long as all excavations were organized rationally by a single company. See the minutes of a meeting of De Beers' directors, 5 February 1886, xerox copy in Smalberger Papers, UCT. And the De Beers Company did itself produce 1.31 carats per load in 1885, although the return dropped to 1.15 carats in 1886 and even less in subsequent years. See Mitchell, *Diamonds and Gold*, p. 8.

142. See the minutes of De Beers' directors' meeting, 5 February 1886, Smalberger Papers, UCT. De Beers changed over to underground production in 1885. See the "Report of the Inspector of Diamond Mines for the Year 1885," *CGHPP*, G40 1886, p. 4.

143. Diamond output from the four mines amounted to 2,312,234 carats in 1883, 2,204,786 carats in 1884, and 2,287,261 carats in 1885, while carat prices

Kimberley Central and its competitors came into full operation—
a development that the Standard Bank's manager expected to take
place by the middle of 1886—then diamond production would likely
expand enormously, carat prices fall, and profit margins narrow or
disappear entirely (particularly in the poorer mines) as the various
companies struggled for supremacy against one another.[144]

"Amalgamation," the chairman of the Kimberley Central Company had pointed out in 1884, even before the development of deep-
level digging exacerbated matters, was "clearly the only remedy"
for the fundamental problem of overproduction.[145] The directors of
the Central feared that if rapid amalgamation did not take place
then the company would become locked in a mutually destructive
struggle with its competitors, particularly with the French Company, the next-largest operation in the Kimberley mine. An attempt
to negotiate a peaceful settlement with the French's directors early
in 1885 did not succeed, though, and the Central then sought to
acquire ownership of properties located in strategically important
parts of the mine and by such means drive the French Company out
of business. The latter company responded in kind, seeking to take
over many of the same operations sought by the Central, and thus
ensued just what the Central's directors had feared: a bidding war—
one in which neither side had much capital to spare—that lasted
through 1885 and into 1886 without resolution.[146]

Amalgamation in the Kimberley mine, once successful, would
threaten the economic prospects of companies in the other three
mines. Whenever the Kimberley Central or the French won their
war, the victor would have the power so to increase diamond production that carat prices would fall to a level at which only the

---

averaged 20s. 5d. in 1883, 23s. 3d. in 1884, and 19s. 6d. in 1885. The Kimberley
mine's contribution to total diamond output fell from 41 percent in 1883 to 29
percent in 1884 and 23 percent in 1885. See the Board for the Protection of Mining
Interests, *Returns of Diamonds September 1st, 1882, to December 31st, 1885*, pp. 26,
30.

144. See the half-yearly reports of the general manager, Standard Bank, to
London, 6 February 1885, p. 39, GMO 3/1/17, and 8 February 1886, p. 47, GMO 3/1/
19, SBA.

145. *Daily Independent*, 11 January 1884.

146. On the Central's initial attempts to negotiate with the French Company,
and the subsequent struggle to take over other mining operations, see the minutes
of the Central's directors' meetings, 13, 17 December 1884, 16, 20, 21 January,
3 February 1885, minute book (directors' meetings) 3 November 1884–26 February
1885, pp. 41, 48, 88, 89–90, 97, 100, 160, KCDM, DBA; and the *Daily Independent*,
31 January, 8 May, 16 June 1885.

Kimberley mine could return a profit. The poorer mines, including De Beers, would then, as the Standard Bank's inspector noted, have "to be shut up," and the company owning Kimberley, secure in its monopoly, could then cut output, raise prices, and win large profits.[147]

To forestall such a development, the directors of companies in De Beers, Dutoitspan, and Bultfontein actively pursued various amalgamation schemes of their own. Rhodes engaged in aggressive takeover tactics in the De Beers mine and formulated a plan to amalgamate all four mines into a single operation. Essentially, he believed that if the De Beers Company acted quickly enough it could acquire ownership of the entire De Beers mine, fully develop deep-level operations in the enlarged property, thereby gain a considerable degree of control over the industry's diamond output, and establish a strong financial base at a time when the Kimberley companies were still struggling in a weak state. His company would then be in a position to pressure the Kimberley companies, and those in Dutoitspan and Bultfontein, to amalgamate on terms beneficial to De Beers—and do so before the Kimberley mine came into full production and forced the poorer mines into bankruptcy.[148] For their part, directors of a number of companies in Dutoitspan and Bultfontein, aware that they could never finance amalgamation on the basis of their own weak operations, sought to interest European investors in the diamond industry as a whole in the hope that they could sell their properties as going concerns before being forced out of business either by Kimberley or De Beers.[149]

The result of such competitive interest in amalgamation and consolidation was, as the local manager of the London and South Africa Exploration Company noted in his annual report for 1885, the opening of the diamond industry "on a new phase and as in 1881 the individual digger gave way to the small Joint Stock Company so the small Joint Stock Company must now give way to greater agglomerations."[150] Such agglomerations included the Kim-

147. See the inspector's report of 22 December 1885, pp. 209, 212, 216, INSP 1/1/86, SBA.

148. See the minutes of De Beers' directors' meeting, 5 February 1886, Smalberger Papers, UCT.

149. Men with large investments in Dutoitspan and Bultfontein, such as Charles Posno, Julius Wernher, and James D'Esterre, were the prime movers behind a plan to float a single large company in Europe in late 1885 to take over the mines. See the discussion of the "Unified" scheme in chapt. 5.

150. J. B. Currey to secretary, London and South Africa Exploration Company, London, 15 March 1886, letter book no. 6, September 1885–July 1886, pp. 599–600, LSAE, DBA.

berley Central, which had a fully paid-up capital of £750,000 in 1885, and De Beers Mining, even larger at £1,000,000, each of which worked nearly an entire mine.[151] The transformation from the early days of diamond digging—when most men had had a capital of no more than a few hundred pounds and often worked claims the size of graves—was striking. Yet one element, the one dearest to the hearts of mining capitalists, remained as meager and ephemeral in 1885 as it had been fifteen years before: profit. Some companies made money in 1885, particularly De Beers Mining, but most did not. Moreover, none of those companies making a profit could count on doing so for long, not, that is, once the Kimberley mine amalgamated into a single operation. The fundamental problem of the industry remained the same in the mid-1880s as it had been in the early 1870s—overproduction because of competition. The only solution to such a problem lay in the elimination of competition and the establishment of a monopoly company in control of the entire industry. But that necessitated a further phase of even more intense competition before a single victor could emerge.[152]

151. For the capital of the companies see their amended Articles of Association, DOK 3/2, 3/5; and Mitchell, *Diamonds and Gold*, p. 8.
152. For discussion of the intensification and demise of competitive production in the later 1880s see chapt. 5.

CHAPTER TWO

# The Origins and Consolidation
# of Black Migrancy, 1870–86

The impact of industrial growth was felt well beyond the confines of the mines, the town, and even of the Cape Colony. Indeed, the most profound changes wrought by the diamond industry were those that affected black societies throughout the subcontinent. For the new mining center had an even more voracious appetite for the labor of men and the agricultural and pastoral output of rural societies than it did for the capital of the Cape and of Europe. Thousands of people, coming from every black society south of the Zambezi River, labored each year in the mines; thousands more sold vast quantities of foodstuffs, firewood, and other goods to the town. Although the initial participation of blacks in production for Kimberley's labor and produce markets was voluntary—at least in the sense that no whites, either at the diamond fields or elsewhere, forced them to produce—this situation changed as the diamond industry grew and its needs changed, and as the British government, acting in response to pressures generated by the rise of the diamond industry, intervened in the subcontinent and conquered most of those black societies hitherto independent. At the same time that the demands of diamond production reordered the organization and control of mining, with small diggers losing out to large industrial capitalists, these demands also caused a fundamental change in Kimberley's rural hinterland, as formerly independent black producers were transformed in many cases into largely landless proletarians.

Yet this latter process was by no means simple or straightforward, marked as it was by considerable variety in the type and intensity of struggle. This chapter examines the ways in which blacks produced for Kimberley, their reasons for doing so, and the means by which they lost their independence—the patterns of their lives determined within two decades of the discovery of diamonds no longer by the work cycles of cultivation and pastoralism but rather by the needs and demands of industrial production.

## THE PRIMACY OF RURAL FACTORS, 1870–75

In the two decades prior to the discovery of diamonds, the productive capacity of rural societies throughout southern Africa was increasingly constrained by a number of pressures. Ecological decay was the most widespread of these. Two highly virulent livestock diseases, redwater fever and lung sickness, spread rapidly in the 1850s and 1860s, decimating the cattle holdings of black pastoralists across the subcontinent—from those of the Tsonga on the east coast to those of the Tlhaping in the west.[1] Drought, while not an uncommon problem in past decades, reached crisis proportions in the early 1860s, further reducing cattle numbers and cutting crop outputs. As with the cattle diseases, this problem was widespread, affecting the Tsonga and the Tlhaping and all the societies located between them, although to varying degrees. The Griqua, who lived in the area where diamonds were soon to be found, perhaps suffered most of all, for their water table dropped, streams and springs dried up, and the fields that they had once cultivated intensively became desiccated. Most Griqua abandoned their lands in the early 1860s and trekked en masse hundreds of miles eastward.[2] Game also de-

1. Both diseases were largely restricted in their effects to the more northerly societies in the 1860s but moved south in the 1870s, reducing the cattle holdings of Zulu, Sotho, and white Natal and Cape pastoralists. For a general account of the spread of redwater fever see the "Supplementary Report of the Commission Appointed ... to Inquire into the Disease of Horned Cattle Known as Redwater," *CGHPP,* G5 1884, pp. 3–4. On the nature of lung sickness see the "Report of the Colonial Veterinary Surgeon on Sheep and Cattle Diseases in the Colony of the Cape of Good Hope," *CGHPP,* G8 1877, pp. 1–6.

2. On drought in Griqualand West see Anon. [W. B. Philip], "The Griquas and Their Exodus," and George Stow, "Griqualand West," *Cape Monthly Magazine,* 2d series 5 (July–Dec. 1872): 71–74, 326–27; J. S. Marais, *The Cape Coloured People, 1652–1937* (Johannesburg, 1968 [1st ed. 1939]), pp. 48–49; Kevin Shillington, "The Impact of the Diamond Discoveries on the Kimberley Hinterland: Class Formation, Colonialism and Resistance among the Tlhaping of Griqualand West in the 1870s," in Shula Marks and Richard Rathbone (eds.), *Industrialization and Social Change in South Africa* (London, 1982), p. 100. On the mass exodus of the Griqua see Robert Ross, *Adam Kok's Griquas: A Study in the Development of Stratification in South Africa* (Cambridge, 1976), chapts. 4–7.

clined, especially on the Highveld, since blacks acquired ever-greater numbers of guns through trade with white merchants and killed animals at a rate faster than that of natural reproduction. By the time of the first diamond discoveries most of the large game south of the Molopo River had been exterminated, and hunters had to travel north toward the Zambezi if they were to have much success.[3]

Pressure from expanding Boer communities added to that of ecological decay, although its effects were largely limited to the Highveld. Like most of the blacks near whom they settled, the Boers of the Orange Free State and the Transvaal Republic were hunters and pastoralists and thus interested in the same natural resources as their black neighbors: game, cattle, and land. Always strong from the time of major white settlement in the 1840s onward, the competition for these resources became intense as population grew while the productive capacity of the Highveld declined. Boer hunters, better armed than their black counterparts, took control of an increasing share of the long-established ivory trade, although in the process they exacerbated the problem of overkilling and forced the trade ever farther northward, beyond the limits of Ngwato settlement in the northwest and the region occupied by Transvaal Boers in the northeast.[4] Moreover, in two wars in the 1850s—against the Pedi and the Tlhaping—Transvaal Boers captured thousands of head of cattle, depleting black herds even before drought and disease took their toll, while in the 1860s the Boers made increasingly vociferous claims to sovereignty over the southern Tswana much at the same time as white settlers moved onto Tswana lands.[5]

3. Stow, "Griqualand West," p. 73; Marais, *The Cape Coloured People*, p. 49; Shillington, "The Impact of the Diamond Discoveries," p. 100; Peter Delius, "Migrant Labour and the Pedi, 1840–80," in Shula Marks and Anthony Atmore (eds.), *Economy and Society in Pre-Industrial South Africa* (London, 1980), p. 303; Neil Parsons, "The Economic History of Khama's Country in Botswana, 1844–1930," in Robin Palmer and Neil Parsons (eds.), *The Roots of Rural Poverty in Central and Southern Africa* (London, 1977), p. 120; Sherilynn Young, "Fertility and Famine: Women's Agriculture in Southern Mozambique," in Palmer and Parsons, *ibid.*, pp. 72–73.

4. Shillington, "The Impact of the Diamond Discoveries," p. 100; Delius, "Migrant Labour and the Pedi, 1840–80," p. 303; Parsons, "The Economic History of Khama's Country," pp. 120–21; Roger Wagner, "Zoutpansberg: The Dynamics of a Hunting Frontier, 1848–67," in Marks and Atmore, *Economy and Society*, pp. 313–49.

5. See the *Evidence Taken at Bloemhof before the Commission Appointed to*

The greatest pressure, however, was exerted against the Sotho. Although unable to defeat Moshoeshoe, whose lands they coveted and whose power they feared, in the 1850s, the Free State Boers were more successful in the 1860s, crushing the Sotho chief and his followers in a devastating war spanning three years, 1865–68. While the Sotho state was saved from total dismemberment by British intervention and the establishment of Basutoland as an imperial possession, much of the most fertile land was lost to the Boers. The British official in charge of the new colony summed up the situation immediately prior to the discovery of diamonds thus: "Their [Sotho] stock had been mostly captured or slaughtered, their ploughs and wagons, houses, clothes, money and movable property captured or destroyed, whilst the people were so dispersed and intermingled that all organization was lost."[6]

The interaction of these pressures—ecological and military—with internal factors exacerbated social and political tensions in many black societies. Cattle loss in particular had an enormous effect, since it meant the near elimination in pastoral societies of the prime means of paying *lobola*, the marriage payment made by a prospective bridegroom to the bride's father. Unable to pay *lobola*, young men could not marry, establish their own homesteads, and become independent of their elders as had been the pattern in the past. Moreover, the combination of cattle loss with existing inheritance practices, such as those of the Tsonga whereby a single male heir received all the property of a homestead on the death of its head, increased social stratification. Those who still had wealth (i.e., cattle) kept it in a few hands; those who did not had no means to acquire any and had to remain in a dependent position far longer than before.[7]

---

*Investigate the Claims of the South African Republic . . . to . . . the Diamond Fields* (Cape Town, 1871), particularly pp. 60–89, 122, 124, 128, 131, 154–57, 163, 193, 278, 280, 304, 315, 320, 324, 341–42; two "Minutes" on Sekhukhune, chief of the Pedi, and relations between his people and the British, contained in the papers of the superintendent of natives, vol. 5, TA; W. Ashton (missionary) to Sir Philip Wodehouse (governor of the Cape), 2 August 1869, quoted in Robertson, *Diamond Fever,* pp. 204–06; D. R. Hunt, "An Account of the Bapedi," *Bantu Studies,* 5 (1931): 275–326; H. O. Mönnig, *The Pedi* (Pretoria, 1967), p. 24; and Peter Delius, *The Land Belongs to Us: The Pedi Polity, the Boers and the British in the Nineteenth-century Transvaal* (Johannesburg, 1983), pp. 30–40, 126–47.

6. C. D. Griffith (governor's agent) to the secretary for native affairs, 31 January 1874, *NABB,* G27 1874, p. 21.

7. On stratification among the Tsonga see Marvin Harris, "Labour Emigration among the Mocambique Thonga: Cultural and Political Factors," *Africa,* 29:1 (1959):

In a different fashion, but with similar results, drought increased stratification among the Tlhaping. Declining rainfall forced the concentration of productive activities into those areas with springs and streams, and control over these water resources was already generally exercised by the wealthier men in the community.[8] In addition, at least two-thirds of the Tlhaping population consisted of hunter-gatherer clients whose own natural sources of subsistence—small game and berries—were, if anything, declining at an even faster rate than were the resources of their cattle-keeping patrons.[9] Growing stratification, however, did not make the powerful and the wealthy in black societies rest any easier, for the combination of declining production, growing Boer incursions, and rising social discontent at this stratification posed a considerable threat to their own position and property. Just as it was in the interests of the young and the poor to seek new means to better their condition, so the chiefs needed new weapons and resources to protect and strengthen their own power as well as rebuild that of their communities.

This combination of decline and discontent encouraged blacks to look for new means to restructure their economic, social, and political relations well before the discovery of diamonds. From the 1840s on, as white settlement and merchant capitalism intruded farther into the interior of the subcontinent, increasing numbers of blacks engaged in market production. By this means they could generate a salable surplus and so acquire those goods that they deemed necessary for this restructuring, cattle and guns. Market production took three forms. First, blacks (the Pedi and Tswana in particular) sold products obtained from the natural surplus of the countryside: ivory, hides, and feathers. But, as noted earlier, there were growing constraints, whether through overkilling or drought, on this trade. Second, blacks (the Pedi, Sotho, and Tlhaping) ex-

---

53–57; and Patrick Harries, "Kinship, Ideology and the Nature of Pre-Colonial Labour Migration from the Delagoa Bay Hinterland to South Africa up to 1895," in Marks and Rathbone, *Industrialization*, pp. 145–50; among the Pedi, see Delius, *The Land Belongs to Us*, pp. 51–52; and among the Sotho, see Leonard Thompson, *Survival in Two Worlds: Moshoeshoe of Lesotho 1786–1870* (Oxford, 1975), pp. 193, 202–03, 258.

   8. Shillington, "The Impact of the Diamond Discoveries," p. 102.

   9. On "serfs" (as contemporary white observers referred to them) in southern Tswana societies, see the *Evidence Taken at Bloemhof*, pp. 180, 194; and A. C. Bailie to the administrator of Griqualand West, 30 July 1876, "Further Correspondence Respecting the Affairs of South Africa," *BPP,* C2220 (1879), p. 47.

panded the areas of land that they had under cultivation, planted higher-producing crops such as maize, and sold the output to Boer and British traders. But this production too was constrained in the 1860s, not only because the new crops were much less drought resistant than those they replaced but also because, with relatively few whites in the interior and poor transport networks, the market for grain was small.[10]

Third, and most important, members of several black societies migrated south in large numbers and sold their labor to whites. Beginning in the 1840s, but only really expanding in the late 1850s and 1860s, a pattern developed of Pedi males, generally under the direction of their headmen, traveling hundreds of miles to labor on the farms and in the towns of the Cape Colony, returning home only after working for several months. The cattle, guns, and blankets that these men brought back with them not only improved their individual economic position, since they were generally the poor men in society to begin with, but also that of the Pedi state, for Sekhukhune, the paramount chief, took a very considerable proportion of these goods in tax.[11] Sotho likewise migrated to work for whites during this period and acquired much the same goods as their northern peers. Moshoeshoe, the Sotho leader, in particular encouraged his subjects to obtain guns in order to protect the state against marauding Boers.[12]

The Tsonga also traveled several hundred miles to work for whites in the 1850s and 1860s, although they chose the closer labor markets of Natal rather than those of the Cape. Sometimes at the direction of their chiefs, sometimes not, they would work for up to two years before returning home with large quantities of sterling; cattle could not be brought back safely through the intervening lands of the Swazi and the Zulu (enemies of the Tsonga), while guns were available locally from Portuguese traders. Because of the ex-

10. On the origins of market production see, e.g., Thompson, *Survival in Two Worlds*, pp. 78, 80, 117, 190–91, 195–96; Shillington, "The Impact of the Diamond Discoveries," pp. 100–02; Delius, "Migrant Labour and the Pedi, 1840–80," p. 305; and *idem*, *The Land Belongs to Us*, pp. 33–34.

11. Mönnig, *The Pedi*, pp. 24–25, 181; Delius, "Migrant Labour and the Pedi, 1840–80," pp. 296–98, 300–01, 305–07.

12. Thompson, *Survival in Two Worlds*, pp. 35, 54, 70, 194–95; *idem*, "Cooperation and Conflict: The High Veld," in Monica Wilson and Leonard Thompson (eds.), *The Oxford History of South Africa* (Oxford, 1969), I, p. 443; Judith Kimble, "Labour Migration in Basutoland, c. 1870–1885," in Marks and Rathbone, *Industrialization*, p. 120.

tent of cattle loss from drought and disease, and the large infusion
of cash from these migrants, money had become an important medium of exchange and of *lobola* among the Tsonga even before the
rise of the diamond industry.[13] Migrant labor, unlike the other forms
of market production engaged in by blacks, did not face increasing
constraints in the late 1860s but new opportunities.

The opening of the diamond fields in 1870 provided a huge new
market for the sale of unskilled labor, one that paid better than any
other in southern Africa. The labor-intensive organization adopted
in the early days of digging demanded the services of thousands of
men. No experience was required; just the ability to handle a pick
and shovel. Moreover, growing competition between claim holders
ensured continued demand for workers throughout the first half of
the decade, pushing pay scales ever higher. Black workers in the
mines could earn wages at least half as much again as those paid
in coastal towns in the Cape Colony and twice or more those ruling
on farms.[14]

Aside from needing unskilled labor for its mines, Kimberley
also required vast amounts of foodstuffs and fuel for its burgeoning
population. While manufactured items such as liquor, sugar, and
tea could be brought up by oxwagon from the coastal ports between

13. Mzila, king of the Gaza state north of the Limpopo River, began negotiations with the British in 1868 to supply Tsonga laborers to Natal. See the "Statement of Umzungulu and Dubule, Messengers from Umzila," 16 August 1870,
enclosure 1 in despatch no. 190, Theophilus Shepstone (secretary of native affairs,
Natal) to Umzila, 18 August 1870, enclosure 2 in no. 190, and St. Vincent Erskine
(agent for the Natal government) to Shepstone, 30 November 1872, enclosure 6 in
no. 190, "Correspondence Relating to Great Britain and Portugal in East Africa,"
*BPP,* C6495 (1891), pp. 198–200, 211–12. For further discussion of the causes and
extent of Tsonga participation in migrant labor see the "Report of the Select Committee Appointed to Consider the Introduction of Native Labourers from Beyond the
Border of the Colony," 13 November 1872, sessional paper no. 12, Legislative Council, Natal; David Leslie, *Among the Zulus and Amatongas* (Edinburgh, 1875), pp. 249,
255, 288; Malyn Newitt, "Migrant Labour and the Development of Mozambique,"
*Societies of Southern Africa,* 4 (1974): 67–76; Patrick Harries, "Labour Migration
from the Delagoa Bay Hinterland to South Africa," *Societies of Southern Africa,* 7
(1977): 61–75; and *idem,* "Slavery, Social Incorporation and Surplus Extraction: The
Nature of Free and Unfree Labour in South-east Africa," *Journal of African History,*
22:3 (1981): 328–29.

14. Wages in Kimberley fluctuated between 5s. and 30s. per week during 1871–
76, with the higher figure becoming the ruling rate in the middle of the decade. Day
laborers in the Cape received an average of 2s. per day, domestic servants (male)
£1 6s. per month, and farm laborers (male) £1 1s. per month. For details on wage
rates in the Cape see the *Cape of Good Hope Blue Book for 1875* (Cape Town, 1876),
p. CC2.

four hundred and seven hundred miles away, the fifty thousand people resident at the diamond fields also needed perishable items—meat, milk, and vegetables—as well as goods such as grain and wood, which at that time could not be transported economically over long distances. Demand for these products was so great that, as with wages, prices rose to levels higher than elsewhere in southern Africa; bread, milk, and vegetables, for example, sold for between four and eight times as much as they did at the Cape. And prices kept rising. Between 1871 and 1873 the price of firewood alone increased sixfold and continued to climb thereafter.[15]

Blacks met these demands for labor and produce. Lieutenant-Governor Southey estimated that fifty thousand men sought work each year in Kimberley in the early 1870s. These men, whose annual earnings totaled at least £500,000, provided the entire labor needs of the diamond industry.[16] Southey further estimated that the value of goods sold annually in Kimberley amounted to £2,500,000. Even allowing for possible exaggeration, and the value of manufactured goods imported by white merchants, the contribution of black producers could not have been worth much less than £1,000,000 per year.[17] In addition, by the middle of the decade at least one thousand black men, along with their families, had settled in the town and were engaged in a wide range of economic activities. These semi-permanent residents included "masons, bricklayers, carpenters, eating-house keepers, cab proprietors and drivers, diggers, overseers, etc."[18] Approximately 10 percent of them owned diamond

15. On the cost of foodstuffs see chapt. 4. With regard to the rising price of firewood see the *Diamond News*, 1 July 1873.

16. Southey to Barkly (governor of the Cape), 30 June 1875, enclosure in despatch no. 1, "Correspondence Relating to the Colonies and States of South Africa; Cape of Good Hope and Griqualand West," *BPP*, C1401 (1876), p. 2. On the wage bill see also the *Diamond News*, 5 December 1872; and the evidence of George Manning contained in the "Report of Lieut-Colonel Crossman," June 1876, Colonial Office Confidential Print African No. 96, p. 34. For various estimates of the number of men working in the mines at any one time see W. Coleman (registrar of contracted servants) to chief clerk, administrator's office, 5 January 1876, GLW 80; the evidence of Manning cited above; and Morton, *South African Diamond Fields*, pp. 15, 25. Any estimate could never be much more than a guess, however, since the labor market was always in flux.

17. Southey to Barkly, 30 June 1875, *BPP,* C1401 (1876), p. 2. The cost price of manufactured goods imported into Kimberley in 1875 was £440,000. See the "Report of Lieut-Colonel Crossman," pp. 87–89. White farmers in the Orange Free State and the Transvaal also supplied agricultural produce to Kimberley.

18. Southey to Barkly, 30 June 1875, *BPP,* C1401 (1876), pp. 2, 3; *idem,* 17 April 1875, GH 12/5. Southey estimated the total number of blacks resident in Kimberley at between three thousand and ten thousand.

claims, most of these situated in the poor Bultfontein mine, which had been largely abandoned by white diggers. Details on these black claim holders are elusive. What can be said for certain is that there were at least 47 black claim holders in the Dutoitspan and Bultfontein mines in 1872, while by 1874 120 out of the 130 claim holders in the latter mine were blacks. In 1879, despite the numerous attempts of whites to get rid of all black claim holders, there were still 20 African diggers carrying out their own digging operations in the Dutoitspan and Bultfontein mines.[19] Such was the extent of black involvement in Kimberley's economy that, within a year of the opening of the mines, every black society south of the Zambezi River, with the exception only of the Venda and of Cetshwayo's Zulu, was represented at the diamond fields, whether by laborers, artisans, or independent businessmen.[20]

Yet there were significant variations in the patterns of participation. As table 2.1 shows, Pedi alone accounted for between half and two-thirds of the black work force.[21] Tsonga and Sotho, the other societies previously engaged in migrant labor, provided a much smaller, although still considerable, contribution. In contrast, as demonstrated by table 2.2, the black communities located closest to the diamond fields provided very few mine workers, no

19. See the *Diamond News*, 27 January 1872, 24 July 1873; "Memorial of Coloured Diggers to Commissioners," 22 March 1872, GLW 26; "List of Native Claimholders Whose Licences Were Suspended," August 1872, GH 12/1; John Salem ("coloured" digger) to the commissioners, 24 July 1872, GLW 28; Inspector Wright (inspector of claims) to J. B. Currey (government secretary), 1 October 1874, GLW 55, petition of black miners and diggers of Bultfontein to Southey, 22 April 1875, GH 12/5; "List of Coloured Owners of Claims in the Dutoitspan and Bultfontein Mines," 1879, GLW 140 (2129).

20. For descriptions of the great variety of blacks at the diamond fields see Gwayi Tyamzashe to Dr. James Stewart, 30 November 1872, quoted in Robert Sieborger, "The Recruitment and Organization of African Labour for the Kimberley Diamond Mines, 1871–1888," (MA, Rhodes University, 1975), p. 2; and Tyamzashe, "The Natives at the Diamond Fields," the *Kaffir Express*, 1 August 1874, p. 5, repr. in Francis Wilson and Dominique Perrot (eds.), *Outlook on a Century: South Africa 1870–1970* (Lovedale, 1972), pp. 19–21. With regard to the absence of the Venda, Delius has suggested that they derived large profits from the ivory trade and therefore did not have to engage in migrant labor, "Migrant Labour and the Pedi Before 1869," *Societies of Southern Africa*, 7 (1977): 44. With regard to the Zulu see below.

21. Nearly all blacks who came to the diamond fields from the northern and eastern Transvaal were officially termed either Mahawa (before 1875) or Secocoeni Basuto (from 1876 on). Lumped together under this term were Pedi, Ndzundza Ndebele, and a number of other peoples who were only distinguished from one another in the official accountings after 1877. Pedi, on the basis of qualitative evidence for the pre-1877 period and statistical returns for the post-1877 period, accounted for the majority of these workers.

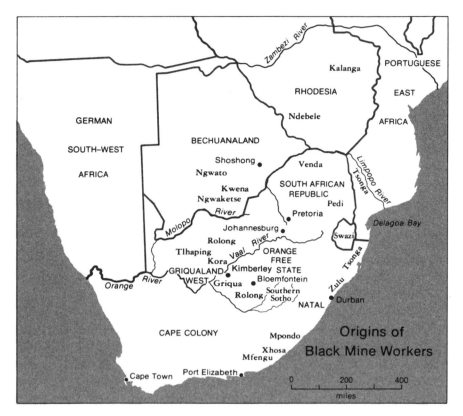

MAP 2.1. Origins of black mine workers

more than a few hundred compared to the thousands who traveled up to a thousand miles to labor in the mines. Kimberley's neighbors did, however, supply most of the town's produce needs. Only the Sotho were a major exception to the general pattern of distant societies supplying labor and neighbors supplying produce, for they were the largest suppliers of grain to Kimberley at the same time as they were the third-largest source of mine workers.

Variations were also apparent in what blacks wanted from Kimberley. High wages were certainly the prime attraction for mine workers, as demonstrated by the speed with which they abandoned the diamond fields every time employers attempted to lower wage rates, just as high prices encouraged rural producers to grow a large surplus. Yet neither laborers nor producers consistently spent their earnings in the same way. With regard to one item frequently purchased—guns—many of Southey's contemporaries, and most

TABLE 2.1    Sources of Black Mine Workers, 1873–76[a] (Percentages)

|              | 1873  | 1874 | 1875 | 1876 |
|--------------|-------|------|------|------|
| Pedi[b]      | 64    | 58   | 62   | 48   |
| Tsonga[c]    | 12    | 15   | 26   | 9    |
| Sotho        | 9     | 5    | 3    | 14   |
| Natal Zulu   | 5     | 4    | 1    | 7    |
| Tlhaping     | 4     | 3    | —    | 8    |
| Griqua       | 1     | —    | —    | —    |
| Other        | 5     | 15[d] | 8   | 14[e] |
| Total number of men in survey[f] | 14,085 | 6,878 | 877 | 12,268 |

SOURCES: GLW 20, 76, 78; *Griqualand West Government Gazette*, 20 October 1877.
[a]Only those people who consistently accounted for more than 1 percent of the work force are listed by name.
[b]All blacks coming from the Transvaal area, of whom Pedi comprised the majority, were referred to as "Mahawa" at the diamond fields.
[c]All blacks coming from southern Mozambique were called "Shangaans."
[d]Kalanga ("Makalaka") from north of the Limpopo accounted for 12 percent.
[e]Kalanga accounted for 7 percent; Kwena for 5 percent.
[f]Only those men who could be identified by their origins are included in the survey.

later scholars, have considered the easy availability of firearms the sole attraction of Kimberley to blacks.[22] This trade must be seen in perspective. Blacks did purchase large numbers of guns at the diamond fields. Between 1872 and 1877 (when the British followed the longstanding lead of the Boers and prohibited all trading in guns with blacks), approximately 150,000 single-barreled guns were imported into the Cape Colony, of which about half were transshipped to Kimberley. Another 3,000 came to the diamond fields from Natal.[23]

22. For some early examples of this point of view see "Fossor," *Twelve Months at the South African Diamond Fields* (London, 1872), p. 31; Payton, *The Diamond Diggings*, p. 146; Boyle, *To the Cape for Diamonds*, pp. 158–60; Morton, *South African Diamond Fields*, p. 15; Matthews, *Incwadi Yami*, p. 187. For two recent expressions of the argument see Delius, "Migrant Labour and the Pedi, 1840–80," pp. 299–300; and Robert Turrell, "Kimberley: Labour and Compounds, 1871–1888," in Marks and Rathbone, *Industrialization*, p. 50.

23. See "Gun Returns," January to June 1873, GLW 48; "Gun Returns," Dutoitspan, 1873 and 1874, GLW 53; "Number of Guns and . . . Gunpowder Introduced into this Province . . . 1st April 1873 to 31st December 1873," GLW 58; Southey to Barkly, 20 February 1874, GLW 183; returns of gun permits for January and February 1875, GLW 76; return of arms and ammunition licensed at Langford in 1875, and in January and March 1876, GLW 88 (1737); *Cape of Good Hope Blue Book for 1872*, p. AA27, *1873*, p. AA58, *1874*, p. AA54, *1875*, p. AA59, *1876*, p. T57. See also the "Return of All Guns and Ammunition Shipped to British and Portuguese Possessions in South Africa . . . from 1874 to 1878," *BPP*, XLIII (150) 709 (1878–79); and Sir Henry Bulwer (lieutenant-governor of Natal) to Sir Michael Hicks Beach (secretary of state for colonies), 11 January 1878, Lanyon Papers, vol. 4a, acc. 596, TA.

TABLE 2.2  Origins of the Black Mine Workers and Distance Traveled to the Mines, 1876

| 0–50 miles | % | 50–150 miles | % | 150–300 miles | % | 300–500 miles | % | 500–1,000 miles | % |
|---|---|---|---|---|---|---|---|---|---|
| Griqua | .4 | Tlhaping | 7.7 | Sotho | 14.2 | Natal Zulu | 6.7 | Pedi | 47.8 |
| Kora | .4 | | | Rolong | .7 | Kwena | 4.7 | Tsonga | 8.9 |
| | | | | | | Cape Colonials[a] | .9 | Kalanga | 7.0 |
| | | | | | | | | Ngwato | .3 |
| | | | | | | | | Ndebele | .1 |
| | .8 | | 7.7 | | 14.9 | | 12.3 | | 64.1 |

SOURCE: GLW 118 (947).

[a]Cape Colonials included, according to the registrar of servants, "'Cape coloured men,' 'Apprentices Mozambiques,' 'Malays,' 'Hottentots,' 'Fingoes,' 'Gonahs,' 'Gaikas,' 'Gcalekas,' 'Tambookies,' 'Amapondas,' & 'Bastards.'"

Although many of these weapons were no doubt acquired for military purposes as they had been in the past, Southey for one believed that most were for "purposes connected with legitimate and beneficial trade," particularly in ostrich feathers and ivory, and considered that the reason blacks came to Kimberley to obtain guns was because there they could quickly earn the money necessary to pay for their purchases.[24]

By 1873, just one year after the gun trade had started in earnest, blacks in Kimberley were already showing great interest in obtaining other goods besides firearms, while by 1876 their purchases of woolen goods alone exceeded in value those of guns.[25] Much greater sums than those spent on guns and blankets were reinvested in the rural economy—in the purchase of livestock to rebuild depleted herds, of ploughs to expand and intensify cultivation of those lands remaining in black hands, and of wagons to transport rural surpluses to market. The Sotho, for example, in four years of working in the mines and selling grain to Kimberley, acquired huge amounts of property (especially livestock), of which guns accounted for but 2.5 percent in value.[26]

Examination of the particular balance of constraints, needs, and opportunities facing each black society in the early 1870s provides an explanation for these varieties in participation and purchase. With regard to those people who did not participate (the Zulu ruled by Cetshwayo) or did so only slightly (the Natal Zulu, blacks from the Cape, and the northern Tswana), relatively prosperous rural conditions and the availability of local markets were the determining factors. Cetshwayo's Zulu, for example, remained in full possession of their lands and had a self-sufficient economy little affected by ecological decay, Boer pressures, or the intrusion of merchant capital. And while Cetshwayo was prepared to send some of his non-Zulu subjects to work in Natal, and to tax them on their return, he forbade the Zulu proper from becoming migrants.[27]

24. Southey to Barkly, 11 April 1874, *CGHPP,* A68 1881, p. 6; and *idem,* 13 August 1874, GLW 188. Southey noted that the Zulu rarely bought firearms at the diamond fields but did occasionally purchase gunpowder. See his letter to Barkly, 15 November 1873, GLW 182.

25. *Diamond Field,* 30 July 1873; "Report of Lieut-Colonel Crossman," 1876, pp. 88–89.

26. *NABB,* G21 1875, p. 4.

27. See Cetshwayo's evidence to the 1883 Commission on Native Laws, *Report of the Government Commission on Native Laws and Customs* (Cape Town, 1883, repr.

In Natal and the Cape economic growth speeded up under the impact of the diamond discoveries, giving rise to considerable local demand for agricultural and pastoral products. Zulu, Mfengu, and Pondo producers chose to meet these demands rather than those of the relatively inaccessible Kimberley market.[28]

In the matter of migrant labor, however, the Cape differed from Natal. The growth of railway construction in the Cape provided a new avenue of employment for thousands of men, with wages close to those paid in Kimberley, which went unmatched in Natal where the colonial administration continued to demand that blacks work for low pay.[29] Furthermore, many of the first white diamond diggers came from Natal and brought their black servants with them. During the 1870s these same employers continued to recruit and contract men in Natal and arrange for their transport to the diamond fields.[30] The result of such differing factors was that thousands of Cape blacks labored on the railway works, but the number going to the diamond mines each year averaged less than a hundred, while several hundred Zulu, most of them recruited, worked annually in

---

1963), minutes of evidence, p. 529. See also Leslie, *Among the Zulus and Amatongas*, p. 288; Sheila van der Horst, *Native Labour in South Africa* (London, 1942), p. 53; Harries, "Labour Migration from the Delagoa Bay Hinterland," p. 66; *idem*, "Slavery, Social Incorporation and Surplus Extraction," pp. 328–29; and J. J. Guy, *The Destruction of the Zulu Kingdom: The Civil War in Zululand, 1879–1884* (London, 1980), pp. 3, 16–18.

28. Van der Horst, *Native Labour,* pp. 103–06; Norman Etherington, *Preachers, Peasants and Politics: Southeast Africa, 1835–1880: African Christian Communities in Natal, Pondoland and Zululand* (London, 1978), p. 20; Colin Bundy, *The Rise and Fall of the South African Peasantry* (Berkeley, 1979), chapt. 3 and pp. 171–76; *idem*, "Peasants in Herschel: A Case Study of a South African Frontier District," in Marks and Atmore, *Economy and Society*, pp. 211–13, 222; William Beinart, "Production and the Material Basis of Chieftainship: Pondoland, c. 1830–1900," in Marks and Atmore, *Economy and Society*, p. 143.

29. On the Cape railways see A. J. Purkis, "The Politics, Capital and Labour of Railway-building in the Cape Colony, 1870–1885," (DPhil, Oxford University, 1978), especially pp. 343, 347–62. On Natal see van der Horst, *Native Labour,* pp. 87–93.

30. On the recruitment of Zulu see the despatch of Barkly to Lord Kimberley (secretary of state for colonies), 29 October 1872, quoted in the *Diamond News*, 1 July 1873; the statements of Tom, January, and Gogo, 30 August and 2 September 1873, GLW 175; Coleman to Southey, 18 November 1873, GLW 71; J. M. Smalberger, "Mrs Help's Zulus and the Politics of Confederation: Southey, Barkly and the Colonial Office, 1872–1876," (unpublished MS, n. d.), Smalberger Papers, UCT. At least one-quarter of the Zulu at the diamond fields were not recruited. Most of these were members of Langalibalele's Hlubi people. On their participation in migrant labor see Southey to Barkly, 19 and 20 November 1873, GLW 182; *idem*, 22 November 1873, GH 12/3; and Etherington, *Preachers, Peasants and Politics*, p. 20.

Kimberley. In total, Cape blacks and Natal Zulu accounted for less than 5 percent of Kimberley's black work force.

There was, however, one general exception to the relative paucity of Zulu, Mfengu, and Pondo coming to the diamond fields: Christian blacks. Christians comprised a majority of the resident black population of artisans and property owners.[31] Under the influence of missionaries such men had, before coming to Kimberley, developed a preference for individual enterprise free from the control of chiefs. Moreover, they had already acquired skills, such as brickmaking and carpentry, and property, such as wagons, much in demand in Kimberley. Skilled workers in the town could earn four or five times as much as in any other urban center, while the transporting of goods to the Kimberley market promised considerable profits. Indeed, all mission stations in Natal reported a huge drop in church attendance in the early 1870s because so many of their wagon-owning members had set off for the diamond fields.[32] John Komali was one such person. A Christian and a wagoner from Natal, Komali arrived in Kimberley in 1873. There he embarked on a new career as a diamond digger with his own claim in the Dutoitspan mine, also working on shares, occasionally as foreman, for various white claim holders in the Kimberley mine. An active churchgoer while at the diamond mines, he was involved in schemes with fellow black Christians to raise money for mission schools in the Cape.[33] Men such as Komali, however, were a very small minority compared with the huge numbers of blacks who labored in the mines or grew crops for Kimberley.

The northern Tswana had limited participation in production

31. See the letter of the Reverend Doxat to his bishop, Easter Monday 1872, printed in the *Quarterly Paper of the Orange Free State Mission*, no. 17, July 1872, pp. 4, 15; Tyamzashe, "The Natives at the Diamond Fields," p. 5; *Diamond News*, 19 June 1873; and the "Annual Return of Canon Gaul for Dutoitspan," 2 November 1881, *Annual Reports*, p. 1121, USPG.

32. Artisans could earn £1 10s. to £2 per day in Kimberley, compared with an average of 7s. in the Cape. See Southey to Barkly, 30 June 1875, enclosure in no. 1, *BPP*, C1401 (1876), p. 3; *Cape of Good Hope Blue Book for 1875*, p. CC2; and on Natal, Etherington, *Preachers, Peasants and Politics*, pp. 20, 125–26.

33. On Komali see the *Diamond News*, 19 June 1873; statements of C. E. Scott, John Purcell, and Abraham, 4 July 1873, GLW 140 (2129); Southey to Barkly, 5 and 10 July 1873, GLW 180. Beinart has argued that the only Pondo to go to the diamond fields were those who were Christians, "Production and the Material Basis of Chieftainship," p. 143. On the participation of Pedi and Sotho Christians in the diamond fields' economy see Delius, *The Land Belongs to Us*, pp. 111, 112, 164–65, 168; and Kimble, "Labour Migration in Basutoland," pp. 133–34.

for Kimberley—they exported no agricultural products southward and their contribution to the mines' work force in the 1872–76 period was considerably less than half that of the Tlhaping alone. Quite apart from their distance (four hundred to six hundred miles) from the diamond fields, making the export of perishable goods impossible, the northern Tswana had only limited agricultural and pastoral resources, since much of their land was infertile and waterless. But the movement of elephant and ostrich hunting northward as a consequence of overkilling in the south meant that the Tswana retained a very considerable share of the profitable ivory and feather trades. In addition, Tswana towns, particularly Shoshong, the capital of the Ngwato chief Khama, located as they were along the major trade route between southern and central Africa, garnered considerable profits as commercial entrepôts. Still, the earning of profits locally did not mean that the Tswana were uninterested in obtaining an additional source of income through wage labor. When a Kimberley labor recruiter visited various Tswana chiefs in 1877 all expressed their willingness to send groups of their hunter-gatherer clients to work in the mines. Yet, as they all pointed out at the time, few if any men could be spared so long as their communities had to suffer the constant armed intrusions of Boers. Khama made clear the financial costs of such outside pressure in a letter to a Boer who had requested safe passage for himself and a group of settlers across Ngwato lands:

> They [Kimberley employers] pay us wages at the Diamond Fields, and then Boers rob us of our honest earnings on our way home. . . . Had it not been for you my people would have gone down in whole towns to work for the English people whereas now I shall only be able to send a few people whom I called from the veld [clients], for we dare not leave our homes either to go to hunt or to work. In this way we are impoverished by you.[34]

Khama, along with the rest of the Tswana chiefs, suggested to the Kimberley recruiter that if the British would only eliminate the Boer threat then thousands of Tswana would go south to work in the mines.[35]

34. Khama to L. M. du Plessis, 11 May 1877, BPP, C2220 (1879), p. 46.
35. On Tswana relations with recruiters from the diamond fields see Palgrave to Southey, 9 November 1874, enclosed in Southey to Barkly, 19 November 1874, GH 28/94 (E140); the letter of Dr. Emile Holub to the Diamond Field, 22 November 1876; and the reports of A. C. Bailie reprinted in BPP, C2220 (1879).

As for Kimberley's black neighbors, most chose to sell produce in the town rather than labor in the mines, although varying access to cultivable land and to means of transport caused considerable differences in their responses to the rise of the new industry in their midst. At first, proximity to diamondiferous ground combined with local knowledge permitted the Griqua, Kora, and Tlhaping to dominate the early years of diamond finds, 1868–69, selling stones picked up from the surface of the land to white traders.[36] The most successful of these black prospectors was Swartboy, a Kora herdsman who in 1868 sold the Star of South Africa for five hundred sheep, ten head of cattle, and a horse. Others, while perhaps not so successful, still made considerable profits with which they purchased livestock and wagons.[37] Few of these blacks made the transition to being claim holders at the river diggings in 1869–70 (where few profits were to be won) or to the dry diggings in 1871 (where blacks faced often violent discrimination by the white diggers). Instead, they sought to make larger and more certain profits in market production and here the differences between them became pronounced. The Griqua, numbering between five hundred and one thousand persons, lacked well-watered land and therefore could not invest their diamond profits in increased agricultural or pastoral production. They did purchase wagons so that they could collect firewood for the Kimberley market but soon depleted the limited resources available on their lands. Preyed upon by white land speculators, once again facing poverty, and lacking any viable alternatives, the Griqua by 1873 had begun to contract in ever-increasing numbers to work in the diamond mines.[38]

The Kora, on the other hand, amounting to some two thousand people, retained access to relatively well-watered lands (claimed by the Berlin Missionary Society) abutting the river diggings along the Vaal. Therefore they could supply perishable goods, such as milk from their large herds of goats, to the local market and reinvest the profits in further livestock purchases. They too acquired wagons so that they could participate in the highly profitable firewood

36. "RJD on the Diamond Fields," 1869, ZC 1/1; Robertson, *Diamond Fever*, pp. 120–60; Shillington, "The Impact of the Diamond Discoveries," p. 103.

37. The Star's white purchaser resold the diamond for £11,500. See Robertson, *Diamond Fever*, pp. 179–82, 184–90.

38. In the eight-month period April–November 1873, 137 male Griqua out of the total population (men, women, and children) of no more than one thousand worked in the mines, "Return of Hands Registered," GLW 71.

trade and had access to better supplies than did the Griqua. With no pressing economic need to work in the mines, and having experimented briefly with such labor early on and rejected it because of the violence used against blacks by white employers, the Kora almost without exception refused to work in the mines in the period 1872–76.[39]

The Tlhaping, ten to fifteen thousand strong, also retained land which, with irrigation, could support increased levels of agricultural and pastoral production. Initially, they used most of their diamond profits to rebuild their livestock herds to levels that more than compensated for the losses of the 1850s and 1860s. They invested their capital more and more in ploughs and wagons to expand agricultural production as well as corner an ever-larger share of the wood trade. They also mobilized the labor of their hunter-gatherer clients for this intensified cultivation. As well as utilizing the labor of these men to supply Kimberley with great quantities of vegetables, maize, and firewood, the Tlhaping did on occasion send surplus workers to the diamond mines. Through the reinvestment of the profits derived from their clients' labor in further expanding production, the Tlhaping had, in the eyes of European observers, become relatively prosperous by the middle 1870s.[40]

The Sotho, beset by even more severe difficulties at the end of the 1860s but possessing far greater resources than did Griqualand West's black inhabitants, produced enormous quantities of agricultural goods for Kimberley and also labored in large numbers in

39. See Dr. G. Wangemann and J. Kampfmeyer *et al.* (for the Committee of the Society for the Furthering of Evangelical Missions amongst the Heathens) to Barkly, 12 September 1872, SGGLW 23; *Diamond News*, 10 March, 20 May, 1 July 1873; *Diamond Field*, 16 June 1875.

40. On Tlhaping relations with the diamond industry see especially, Stow, "Griqualand West," p. 77; *Diamond News*, 10 March 1873; Southey to Barkly, 24 August 1873, GLW 181; W. Coleman, "Report of the Native Labour Department in the Year 1876," *Griqualand West Government Gazette*, 20 October 1877; A. C. Bailie's reports on his recruiting mission printed in *BPP*, C2220 (1879); "Memorandum by Captain Harrel, Late 109th Regt., Specially Employed, Cis-Molopo, Addressed to his Honour the Acting Administrator, Griqualand West," 27 April 1880, "Reports by Colonel Warren, R.E., C.M.G., and Captain Harrel (late 89th Regiment), on the Affairs of Bechuanaland, Dated April 3rd, 1879, and April 27th, 1880," *BPP*, C3635 (1883); Shillington, "The Impact of the Diamond Discoveries." The southern Tswana Rolong people also participated in trade with Kimberley. On their activities see Harrel's "Memorandum"; and, for the experiences of a Rolong family at the diamond fields, Z. K. Matthews, *Freedom for My People: The Autobiography of Z. K. Matthews: Southern Africa, 1901 to 1968* (London, 1981), chapt. 1.

the mines. The war of 1865–68 had left the Sotho bereft of much of their arable land and of all of their livestock and movable property. In 1870 the Cape Colony officials who administered Basutoland added a further imposition of their own; an annual tax of 10s. on each hut owned by blacks. The officials hoped that this tax would not only provide revenue for their administration but also, by encouraging individual production and accumulation, undermine the power of the chiefs whom they considered reactionary and possibly rebellious influences. To accelerate the introduction of a market economy and to obtain men for the labor-hungry Cape, the officials required that the tax be paid in cash; goods proffered as payment in kind would only be accepted at well below their market value. Those men who could not pay the tax were required to seek work in the Cape.[41]

The Sotho responded to these new pressures in two ways. They took advantage of the fact that they still had considerable areas of fertile and well-watered land to raise large amounts of grain, enough by 1871 to supply their own needs as well as those of the diamond fields.[42] Their lack of wagons did not impede the marketing of this output, since Boers and other white traders came to Basutoland to purchase the grain and then transported it themselves to the Orange Free State and Kimberley.[43] The profits from this trade were sufficient to enable the Sotho not only to pay the hut tax entirely in cash by 1872 but also to purchase large numbers of livestock, ploughs, and wagons and so further expand rural production.[44]

At the same time that they increased agricultural production, the Sotho engaged more and more in migrant labor. Approximately three thousand went to the diamond fields in 1872 and at least another sixty-five hundred to the Cape and the Free State. Even more went the following year, while by 1875, as one official noted, "3 out of 4" able-bodied Sotho males annually sought employment outside

41. High commissioner to J. H. Bowker (resident magistrate), 25 April 1870, "Basutoland Records," V, p. 478; J. Austen (resident magistrate, Cornet Spruit) to high commissioner's agent, 26 January 1871, governor's agent to colonial secretary, 1 May 1872, ibid., VI, pp. 35, 48, 455; NABB, G27 1873, pp. 8–9, G27 1874, pp. 22–23.

42. On the size of grain production see C. Griffith (governor's agent) to colonial secretary, 26 August 1872, "Basutoland Records," VI, pp. 498–99.

43. NABB, G27 1873, pp. 2, 5, G27 1874, pp. 23, 32, 34, G16 1876, p. 7.

44. On the relative ease with which Sotho paid their hut tax see, NABB, G27 1873, pp. 1–3, 6–8, G27 1874, pp. 23, 29, 32, 34, 35, G21 1875, pp. 6, 9.

Basutoland.[45] Some acquired guns, whether at the mines or at the Cape railway works; most, especially those who worked in the Cape and the Free State, bought livestock with their earnings. There was considerable dispute between officials of the Basutoland administration and Sotho chiefs, and among the chiefs themselves, as to whether these men were sent to the diamond fields to acquire weapons or not. The officials claimed that men were ordered to work in the mines and to purchase guns by chiefs who opposed colonial rule. Those chiefs who supported the administration tended to go along with this point of view. Those opposed to British rule denied that they sent men off to rearm, claiming instead that migrants went of their own free will to obtain guns for hunting or to prove their manhood.[46]

Quite apart from exporting their labor, each of those three out of four Sotho men who migrated also produced annually "with the help of their women from 30 to 40 bags of grain per household. . . ." In large part, the adoption of a new technology permitted this concurrent expansion of agriculture and migrant labor. As the same official quoted above noted, "the use of the plough instead of the Kafir pick has enabled the Basutos either to hire ploughmen whilst they went to work, or to proceed to the Free State after a few days' ploughing themselves."[47] Furthermore, high-paying migrant labor, in conjunction with the profits earned from grain sales, enabled the Sotho to accumulate property at a much faster rate than if they had relied upon one form of income alone. Indeed, so considerable were the profits from such dual production that in the four years after the opening of the Kimberley diamond fields in 1870 the Sotho more than made up for their losses in the 1860s by acquiring over £1,000,000 worth of livestock and other property.[48]

The Pedi and the Tsonga, not having managed to alleviate the

45. See the *Diamond News*, 19 December 1873; the returns of labor contained in GLW 20; and the *NABB*, G27 1873, pp. 2, 4, 6, 29–30, G27 1874, pp. 35–36, and G16 1876, p. 8.

46. On these issues see Southey to Barkly, 18 January 1873, GLW 180; Griffith to colonial secretary, 12 March 1873, Tsekelo Moshoeshoe to Griffith, 27 June 1873, Griffith to colonial secretary, 12 July 1873, Griffith's report of a *pitso* (public meeting) convened with the chiefs, 20 August 1873, Griffith to secretary for native affairs, 30 August 1873, NA 272; *NABB*, G27 1873, pp. 2, 6, G27 1874, pp. 22–23, 31, 34, G21 1875, p. 7. See also Kimble, "Labour Migration in Basutoland," pp. 131–33.

47. Emile Rolland (assistant resident magistrate, Mafeteng) to Griffith, 31 December 1875, *NABB*, G16 1876, pp. 8, 9.

48. *NABB*, G21 1875, p. 4, G16 1876, pp. 7, 18–19.

pressures that had led to their participation in migrant labor in the first place, shifted the sale of their labor in large part from the Cape and Natal markets to the more accessible (although still six hundred to one thousand miles from their homes) and profitable ones of the diamond fields in the early 1870s. Acquisition of guns by the Pedi had only engendered even greater Boer hostility, while cattle purchases by migrants had not been sufficient to replace the beasts lost through disease, drought, and raiding. Moreover, the financial contribution of migrants had become an increasingly important source of revenue for the Pedi state. As a result, not only did men go to the diamond fields in the early 1870s to acquire guns and cash for cattle purchases, but their paramount chief, Sekhukhune, strongly encouraged this migration. He even went so far as to enter into an agreement with a Kimberley labor recruiter to supply several thousand men to the mines each year in exchange for a payment to himself of £1 per man. Although this particular agreement proved abortive, it did not hinder the flow of Pedi to Kimberley, many thousands of whom worked in the mines throughout the 1870s.[49]

Migrant labor was equally important to the Tsonga, referred to as Shangaans at the diamond fields on the assumption that they were all subjects of the Gaza chief, Soshangane. Many of the men coming to the mines, however, appear not to have been from the Gaza state but from Tsonga societies in southern Mozambique.[50] Continuing ecological constraints prevented most homesteads in

49. On the recruiting agreement see the "Memorandum of an Arrangement Made by Mr John Edwards with Sekukune, Paramount Chief of Sequati's People on the 13th August 1873," GLW 17; and Southey to Barkly, 6 March 1875, GLW 184. Southey prohibited the arrangement because he considered the share of taxation for Sekhukhune to be excessive. See also Delius, "Migrant Labour and the Pedi, 1840–80," pp. 299–300, 302, 307–08, who argues that Sekhukhune was trying to consolidate his own power within Pedi society by this move.

50. On Tsonga participation in migrant labor in the early 1870s see the "Correspondence on Bill No. 18 1869, for Facilitating the Obtaining of Native Labour," document no. 35, 1870–71, Selected Documents Presented, Legislative Council Natal, 1866–74; "Report of the Select Committee Appointed to Consider the Introduction of Native Labourers from Beyond the Border of the Colony," L. C. no. 12, 13 November 1872, Sessional Papers, Legislative Council Natal, 1872; Harris, "Labour Emigration among the Mocambique Thonga," p. 53; Newitt, "Migrant Labour and the Development of Mozambique," p. 68; Harries, "Labour Migration from the Delagoa Bay Hinterland," pp. 61–75; idem, "Kinship, Ideology and Labour Migration," pp. 151–53. I have not discussed here the participation of blacks from present-day Zimbabwe in Kimberley's economy but do so briefly in my dissertation, "The Making of a Monopoly: Kimberley and the South African Diamond Industry, 1870–95," (PhD, Yale University, 1982), pp. 103–04.

these societies from being self-sufficient. The use of money to pay *lobola* for brides and as the prime medium of exchange made a continued supply of sterling necessary, and since the Tsonga lacked the resources to produce an agricultural or pastoral surplus, migrancy offered the only means for its acquisition. Chiefs encouraged this migrancy: with the loss of most cattle, taxes levied on returning laborers provided their major source of revenue. Beginning in 1870—known as the year of the *diaman* in southern Mozambique—the Tsonga shifted their labor to the diamond fields. Although they did not completely abandon Natal, growing numbers chose to work in Kimberley because there they could earn as much in six months as they could in a year or two elsewhere, they could do so without binding themselves to long-term contracts (as they had to if they chose to travel by subsidized ship passage from Delagoa Bay to Natal), and they did not have to risk the loss of their earnings on the journey home (as they did when they traveled through the hostile territories of the Swazi and the Zulu).

Far from intervening to propel blacks into the mines, whites (other than those at the diamond fields) sought actively to prevent their migration to Griqualand West in the early 1870s. Boers in the Transvaal and the Free State opposed the movement of blacks from or through their territories en route to Kimberley; they wanted to retain the labor of these men for their own farms, and they feared the power of newly armed migrants. Therefore they attempted at first to curtail and when that failed to control this flow. Transvaalers and Free Staters alike introduced pass laws requiring that all black travelers pay a cash transit or exit tax; they tried to force those who could not pay to work out the fines imposed as farm laborers; and they attempted to disarm the men returning home from Kimberley. All such attempts at control, while frequently violent in practice, had little effect in the long term, since the thousands upon thousands of migrants constantly on the move through the republics far outnumbered, and could easily evade, the few officials sent out to impede their progress.[51] Officials in Basutoland, the Cape, and Natal likewise feared the loss of their laborers to the mines: those in Ba-

---

51. For cases of harassment see, for example, the statement of Francis Umtwana, 16 January 1873, GH 12/3; J. W. Collins to Inspector Percy, 1 June 1874, GLW 66; Southey to Barkly, 16 January 1875, GH 28/95; *Diamond Field*, 21 May 1873; Smalberger, "Mrs Help's Zulus"; Sieborger, "The Recruitment of African Labour," pp. 43–47, 52–57.

sutoland because they wanted the supply to go to the Cape only; those in the Cape and Natal because the rise of the diamond industry had spurred economic growth throughout southern Africa and increased their own need for laborers. Consequently, officials in Basutoland used their influence to try and steer prospective migrants to the south, while those in the Cape and Natal attempted to retain what black labor supplies they already had and to acquire more, either by raising wages to levels competitive with those paid in the diamond industry or through various recruitment schemes.[52]

Officials and private individuals in Kimberley, on the other hand, eagerly sought black participation in the diamond industry but found that they could do little to regulate the supply of migrants. Prior to the later 1870s, the practical authority of the Griqualand West administration barely extended beyond Kimberley's urban boundaries. Southey did attempt to manipulate the supply of labor by increasing the tax on guns, in the hope that men would then have to stay longer to earn the price of a firearm, and by sending representatives on recruiting missions to Tswana and other chiefs to the north of Kimberley. Neither measure had much success. The gun tax showed no appreciable effect on the length of migrants' stay at the diamond fields, while the recruiting missions produced many expressions of chiefly goodwill but no more than a few hundred men. Attempts by private individuals to recruit laborers were even more dismal failures. Lacking financial resources and never needing more than a dozen or so men at any one time, the small diggers could neither finance elaborate recruitment missions nor come to any collective agreement as to their labor needs and the conditions that they were prepared to offer. Instead, claim holders took their chances in the urban labor market and largely ignored the rural homes of their workers. The limited role that whites played directly in securing laborers for the mines in the early 1870s is evident in the small proportion of migrants who came from white-ruled

52. On Basutoland see, e.g., Griffith's speech to a *pitso*, 20 August 1873, NA 272; and his annual report in *NABB*, G27 1873, p. 2. On Natal's demand for labor see the "Report of the Select Committee," 13 November 1873, L.C. no. 12, Sessional Papers, Legislative Council Natal, 1872; and Norman Etherington, "Labour Supply and the Genesis of South African Confederation in the 1870s," *Journal of African History*, 20:2 (1979): 236, 241. For the Cape see the "Correspondence on the Subject of the Introduction of Labour from the Territory Beyond the Transvaal Republic," *CGHPP*, A16 1875; and Sieborger, "The Recruitment of African Labour," pp. 72–73; and for labor shortage in general in southern Africa, van der Horst, *Native Labour*, pp. 100–02; and de Kiewiet, *The Imperial Factor*, pp. 157–64.

areas—never more than 20 percent of the work force and sometimes as little as 5 percent.[53]

Blacks retained considerable autonomy in their movements to, from, and within Kimberley prior to the later 1870s. Mine workers arrived in and left the town largely in accord with the demands of agricultural cycles, for none were as yet fully proletarianized. The length of their stay generally reflected the distance they had traveled to reach the mines: three to six months in the case of men coming five hundred miles or more, anywhere from two weeks to two months for those traveling less.[54] Such stays could be suddenly cut short if, for example, the white diggers attempted to lower wages or if outside military pressures threatened rural societies. In such cases migrant workers were likely to leave the diamond fields en masse.[55] Furthermore, blacks refused to engage themselves to any one employer for the entire duration of their stay in Kimberley, universally preferring short contracts (of one to two months) in order to protect their bargaining power in a highly fluid labor market.[56] By the use of such measures, black mine workers quintupled their wages between 1871 and 1875.[57]

Yet once involved in Kimberley's market economy blacks could not easily withdraw, since the very extent of their involvement had altered fundamentally the organization of rural production. In the early 1870s, for example, Tswana earned £100,000 annually from their exports to the diamond fields, Sotho at least £500,000, while a majority of Pedi males and a large proportion of Tsonga labored each year in the mines. The Pedi population was estimated to consist of at least fifteen thousand adult males of "fighting age" in 1878 while the number registering to work in the mines averaged around

53. On the tax see Southey to Barkly, 4 February 1873, GLW 180. The various recruitment schemes are summarized in Sieborger, "The Recruitment of African Labour," pp. 60–67.

54. Coleman to Currey, 4 February 1873, GLW 71; Southey to Barkly, 15 November 1873, GLW 182; Coleman to Currey, 11 March 1874, GLW 55; J. B. Currey, "The Diamond Fields of Griqualand West," *Journal of the Society of Arts*, 24 (17 March 1876), p. 378.

55. See the *Diamond Field*, 19 November 1873 and 4 August 1876, for two examples of mass departures.

56. See the return of contracts entered into by "servants" in Kimberley between October 1873 and January 1874, GLW 20. Of the 13,436 contracts, more than 40 percent were for one month or less, 27 percent for two months, 24 percent for three months, and the remaining 9 percent for four months or more.

57. The average wage rose from 5s. per week plus food in 1871 to 5s. per day plus food in 1875. Lanyon to Carnarvon, 18 December 1875, CO(m) 107/8 (1569).

six thousand annually in the early 1870s and closer to ten thousand in the later 1870s and early 1880s. An average of fifteen hundred Tsonga registered each year in the early 1870s, while upwards of eight thousand did so after 1876. Since blacks and white employers alike regularly avoided labor-registration procedures, such statistics give only a very general indication of the numbers involved.[58]

The gearing of economic activities to export production could not fail to have major effects. Some natural resources were eliminated entirely. A swath of extermination and deforestation swept outward from Kimberley as the town's meat and fuel markets consumed the game and trees of Griqualand West and beyond at a rate faster than they could be reproduced. Tlhaping clients had depended on the game for their subsistence, Griqua on timber as their sole trade item; as a result of the loss, each group was increasingly forced into labor for others.[59] In addition, there was a reallocation of land and labor resources from pastoral activities to more profitable cultivation and migrant labor. Among the Tlhaping and the Sotho, for example, cultivation became so important that nearly all arable land was cropped, and pastoral activities were pushed to the very margins of settlement in the least desirable areas. The Tsonga, on the other hand, lacking such arable land, invested heavily in the export of their labor, so that agriculture declined, making migrancy an ever more important supplier of income.[60]

The growth of market production also exacerbated conflict between chiefs and commoners. With pastoralism chiefs, through their ownership of all cattle, had controlled production and retained all surpluses; not so with the export trade to Kimberley. Commoners could now accumulate property by cultivating their own fields and selling their own labor, since these activities, and the proceeds from them, were customarily regarded as being under the

58. On the extent of Tswana production see the "Memorandum by Captain Harrel," *BPP,* C3635 (1883). On the Sotho see Colin Murray, *Families Divided: The Impact of Migrant Labour in Lesotho* (Cambridge, 1981), p. 12. On the Pedi see, Coleman to colonial secretary, 18 April 1878, GLW 118 (947).

59. See, e.g., the *Diamond News,* 1 July 1873; the *Diamond Field,* 28 October 1874; and Shillington, "The Impact of the Diamond Discoveries," p. 105.

60. On the marginalization of Sotho pastoralism see *NABB,* G16 1876, p. 14, G12 1877, p. 14, G17 1878, pp. 8, 20, G33 1879, p. 13; on that of the Tlhaping see Shillington, "The Impact of the Diamond Discoveries," pp. 105–06; and on the decline of Tsonga agriculture see Harries, "Kinship, Ideology and Labour Migration," p. 153.

control of the individual. Such a change in the control of production and distribution of surpluses threatened to cut chiefs off from the great profits being earned and at the same time undermine their position within society. As one official noted in 1872 with regard to the Sotho, "The common people find that they can possess property in spite of their chiefs, and acquire it more surely and quickly by industry than begging from their chiefs. They are therefore everywhere making themselves independent of their chiefs . . . the people being no longer bound to them either by interest or fear."[61] In response to this threat, chiefs took various measures to obtain a share of the new profits and to reinforce their power. They taxed returning migrant workers (in the case of every society under study in this chapter); they taxed cultivators (as Sotho chiefs did, indirectly, by collecting the hut tax for the Cape administrators of Basutoland in return for a percentage of the payments made); they raised the price of *lobola* for brides (as the Tsonga chiefs did threefold in the 1870s in an attempt to slow down the rate at which young men could set up independent households).[62] Thus new bonds of obligation were forged, no longer based on the control of cattle but of the proceeds of market production.

The forging of such bonds in rural societies further tied blacks to market production. For those societies in which money became the prime means of exchange in the early 1870s—the Tsonga and the Sotho, for example—continued supplies of sterling were a necessity. Without them *lobola* payments could not be made, obligations to elders met, nor the states' revenues maintained. Moreover, while the investment of capital in manufactured goods like ploughs, harrows, and wagons had transformed agriculture, a surplus could only be produced so long as the process of investment in new technology continued, especially since ecological constraints made cultivation such a risky business. Manufactured products too became increasingly important in the realm of consumption. As one official noted of the Sotho, in a statement that had relevance to all of Kimberley's market producers, "[they] are beginning to find, with their enlarged means, enlarged requirements and diversified wants."

61. *NABB*, G27 1873, pp. 8–9.
62. On Sotho chiefs and taxation see, e.g., *NABB*, G13 1880, pp. 46–47, 54, 61; and on the Tsonga chiefs see Harries, "Kinship, Ideology and Labour Migration," pp. 151–52.

These wants were many—textiles, guns, and processed foodstuffs, which were in demand throughout the subcontinent.[63]

But market production had potentially weak foundations. Kimberley's agricultural suppliers had only limited areas of land to cultivate. Moreover, the ecological constraints of the 1860s did not disappear in the 1870s. Drought, for example, destroyed much of Basutoland's wheat crop in 1873 and in the following year the late arrival of spring rains also reduced yields.[64] The Sotho still made a profit from the sale of their remaining harvest but only because heavy demand from the diamond fields in conjunction with the limited supply available pushed prices upward. Similarly, the high wages of black mine workers were the result of demand exceeding supply. Blacks could withdraw their labor if wage levels were threatened because economic conditions were not yet so harsh throughout the subcontinent that all rural dwellers had to sell their labor to survive, nor was Kimberley the only market for their labor. In essence, the prosperity evident in so many black societies in the mid-1870s rested on three requirements: that urban demand for rural output remain high; that black communities retain the ability to produce a salable surplus; and that blacks have options available so as not to be forced to sell just one product in any one market.

## THE INTERACTION OF INDUSTRIAL AND RURAL CHANGE, 1876–86

From the mid-1870s on, Kimberley's needs and demands impinged to an ever-greater extent on black communities as the diamond industry passed through a decade of stress and restructuring. The large capitalists who took charge of mining sought to strengthen the shaky foundations of their enterprise through a two-part process: cut competition in the mines by eliminating small claim holders, and reduce production costs by obtaining agricultural and labor supplies at the lowest possible price. In both endeavors the capitalists successfully sought state aid. The spillover into the

63. *NABB*, G27 1873, p. 2. In 1872, the main purchases of Sotho within Basutoland had consisted of "blankets, ready made clothing, handkerchiefs, beads, copper wire, tobacco, sugar, rice, soap, salt, ploughs, spades, axes, hoes." Griffith to colonial secretary, 26 August 1872, "Basutoland Records," VI, p. 498.

64. *NABB*, G27 1874, pp. 24, 36, G21 1875, pp. 6, 8, 9. On increasing problems with rainfall in Pedi lands in the early 1870s see Delius, "Migrant Labour and the Pedi, 1840–80," p. 305.

PLATE 2.1   Before and after working in the mines,
1873 (*The Graphic*, 22 December 1873)

PLATE 2.2   Arriving at the diamond fields
(Williams, *The Diamond Mines of
South Africa*, vol. 1, p. 188)

PLATE 2.3   Zulu workmen, Dutoitspan mine
(Cape Archives, AG 4760)

countryside of this struggle for profitability in the mines forged additional bonds, beyond those already created within black societies, between rural producers and their urban market, and between migrant workers and their industrial workplace. By 1885, after a decade of often ferocious struggle, industrial production had largely imposed its demands not only on Kimberley's immediate rural hinterland but also well beyond the borders of the Cape Colony.

Beginning in 1876, the relationship between Kimberley's demands (for food as well as labor) and black suppliers began to change to the detriment of black societies. With the era of small-scale production in the mines reaching its nadir in the depression of mid-1876, thousands of people moved away from the diamond fields, and Kimberley was left with less than half its earlier population.[65] Since the demand for foodstuffs fell precipitously, black growers inevitably felt the pinch. Basutoland's grain trade, for example, thriving in 1875, was "very slack and dull" by the end of 1876, and more and more men were engaging in migrant labor rather than in agricultural production.[66] The proportion of Sotho and Tlhaping, Kimberley's main agricultural suppliers, working in the mines in 1876 was at least triple that of the previous year.[67] Such increase in the labor supply, in conjunction with an absence of mining profits, encouraged the white claim holders unilaterally to cut black wages in half in late June 1876, with unexpected results. More than half the black workers at the mines chose to take their labor elsewhere, particularly to the railway works in the Cape. A Boer attack on the Pedi state at the same time further reduced Kimberley's work force by several thousand men. Within one month of the wage cut the number of black laborers in the mines had fallen by half; within two months the number of men arriving to work was one-fiftieth of what it had been before the cut.[68]

65. "Results of the Census Recently Taken in the Province of Griqualand West," *CGHPP*, A14 1877; evidence of A. T. Goodchild in the "First Report of the Select Committee Appointed to Consider and Report on the Griqualand West Association Bill," 12 June 1877, p. 10, GH 12/4.

66. *NABB*, G12 1877, pp. 3, 4, 8, 13.

67. For the returns of blacks working in the mines in 1875 (figures for two months only) and 1876 see GLW 20; and the *Griqualand West Government Gazette*, 20 October 1877.

68. On the wage-reduction scheme and its failure see chapt. 3. On the Pedi see the *Diamond Field*, 4 August 1876; and Delius, *The Land Belongs to Us*, pp. 205–12. See also *NABB*, G12 1877, p. 8; and Purkis, "The Politics of Railway-Building," pp. 392–93.

In the final quarter of 1876, however, the large capitalists who increasingly dominated the mining industry raised wages to levels higher than they had been before the cut was imposed. Blacks soon responded to these improved terms. By December several hundred men were arriving in Kimberley each month, by the beginning of 1877 several thousand. Sotho predominated, accounting for half to two-thirds of those contracting to work—a proportion far higher than they had ever accounted for in the past.[69] Drought, affecting the northeast Transvaal from the end of 1876 and Basutoland from mid-1877, propelled even more workers into the mines.[70] Indeed, such was the increase in the supply of labor to Kimberley that whites began to believe, in the latter half of 1877, that they might finally obtain a permanent surplus of workers sufficient to enable them to cut wages in half once and for all.[71]

But high wages and drought were not foundations on which employers could hope to build the sort of labor policy that they wanted in the long term: the one factor was too expensive, the other too uncertain. Reducing the ability of blacks to produce a surplus (or even their own subsistence needs) in the rural areas, and at the same time introducing new financial impositions to force men out to work, was another matter, one that promised employers what they had wanted all along: labor that was not only plentiful but cheap as well.

The struggle for the control of rural resources took place first in Griqualand West. Although British annexation of Griqualand West in 1871 had been legally based on recognition of Griqua sovereignty over the whole territory, local whites soon challenged black ownership of the land. Officials believed that the colony would be best developed by white farmers, and land speculators hoped both to acquire all the potentially diamondiferous areas they could find and to monopolize the supply trade with Kimberley. The issue of land ownership was clouded by the conflicting claims of the Griqua, the Tlhaping, and the Kora and further complicated by the existence of white-held Orange Free State titles inherited from the period

---

69. See the monthly returns published in the *Griqualand West Government Gazette.*

70. *Diamond News,* 9, 29 January, 27 February 1877; *NABB,* G17 1878, pp. 5, 10, 13, 15; Delius, *The Land Belongs to Us,* pp. 208–09, 229–30.

71. See, e.g., the *Diamond News,* 15 September 1877.

prior to 1870, when the Boers had claimed sovereignty.[72] In May 1876, a Kimberley land court attempted to impose clarity on this confusion by rejecting most Griqua and Kora land claims (and thus, in effect, the legal basis of annexation), acknowledging the validity of a few Tlhaping claims, and recognizing most of those made by whites on the basis of Free State titles.[73]

With the third of Griqualand West located closest to Kimberley then legally placed in white hands, the colony's administrator, Colonel Owen Lanyon, next sought to satisfy the demands of these landowners, and of mine claim holders, for more labor by reallocating the remaining land. In November 1876, at a time of serious labor shortage in Kimberley, Colonel Lanyon proposed the establishment of a series of rural locations for blacks, each location small enough so that it could not be self-sufficient, all carefully dispersed throughout the countryside in such a manner that they could be used as labor reserves for the newly established white farmers, and with white magistrates in control so that the power of chiefs could be curtailed. In the survey that took place to establish these locations, approximately one-tenth of Griqualand West's land area was allocated to blacks, the rest went to whites.[74]

Black resistance to this extension of colonial rule was soon overcome, although not without armed conflict. The legal battle culminating in the land-court decision absorbed much of the capital of the various black claimants, especially of the Griqua, forcing them to sell more land (at reduced prices because of its disputed title) to pay their bills.[75] Some Griqua who attempted to prevent the loss of their land by pulling up surveyors' pegs only delayed momentarily a process that the local colonial officials were determined to complete. Furthermore, Griqualand West's white rulers disregarded the claims of chiefs to sovereignty over the indigenous inhabitants of the area. Thus it was that Andries Waterboer, the Griqua leader at whose request Griqualand West had been annexed

72. The background to the land issue is discussed thoroughly in the "Report on the Land Question in Griqualand West by Lieut-Colonel Charles Warren, R.E., C.M.G.," Colonial Office, June 1880.

73. *Ibid.*, pp. 136–37.

74. On the development of the location policy see the report by F. H. Orpen (surveyor-general, Griqualand West), 12 December 1876, GLW 7 (237); Lanyon to Barkly, 22 November 1876, CO(m) 107/2 (15277); and Lanyon's instructions to Orpen, 15 February 1877, CO(m) 107/4 (4452). For a view critical of the amount of land allocated to blacks see Charles Warren's report.

75. "Report on the Land Question by Warren," p. 13.

in 1870, was arrested and imprisoned in 1876 when he attempted to free from a prison work gang some of his subjects whom he believed had been wrongfully detained and badly treated by the British.[76] Growing discontent over land ownership and the rights of chiefs to deal with their own subjects erupted in a small-scale rebellion in 1878 when numbers of Kora, Griqua, and Tlhaping, led by unsuccessful land claimants and chiefs, but not supported by those blacks who had the closest trading links with the diamond fields, rose against British rule in a series of sporadic attacks on white traders and land surveyors. After a brief struggle, the uprising was crushed. The losers' stock was confiscated and much of their property destroyed, and hundreds of men, women, and children were taken to Kimberley as prisoners of war, forced to work as mine laborers and domestic servants.[77]

Defeat confirmed the administration's earlier reallocation of resources. The majority of Griqualand West's black inhabitants were placed in the previously surveyed locations; those not in the locations, perhaps amounting to one-quarter of the black population, dwelt as servants on white farms.[78] Some of the location dwellers continued to grow market crops on their limited and poorly watered lands, but droughts became progressively severe at the end of the 1870s, greatly restricting agricultural output. Hundreds also engaged in the wood trade with the mines, but in 1880 the administration, partly in fear of increasing deforestation, began to prohibit the collection of timber from Crown lands.[79] In 1879 the

76. *Diamond Field*, 4 April 1876; Barkly to Carnarvon, 16 April 1877, CO(m) 107/4 (5373).

77. On the rebel leaders see, "Report on the Land Question by Warren," p. 19; Teresa Strauss, *War along the Orange: The Korana and the Northern Border Wars of 1868–69 and 1878–79* (Cape Town, 1979), pp. 71–72; and Shillington, "The Impact of the Diamond Discoveries," pp. 106–07, 110–12. On the fate of the POWs, most of whom soon deserted, see Coleman to acting colonial secretary, 14 December 1878, GLW 126 (2663); the "List of Contracts Entered into by Female Prisoners of War," GH 29/6; and correspondence between the Cape and British governments published in "Further Correspondence Respecting the Affairs of South Africa," *BPP*, C2252 (1879), pp. 4–5, C2367 (1879), p. 82, and C2374 (1879), p. 151. On the Griqua uprising in general see also, I. B. Sutton, "The 1878 Rebellion in Griqualand West and Adjacent Territories," (PhD, SOAS, 1975).

78. "Report on the Land Question by Warren," pp. 18–19; *NABB*, G20 1881, pp. 127–30.

79. T. Green (inspector of locations) to C. Marshall (civil commissioner, Hay), 12 July 1880, GLW 160 (1992); F. R. Thompson (inspector of locations) to W. Franklin (civil commissioner, Barkly West), 8 July 1880, GLW 160 (2052); E. Roux (inspector of locations) to Franklin, 21 July 1880, GLW 161 (2197); *NABB*, G20 1881, pp. 127–30.

administration added a further incentive to participation in migrant labor by introducing a hut tax. With poverty and destitution becoming widespread, although not yet universal, more and more men sought work on the white farms and in the mines. In one of the areas of heaviest black settlement, for example, the inspector of locations noted in 1880 that "The greater part of the natives (young men) proceed to work in Kimberley for three to six months at a time . . . leaving their wives and children to take care of their stock etc."[80] Migrant labor, carried out under the surveillance and control of location inspectors and local magistrates, had thus become an integral part of the rural life of Griqualand West's black inhabitants within a decade of the establishment of the Kimberley diamond industry.

But Griqualand West, with its small black population, could never supply more than a tiny fraction of the diamond industry's labor needs. In 1880, for example, the Griqua, Kora, and Tlhaping resident in the colony, mostly landless and subject to taxation, still contributed less than 4 percent of the work force in the mines.[81] If the diamond industry was to secure cheaply its main supplies of labor then the pattern of British imperial intervention, the subjugation of African states, and the wresting of control over rural resources by whites from blacks would have to be repeated elsewhere in southern Africa.

The concern of Kimberley's claim holders over the supply and cost of black labor was increasingly shared in the mid to later 1870s by white employers elsewhere in southern Africa, particularly those located in the Cape and Natal. The development of the diamond industry had spurred economic growth in both colonies, and as a result the demand for black labor rose enormously on farms producing for expanding markets, in growing towns, and on large-scale public-works projects. The price of this labor also increased, since urban employers and railway builders had to match (or at least come close to) the wages paid in Kimberley if they were to attract black workers from rural areas and not lose them to the mines. White farmers were affected most of all by these developments, because they did not want to (and were perhaps not able to) match the higher wage rates—and thus lost many of their laborers to ur-

80. Green to Marshall, 12 July 1880, GLW 160 (1992).
81. See the "Return of New and Old Hands Registered at Kimberley and Du Toit's Pan during the Year 1880," *NABB*, G20 1881, pp. 132–33.

ban employers. Despite the differential impact of these developments, all white employers believed that black labor was too expensive, that there was not enough of it, and that until these problems were solved their own economic success, indeed their very survival, hung in the balance.[82]

Although the recruitment of blacks from beyond the borders of Britain's colonies had been seen as providing a partial solution to labor problems in the early to mid-1870s, by the latter half of the decade there was growing support, among both private employers and local officials, for the view that colonial borders should be expanded, much greater numbers of blacks brought under British rule, and labor problems solved by imperial action. Recruiting missions, particularly those carried out to the north of Griqualand West and the Transvaal, had had little success. As noted earlier, Boer military pressures prevented many blacks from leaving their rural homes. Besides, the only way recruiters could ever attract men was by offering high wages.[83] The expansion of colonial rule, however, promised the elimination of constraints on black participation in wage labor and the opening up of vast new supplies of men. One Griqualand official, for example, argued with regard to the Tswana that if British control were extended northward such a move would not only eliminate the Boer threat to blacks but also free the Tswana's hunter-gatherer clients from their masters, with the result that "the most industrious [clients] would at once come and seek employment here [Kimberley], while their present masters would be forced to do at last the work now done by their slaves."[84]

Another proponent of an expansionist policy was the secretary of native affairs in Natal, Theophilus Shepstone. Shepstone, moreover, exerted considerable influence on the formulation by the British colonial secretary, Lord Carnarvon, of a policy of confederation for the Boer states and the British colonies in the mid to later 1870s. Central to the confederation policy was the belief that British in-

82. See the "Report of the Select Committee Appointed to Consider . . . the Supply of the [Cape] Labour Market," *CGHPP*, A26 1879; and Etherington, "Labour Supply and South African Confederation," pp. 239–45; as well as the discussions of labor shortage by de Kiewiet and van der Horst referred to in note 52.

83. On the necessity of paying high wages see, e.g., the "Report of the Commission upon the Griqualand West Labour Question," Government Notice No. 102 of 1876, GH 12/7.

84. J. D. Barry (judge) to Bartle Frere (governor of the Cape), 19 May 1877, ZT 1/1/1, vol. 2, Lanyon Papers. On Lanyon's support for territorial expansion see Etherington, "Labour Supply and South African Confederation," p. 244.

tervention in southern Africa, preferably diplomatic, was necessary to bring the various white states into some form of union and thus permit the establishment of a "uniform native policy" to regulate relations between black and white in southern Africa.[85]

When diplomacy failed, more forceful measures were adopted. In April 1877 Shepstone annexed the Transvaal, which was teetering on the edge of collapse after a disastrous war against the Pedi. A series of wars by British and colonial troops followed: against Xhosa on the Cape's eastern frontier in 1877-78; against Sekhukhune's Pedi in 1877-79; against Cetshwayo's Zulu in 1879; and against the Sotho from 1880 onward. Only the Sotho staved off their attackers, at considerable cost in lives and property; in each of the other wars the blacks were defeated, their leaders deposed, and many of their resources reallocated, generally to whites. In particular, the economic and political autonomy of the two most powerful black states in the subcontinent was destroyed: the Pedi were dispossessed of most of their cattle and land and were subjected to hut taxes; the Zulu were divided into thirteen separate weak units where there had been but a single powerful state before.

Although white employers in Kimberley had hoped that the destruction of black autonomy would in the long term solve their labor problems, in the short term war brought nothing but increased difficulties. The supply of workers to the mines was constantly interrupted by men leaving Kimberley to fight. Between 1877 and 1879 the proportion of Pedi in the mines' work force rose and fell in accord with the rhythms of hostilities, but it declined from being one-half of the overall force to less than one-third. The situation was the same among the Sotho. Accounting for one-third of the mine workers in 1877, their numbers dropped as war threatened; by the time hostilities erupted in 1880-81 they formed only one-tenth of the work force. Much of the slack was taken up by the Tsonga, the only people who did not suffer from increased imperial attentions in the later 1870s. Their proportion of the work force

85. On the linkage of Shepstone, Carnarvon, labor supply, and confederation see Anthony Atmore and Shula Marks, "The Imperial Factor in South Africa in the Nineteenth Century: Towards a Reassessment," *The Journal of Imperial and Commonwealth History*, 3:1 (1974): 123-27, 137-38; Etherington, "Labour Supply and South African Confederation," pp. 245-53; and R. L. Cope, "Strategic and Socioeconomic Explanations for Carnarvon's South African Confederation Policy," *History in Africa*, 13 (1986): 13-34. See also Delius, *The Land Belongs to Us*, pp. 217-22; and Guy, *The Destruction of the Zulu Kingdom*, pp. 41-45.

more than tripled between 1877 and 1878 (from 9 percent to 31 percent), and they continued to account for close to one-third of Kimberley's mine workers until 1883. Yet to attract these men Kimberley's employers had to keep raising wages, so that by the end of the 1870s they were the highest that they had ever been.[86]

The end of most hostilities by 1880, with the exception of the Cape-Sotho war, did not bring any major relief to Kimberley's labor problems. Although white rule was extended over most blacks in the Cape and Natal, officials in both these colonies wanted to retain the labor of their black subjects for local industries and not have it disappear to the diamond fields. Therefore, magistrates pressured those blacks living in localities under their control to seek work in the colonies rather than in the mines.[87] Only in the Transvaal did the new colonial administration work to assist Kimberley employers with their labor needs, and that was largely because Colonel Lanyon replaced Shepstone as administrator of the conquered territory in 1879. Lanyon brought to his new appointment the same zealous concern for Kimberley's labor supply that he had exhibited as administrator of Griqualand West. To increase the number of men migrating to the mines he repealed the transit taxes previously levied on southward-bound workers, negotiated with Kimberley labor agents to assist them in their recruitment schemes, and enforced the collection of hut taxes in a far more rigorous manner than had his Boer predecessors. He carried out these measures with such vigor that in the latter half of 1880, with Kimberley's employers crying out for men to replace those gone to fight in the Cape-

86. For the monthly returns of contracted workers in 1877–79 see the *Griqualand West Government Gazette*. For later returns see *NABB*, G20 1881, pp. 132–33, G33 1882, pp. 182–83, G8 1883, pp. 10–11; and NA 195, 198. On the effects of war and drought on the supply of Sotho see *NABB*, G33 1879, pp. 12, 14, 17, 19, 20, G13 1880, pp. 10, 21, 22–23, 24, 25, 37, G20 1881, p. 130. Hostilities between the British and the Zulu also made it more difficult for the Tsonga to travel to Natal, thus steering them toward the diamond fields. See the following documents on Natal's problems with the supply of Tsonga labor: CSO 620 (4462/1877), 677 (2882/1878, 3073/1878, 3811/1878), 682 (472/1879), 726 (4977/1879), SNA 1/1/38 (243/1880, 247/1880), NAD.

87. In Natal, for example, the administration strictly enforced the collection of extra taxes from all those blacks who chose to work outside the colony. See the circular sent to all magistrates, 13 November 1878, SNA 1/1159 (65/1883), NAD. The Cape attempted to alleviate its labor needs in part by recruiting men in southern Mozambique. See the correspondence on these efforts in PWD 2/124, 2/144, 2/146, and 2/161. For an overview of the efforts made by Cape and Natal officials to acquire black labor see van der Horst, *Native Labour*, pp. 110–22.

Sotho war, he was credited with having supplied ten thousand more Pedi than would normally have sought work in the mines.[88]

But Lanyon alone could not solve the problems of the diamond industry. The Transvaal won back its independence in 1881, after defeating the British in the battle of Majuba Hill, while in Kimberley the supply and cost of labor was made ever more critical by the appalling conditions for blacks on the one hand and the establishment of numerous joint stock companies on the other. Accidents in the mines had increased as the diggings became deeper. Pneumonia, dysentery, and various "fevers" became more virulent because of poor sanitation and inadequate housing. Medical care was virtually nonexistent. White employers almost universally refused to send their sick workers to doctors, preferring to find new men rather than pay for the treatment of the old. And even if the employers did send their men to be treated, the hospital facilities for blacks in Kimberley were vilely inadequate—officially described as "dilapidated" and "filthy" in 1876, the "Native ward" of the Kimberley hospital was still operated in 1881 "in defiance of all sanitary laws," with the result that at least one-third of those admitted died.[89] Such conditions produced an annual black death rate of over eighty persons per thousand head of population in Kimberley, a rate at least half as high again as that of Calcutta, the city popularly viewed at the time as the most unhealthy in the British Empire.[90] Such conditions could not help but dissuade men from coming to

88. Hut taxes had been imposed by the Boers but never collected with much effect. In 1876, e.g., the Boer administration had collected only £1,427 in taxes; within a year of his appointment Lanyon had collected £33,690. See the memorandum of H. Shepstone, 17 October 1879, SN 1 (312/1879), TA; Lanyon to acting administrator (Griqualand West), 16 April 1880, GLW 17 (9); two minutes of 15 February and 27 April 1880, the latter of which contains a copy of Lanyon's new tax law (no. 6 of 1880), SN 3 (64/80, 161/80), TA; Coleman to colonial secretary, 11 December 1880, CO 3344; and NABB, G20 1881, p. 130.

89. On hospital facilities for blacks in Kimberley see Lanyon to Carnarvon, 18 December 1875, CO(m) 107/3 (1569); Dr. Grimmer to chief clerk, 20 September 1876, GLW 94 (2835); memorandum of John X. Merriman on Kimberley hospitals, 10 October 1881, CO 3357; and the Daily Independent, 23 September 1881, 27 December 1882. By 1883 it was common practice for employers to have their sick employees carted off to the Kimberley jail as vagrants, thus overburdening its minimal health-care facilities. See the report of the jail superintendent, 4 August 1883, CO 3434.

90. On death rates in Kimberley see, e.g., the Griqualand West Government Gazette, 1 September 1877; Diamond News, 25 January, 4, 29 March, 1 April 1879; Daily Independent, 21 January 1882. The death rate in Calcutta in the late 1870s was 52/1,000, that of London, 23/1,000.

the mines. Added to this was the havoc played with the labor market by the proliferation of joint stock companies in 1880–81. In the shakedown period that followed their founding, the owners of these companies competed viciously against one another for whatever labor was available, bidding wage rates ever higher.

The result of this combination of factors was that at the same time that employers complained of a great scarcity of workers in 1880, 1881, and early 1882 when competition between the companies was at its most ferocious, black wages rose to the highest levels they were ever to reach (up to £2 or more per week), and more migrants—including those thousands of Pedi sent down by Lanyon, and even greater numbers of Tsonga—contracted to work in the mines than at any time in the past, risking ill health for the considerable financial returns that they could earn.[91]

To alleviate the problems of high wages, Kimberley's industrialists sought to tap new sources of men through recruitment in rural areas. Prior to 1880, labor recruitment had been limited largely to "touting"—the practice whereby white labor agents met arriving migrants on the outskirts of Kimberley, engaged them as "contracted servants" and then resold their contracts to mining employers in the town.[92] From 1880 on, however, many of the mining companies either sent out their own recruiters or made arrangements with independent labor agents in the areas from which the migrant workers came. The relatively small Birbeck Mining Company, for example, in what was little more than an expansion of "touting," sent a recruiter northward into the Transvaal to contract men already on their way along the roads to the diamond fields.[93] The much larger Kimberley Central Company made more permanent arrangements for its own labor supply by contracting with agents in Natal, particularly with members of Theophilus Shepstone's family who already had considerable experience in recruiting men for employers in that colony, and with recruiters in the

91. On wage rates see the *Daily Independent*, 28, 30 November 1881, 11 February 1882. On labor statistics see, *NABB*, G20 1881, pp. 132–33, G33 1882, pp. 182–83.

92. By the end of the 1870s, most blacks coming to the diamond fields entered into contracts with labor touts while on the roads leading to Kimberley. See the *Diamond News*, 4 December 1879.

93. On the Birbeck Company see C. T. Davis (labor recruiter) to G. Hall (manager of the Birbeck), 18 August 1881, letters received, Jan. 1881–March 1883, Birbeck Mining Company Limited, CR 6/1, and the bankruptcy papers contained in the same file.

Portuguese-ruled areas of Mozambique. Still, such arrangements were not particularly successful. Although the recruits were engaged at rates of pay substantially lower, and for contracts considerably longer, than those ruling in the diamond fields, once in the town they readily ascertained the true state of affairs, broke their contracts, and sought work with higher-paying employers. Largely as a result of such problems with the supply of labor the Birbeck Company went bankrupt, and the Kimberley Central was forced to keep on raising its wages to levels higher than those offered by any of its competitors.[94]

But changes resulting from the ongoing process of consolidation in the diamond industry began to tip the scales against blacks. The depression that hit the industry in late 1882 and bankrupted more than half the mining companies reduced the demand for labor. As table 2.3 shows, the number of black employees fell by half in 1883. Furthermore, with a relative surplus of labor on their hands, employers generally chose to rehire current employees when the latter completed their contracts rather than replace them with newly arrived inexperienced men. The result, as demonstrated by table 2.4, was that 85 to 90 percent of the post-1882 work force consisted of long-term employees. With turnover drastically reduced, a much smaller number of new arrivals annually could keep the mines adequately supplied with labor. Though thirty thousand new hands had been deemed insufficient to meet the needs of Kimberley's industrialists in 1882, five thousand were considered about enough in 1883.[95] Moreover, employers took advantage of the changing balance of supply and demand to reduce wages by up to 50 percent.[96] Even so, the industrialists felt that such a profitable state

94. On the recruitment measures taken by the Kimberley Central Company see the *Daily Independent*, 6 December 1881; the *Griqualand West Investor's Guardian*, 8 December 1881; and Sieborger, "The Recruitment of African Labour," pp. 86, 88–89. On the involvement of Theophilus Shepstone and his family in labor recruitment, both for the diamond fields and for Natal, see Bulwer to Hicks Beach, 23 August 1878, despatch no. 66, and the report on the "Employment of Native Labourers in Natal," by the attorney general, M. A. Gallwey, 22 August 1878, enclosure 1 in no. 66, *BPP*, C2220 (1879), pp. 171–72; evidence of H. J. Feltham and S. Marks contained in the "Report of the Select Committee on Illicit Diamond Buying in Griqualand West," *CGHPP*, A9 1882, pp. 3, 21, 42. On recruitment in Natal and Mozambique in general see the minutes contained in SNA 1/1/37 (186/1880), CSO 820 (3293/1881), CSO 837 (2832/1881), CSO 840 (289/1882), NAD; and the correspondence from labor agents contained in PWD 2/144, 2/146, 2/161.
95. *NABB*, G8 1883, pp. 5, 7, G3 1884, p. 28.
96. *Daily Independent*, 17 January 1883.

was only a passing phase: demand for labor would no doubt exceed supply, and wages would rise again once the depression ended and production returned to its former levels.

An outbreak of smallpox in Kimberley late in 1883 threatened to confirm the industrialists' worst fears of a return to the bad old days of labor shortage. To offset the devastating effect that public knowledge of such a disease was likely to have on the supply of labor, the industrialists immediately denied (and continued to do so for several months) that the disease afflicting their employees was smallpox. Rather, they supported the claims of a number of local doctors, most of whom had financial interests in mining, that the rapidly spreading illness was neither contagious nor harmful and that it was a peculiarly black ailment quite unlikely to affect whites. The employers provided no medical care for their workers and did not allow any of them to be treated. Instead, they kept sick and healthy cooped up together on company premises. Inevitably, the disease reached epidemic proportions, spreading not only through the mines but into the town as well. It was only at that stage, when large numbers of whites fell ill, that the town's medical

TABLE 2.3   Average Number of Black Mine Workers, 1881–85

| Mine | 1881 | 1882 | 1883 | 1884 | 1885 |
|------|------|------|------|------|------|
| Kimberley | 3,000 | 4,000 | 2,000 | 1,500 | 1,500 |
| De Beers | 2,000 | 2,000 | 1,260 | 1,700 | 1,700 |
| Dutoitspan | 8,000 | 3,235 | 2,800 | 3,300 | 4,500 |
| Bultfontein | 4,000 | 2,685 | 2,300 | 2,500 | 3,600 |
| Total | 17,000 | 11,920 | 8,360 | 9,000 | 11,300 |

SOURCES: *CGHPP,* G34 1883, p. 29, G11 1890, p. 38.

TABLE 2.4   Old and New Hands in the Black Work Force, 1879–85
(As a Percentage of Contracted Black Workers)

| | 1879 | 1880 | 1881 | 1882 | 1883 | 1884 | 1885 |
|------|------|------|------|------|------|------|------|
| Kimberley and De Beers | | | | | | | |
| New Hands | 22 | 29 | 26 | 17 | 9 | 18 | (17) |
| Old Hands | 78 | 71 | 74 | 83 | 91 | 82 | (83) |
| Dutoitspan and Bultfontein | | | | | | | |
| New Hands | 50 | 47 | 41 | 42 | (10) | (8) | (14) |
| Old Hands | 50 | 53 | 59 | 58 | (90) | (92) | (86) |

SOURCES: NA 195, 198, 202; *CGHPP,* G20 1881, G33 1882, G8 1883. Percentages in parentheses are based on part-year returns.

officer of health was able to have his diagnosis of the disease as smallpox officially accepted, quarantine measures imposed, and steps taken to care for the sick. Because of the delay, however, the toll was enormous: 2,214 cases of smallpox between October 1883 and the end of 1884, of which more than one-quarter were fatal.[97]

Nonetheless, such high levels of mortality did not have a significant effect on Kimberley's labor supply. With even more new hands contracted in 1884 than in 1883, the registrar of servants concluded that the labor market was quite well supplied.[98] In large part, this lack of a negative impact reflected the fact that with Kimberley's labor needs so much less than what they had been in the past there were more than enough men available who were ready to work in the mines no matter how bad the conditions, particularly given declining conditions in white-ruled rural areas. Indeed, of all Kimberley's migrant workers the only ones noticeably to shift the sale of their labor elsewhere at the time of the smallpox epidemic were the Tsonga, who alone were still outside the ambit of imperial control: their proportion of the work force fell from 26 percent in 1883 to 11 percent in 1884.[99]

The continued participation of blacks in wage labor in Kimberley's mines, despite waning conditions in the workplace and in the town, reflected in large measure the destructive impact of white rule on rural societies. In Griqualand West, for example, conditions in the rural locations had become critical by 1883-84. Smallpox and syphilis were widespread, the wood trade was largely at an end with most of the trees cut down or out of bounds to blacks, and crops were destroyed by severe droughts in both years. Starvation, as one colonial official noted, forced many people "to seek labour."[100]

97. For a discussion of the smallpox epidemic by the Kimberley medical officer of health see Hans Sauer, *Ex Africa* (London, 1937), pp. 72-92. See also the annual reports of the Kimberley district surgeon, *CGHPP*, G67 1884, p. 17, and G19 1885, p. 23; and Matthews, *Incwadi Yami*, pp. 108-11.

98. *NABB*, G2 1885, p. 206.

99. For statistics on the men registering see NA 195 and 198. On the shift of Tsonga from the diamond fields to the Natal labor market see CSO 958 (1552/1884), 978 (3561/1884), NAD. By the mid-1880s more than half the adult male population of the Tsonga were, at any one time, engaged in migrant labor. See C. R. Saunders (agent of the Natal government) to secretary of native affairs, Natal, 17 November 1887, enclosure in no. 21A, "Further Correspondence Respecting the Affairs of Swaziland and Tongaland," *BPP*, C6200 (1890), pp. 46, 48; and Harries, "Kinship, Ideology and Labour Migration," pp. 153, 154, 156-58.

100. *NABB*, G3 1884, p. 9. For descriptions of the difficult conditions facing blacks in Griqualand West see also, *NABB*, G8 1883, pp. 8, 18, 121, G3 1884, pp. 7, 8, 9, G2 1885, pp. 7, 8, 25; and the annual reports of the district surgeons, *CGHPP*, G91 1883, pp. 14, 50, 53-54, G67 1884, pp. 6, 15, G19 1885, pp. 4, 19, 20.

In Basutoland, the Sotho were likewise brought face to face with the prospect of famine by the combination of growing population pressures on limited land resources, the legacy of destruction from the recent war with the Cape, and severe droughts in 1883 and 1884. Thousands migrated, largely to seek work on the farms of the Cape and the Orange Free State but also in the diamond mines.[101] In the Transvaal the Boers, who had freed themselves from British rule in 1881, consolidated white rule in 1882–83 with the conquest of the Ndzundza Ndebele, their former allies in wars against the Pedi, and building upon the bureaucratic structures put in place by Lanyon they imposed harsh hut-tax collection measures on all their now largely landless and impoverished black subjects.[102]

Seeking even more land and labor, whites also intruded to an increasing extent on the lands of the Tswana. A number of wars broke out among the Tswana in the late 1870s and early 1880s, primarily because of increasing internal pressures for land resulting from the expansion of British rule to the northeastern margins of Griqualand West and Boer settlement on the westernmost borders of the Transvaal. Whites—English speculators and Boer farmers—allied themselves with various Tswana factions, offering their armed support in territorial disputes in return for land grants. The process soon got out of hand as the white freebooters usurped the power of their supposed black masters. By 1883, Boer mercenaries had taken control of most of the lands of the Tlhaping and Rolong and had established the independent states of Goshen and Stellaland. In the face of such dispossession, many Tswana turned to migrant labor as their ability to produce not only market goods but even their own subsistence needs steadily declined.[103]

The undercutting of rural autonomy became even more pronounced in the mid-1880s as Kimberley's industrialists took measures that impinged directly on black societies. First to feel the pressure were the southern Tswana. Ignoring the claims of the Goshen and Stellaland Boers, the British annexed the territories of the Tswana south of the Molopo River in 1884 and established a protectorate over those north of the river. The Tlhaping and Rolong

101. See, e.g., *NABB*, G3 1884, pp. 84, 86, 89, 91, 92–93, 95; and Robert Germond, *Chronicles of Basutoland* (Morija, 1967), chaps. 35–37, especially pp. 464–71.
102. See, e.g., Delius, *The Land Belongs to Us*, pp. 246, 251–52.
103. See, e.g., the "Report of the Commissioners Appointed to Determine Land Claims and to Effect a Land Settlement in British Bechuanaland," *BPP*, C4889 (1886), pp. 24–28, 35, 63–65, 69–72, 85–92.

did not get their lands back, however, for Cecil Rhodes, who had largely engineered the annexation of what had become British Bechuanaland, promised the Boers that they could keep the lands that they had seized from the Tswana so long as they acquiesced peacefully in accepting British overrule. As an industrialist Rhodes was interested in Tswana labor, not Tswana land, the loss of which would further augment the supply of labor. In early 1886 a land commission confirmed Rhodes' agreement by accepting the majority of white claims and rejecting most of those made by blacks. The Tswana were left with legal title to less than 10 percent of their former lands. Later in the same year, the new administrators of British Bechuanaland introduced a hut tax, to be paid in "sterling coin," in an effort to raise revenue to pay for their government and to force blacks to work for whites.[104]

Even before the southern Tswana had been legally dispossessed of most of their lands, the opening of a railway from the Cape coast to Kimberley in November 1885 had already reduced the market options open to Kimberley's black producers. Rhodes had taken a leading role in having the railway built, largely because he believed that only with a rail connection to the Cape would the diamond industry be able to free itself from dependence on expensive supplies of local wood and produce and bring up cheaper goods from the south.[105] The effects of the railway's opening were much as Rhodes had hoped. Fuel costs dropped as wood traders lowered their prices to remain competitive with Cape coal,[106] and grain prices fell even more precipitously because the rail link permitted American imports to be brought to the diamond fields for less than the cost of bringing Sotho crops by wagon across the Free State. With such competition from outside suppliers there were no longer

104. See *BPP*, C4889 (1886); Owen Watkins to J. Kilner, 12 May 1886, "Proclamation [re hut tax] by Sir Hercules Robinson (governor of British Bechuanaland)," 20 August 1886, in "Further Correspondence Respecting the Affairs of the Transvaal and Adjacent Territories," *BPP*, C4890 (1886), pp. 15, 55; and Williams, *Cecil Rhodes*, chapt. 8.

105. On Rhodes and the railway see, e.g., Rhodes to Merriman, 16 May 1880, Merriman Papers, 1880/27; and Jean van der Poel, *Railway and Customs Policies in South Africa, 1885-1910* (London, 1933), pp. 9-10.

106. The wood trade, which was largely concentrated in British Bechuanaland, did not stop entirely, since even with lower prices blacks could still make some money by supplying the Kimberley market. See the "Annual Report of the Civil Commissioner and Resident Magistrate, Vryburg," 21 September 1886, *BPP*, C4956 (1887), p. 98; "Report of the Acting Administrator [British Bechuanaland] for the Year Ended 30th September 1888," *BPP*, C5620-2 (1889), pp. 9-10, 32, 49; and "Annual Reports [British Bechuanaland] for 1892-93," *BPP*, C6857-50 (1893-94), pp. 6, 17.

large profits to be won in the Kimberley marketplace by black producers. The elimination of the Kimberley grain market, on top of land shortages and ecological problems, left Basutoland's once successful agricultural producers impoverished by the second half of the 1880s.[107]

Kimberley's industrialists, taking advantage of this conjunction of low demand for black produce and labor and worsening rural conditions, sought next to consolidate their control over the supply and price of black labor. In 1885 and 1886, the three largest companies in the mines began the practice of engaging only recruited men for their work forces rather than contracting those who had traveled independently to the diamond fields. The companies obtained these recruits either by direct negotiation with chiefs (who were paid for each man thus obtained) or through established labor agents. The French Company used the services of a former police superintendent from Durban who had recruited Zulu as prison guards for the Kimberley jail throughout the 1870s and early 1880s; the Kimberley Central Company continued its association with the Shepstone family; and the De Beers Company hired the former superintendent of native locations in Griqualand West to make, successfully as it turned out, "arrangements with the chiefs of Basutoland, Bechuanaland and the Transvaal for a continuous supply of men." All the recruits were offered much poorer terms than the men whom they replaced: they had to agree to contracts of six to twelve months duration rather than three to six; they had to remain in fenced compounds on their employers' properties for the entire term of the contract; and they had to accept wages half those paid formerly. Since these three companies exercised an effective monopoly over the Kimberley job market, most smaller operations having long since gone bankrupt or been taken over, black migrants had little choice but to agree to these new terms and work or to refuse and have no job. Enough chose the former option for the work forces of the mining companies to consist almost entirely of recruited men by the end of 1886—and for there to be few employer complaints about the shortage or price of labor.[108]

107. Germond, *Chronicles of Basutoland*, pp. 469–70; Purkis, "The Politics of Railway-building," p. 430; Murray, *Families Divided*, p. 12.

108. Minutes of directors' meetings, Kimberley Central Diamond Mining Company Limited, 2 February, 20 November 1885, KCDM, DBA; *Diamond Fields Advertiser*, 19 January 1885; evidence of F. R. Thompson, contained in the "Report of the Commissioners . . . upon the Diamond Trade Acts," *CGHPP*, G3 1888, p. 8; Nancy

CONCLUSION

The introduction of full-scale recruitment of labor and of closed compounds did not mark the end of the struggle between employer and employee, white and black, over the terms and conditions of labor. Indeed, conflict continued taking a multitude of new forms in the compounds.[109] Nor could the supply of labor be counted on to remain constant, no matter how far conditions deteriorated in the workplace. For example, one Bechuanaland official reported in 1887 that the Tlhaping under his control went in large numbers to Kimberley, albeit "forced to go to the Fields to earn money to pay hut tax," yet greatly benefiting from the compound system since they could save their earnings rather than dissipate them in the town on liquor. Only two years later, however, the same official noted that his charges now worked for farmers in the Transvaal and the Free State in preference to going to the diamond mines, for "they would sooner go to prison than into the compound, where they are beaten, knocked about, and worse treated by the white overseers than they are in prison."[110]

But 1886 was something of a watershed all the same because the changes effected in the relationship between Kimberley and its rural hinterland by that time had been quite fundamental. After fifteen years of constant struggle, the diamond industry had clearly left its imprint on black societies both in terms of what it wanted from them and how it took it. Voluntary participation in mine labor had been largely replaced by relatively forced engagement, with 80 percent of Kimberley's mine workers in the mid-1880s coming from areas under white rule. Production of a wide range of products for the Kimberley marketplace had largely declined to dependence on the export of a single devalued staple—labor. The demands of agricultural production had been usurped by those of industrial pro-

---

Rouillard, *Matabele Thompson: An Autobiography* (London, n. d. [1936]), pp. 81, 83. On recruiting missions carried out by Shepstone and the ex-police superintendent for other mining companies see, SNA 1/1/78 (840/1884), 1/1/81 (107/1885), 1/1/91 (411/1886), NAD; H. Eckstein to Mr. Lewis, 14 August 1886, and Eckstein to J. McDonald, 12 November 1886, HE 124, pp. 109, 206, BRA.

109. See chapt. 6.

110. See the annual reports of the civil commissioner and resident magistrate for Taungs, 7 September 1887, in "Further Correspondence Respecting the Affairs of Bechuanaland and Adjacent Territories," *BPP,* C5363 (1888), p. 32; and 30 September 1889, in the "Report of the Administrator of British Bechuanaland for the Year Ended 30th September 1889," *BPP,* C5897–27 (1890), p. 47.

duction, with the mines monopolizing the labor of men for a year or more at a time. Moreover, in molding black societies to fit the needs of industrial production, the diamond industry prepared the way for the much greater labor demands that were to develop in the gold industry on the Rand. Just as Kimberley drew well over two-thirds of its workers from the Pedi and the Tsonga in the mid-1880s so thereafter did the Rand, while the remainder of the gold mines' work force was derived from the same sources as those of the diamond industry. Without a viable agricultural base in their home areas and required to pay taxes, thousands moved on to sell their labor in this vast new market if they could not find work in Kimberley, where wage rates even at their reduced levels remained considerably higher than those paid elsewhere in southern Africa, or if they chose not to live in closed compounds.[111]

111. In the later 1880s the wages of black workers in the diamond mines averaged between 18s. and £1 10s. per week, considerably higher than those paid in the Cape, where the average was less than £1 per month. In the gold mines wages for blacks averaged £2 to £3 per month, although considerable pressure was exerted by employers to lower these rates. For Kimberley and Cape wage rates see *CGHPP*, G11 1890, p. 39, C1 1892, pp. 3–4. For wages in the gold mines see the Witwatersrand Chamber of Mines, *First Annual Report [for 1889]* (Johannesburg, 1890), p. 10; and van der Horst, *Native Labour*, pp. 128–33. On the sources of labor for the diamond mines up to 1885 (the last year for which breakdowns by place of origin appear to be available in the Cape Archive collections) see NA 202 and 205. On the gold mines see Francis Wilson, *Labour in the South African Gold Mines, 1911–1969* (Cambridge, 1972), p. 70.

# CHAPTER THREE

# Workers as Criminals: The Rule of Law, 1870–86

The struggle between black and white in the workplace and the town was no less intense than that which went on beyond Kimberley's urban limits. The early white diggers, and the companies that replaced them, sought to consolidate their often shaky financial position at the expense of blacks by preventing them from legally owning diamonds and by subjecting mine laborers to strict discipline. Whites believed that at base all their problems were caused by blacks—by their theft of diamonds and by their over-high labor costs. Moreover, the black laborers resisted the efforts of their white employers to cut costs: they broke contracts and "deserted"; they resisted wage cuts and harsher disciplinary measures; they played employers off against one another; and (or so their employers believed) they displayed a distressing irreverence to the sanctity of private property by taking and selling diamonds themselves.

Unable to unite and agree on a single course of action in order to break worker resistance, employers turned to the state to help them in this struggle. In particular, they saw in the law the means by which black labor could be brought under control. Indeed, during the first two decades of diamond mining the legal system played a crucial role in elaborating and maintaining the rule of inequality in Kimberley—of capitalist over worker and of white over black. White employers sought to discipline their work force through legislative means and did so with such thoroughness and success that they created a pervasive ideological equation of black workers with criminals, which effectively split an emergent white working class

110

from the black. White workers, subject to a much less rigorous, although still onerous, set of controls, contrasted their perceived respectability to the ascribed criminal tendencies of black workers and drew away. Mining capital, with increasing access to the state and its lawmaking functions, manipulated the fears and insecurities of the white workers and obtained dominance over labor through this racial split.

Yet the struggle between white capital and black labor in the mines was by no means easy. For fifteen years black and white fought against each other, in the workplace and in the town, but slowly the employers, assisted by the state and its legal apparatus, won out. By the time the owners of the mines gained firm control over their laborers they had created the most basic institutions that were to shape the lives of black workers in South African cities: the labor registration office, the location, the compound, and the jail. Ideologically, the diamond capitalists came to define the black worker not as a legitimate part of an economic structure or of a growing city but as a presumptive criminal. Institutionally, their efforts came to embrace not only the workplace but the entire town. Above all, capital and the state shaped a pattern of movement for black workers, exercising tight control over how they went between work and rest, between jobs, between city and country, and asserting (slowly and with great difficulty) control over the space and time through which black workers moved. Kimberley became for black workers a new kind of urban structure built in the interests of labor control and sanctioned by the rule of law.


EARLY DEVELOPMENTS, 1870–75

White claim holders, most of them unable to make a living in the gamble that was diamond mining, early on decided that the root cause of their problems lay with black labor; with its supply, its cost, its control, and its apparent tendency to steal. First reports of the diggings had made little comment on difficulties with the work force. In 1870 and 1871 labor was generally plentiful, and diggers expressed little concern about discipline or theft. Yet by early 1872, with the move in operations to the dry diggings and the onset of difficult times, the three commissioners who administered the diamond fields believed that the future prosperity of mining was almost totally dependent on obtaining a "constant supply of native labor" and feared that the numbers available were already inadequate.[1] The number of black workers at the mines also fluctuated throughout the year, creating further difficulties. In winter, when temperatures often fell below freezing, many men left the diamond fields; they also left periodically to plant and harvest their crops, causing intermittent periods of critical labor shortage. In short, white employers had little control over the movement of black labor.

Nor could they control its cost. The intense and unregulated competition for black workers that resulted from the greater labor demands of the dry diggings doubled wages by 1872. With weekly wages averaging 10s., and food provided in addition, one local newspaper estimated that at least £45,000 was paid out each month to the twelve thousand black workers who had officially registered to work in the mines. Black labor, the *Diamond News* argued, apart from being "the most expensive in the world" was also "the most unmanageable."[2] Indeed, there was growing concern with the almost constant refusal of employees ("servants" in the popular and legal terminology of the time) to obey what were deemed to be the "lawful commands" of the employers ("masters"). White diggers were also greatly concerned in 1872 at the extent to which their workers appeared to steal diamonds and attributed much of their own financial failure to the widespread nature of the problem. The diggers believed that in order to achieve economic success measures would have to be taken to assist in the supply and control of labor, to lower its cost and to end its thieving.[3]

In the first few years of the diamond industry, discipline of the work force was more a matter of employer violence than the rule of law. Flogging with a *sjambok* (a leather whip) or tent rope, or striking with the fists, were common methods but ones with major drawbacks. Such violence had a negative impact on the supply of labor. An abused worker could easily "desert" his employer and find a job with another claim holder or could leave the diamond fields altogether and so increase the competition for the remaining pool of workers. Richard Southey, the lieutenant-governor from 1873 to 1875, considered that one of the major causes of the poor supply of

1. Commissioners to colonial secretary, Cape Town, 22 February 1872, GH 12/1.
2. *Diamond News*, 5 December 1872, 25 February 1873.
3. See, e.g., the *Diamond Field*, 4 July 1872.

labor during his administration had been the legacy of violence of the first few years of mining.[4]

In consolidating its authority in Griqualand West, the British administration began to punish those who took the law into their own hands. In July 1872, a white digger was brought before the magistrate's court after having flogged two of his black employees whom he suspected of diamond theft, leaving them naked and bound in the open air on a winter's night, causing the death of one of the men. Found guilty by the jury only of common assault, and that committed under "great provocation," he was, however, sentenced by the judge to six months' hard labor without the option of a fine. The relative severity of this sentence, in a community in which crimes of violence against blacks had not been punished in the past except perhaps by the imposition of small fines, shocked Kimberley's residents. One local newspaper, the *Diamond Field*, claimed that the sentence had "done more to defeat the ends of justice than uphold the dignity of the law."[5] Still, it was becoming obvious to Kimberley's white population that individual acts of violence could do little to solve the problems of the supply and cost of black labor.

Digger combinations had hardly any more success than individual actions in overcoming these problems. With so many diggers (approximately five thousand in 1872) competing as employers there was never any possibility that they could reach and enforce consensus on labor policies. The main drawback to any policy of extending controls over the work force was that in response to such efforts black laborers would quit the mines. In the middle of June 1872, with a depressed economic situation, the white employers did initially unite to lower the rate of wages to 6s. per week and to make payments on a monthly basis, with one week's wages always held in arrears in an attempt to cut costs and reduce desertion. They also agreed to fine any of their number who broke the agreement. At a mass public meeting, the diggers told the black workers of this agreement and stated that any laborers who did not accept the new conditions would be driven from the diamond fields. It was the middle of winter and food would be scarce on any homeward journey.[6]

4. Southey to Barkly, 26 April 1873, GLW 180.
5. 12 September 1872.
6. *Diamond News*, 19 June, 3 July 1872; *Diamond Field*, 4 July 1872.

The scheme was a fiasco. Within one week of the announcement the demand for labor far exceeded the heavily depleted supply resulting from hundreds of laborers having rejected the new conditions and abandoned Kimberley. Digger unity quickly fell into disarray as employers competed for the remaining workers, so that wages soon rose again to 10s., the idea of monthly payments was dropped, and most whites resigned themselves to the fact that black wages were sure to rise even higher in the near future.[7] Unanimity among the diggers had little chance of success so long as blacks could afford to leave the diamond fields, and so long as the units of production in the mines (the claims and portions of claims) remained small, numerous, and in competition for the same limited supply of labor.

The *Diamond Field* had earlier suggested a possible solution to these problems through the use of law to control the work force. It had argued that "natives" had to live "under a kind of patriarchal system," otherwise they would become "loafers, thieves and drunkards." The relative freedom of the black laborers on the fields, in comparison with the strict controls of their own communities, made them disrespectful of the diggers. What was needed was a system of control as strict and authoritarian as that which it believed chiefs exercised in the men's home communities.[8]

Employers wanted laws to regulate every aspect of the behavior of their workers. In March 1872 the residents of Kimberley presented to the commissioners a memorial listing those controls that they wished made law:[9]

1. No "Kafir or other colored person" to hold a digging license unless supported by fifty white claim holders.

2. All employers to have written contracts with their servants registered before a government official.

3. No contracts of less than three months.

4. On discharge of each servant the employer to endorse the servant's ticket of service as to the satisfactory completion of contractual obligations.

5. No unemployed native laborer to be permitted in the camp longer than forty-eight hours after discharge.

6. All employers and constables to have the right to search

7. *Diamond News*, 17 July 1872.

8. 28 December 1871. See also the issues of 2 May, 25 July, 8, 22 August 1872.

9. "Memorial of the Residents of Colesberg Kopje (Kimberley)," 23 February 1872, enclosure in commissioners to colonial secretary, 20 March 1872, GH 12/1.

servants at any time. Any "native or colored person" found to have a diamond in his possession for which he could not "satisfactorily account" to be liable to a sentence of at least fifty lashes.

7. Any person (who was not a registered claim holder) convicted of having purchased a diamond from a "native or colored servant" to receive fifty lashes in public, have his property confiscated, and be expelled from the diamond fields.

8. A fine of £25 or one month's imprisonment for anyone inducing a servant to leave his master.

9. Police to patrol the countryside to check that servants were properly registered.

10. All diamonds found on any natives leaving the fields to be regarded as the property of their last master.

11. No liquor to be sold to servants except with the written permission of their masters.

12. Any person caught stealing diamonds to be liable to up to fifty lashes and three years' imprisonment.

13. No native to be allowed to move about the camp after 8:00 P.M.

Over the course of the next few months the diggers persuaded the commissioners to give their proposals legal force. When peaceful measures had little effect they resorted to violence, burning the tents of black claim holders, attempting to lynch black men suspected of stealing diamonds, and on occasion rioting. In the face of increasing social disorder, and unwilling and unable to go to the expense and trouble necessary to repress the agitation, the commissioners wrote most of the diggers' demands into law, although the Colonial Office, upholding the principle that no British subject (such as those blacks who came from Basutoland, the Cape Colony and Natal) should be legally discriminated against on the basis of color, eliminated the references to "natives" and "colored persons" and substituted the term "servant."[10]

Government Notice 68 of July 1872 established a servant's registry office and ordered the construction of a depot at which all arriving black laborers would be required to register and obtain a daily pass until they had secured employment. This pass, and another given upon getting a job, had to be carried at all times and shown "to anyone who may demand it"; failure to do so by the black

10. See Smalberger, "The Role of the Diamond-mining Industry," pp. 419–34.

pass holder would render him liable to arrest. The notice required that upon leaving the fields the laborer obtain a third pass, certifying that he had carried out his employment obligations satisfactorily. Workers were required to remain on their employer's premises after 9:00 P.M. Any employer who attempted to engage workers other than through the registry office would be liable to a fine of £10 and three months' imprisonment.[11] The administration, responding to the pressure of the employers, had begun to shape legal controls over what workers did in the workplace and the town.

One month later the pass law was further elaborated. Under the regulations instituted by Proclamation 14 of August 1872, all so-called servants upon registering for employment at the registry office were to be given a certificate stating the duration of their contract and the rate of wages they were to receive. They were required, under penalty of a £5 fine or two months' imprisonment, to produce this certificate for any "justice of the peace, field-cornet, police officer, constable, or registered holder of a claim" who asked to see it. This was the fate of anyone discovered without the pass:

> Any person who shall be found wandering or loitering about within the precincts of any camp without a pass signed by his master or by a magistrate or justice of the peace, and without being able to give a good and satisfactory account of himself, may be arrested by any police officer or constable without a warrant, and taken before the magistrate of the district, and shall be liable to be punished by fine not exceeding five pounds, by imprisonment with or without hard labour and with or without spare diet for any period not exeeding three months, or by corporal punishment in any number of lashes not exceeding twenty-five.

The surveillance of the law extended to the servant's body as well as his movements. Any master could search the person, residence, or property of his servants at any time without a warrant while they were in his employ, and within two hours after they had left his service. All diamonds found in the possession of a servant were deemed to be the property of his master, or if he were currently out of work then of his former master. Any servant found guilty of diamond theft could be flogged, up to a maximum of fifty lashes, and be sentenced to twelve months' hard labor. Although this legislation

11. *Statute Law of Griqualand West* (Cape Town, 1882), pp. 63–64.

was intended to regulate black labor, like Government Notice 68 it did not use racially discriminatory language. Black workers were always referred to as "servants," never as "natives," and thus the law remained, in language at least, color-blind.[12]

Language was one thing, however, actions quite another. The police and courts took vigorous steps to enforce the laws regulating worker behavior. The police patrolled the outskirts of the mining camps checking that departing black workers had the requisite passes and often searching them for stolen diamonds.[13] Within the camps, the police patrolled the streets, making pass checks on blacks as they sought to discover so-called deserters. In 1872, for example, the Kimberley Magistrate's Court dealt with over 4,760 criminal cases, and the most common offense by far was "desertion of employment" by black workers. Those found guilty were generally flogged ten to twelve times with a cat-o'-nine-tails and then sent back to their employer. Typical cases included those of prisoner 4409, known as Sunday, who was convicted in February 1873 of "desertion" and received twelve lashes, and prisoners 4523 and 4524, Jacob and Buffalo, who each received eleven lashes for the same offense. For the lesser crime of being in camp without a pass, prisoners 4670, 4671, 4672, and 4673 (Jimmy, Hans, Jim, and Boy) each received the option of a fine or three lashes. Such were the typical sentences of the time.[14]

Yet most of the diggers did not believe that the state's efforts at control went far enough. Although labor registration had been carried out on a large scale in 1873 with fifty-one thousand men contracted, in 1874 the number registered dropped to forty-three thousand.[15] Most whites believed by the end of 1874 that registra-

---

12. *Ibid.*, pp. 26–32, Proclamation 14, August 1872.

13. For example, in December 1872 between 1,100 and 1,500 departing laborers were stopped and checked for exit passes. The 275 men who did not possess that document were brought back to the registry office so that officials could check that they had fulfilled their contractual obligations. Most of them had not, for 250 were fined 2s. 6d. each and another 18 received six lashes each in addition to a fine. W. Coleman (registrar) to J. Currey (government secretary), 4 March 1873, GLW 71; *Diamond Field*, 9 January 1873; Cape *Argus*, 14 January 1873.

14. Sergeant Bradshaw to government secretary, 27 October 1874, GH 12/4; Criminal Record Books, Kimberley Magistrate's Court, January 1872–19 February 1873, 1/KIM ADD1/1/2/1, ADD1/1/2/2. Imprisonment as a punishment was generally restricted to whites.

15. See the statements of W. Coleman, 29 July 1874, 22, 24 February 1875, and of J. E. House (registrar, Dutoitspan), 24 February 1875, GLW 20.

tion—the basis of the system of labor control introduced in 1872—
no longer served their purposes.[16] Employers argued that they did
not register their servants since these men still constantly deserted,
generally eluding the best efforts of the police. In fact, the employers
were particularly annoyed at having paid a fee to register their
employees only to see them desert still in possession of the contract
document that guaranteed its bearer relatively free movement
about the diamond fields. And so the laborers found new ways to
evade the attempts to control their time and labor, while all their
employers could do was complain about the ineffectiveness of the
police's attempts to enforce the law.[17]

At the same time, employers remained obsessed with the theft
of diamonds, especially as the industry entered a severe depression
in 1874. In August of that year white diamond diggers met together
in a mass public meeting to complain of the presence of "swell
niggers" on the fields who, those in attendance claimed, were profiting
from illegal activities while they themselves, the "rightful" owners
of the diamonds, could not make a living.[18] Whites argued that
blacks should be prevented from holding claims not simply because
of their desire to eliminate competitors in the mines but also because they felt that black diggers undermined their control over
labor by acting as fronts for the fencing of stolen diamonds. Im-
plicitly defining a black digger as a criminal, white employers objected to the British administration's refusal to enact racially
discriminatory legislation and suggested that it was being unduly
influenced by the Aborigines Protection Society in London. Instead
of conspiring to "elevate in one day the servant to equality as re-
gards the right to hold property with his master," wrote an editorialist in the *Diamond Field*, the state should enforce "class
legislation, restrictive laws, and the holding in check of the coloured races till by education they are fit to be our equals. . . ."[19]

It seemed to many of the white employers that, having secured
legislation to protect their interests, the state, rather than coming
to their aid at a time of economic hardship, was opposing them by

16. See the letters of the registrar, Kimberley, to government secretary of 12
and 18 December 1874, GLW 71. On 13 January 1875, the *Diamond Field* referred
to registration as a "farce."

17. Registrar to government secretary, 18 November 1874, GLW 55; *Diamond
Field*, 7, 14, 28 November 1874.

18. *Diamond Field*, 14 August 1874; *Diamond News*, 18 August 1874.

19. 28 November 1874.

refusing to recognize reality and sanction racially discriminatory laws. Dissident diggers armed themselves and drilled in public, challenging the authority of Lieutenant-Governor Southey. Southey, in response, not only refused their demands for racial laws but also stated that he was ready to arm blacks to defend law and order and put down the "rebels." As noted in chapter 1, the Black Flag affair was only settled with the arrival of troops from Cape Town who disarmed the rebels. Southey, however, did not long outlast his enemies, for within a few months the Colonial Office replaced him and his administration with men deemed more in tune with the local community.

In sum, three factors prevented the successful extension of legal controls over the black work force in the first half of the 1870s. First, and most important, the small-scale, mutually competitive nature of the units of production made them economically unstable and prevented the formation of effective combinations of employers over any extended period. Second, the state, in the form of the colonial administration, seemed to be acting indecisively, enacting legal instruments of labor control but blunting them in the name of abstract principles of the universality of law. Third, and closely related to the second factor, criminal sanctions could not be applied effectively against black workers because of the physical weakness of the state apparatus; there were too few police, not enough jails, and the courts were overburdened.

## A PERIOD OF TRANSITION, 1876–80

In the second half of the 1870s major changes took place in the diamond industry and in the nature of the state, changes that had a considerable impact on labor. The unit of production in the industry became steadily larger as combinations of claims were brought into single ownerships. The owners and managers of these larger units, in order to protect their considerable investments in property and machinery, sought greater controls over labor. In this enterprise they were assisted energetically by the state which, with a greater economic stake of its own in diamond mining, sought to secure and protect the profitability of the industry. But complete control over labor could only be approached, not achieved, during this period. Despite the support of the state, the structure of the industry suffered from internal contradictions that prevented the mining capitalists from securing the degree of control over labor which they desired.

The large claim holdings differed from the smaller operations both in their scale of operations and in their organization of production. Much greater use was made of machinery and a more thorough and carefully organized coordination of machine and man power became necessary. Machines, in which the large claim holders had invested hundreds of thousands of pounds, were obviously worked more effectively by men who knew what they were doing, thus placing a premium on skill and experience in the work force that had not been particularly valued before. The large claim holders had an even greater incentive than their predecessors to make sure that black laborers worked their full contract period and did not take their skills elsewhere. The enlarged scale of operations made it necessary for the claim holder to delegate some of his supervisory functions over black workers to a new class of employee, the white overseer. Such transformations in the organization of production introduced new tensions into the changing relations of capital and labor at the diamond fields, relations that the state took a much more active role in regulating than it had in the past.[20]

The state had a considerable financial interest in the success of the diamond industry. By 1876 diamonds were the largest item in the Cape Colony's exports, and their discovery had been the major factor in enabling the Cape to recover from the depression of the late 1860s. More immediately, in 1875 the British administration purchased the Vooruitzigt farm, which contained the Kimberley and De Beers mines and the town of Kimberley, for £100,000. As Colonel Lanyon, the new administrator of Griqualand West, put matters, the state was now the "proprietor" of the town and consequently it was "very expedient" to facilitate the working of the mines "so as to induce as many workers as possible to remain, and thus to enhance the value of the property."[21] Moreover, the enforcement of black-labor regulations, apart from improving the supply of labor, would through fines and fees provide a considerable amount of income for an administration desperately in need of more revenue. Indeed, within one year of taking office Lanyon, by strictly en-

20. For a description of one of these new operations see the *Diamond News*, 13 March 1877.
21. Lanyon to Barkly, 25 January 1877, GH 12/8.

forcing the existing laws, had doubled the state's income from labor-registration fees.[22]

The general coincidence of interest between state and industry with regard to black labor was given practical form in early 1876 when Lanyon established a commission "to enquire into and report upon the supply and demand for native labour." The deliberations of this body dominated public affairs during the first quarter of the year as large numbers of employers made their needs known. In May the commission reported its findings along with a recommendation for the establishment of an elaborate administrative structure to control the supply of labor. Its proposals included measures to provide safe passage for blacks coming to the diamond fields, severe penalties for persons enticing servants to desert, and stress on the need for the strict enforcement of a vagrancy law in order to keep blacks in Kimberley under continuous control.[23]

Lanyon's attempt to give these proposals a legal basis foundered, however, on the continued opposition of the Colonial Office to racially discriminatory legislation. In 1876, Lanyon enacted a new law to replace the older statutes (Government Notice 68 and Proclamation 14) in which he did away with the use of the euphemistic "servant" and substituted "native" to refer to black laborers. He defined the latter term "to mean any member of any South African tribe" whether British subject or not. Since the previous laws had essentially secured "the reality while avoiding the appearance of class legislation," Lanyon's attorney general considered that the new ordinance would eliminate much legal hypocrisy and be easier to enforce. But the Colonial Office, continuing to insist that race not be made a legal category, did not go along with the reasoning of Lanyon and disallowed the ordinance.[24]

Yet Whitehall's respect for the niceties of the language of the law had little impact on legal practice in Kimberley, particularly since Lanyon was prepared to take a far more active role than his

22. "Table of Actual Revenue and Expenditure in the Province of Griqualand West 1870 to 1879," GH 21/2.

23. "Report of the Commission upon the Griqualand Labour Question," Government Notice 102 (1876), enclosure in Lanyon to Barkly, 1 June 1876, GH 12/7.

24. See the "Ordinance to Provide for the Better Protection of Native Labourers, and to Amend the Laws Regulating the Rights and Duties of Masters and Servants in the Province of Griqualand West and for Other Purposes," no. 10, 1876; and the comments of S. G. Shippard (attorney general), enclosed in Lanyon to Barkly, 15 March 1877, GLW 8.

predecessor in using the agencies of the state to help regulate the labor market. An example of the new activism is supplied by the experience of one white employer, H. Green of the Dutoitspan mine. In May 1876 Green wrote to Lanyon complaining of the great difficulty he had in obtaining labor at a time when numerous unemployed men were holding out for higher wages. Green made a simple request to the administrator: "Could not the police put a little gentle pressure on these gentlemen to oblige them to enter service?" Lanyon responded with a note to the inspector of police requesting that a series of pass raids be made and the unemployed arrested. The inspector agreed to make a raid the following Sunday, when he knew that the unemployed would be "loafing about," although he was somewhat concerned by the fact that the jail at Dutoitspan was already full and could not accommodate any more prisoners.[25]

Green's success in getting police assistance was not an isolated case; in 1876 police activity on behalf of employers increased at a quickening pace. The police force grew from 44 officers and men in January to 112 by September. Moreover, the colonial secretary in Cape Town backed up Lanyon's efforts by ordering the Kimberley inspector of police to "be very particular for the future in strictly enforcing the law which obliges *all* natives to register and obtain a pass," while in the same year Lanyon contracted with the former head of Durban's municipal police to obtain a supply of Zulu to work as jail guards and to detect crime in the "Kafir community."[26]

Arrests increased dramatically. In the first six months of 1875, there were 1,396 blacks and 131 whites arrested; in the first six months of 1876 arrests rose to 3,131 blacks and 384 whites. Most of the increase in white arrests was accounted for by a greater number of individuals being charged with "lying drunk in the streets." With regard to the arrests of blacks, the greatest increase was in the number charged with being "in camp without passes," from 95

25. H. Green to Lanyon, 2 May 1876, GLW 86; Lanyon to Percy (inspector of police), 16 May 1876, and the reply of Percy, 17 May, GLW 87 (1524). J. Stanton, the digger who had flogged his servant to death in 1872 and been sentenced to six months in jail (a sentence that was not carried out), also complained at the same time as Green about the nonregistration of laborers. See Coleman to Percy, 3 May 1876, GLW 86.

26. Colonial secretary to inspector of police, 7 January 1876, GLW 80; Lanyon to Barkly, 26 February 1876, GH 29/1, enclosure 38; Barkly to secretary of state, 9 February 1876, and Barkly to Carnarvon, 10 April 1876, GH 25/1; Lanyon to Barkly, 15 June 1876, GH 29/2, enclosure 64; Percy to chief clerk, 15 September 1876, GLW 93 (2770).

in 1875 to 971 in 1876. Arrests for "neglect of duty to masters" increased from 99 in 1875 to 257 in 1876; for "desertion of service" from 174 to 300; for "lying drunk in the street" from 83 to 320.[27] Both Lanyon and his inspector of police considered that the greater number of arrests did not reflect any major rise in the amount of crime in Kimberley but rather was a product of the new strength and activism of the police force.[28]

Throughout the remainder of the decade the police continued to harass black workers in Kimberley. They made constant checks on men in the street, requiring them to show their passes, and regular Sunday raids on those areas with a large black population, in an attempt to cut down the circulation of labor through desertion and to make sure that no blacks were in the town who did not have official permission to be there. These police actions were by necessity carried out on a random basis, since it was physically impossible to check that every black person had a pass. Yet the randomness of these mechanisms of worker control assisted the police in creating a climate of insecurity and fear. The very arbitrariness of law enforcement contributed to the disciplining of the members of the first generation of a new working class.

The courts adopted rapid procedures in determining guilt and passing sentence, essential developments considering the number of cases with which they were deluged. In a single day in January 1876, for example, 107 cases came before the Kimberley Magistrate's Court; on 5 November 1877, 115 cases were dealt with; on 28 January 1878, over 150. In such circumstances the time available to determine guilt or innocence was extremely limited, and the magistrates generally accepted the evidence of the arresting officers as adequate proof of guilt.[29]

Sentencing was punitive. One magistrate, in attempting to decrease the number of people brought before him each week charged with pass offenses, doubled the penalty from a 10s. fine or two weeks'

27. Most of these arrests took place in May and June at the same time as the employers were attempting to lower wages. See the "General Summary of Offenses Committed at Kimberley and Tried at the Resident Magistrate's Court during the Half Year Ending 30th June 1875," and the similar summary for the half year ending 30th June 1876, enclosures in Percy to chief clerk, 15 September 1876, GLW 93 (2770).

28. Percy to chief clerk, 15 September 1876, GLW 93 (2770); *Diamond News*, 21 September 1876.

29. *Diamond News*, 6 November 1877, 29 January 1878.

hard labor to a 20s. fine or one month's hard labor (with eighteen days on a rice-water diet) and even considered doing away with the option of a fine. Yet, while increasing the burden on those arrested, this measure had little apparent effect on the number charged.[30]

The production-line techniques of the courts were further refined in 1879 with the establishment of the Police Magistrate's Court. This court dealt with those people, almost all of whom were black, charged with offenses under the 1872 pass-law ordinances and the 1856 Cape Colony Masters and Servants Act. In the first year of operation of this new system only 952 cases came before the Kimberley Magistrate's Court, while 4,359 were adjudicated by the Police Magistrate's Court. As the name implies, the latter was essentially an institution for disciplining those brought before it, doing without a jury system and aiming at a rapid turnover of cases.[31]

Despite the repressive activities of the police and courts, the total control desired by the white employers over their black workers remained as elusive as ever. Though the energy of the police had resulted in a great increase in labor registration in 1876, employers were still dissatisfied. When claim holders, beset by harsh economic conditions, decided in 1876 unilaterally to cancel the contracts that they had made with their black employees and reduce wages by half, they had to stand by helplessly as more than half the mines' work force left Kimberley. The police could do nothing to prevent such an exodus.[32] As a result of these experiences, employers' dislike of the registration system grew to such an extent that by 1880 they generally considered it useless as a means to regulate the supply and behavior of workers.[33] Yet, as the *Daily Independent* pointed out, this failure had more to do with the competitiveness of the employers and their inability to act in concert than with any shortcomings in the strict enforcement of the law. In practice, employers often ignored the registration legislation that they had so energetically pushed for and attempted to obtain workers by means that they had had declared illegal—such as encouraging men to desert

30. *Ibid.*, 6 November 1877.

31. Criminal Record Book, Kimberley Magistrate's Court, 1879, 1/KIM ADD1/1/2/27; Criminal Record Book, Police Magistrate's Court, 1879, 1/KIM ADD2/1/2/3.

32. *Daily Independent*, 29 June 1876; *Diamond News*, 15, 18, 20, 29 July, 3, 8, 24 August 1876.

33. *Diamond News*, 13 April 1876, 11 January 1877; *Daily Independent*, 13, 15, 18, 24, 25 September 1880.

the employ of competing mining companies in exchange for better conditions and rates of pay at their own operations.[34]

The employers' readiness to evade the law themselves also reflected an awareness that its strict application could have a detrimental effect on the supply of labor. The problem was best summed up in an editorial in the *Diamond News*. As the editorialist noted, the courts were constantly crowded with blacks "arrested nominally for being without passes, but really because they were suspected of being deserters." The police had stationed men outside the office of the registrar of servants to arrest groups of black men who had come to get passes, on the vaguest suspicion that they might be deserters. The process became a "burlesque of an extremely stupid order," since men were being arrested, knocked about by the police, and placed in an extremely overcrowded jail for a night, then set free the next day to search for employment again. These police practices, the editorialist argued, not only took workers away from their employers for brief but annoying periods (as when men who had left their passes in the safe keeping of their employers—a common practice—were arrested), but also suggested to those same workers that the law was unjust.[35]

Another commentator on the regulation of blacks in Kimberley, the local correspondent for the Cape *Argus*, argued that the main problem with the rule of law in the town was the contradiction that existed between extremely restrictive laws and the inconsistent ways in which they were enforced. The police might make a raid on some area of the town and arrest several hundred people for being without passes. But the legislation was so all encompassing that there was no possible way that everybody not in compliance with the provisions of the law could be punished. Some laws were laxly enforced, such as an 1879 regulation requiring employers to feed their employees on company properties. Yet the police strictly enforced a law preventing black workers from going to "Kafir eating-

34. See the issues of the *Daily Independent* referred to in the previous note; and see also the *Diamond News*, 27 September 1877.

35. 3 November 1877. For further discussion of the drawbacks of police actions see George Champion to W. H. Ravenscroft (acting government secretary), 6 March 1877, and the note attached by R. Scholtz, 20 March 1877, GLW 101 (675); W. H. Bevan (vicar) to the administrator of Griqualand West, 28 January 1878, and the reply of the colonial secretary, 9 February 1878, GLW 114 (165); Coleman to acting colonial secretary, 17 April 1877, GLW 102 (947); and *idem*, 29 November 1877, GLW 111 (2766).

houses" (which were the main source of meals for workers), out of fear that such places were centers of illicit dealing in diamonds. Men could thus remain at the workplace without food or go into town and risk arrest. The *Argus* correspondent argued that with such a state of affairs the actions of the police could seem "capricious and tyrannical" to those affected by them rather than regular and just. The worker soon realized that in dealing with the law and its agents the only lesson to be learned was not to get caught.[36]

Such arbitrary application of the law, combined with the constant failure of many employers to fulfil their contractual obligations to their black workers, had a counterproductive effect on the supply of labor. For example, one of the leading industrialists in Kimberley, J. B. Robinson, reported that when he attempted to enforce the 1879 regulation and make his black employees eat on company premises, two-thirds of them left and sought work with other employers who were not so ready to uphold the law.[37] The registrar of servants reported to the colonial secretary that black workers were constantly coming to his office to complain of the nonpayment of their wages by employers. He cited the case of John, a black laborer who had come to him with just such a complaint. Coleman noted that John had gone to court to pursue the issue but that the case had become entangled in procedural delays. Since John had neither the time nor the money to pursue his case, Coleman expected that he would "make up his mind to lose his money & quit the Fields in disgust" like many before him.[38] Thus black workers, in response to harassment by police and employers and subjected to courtroom practices that gave little heed to their concerns, took themselves and their labor away from the diamond fields.

In an attempt to ameliorate the worst effects of these pressures on workers, and so protect the supply of labor, Lanyon in 1877 created a new civil-service position, that of protector of contracted servants. Lanyon insisted that nonpayment of wages and ineffective court practices caused injury to the "good name" of the diamond fields among the "tribes of the interior." The new protector's duties were "to attend the Magistrates' Court every day [and] defend all cases in which natives are concerned, except criminal ones, to pre-

36. Reprinted in the *Diamond News*, 20 April 1880.
37. *Ibid.*, 23 October, 6 November 1879.
38. Coleman to acting colonial secretary, 28 August, 13 September 1877, GLW 107 (1958), 108 (2126).

vent them falling into the hands of [law] Agents who act unscrupulously towards them, and extort money from them and their friends outside, to investigate and settle all cases in dispute between master and servant, to enforce payment of wages and to look after the interests of the natives in every way." In short, the protector would put a check on the actions of disreputable employers and the worst excesses of the courts.[39]

The first protector—who was also the labor registrar—had some limited success. In October 1879, for example, he defended 79 men appearing before the police magistrate and managed to have the charges dismissed in 29 of the cases. Among those dismissed were Adrian, who, because of the presence of the protector, was given the opportunity to explain that he was "in camp without a pass" because he had come to attend the funeral of his child, and Hendrik, who pointed out that he did not have a pass allowing him to seek employment because he had only come to Kimberley to sell some sheep. Previously, such men had seldom been given the opportunity to explain their actions before being summarily convicted.[40]

There were far too many cases for one official to deal with on a part-time basis, however. The *Argus* correspondent, writing well after the appointment of the protector, concluded that the supply of labor was steadily decreasing in reaction to the practices of the police and the courts: "Everyone knows the extraordinary freemasonry and the rapidity of communicating information possessed by the Kafir race, and this source [of labor] is nearly dried up by the lugubrious reports which are daily being taken away by parties leaving the Fields." He cited two examples: first, the case of some Swazi who, after traveling hundreds of miles to work in the mines, turned back within sight of Kimberley discouraged by the reports of working and living conditions that they received from departing laborers; second, the case of an old chief in Thaba 'Nchu who, when approached by a labor recruiter, "absolutely refused [to supply any men], saying that never again would he send any of his tribe to the Diamond-fields, for all those who had been there came back maimed

---

39. Lanyon to Bartle Frere (governor of the Cape), 14 September 1877, GLW 9 (139); Coleman, "Minute on the 'Protector of Natives' and 'Native Registry Office' for the Information of His Honour the Acting Administrator," 18 September 1880, GLW 163 (2654).

40. For these and other cases see the "Return of All Cases Tried in the Court of the Police Magistrate and Defended by the Protector of Natives during the Month of October 1879," GLW 147.

and useless in body, and corrupted in mind." Lanyon's partial measures to improve the harsh and arbitrary rule of employers and the courts had not been sufficient to counter the detrimental effects of these factors on the supply of labor.[41]

At the same time that the state was rigorously enforcing laws that had generally been introduced prior to the mid-1870s, the large claim holders and company men who grew in importance in the diamond industry after 1875 moved to protect their investments and to secure maximum profits by attempting to extend the compass of the law into further areas of the lives of their employees. Initially, they tried to introduce a system of strip searching that would apply to all workers, white as well as black. Subsequently, they pressed for closer regulation by the state of those parts of the urban area inhabited by blacks.

Industrialists led the agitation for searching. Julius Wernher, the manager of the largest mining company in Kimberley, argued that the diamond industry's profitability was severely undermined by theft. He claimed that at least three-fifths of the mines' production was stolen by workers and suggested that the problem could be totally eliminated only so long as all employees were searched every time they left the mines.[42] His emphasis on the economic threat of illicit dealing provided a strong ideological argument that was to be returned to again and again throughout the agitation for the introduction of searching. The *Diamond News* made typical use of this argument when it claimed that no "honest man" would object to being searched "because every honest man, be he black or white, will heartily concur in any measure which will lead to the conviction of the guilty, even though at some personal inconvenience."[43] As a result of the industrialists' demands, the state introduced Ordinance 11 of 1880 to provide the legal basis for the establishment of a comprehensive system of searching of all workers at every mine.

But Ordinance 11 was not enforced in 1880. The major barrier to the imposition of searching at that time was the shortage of labor caused by disturbances in the two areas that supplied most of Kimberley's workers, Basutoland and the Transvaal. No employer was

41. *Diamond News*, 20 April 1880.
42. *Ibid.*, 16 May 1878. Wernher was manager of the Griqualand Diamond Mining Company.
43. 4 May 1878.

going to put at risk his economic survival by applying additional punitive controls over workers who had already made known their opposition to the ones in force.

The second reason for the nonenforcement of searching was the opposition of the white overseers. These men held several public meetings to denounce the proposed system, petitioned the government to prohibit its application to white workers, and sought support for their case from other members of Kimberley's white community. The winning of this support was assisted by the conflicting needs of different claim holders and companies and the considerations of local politics, which forced some claim holders to back up the overseers' complaints. George Bottomley, for example, a large claim holder, had at first been an enthusiastic supporter of the searching scheme. Though he owned large amounts of mining property, however, he was still a relatively small employer of white labor, with perhaps no more than five to ten white men working for him, whereas Wernher's company employed well over fifty white overseers. The relationship between smaller employer and white employee was a more personal one, especially since both had the common experience of being or having been a claim holder. And the smaller operations, with none of the capital resources of the larger companies, could not afford to ride out a strike. In addition, the white workers formed a large proportion of the local electorate, an important factor in Bottomley's decision to change sides, since he had considerable political aspirations.[44]

In contrast, proposed regulations affecting only blacks failed to create any dissension among white capitalists and overseers. The second measure of labor regulation that the industrialists wished introduced in the later 1870s—closer control of the urban dwelling areas of blacks and the establishment of municipal locations—reflected a desire to extend the controls of the workplace throughout the urban community and so ensure a regular and disciplined movement of black labor within the town. In pressing for the introduction of such urban controls, the industrialists made constant use of a now familiar argument: all blacks were thieves. Indeed, throughout the later 1870s the press in Kimberley continually claimed that there was extensive trafficking in illegal diamonds in those parts of the town populated mainly by blacks.[45] George Bot-

44. *Diamond News*, 29 July 1880.
45. See, e.g., the *Daily Independent*, 29 June 1876, 2 May 1878; and the *Diamond News*, 17 July 1877, 9 December 1879, 3 April 1880.

tomley used this same argument when he suggested to the Kimberley borough council that a municipal superintendent of locations be appointed. This official could regulate areas in which blacks lived, maintain order, and ensure that only people employed through the labor registry office were permitted to remain in the town. Such a new form of regulation would, claimed Bottomley, check diamond theft and alleviate the labor supply problems of the industry; "natives would be restrained, and their character, habits and occupation known."[46]

The logic of Bottomley's argument lay in his idea that ultimately all black workers in Kimberley, during every moment of their temporary residence in the town, should be under the surveillance and control of either an employer, a civil servant, a policeman, a jailer, or a municipal officer. This control would ensure a regular movement of the workers from first entry into the urban area to the registry office, to an employer, to a location (while employed but not living on an employer's premises, or unemployed but with a pass permitting its holder to look for a job), to another employer, and then back out of the town a few months later once the period of contracted labor had been completed. Desertion would be prevented because there would be no unregulated area in the town to which any black could escape.

The bylaws of the Kimberley Town Council, drawn up in 1878, made provision for the appointment of a superintendent of locations. His duties included laying out the locations, numbering each and every hut, preparing a register of all location residents, and checking for passes to ensure that all the location inhabitants had an officially sanctioned means of earning a living. When the Cape government passed control of its existing locations, which had been largely unsupervised, to the council in 1880, the superintendent strictly enforced these regulations. In his first six months in office he had 643 blacks arrested for transgressing location rules. Still, he found it quite impossible to achieve the degree of control over location residents that the regulations made theoretically possible. With a problem of labor shortage at the time, most employers ignored the labor-registration system. The superintendent for his part was dependent on the labor-registration system working smoothly so that he could effectively enforce the location regulations. He could not harass men for passes if their employers refused to give

46. *Diamond News*, 14 March 1878.

them any without causing yet further difficulties with the supply of labor. In addition, not all blacks were as yet forced to live in the locations. In short, the scheme could not work as effectively as intended so long as the competition for labor remained intense. But disgruntled employers continued to complain that "loiterers" always found refuge in the locations and thus evaded their "responsibility" to labor in the mines.[47]

By the beginning of the 1880s, neither the repressive activities of state agencies nor the attempted extension of labor control beyond the workplace had succeeded in securing a system of regulation that satisfied the white employers who controlled the mining industry. This failure was due to a number of factors. First, despite the increasing penetration of the state into the workplace, the locations, and the town as a whole, the British Colonial Office was not prepared to sanction "class" (meaning color) legislation. Second, the mechanics of repression could not work successfully so long as the demand for cheap labor exceeded the supply of men willing to work for the wages offered. Third, so long as the industry remained relatively competitive, workers could always play employers off against each other. That none of the schemes to control workers were successful did not, however, prevent them from being very oppressive in practice. In sum, the state had become increasingly sympathetic to industrialists and the industry was being transformed from a collection of small holdings into a series of much larger operations, yet in neither case had the development gone far enough to allow for the successful application of strict control over labor.

## INDUSTRY OFFENSIVE, 1881–85

Changes in the structure of the diamond industry in the 1880s led to the extension by industrialists and the state of much greater controls over black labor. Within the industry, the major structural crisis extending from 1882 well into the mid-1880s was resolved through the elimination of many of the smaller joint stock companies and the increasing dominance of a few very large companies.

47. "Bye-Laws of the Kimberley Town Council," 1878, section VII, Native Locations, GH 10/14. For details on the actions of the superintendent see the *Daily Independent*, 10 June, 15 July, 3 September, 28 October 1881. For complaints of idlers and vagrants see the same newspaper, 15 July and 23 September 1881.

Parallel changes in the nature of the state, with colonial rule largely replaced by representative government, allowed the industrialists who controlled these large companies to gain greater access to Parliament and to the making of legislation. They used this access to extend their power in Kimberley and increase their control over both the black and the white work force in the mines. At first this control was applied through greater police activity against blacks, but the total control desired remained elusive so long as there remained a shortage of cheap black labor and so long as the company men could not agree on which policies to adopt.

Another product of the 1882 depression, however (apart from the bankruptcy of many of the smaller companies), was a reduced demand for black workers. In fact, the number of black laborers employed in the industry was halved. The operators of the largest mining companies took advantage of this situation of relative labor surplus to introduce a new form of labor regulation that lay under their direct control—the establishment of closed compounds. This they used in conjunction with continued reliance on the regulatory apparatus of the state: the police, the courts, the jails, the locations and the newly established De Beers convict station. Industrialists, by the mid-1880s, were able, much as Bottomley had envisaged, to maintain their black workers in a continual round between compounds, locations, jails, and entry to and exit from the town. In sum, criminal law and public and private institutions for regulation and incarceration were integrated into a complex system of labor control.

The majority of the seventy or so joint stock companies established in 1880–81 suffered from a combination of often crippling constraints. First, few companies kept any of their capital in reserve to meet unexpected working expenses. Second, open-cast mining was becoming increasingly difficult, with many of the companies working at different depths and undercutting each other's operations. Third, the price of diamonds fluctuated downward from late 1882 to 1888. The fourth constraint, and the one regarded as the most severe at the time, was the continuing shortage of cheap black labor.

While most of the companies formed in 1880 and 1881 were relatively small, a number of significantly larger operations were established at the same time. These included J. B. Robinson's Griqualand West Diamond Mining Company, Cecil Rhodes' De Beers

Mining Company, and George Bottomley's Kimberley Central Diamond Mining Company. The company founders, Kimberley's leading industrialists, believed that the fate of those companies that had failed, of which the small operations had formed a disproportionate number, would soon befall them if they did not act to eliminate the various constraints on the diamond industry. Only the fourth constraint, though, the supply of cheap black labor, seemed (potentially at least) within their control.[48] Therefore, in 1882 the industrialists sought to implement new controls to discipline their black work force and make it accept those industrial demands—such as regular attendance at work and the fulfilment of all contractual obligations—that had been important in the past but were now critical to the financial success of mechanized production. And once again industrialists sought to harness the state in this renewed attempt to control the movements of black workers in Kimberley.

At much the same time that the structure of the industry changed so too did that of the state. In 1880 the Cape Colony annexed Griqualand West, abolished the office of administrator, and the Cape Parliament became responsible for enacting legislation for the territory. While the British Colonial Office still exercised ultimate authority through the governor of the Cape, Kimberley was no longer under the direct jurisdiction of officials of the colonial service. Parliament in Cape Town now became the main forum in which Kimberley's residents expressed their concerns and sought political remedies.

Kimberley's first parliamentary election, in March 1881, centered on the problem of black labor. At least it did so after the publication of J. B. Robinson's election manifesto. Robinson held out to the community the promise of prosperity, happiness, and civilization, but warned that the realization of this rosy future was dependent on the supply and treatment of black labor. He warned that while black labor could be treated humanely and fairly, blacks still had to be taught "to respect the laws of *meum* and *tuum*," that is, to know their place. This respect, he felt, could be achieved successfully through the strict enforcement of existing legislation such as the pass and masters' and servants' laws. With this firm statement of an opinion widely held by most whites in the community, and

---

48. For a discussion of a similar situation with regard to costs and labor on the building of the Cape railway see Purkis, "The Politics of Railway-building," p. 403.

most fervently of all by industrialists, Robinson was elected to Parliament along with his fellow nascent magnate, Cecil Rhodes.[49]

The problem of illicit dealing in diamonds was the first major issue brought to Parliament by the Kimberley members. Within a year of their election they sought to solve this problem through the establishment of a select committee to investigate the issue and suggest legislative remedies.[50] The old beliefs that blacks were natural thieves and that they were grievously damaging the industry— allegedly stealing one-third to one-half of all diamonds—became more acute in the crisis of 1881–82 and took on a new dimension with the restructuring of the companies. One witness appearing before the select committee bluntly demanded exceptional legislation "in the interests of the special class who are engaged in mining. . . . a class [once] consisting merely of diggers; but now . . . [consisting of] the shareholders in the Joint Stock Companies. . . ." Most of the witnesses wanted to force black workers to submit to body searches, to work naked, to be confined to compounds, and to be flogged if caught stealing.[51] The select committee accepted most such recommendations, as did Parliament with the passage of the Diamond Trade Act in 1882.[52]

Under this act those accused of illicit diamond buying (IDB) were presumed guilty until they could prove their innocence. The legislation provided for the establishment of a special court to try those accused of IDB, this court to be presided over by a judge assisted by two magistrates but without a jury. People found guilty of IDB were subject to very severe penalties: whites faced prison terms of up to fifteen years, fines of up to £1,000, and the possibility of permanent banishment from Griqualand West; blacks could expect to be flogged in addition to the preceding punishments.[53]

49. *Daily Independent,* 19 February 1881.

50. Rhodes chaired the Select Committee on Illicit Diamond Buying in Griqualand West; Robinson and another Kimberley parliamentarian were members of the committee.

51. Evidence of H. J. Feltham (quoted), S. Marks, and Francis Baring-Gould, in the "Report of the Select Committee on Illicit Diamond Buying in Griqualand West," *CGHPP,* A9 1882, pp.3, 6–8, 12, 20, 105. Marks in fact had his contracted black employees work in the nude, see pp. 20, 22, 24, 30, 31. For public comments about the problem of IDB see the *Daily Independent,* 16 February, 18 June, 1, 15 July, 18, 22 August, 1, 4 October, 12, 16, 23 November 1881, 2 February, 10, 13, 14, 15, 21, 27 April, 8, 10 May, 20 July, 5 August 1882.

52. See the committee's report in *CGHPP,* A9 1882, pp. iii–iv. See also Act 48 of 1882.

53. Act 48 of 1882.

At the same time, the Kimberley police force was increased, from the 73 white officers to which it had fallen, to 105 by the end of 1882 and 150 in subsequent years. An independent detective department was established—staffed by a chief detective, 3 white detectives, and 40 black—to concentrate on IDB.[54] These detectives made considerable use of "trapping" to catch those thought likely to succumb to the temptation of illicit profits, a practice that made the department much villified by Kimberley's white and black residents.[55]

Furthermore, although the law's language remained color-blind, its practice certainly was not. As the civil commissioner for Kimberley put matters in his annual report for 1882, in interpreting laws regulating relations between masters and servants officials looked upon "every Native, but no European . . . as a servant. . . ." Thus it was that only blacks had to carry passes or pay a hospital tax, burdens that in theory all wage employees whatever their color were supposed to bear.[56]

Such energetic and racially discriminatory enforcement of the laws resulted in a great increase in police harassment, arrests, and convictions. As table 3.1 shows, the number of people arrested in Kimberley reached extremely high levels in the early to mid-1880s, markedly so given that the urban population was declining during this same period. A comparative survey of arrest rates between several English cities and Cape Town, conducted in 1884 by the Cape commissioners of police, found that the average number of arrests made by an individual police officer ranged from 53 in Liverpool to 45 in Cape Town, 43 in Newcastle, and 29 in Manchester. Kimberley, by comparison, had an arrest rate of between 114 and 160 persons per police officer in 1882 and stayed close to that figure for the remainder of the 1880s. The total number of arrests in Kimberley in 1882 amounted to almost half the total for Manchester, a city with

54. The police reforms were based on the suggestions made by an officer brought over from Scotland Yard and were sanctioned by the Cape governor in 1882. See the "Reports on the Kimberley Police and Detective Department by Bernard V. Shaw," *CGHPP,* G77 1882, pp. 7, 9, 15, 20–26. Detectives had been employed by the police force since 1874, but in 1882 a completely separate force was established. On the implementation of Shaw's recommendations see the "Report by the Commissioners of Police for 1882," *CGHPP,* G100 1883, p. 27. For later years see the following annual reports, G51 1884, G12 1885, G11 1886, G7 1887.

55. For a discussion of trapping practices see the memorandum of Captain Harrel, 30 November 1880, CO 3344 (98).

56. *NABB,* G8 1883, p. 4.

TABLE 3.1    Arrest and Conviction Rates, 1875–89

| Year | Total Arrests (A) | Summarily Convicted (B) | B as % of A |
|------|-------------------|--------------------------|-------------|
| 1875 | 1,527 (6 months)  | 867 (6 months)           | 56.7 |
| 1876 | 8,646             | 5,679                    | 65.7 |
| 1882 | 2,012 (2 months)  | 1,329 (2 months)         | 66 |
| 1883 | 14,003            | 10,934                   | 78 |
| 1884 | 14,144            | 11,195                   | 79.1 |
| 1885 | 16,214            | 12,948                   | 79.8 |
| 1886 | 16,359            | 13,129                   | 80.2 |
| 1887 | 14,886            | 11,321                   | 76 |
| 1888 | 13,520            | 10,494                   | 77.6 |
| 1889 | 10,788            | 8,262                    | 76.5 |

SOURCES: GLW 93 (2770); CO 3575, 3605, 3631, 3656; *CGHPP*, G77 1882, G12 1885.

at least five times the population. Even in a South African context the number of arrests in Kimberley was extraordinarily high. Cape Town, for example, a community of roughly similar size to that of Kimberley, recorded only one-third the number of arrests made by the Kimberley police.[57] Many of these arrests were made during raids for pass-law offenders. Often 30 to 100 people would be picked up in a sweep; on one occasion later in the decade 286 offenders were arrested in a single day.[58] Much of the cause of this high rate of arrests was attributable, as it had been before when Lanyon had taken office in 1876, to the greater activities of the police rather than to any increase in crime.

Most of the arrests, as table 3.2 reveals, were for relatively minor crimes, largely transgressions against the various laws that regulated black labor. While pass-law offenses accounted for the single largest number of arrests, almost as many again came within the categories of breach of the peace, municipal bylaws (generally relating to location regulations), committing a nuisance (usually

57. The figures for the English cities are based on arrest statistics for 1881, those for Cape Town on 1884 returns. See the "Report by Commissioners of Police for 1884," *CGHPP*, G12 1885, p. 11. For Kimberley arrest statistics see *CGHPP*, G77 1882; G12 1885, p. 29; and the *Daily Independent*, 15 February 1887. It is difficult to compare population size. Manchester had 354,000 inhabitants in 1884, Cape Town approximately 80,000. Kimberley, by contrast, had a population of only 20,000 (of whom about half were black) at any one time, but it had a constant procession of blacks moving into and out of the town as they sought work and completed their contracts. Therefore, the population comparison has been based on the police's own estimate of the number of people they had to deal with on the diamond fields—70,000.

58. For details on police and court practices see the "Report of the Committee on Convicts and Gaols," *CGHPP*, G2 1888.

urinating in public by blacks in a town that provided no public lavatories), and the other offenses listed in section II of the table. The penalties for these offenses were a considerable burden on those convicted—generally fines ranging from 10s. to 40s. or the option of choosing a jail sentence ranging from one week's to one month's hard labor.

Justice in the courts was generally summary for pass-law offenders. They were arraigned in batches, sometimes of up to fifty people, before the police magistrate, allowed to plead guilty (as they were expected to do), and sentenced en bloc. The superintendent of the Kimberley jail, who attended the court in an official capacity, reported that the longest trial that he had witnessed had lasted no more than ten minutes.[59]

The summary processing by the Police Magistrate's Court resulted in a high rate of convictions. In 1882, 76 percent of all cases brought before the court resulted in conviction. The Kimberley Magistrate's Court by comparison had a conviction rate of only 23 percent. In addition, the number discharged without conviction by all the courts in Kimberley declined, from 35.5 percent of all cases in 1875 to 22.8 percent in 1882.[60] Essentially enforcing summary punishment against those who were suspected of being recalcitrant workers, the courts acted as an adjunct to the employers.

Yet the severe application of state power in 1882 could not alone provide a complete system of labor control, for much the same reason that it had failed in the past—the structure of the diamond industry with its large number of employers and shortage of black labor. Many employers, competing desperately against each other for the same black workers, evaded the regulations and encouraged men to desert to their operations. An attempt by a number of companies collectively to lower wages in late 1882 completely failed when other companies refused to participate.[61] After all, the small companies could not afford to put their labor supply at risk while those companies that worked at greater, and therefore more dan-

---

59. *Ibid.*, pp. ii, 3.
60. *CGHPP,* G77 1882.
61. *Daily Independent,* 28 August 1882. For details on the scheme see A. W. Davis to directors of the Eagle Diamond Mining Company of De Beers Mine Limited, 18 August 1882, CR 6/4. Similar schemes had failed in late 1881 and early 1882. See the *Daily Independent,* 10 October, 23, 28 November 1881, 11 February 1882; and the *Griqualand West Investor's Guardian,* 24 November, 1 December 1881.

TABLE 3.2  Arrests by Crime, 1875–88

| Crime | 1875ᵃ | 1876ᵃ | 1882ᵇ | 1884 | 1885 | 1886 | 1887 | 1888 |
|---|---|---|---|---|---|---|---|---|
| *Section I: Pass offenses* | | | | | | | | |
| Loitering without a pass | 95 | 971 | 658 | 5,337 | 6,325 | 6,274 | 6,071 | 4,105 |
| Loitering without a special pass | | | | 819 | 229 | 127 | 94 | 189 |
| Loitering after hours | | | | 54 | 47 | 136 | — | .148 |
| Subtotal | 95 | 971 | 658 | 6,210 | 6,601 | 6,537 | 6,165 | 4,442 |
| As a percentage of total arrests | 6.2 | 24.2 | 32.7 | 43.9 | 40.7 | 40.0 | 41.4 | 32.8 |
| *Section II: Other offenses mainly relating to black labor* | | | | | | | | |
| Breach of the peace | 246 | 386 | 135 | 300 | 298 | — | — | — |
| Bylaws, municipal | — | — | 25 | 560 | 817 | 950 | 554 | 654 |
| Committing a nuisance | 80 | 150 | — | 637 | 466 | — | — | — |
| Desertion | 174 | 300 | — | 402 | — | 179 | 304 | — |
| Drunk | 83 | 320 | — | 2,248 | 2,110 | 2,488 | 2,585 | 3,287 |
| Masters and servants | — | — | 324 | — | 507 | 399 | 277 | 207 |
| Neglect of duty to master | 99 | 257 | — | 67 | — | — | — | — |
| Searching regulations | — | — | — | 565 | 1,245 | 1,133 | 534 | 421 |
| Vagrancy | — | 1— | — | 1.59 | .108 | 1,124 | 161 | 1,132 |
| Subtotal | 682 | 1,413 | 484 | 4,838 | 5,551 | 5,273 | 4,415 | 4,701 |
| As a percentage of total arrests | 44.7 | 35.7 | 24.6 | 34.2 | 34.2 | 32.2 | 29.7 | 34.8 |
| *Section III: Other offenses* | | | | | | | | |
| Assault | 153 | 256 | 136 | 702 | 672 | 815 | 699 | 727 |
| Murder | 3 | 4 | 7 | 17 | 38 | 42 | — | 27 |
| Theft | 233 | 376 | 144 | 969 | 1,324 | 1,172 | 1,093 | 1,050 |
| IDB related | 66 | 105 | 43 | 203 | 244 | 206 | 181 | 202 |
| Miscellaneous | 295 | .882 | 540 | 1,205 | 1,784 | 2,314 | 2,333 | 2,371 |
| Subtotal | 750 | 1,623 | 870 | 3,096 | 4,062 | 4,549 | 4,306 | 4,377 |
| As a percentage of total arrests | 49.1 | 40.5 | 43.2 | 21.9 | 25.1 | 27.8 | 28.9 | 32.4 |

SOURCES: GLW 93 (2770); CO 3575, 3606, 3631; *CGHPP*, G77 1882, G12 1885.
ᵃFirst six months only.  ᵇFirst two months only.

gerous, depths also had problems in getting workers.[62] Black wages
continued to rise rather than fall. And IDB, in the eyes of the industrialists, remained as prevalent as ever, although the only proof of
its continuance was the limited number of arrests made by trapping—a situation which only proved, according to those same industrialists, that the law was ineffective rather than that the
problem was less severe than they had claimed. In sum, by the end
of 1882 the expansion of state activity had largely failed to solve
the problems of IDB and of the cost, supply, and disciplining of the
black labor force.

The collapse of the European diamond market in late 1882, and
the consequent fall in the price of diamonds, accelerated changes
in the organization of the diamond industry. Most of the smaller
companies had gone bankrupt by the end of 1883, and the large
companies were left more dominant than they had ever been before.
The De Beers and Kimberley Central companies in particular not
only survived the crash but used their considerable financial resources to buy up the properties of their ailing competitors.

The structure of the black work force also changed dramatically between 1882 and 1883. Only half as many laborers were
needed as in the past, and most of those kept on were old hands,
since the employers preferred men who had already worked in the
mines, had acquired some skills, and who were accustomed if not
necessarily agreeable, to the disciplinary demands of industrial labor. Thus, in a very short time, a labor shortage was replaced by a
relative (although still limited) labor surplus.

The conjunction of changes in the structure of the diamond
industry and the black work force, together with declining receipts
and the continuing high cost of labor as a proportion of working
expenses (running at 25–40 percent in 1882), led industrialists to
mount another offensive against labor. This offensive, backed up by
the state, took two forms: the establishment of a system of strip
searching of black workers (and partial inspection of white) in 1883,
and the introduction of closed compounds in 1885.

The searching system, enacted into law by a proclamation of
the governor of the Cape in early 1883, followed the recommendations made by mining men (especially George Bottomley and J. B.
Robinson) for a set of rules "to establish a system of search in and

62. For a discussion of the problems of different companies see the *Daily Independent*, 29 August 1882.

around the Mines . . . with a view to the better control of the Native Population generally. . . ."[63] All workers below the rank of manager had to enter and exit the mines through a limited number of guarded entryways each with a search house (with separate ones for black and white workers). Blacks had to strip naked each time they passed through and be prepared to undergo intimate and degrading body searches. Whites did not have to take off their clothes and only had to undergo a limited visual inspection. The purpose of the search system was to eliminate theft by keeping all unauthorized people out of the mines and preventing anyone from exiting with diamonds concealed on his person. It was also intended to discipline the workers in the time requirements of their employers by making them enter the mines through the search houses at the same time and preventing them from leaving the mines unless they were permitted to do so by their employers.

But even with a relative labor surplus and a greater sense of cohesion among the large companies the scheme did not succeed to the extent that its promoters wished. It was physically impossible for the limited number of searchers whom the employers hired to search eight thousand black workers twice a day (on leaving the mine for lunch and at the end of the work day). Nor did all the companies force the workers to wear the sack that had earlier been agreed upon as the common uniform for all black laborers. Indeed, some companies allowed their men a choice of uniforms—the most popular being flour bags—in an attempt to prevent disgruntled workers from deserting and to attract men from other companies to work for them.[64]

Very few diamonds were ever found in the searching houses, even though they were in operation throughout the rest of 1883 and well into the mid-1880s.[65] Still, industrialists continued to favor searching as a means of labor control and with this aim in mind extended the practical requirements of the searching system to white workers in late 1883 and early 1884, in an attempt to break the power of white labor organization at the diamond fields and to

63. Proclamation 1, 1883. For Bottomley's role see the "Report of the Joint Committee . . . and Draft of Searching Rules and Regulations," Kimberley, 19 May 1882, Smalberger Papers, UCT. For Robinson's role see the *Daily Independent*, 10 January 1883.
64. *Daily Independent*, 2, 8 March 1883.
65. For complaints of the lack of finds see the *Daily Independent*, 1, 10, 12, 21, 23 October 1884.

subject all workers, irrespective of race, to various levels of control, an attempt that was ultimately successful.[66]

Buoyed by their success in the struggle with white workers, industrialists in 1884 contemplated the introduction of a further measure of labor control over black workers—closed compounds.[67] By then most companies already housed their black employees in compounds on their own properties. The men, however, were free to come and go after working hours and to make their own way to and from work. On occasion companies would request the police to discipline their workers, as the French Company did in October 1883 when it asked the police to go to its compound and arrest the men there for being late for work, but such measures were unsatisfactory, since they could never be carried out in a thorough and consistent manner.[68] Closed compounding, which promised total control over black workers through their incarceration in fenced and guarded institutions, seemed the ideal system to prevent theft and to discipline labor.

The government inspector of diamond mines gave the clearest exposition of what was hoped for by the introduction of closed compounding. In his annual report for 1884 he stated his belief that all workers should be compounded, although he felt that whites should be in "small detached cottages with gardens attached and with a central mess and reading room" rather than in barracks. Black and white workers, whether in cottages or barracks, would be physically separated from the rest of society, and from each other, and would be thoroughly searched before being allowed to leave their places of confinement. The greatest benefits of compounding, the inspector believed, lay in the regulation and discipline that it would establish on a day-to-day basis in the mines:

> By establishing a regular chain of responsibility among the employes in dividing the Kafirs into nominal squads and placing each squad under a particular overseer, so many overseers under the direct control of a particular sub-manager or foreman, and all under the manager of the claims or floors respectively; a most thorough control and supervision of all their [employers'] servants would be provided.

66. See chapt. 4.
67. The introduction of compounds had been widely discussed in 1882. See the reports of Inspector Shaw referred to earlier; also *CGHPP*, A9 1882.
68. *Daily Independent*, 12 October 1883.

The squads of Kafirs could be marched to and from the mines or floors by their overseers in charge, who would also look after them while at work, search them as necessary, and be responsible to the sub-manager or foreman for their presence and conduct at work and for their general well-being; the sub-managers or foremen being in turn responsible to their own managers and these to the Company or employer...."[69]

In short, the mining industry should be thoroughly self-contained.

Four factors largely explain the great support among industrialists in 1884 for the introduction of a system of closed compounding. First, as mentioned above, the searching system had apparently failed to eliminate IDB. Second, three of the largest companies in the mines (De Beers, Kimberley Central, and French) were moving from open-cast to deep-level digging. This type of production, with its sophisticated technology and large capital investment, required a regular and disciplined supply of labor so that the machinery could be worked efficiently and to capacity. Third, labor was in a relatively weak position. White labor organization had been effectively broken by a combination of industry and state power in May when six white workers had been shot to death in a confrontation with the police and the industrialists.[70] With regard to black labor, the chairman of the European Diamond Company summed up the situation when he suggested that dealing with blacks was essentially "a question of supply and demand" and that if the supply was plentiful, or at least adequate (as it was), then "You can do what you like with your boys...."[71] Fourth, by late 1884 the Kimberley and De Beers mines, the two most important mines at the diamond fields, were under the complete control of the Kimberley Central, De Beers, and French companies. So long as these companies could agree to work together in introducing a new system of labor control, they could ensure its successful implementation through the dominance that they exerted over the labor market. There were few operations in Kimberley that these companies, or others that supported them, did not control, and thus they had a virtual monopoly over the job market.

The three companies, along with a number of others, estab-

69. "Report of the Inspector of Diamond Mines for the Year 1884," *CGHPP,* G28 1885, p. 12.
70. See chapt. 4.
71. *Daily Independent,* 21 October 1884.

PLATE 3.1   De Beers compound, 1894 (Johannesburg Public Library)

PLATE 3.2   Inmates of the De Beers compound (Cape Archives, AG 5997)

lished closed compounds for their black workers in 1885 and 1886. In January 1885, the French Company placed 110 black laborers in a set of barracks that they were not permitted to leave, except to go to work, for the duration of their six-month contracts. The Kimberley Central followed suit two months later with a compound for four hundred black employees, while later in the same year two companies in the Bultfontein mine compounded their laborers. The De Beers Company closed its compounds in mid-1886. Although the men employed by the Kimberley Central and De Beers companies at first refused to accept these new conditions, they were soon replaced by men recruited directly from rural societies (rather than engaged in the Kimberley urban labor market) and their strikes were broken.[72]

Throughout the middle 1880s the state gave considerable support to the industrialists in their attempts to subject black workers to ever more restrictive controls. In June 1884, the Kimberley commissioner of police wrote to the men who managed the Dutoitspan Mine that he wanted to do "all in [his] power to assist the Mining Interest" and suggested that to eliminate the problem of Monday-morning absenteeism each company should appoint an overseer "to accompany constables [to the locations], and point out . . . boys [absent from work], and have them arrested for . . . Neglecting their Master's Work."[73] Reference back to table 3.1 shows the extent of the police's energy, with the greatest number of arrests being made between 1883 and 1887, years when the laboring population was considerably smaller than it had been earlier. Table 3.2 shows that the percentage of arrests for offenses mainly relating to black laborers (sections I and II) increased from 57 percent of total arrests in 1882 to 78 percent in 1884 and then hovered around 70 percent for the next three years. The conviction rate also increased during the same period, with a 15 percent jump between 1882 and 1883 and a further rise in subsequent years.

72. *Diamond Fields Advertiser,* 19 January, 28 April 1885; *Daily Independent,* 27, 28 April, 7 September 1885; "Report of the Inspector of Diamond Mines for the Year 1885," *CGHPP,* G40 1886, pp. 12–13, 19; Rouillard, *Matabele Thompson,* pp. 81, 83; J. M. Smalberger, "I.D.B. and the Mining Compound System in the 1880s," *South African Journal of Economics,* 42:4 (1974): 411.

73. E. Christian to secretary of the Dutoitspan Mining Board, 20 June 1884, letters received, November 1883–November 1884, DTMB, DBA. The policy was carried out strictly. In one instance in February 1885, 297 men were arrested at the Bultfontein location for having passes but not being at work, *Daily Independent,* 24 February 1885.

By 1886 state and capital had established an extensive system of labor control in Kimberley. Black workers were subjected to a mesh of criminal laws and a maze of institutional controls. Along with the closed compounds, the jail remained a primary agent of worker control. Kimberley's jail was the largest in the Cape Colony, with a daily average of 658 inmates, seven times the number incarcerated in Cape Town's jail. In 1884 the De Beers Mining Company had negotiated with the state to establish a privately controlled convict station and used the labor of the inmates to carry out most of its surface-mining operations. The inspector of diamond mines considered "these convict barracks . . . the perfection of the compound system," since in return for housing and feeding the convicts, and paying a small fee to the Cape government, the De Beers Company obtained the compulsory labor of several hundred men, all of them subject to strict prison discipline while at work.[74] In addition, Kimberley's urban locations were strictly regulated by the Town Council: constant raids were made to check that all inhabitants had passes; hut taxes were regularly collected; and the council announced plans not only to force "coolies" (Indians), Chinese, and Malays to live in locations but also to remove all the locations to the outskirts of the town so that there would be no urban intermixture of white and black dwellings.[75]

The interacting and often contradictory effects of these forms of labor and race regulation were well described by one visitor to Kimberley in 1885:

> The Kaffir cannot understand the mixed treatment to which he is subjected. Those interested in encouraging the illicit diamond-trade employ him as a purveyor of stolen goods. Those interested in putting down the illegal traffic employ him as a spy [or trap] to get innocent people convicted. And yet if a Kaffir happens to come into town looking for work, and knowing nothing of the white man's laws innocently enters the streets "naked, and not ashamed," he is immediately arrested and "fined" [then imprisoned for a month or two because he had no money

74. See the "Report of the Inspector of Diamond Mines for the Year 1885," *CGHPP,* G40 1886, pp. 11–12; and E. A. Judge (civil commissioner) to under colonial secretary, 14 April 1886, CO 3526.

75. See on these matters "A Bill to Explain and Alter Certain Provisions of the Kimberley Borough Act, No. 11 of 1883, and to Increase the Powers of the Borough Council of Kimberley," along with considerable amounts of correspondence on the subject of locations, in LND 1/222. See also *NABB,* G2 1885, p. 209.

and, when let out, if he does not find a master the same day arrested again, this time as a vagrant, and put back in jail for a day or two]. . . . The poor wretch is bewildered, and falls violently in love with the white man and his customs, and takes care to get somebody to give him a piece of paper certifying that he is in a situation. He then goes to seek for some Kaffir friends of his at the mines, and finds his way into a compound. Arrested for being there without permission, or with "unlawful intent," he is charged, fined and eventually gravitates again to the prison. Having served his time he will probably return to his "master," but finds that as he has been away "without leave" for a week, his "occupation [is] gone" and the joyous round of the police-station, court-house, and prisoner's cell begins once more.[76]

Although this description exaggerates the passive and uncomprehending nature of black reactions to the institutions and controls with which they came into contact, it does convey the extent to which regulation of nearly every aspect of a black worker's life and behavior in the workplace and the town had been achieved by Kimberley's industrialists by the mid-1880s. Indeed, there was little discernible difference between the workplace, the compound, the location, and the jail in Kimberley; all were part and parcel of the same system of labor control.

76. Gilarmi Farini, *Through the Kalahari Desert* (London, 1886), pp. 27–28. See also Coleman's report on the problems facing blacks in Kimberley, *NABB*, G2 1885, pp. 206–10.

CHAPTER FOUR

# White Mine Workers, Economic Struggle, and Labor Consciousness, 1875–84

Kimberley was riven with conflict in the late 1870s and early 1880s. As the diamond industry lurched from a system based on individual small-scale production to one dominated by large public companies, bitter division and struggle erupted within society—between small and large mining capitalists, capital and labor, white labor and black labor, and white skilled and unskilled labor. During the course of the transition from small-scale production to company control between the middle 1870s and the middle 1880s, a white working class formed, grew conscious of its antagonistic relationship to mining capital, developed trade unions, and resisted the attempts of industrialists to subject its members to the same oppressive treatment accorded black labor. The combined forces of industrial capital and the state, however, finally overwhelmed the resistance of white workers and forced them to submit to the control of Kimberley's industrialists.

Discussion of three interrelated topics is central to an examination of the white working-class experience. The first is the role of technological change in the mining industry, particularly with regard to its effects on production and property ownership. The second topic is the impact of this change and the resulting policies instituted by the industry on the structure, and the material conditions of life, of the working class with regard, for example, to such issues as the size of the work force, skill requirements of workers, hours of labor, wage levels, property accumulation, health, and mortality. The third point is the combined effect of technological

147

change and varying material conditions on the developing consciousness of the workers. Identification of the emergence and specific form of class consciousness can best be done through the prism of struggle; by examining the reactions of white workers to wage reductions, unemployment, poverty and the development of mutual-benefit societies, trade unions, and other worker-protection organizations.

## THE ORIGINS OF THE WHITE WORK FORCE

Changes in claim holding and technology in the middle 1870s produced a white work force. Before 1876, with production in the hands of small claim holders (nearly all of whom were white), all wage labor in the mines had been done by black workers. Each claim holder, perhaps assisted by one or two partners, or working someone else's claims on shares, had supervised his own work force of ten to twenty black laborers. White men rarely sold their labor. Their services were generally not required since black labor was cheaper, and most supervisory functions could be performed by the diggers themselves. But the growth of larger units of production, and the increasing sophistication of machine working, encouraged the growth of two new elements in the mine work force: white supervisory workers and white skilled miners and artisans.

The development of a supervisory group of white workers was a direct result of the expansion of the scale of production. In the later 1870s it was quite common for the larger claim holders and companies to employ one hundred or more black laborers. Most employers believed that their black employees were both lazy and thieves; all considered that the elimination of diamond theft was crucial to the profitable working of the industry. Since employers could not personally supervise all their black employees, they hired white men to undertake that task for them. Generally one white man was hired to oversee the work of every ten black laborers. In 1877, Solz and Company, one of the growing number of private companies on the diamond fields, employed between 5 and 8 white overseers and 80 black laborers. In 1881, reflecting the increased scale of working, the Kimberley Central Company had 93 white overseers supervising the work of 902 blacks.[1] In sum, whites en-

1. For Solz and Company see the *Diamond News*, 13, 20 March 1877, and chapt. 1. For the Kimberley Central Company see its second annual report (for the year ending 30 April 1882) published in the *Daily Independent*, 30 May 1882.

gaged in wage labor, but as supervisors of black workers, not as laborers themselves.[2]

White men were hired as overseers because they were considered trustworthy, and the main reason why they were so regarded was because many of them were former claim holders. Overseeing as a job was, in fact, little different from the work done by small claim holders—watching laborers to make sure that they worked and did not steal. Thus, former claim holders, generally lacking any other marketable skills, were perfectly suited to the work. In addition, they shared the attitudes of their new employers (often fellow claim holders in the pre-1876 period) to black labor. As claim holders themselves, they had been just as concerned about productivity and theft. Moreover, most of those failed claim holders who became overseers blamed blacks for their misfortune, sharing the belief of their employers that diamond theft was the critical factor in profitable working. Believing that they had already lost one living through such theft, the claim holders-cum-overseers were not ready to lose a second occupation to the same cause.

The demand for skilled labor grew in proportion to the expansion and increasing elaboration of mechanization. In the later 1870s, most of the larger companies employed one or two engine drivers and possibly a mechanic to run their hauling and pumping engines; Solz and Company, for example, had two engine drivers in 1878. The number of skilled workers and the skills required, however, expanded rapidly, particularly after the establishment of joint stock companies in 1880 and 1881. The establishment of such companies attracted huge amounts of investment capital, much of which was spent on expanding the scale of working and on importing considerable amounts of machinery. The Kimberley Central Company, the largest operation in the Kimberley mine in 1881, employed in addition to the 93 overseers mentioned above an engineer, 5 gear managers, 2 box keepers, 5 miners, 4 plate layers, 15 engine drivers, 4 fitters, 7 carpenters, 3 blacksmiths, 2 strikers, and a wire splicer. Therefore skilled workers, just under 50 in number, comprised one-third of the company's white work force a bare five years after whites first entered wage labor. By 1883, skilled workers accounted for 56 percent of the white workers in the mine and 38 percent on the floors, showing that the mine work force as a whole

2. Some whites did work as laborers but only rarely and then generally because blacks were not available.

had followed the pattern set by the Kimberley Central Company. In the Dutoitspan mine, by contrast, the respective figures were 25 percent and 36 percent, reflecting the use of less mechanized technology.[3]

Unlike the overseers, who had generally been at the diamond fields since the days of small holdings, most of the skilled workers were newly arrived in the late 1870s and early 1880s. They did not come in anticipation of making a fortune but rather to make a good living from the high wages paid and to support their families who generally remained behind in Great Britain. Few details exist on these men. Their experiences were not nearly so romantically adventurous as those of the early diggers. But at least two groups can be discerned within the relatively anonymous mass: the men who came from the tin mines of Cornwall and those from the coal mines of Cumberland.

The Cornish miners came to Kimberley to escape the effects of a depression in the tin industry. Between 1873 and 1878 more than half the Cornish tin mines ceased operations, reducing the number of miners by almost the same proportion—from more than twenty-six thousand to less than fourteen thousand. The closing of these mines resulted in mass poverty and starvation, and many of the unemployed migrated, to North America and South Africa in particular. Many came to the diamond fields because the mines' demand for labor and the high wages paid were well known. Furthermore, the mining engineer hired by the Kimberley Mining Board in 1874, Francis Oats, came from a prominent Cornish mining family and probably assisted in the recruitment of his fellow countrymen.[4] No statistics exist for the number of Cornish miners who came to Kimberley, although some evidence of their importance exists in the

3. See the second annual report of the Kimberley Central Company in the *Daily Independent*, 30 May 1882; and the "Report of the Inspector of Diamond Mines for the Year 1883," *CGHPP*, G30, 1884, p. 7. For general reports on the increase in the use of machinery and the employment of skilled labor in the mines see Captain Charles Warren, "Result of an Enquiry . . . into the Work now in Progress in the Kimberley Mine . . . ," (1879), Royal Commonwealth Society Library; J. B. Finlason, "The Diamond Mines of the Cape Colony," (n. d.); North, "A Valuable and Interesting Paper," (1878); and Thomas Kitto, "Report on the Diamond Mines of Griqualand West," (1879), the last three all in the Smalberger Papers, UCT. Kitto's reports were also published in the *Griqualand West Government Gazette*, 15 August, 5, 19 September 1879.

4. D. B. Barton, *Essays in Cornish Mining History* (Truro, 1968), pp. 60, 65; idem, *A History of Tin Mining and Smelting in Cornwall* (Truro, 1967), pp. 173–75.

details of one incident, the De Beers mine fire of 1888. That fire, which affected the entire mine, caused the deaths of one-third of the underground white work force. Of the twenty-four miners killed, seven had been born in Cornwall, most in the village of St. Just, and most left widows and orphans still in their home towns.[5]

Another seven of those killed in the De Beers fire had been born in Cumberland. The coal-mining communities of west Cumberland provided numerous emigrants to the diamond fields, men searching, much like the Cornishmen, for jobs and higher wages to support their families left behind. And like the Cornishmen, the miners from Cumberland came from industrial communities where they had had considerable experience of wage labor and of struggles with their bosses.[6]

Skilled white workers and overseers were divided from each other in several important ways. First, skilled workers had a heritage of wage labor that extended over many generations. Most overseers, on the other hand, were from the middle class, and their most immediate work experience at the diamond fields had been as employers of labor. Second, skilled workers came to Kimberley to do much the same sort of work that they had done before in their working lives. For overseers, supervising black workers was not a chosen occupation. The origins of their situation lay in the parallel processes of property accumulation and property loss as capitalists took over the mines and small holders were forced by economic necessity into wage labor. Third, skilled workers had limited contact in the workplace with blacks, except in occasionally requiring their services as laborers. The basis of the overseer's occupation, however, was surveillance of men presumed to be thieves—thieves who they believed had deprived them of their own economic independence.

The rapidity of the transition from small-scale production to capitalist enterprise was reflected in the growth of the white work force. Within a year of the repeal of the claim-limitation law in

5. For biographical details on the white mine workers see the list of the dead contained in "De Beers Mine Fire, 1888," file 82, De Beers reel 44A, DBA. For a description of the fire, which also killed 178 black laborers, see Williams, *The Diamond Mines*, II, pp. 28–40; and Brian Roberts, *Kimberley: Turbulent City* (Cape Town, 1976), pp. 268–69.

6. *Ibid.* For various descriptions of life in the mining communities of Great Britain see Raphael Samuel (ed.), *Miners, Quarreymen and Saltworkers* (London, 1977).

1876, the white work force in the mines amounted to approximately one thousand men. They accounted for one-third of the white adult male population of Kimberley.[7] By 1881, the number of white wage earners in the mines had increased to nearly three thousand.[8]

Work conditions in the mines were onerous. The hours of labor were very long, stretching from dawn to dusk five days a week, with a half day's work on Saturdays. In summer this meant a work day of at least twelve hours (6:00 A.M. to 6:00 P.M.), plus travel time of an hour or so to and from the workplace.[9] Daily labor was made more difficult by the extreme variability of the climate. In summer temperatures frequently reached well over 90° F; in winter they were just as likely to go below freezing. With such conditions even overseeing, despite its limited physical demands, was an unpleasant occupation.

A large number of mining accidents added to the difficulties of the workers. The introduction of large-scale company working in the later 1870s did not eliminate the problems of reef falls and flooding. On the contrary, it exacerbated them, since the new companies competed even more ferociously against one another than had the small holders. There were constant problems with claim undercutting leading to cave-ins and reef falls, flooding of competitor's claims, and unregulated blasting. All workers, black and white, suffered severely from this competition, particularly in the deepest mine, Kimberley. The government inspector of mines noted in a report in 1880 that claim holders, having no legal obligation to compensate injured miners or the heirs of those killed, had their men work in extremely dangerous conditions, confident that they could not be held responsible for the many fatalities that resulted.[10]

The risk of injury and death in the workplace was compounded by unsanitary conditions in the township. An 1879 report of the municipal sanitary inspector singled out ineffective human-waste

7. *Diamond News*, 24 April 1877, quoting an estimate of Oats'. For various population breakdowns (by age, race, and sex), see the "Results of the Census Taken in the Province of Griqualand West, 1877," enclosed in GH 12/14; H. J. Vickers, *Griqualand West, Its Area, Population, Commerce and General Statistics* (Kimberley, 1879), pp. 4–5; and *Turner's Kimberley, Old De Beers, Dutoitspan, Bultfontein and Barkly Directory and Guide* (Kimberley, 1878).

8. See the table in the "Report of the Inspector of Diamond Mines for the Year 1889," *CGHPP*, G11 1890, p. 38.

9. See the reports of Finlason *et al.* referred to in note 3.

10. H. Ward to acting colonial secretary, 19 July 1880, GLW 160 (2008).

disposal as a major cause of illness. Cesspits had been used in the past throughout the town. By 1879, not only were these all full but in many cases "fermenting and bubbling up." The three cemeteries for blacks within the municipality caused further problems. In these the dead were placed in shallow graves without coffins. As the sanitary inspector noted, this was a considerable health hazard, since rains caused rapid decomposition and passage of the resulting "putrefying mass" into the ground water and eventually the drinking water of the town. The result was a constant threat of dysentery and typhoid. Of the 262 whites, adults and children, who died in 1878, 51 died from zymotic diseases (remittent fever and dysentery) and 36 from lung diseases (bronchitis, pneumonia, pthisis, and pleurisy), reflecting the combined effects of poor sanitation, a strenuous climate, and difficult working conditions.[11] Because of such problems, Kimberley had an appallingly high white death rate—40.5 per thousand in 1878—considering the general youth of the population and the fact that even industrialized cities such as London had rates of only 23 to 25 deaths per thousand head of population.[12] Such high rates of illness and mortality meant that most individuals (and families in particular, since the death rate of children was far higher than that of adults) could expect to face the emotional and financial costs of sickness and death as a relatively frequent aspect of their existence.

Work conditions might have been bad, but wages appeared high at the time. They were much higher than the wages paid for comparable work in the Cape or in Great Britain. In 1878, white wages in the diamond mines ranged between £3 and £6 per week, the lower rate being for overseers and the higher for skilled men.[13] These rates increased during the next few years, although the differential remained much the same. By 1882, overseers were earning £5 per week and engine drivers and mechanics between £7 10s. and £8.[14]

11. *Diamond News*, 29 March 1879.

12. *Ibid.*, 25 January, 1 April 1879. For further statistics on death rates for the total population and broken down by race see reports in the following issues of the *Diamond News*, 23 November 1876, 6 February, 4 September 1877, 25 January, 4, 29 March 1879; and in the *Daily Independent*, 21 January 1879, 21 January 1881, 20 January 1883, 15 January 1886. By 1886 the combined death rate for blacks and whites in Kimberley was 25/1,000, *Daily Independent*, 10 February 1887.

13. The figures are from Trollope, *South Africa*, II, p. 171.

14. "Report of the Inspector of Diamond Mines for the Year 1882," *CGHPP*, G34 1883, p. 6.

These wages were at least twice those paid in most parts of the
Cape and two to three times those paid in Britain.[15]

Such high wages were a deceptive index of economic well-
being, however, since the cost of living in Kimberley was very high.
Prices for foodstuffs were at least twice those charged in Cape Town,
largely because of the great costs of transportation and the inflationary atmosphere of the fields. Staples were particularly expensive.
Bread was 1s. for a one-pound loaf in Kimberley; in Cape Town the
same loaf cost 3d.; rice cost 1s. a pound instead of 2d.; milk was
2s. a quart rather than 3d.; Cape wine or brandy, a popular necessity on the fields, 12s. to 14s. per gallon rather than the 3s. charged
at the Cape. Vegetables in Kimberley, brought in from considerable
distances, fetched enormous prices; it was quite common for cau-
liflowers and cabbages to sell for 2s. to 3s. each. Meat was the only
cheap food in Kimberley. Prices averaged between 6d. and 10d. per
pound, much the same as was charged in Cape Town.[16] The minimum food requirements necessary to support a single white adult
male worker in Kimberley would have cost at least 26s. per week.[17]
To this sum should be added another 15s. to 20s. per week for fuel
and lodging, and 5s. to 10s. for such services as laundering and
medical treatment—a total weekly expenditure of between £2 10s.
and £2 16s. This is a subsistence estimate for a single man in the
middle to later 1870s, when the basic wage for an unskilled white
worker was £3 per week; it makes no allowance for the extra cost
of dependents.[18]

These high living costs meant that the majority of working families in Kimberley had to struggle hard merely to subsist. One over-

15. For wages in the Cape in 1884, e.g., see the *Blue Book for the Colony of the
Cape of Good Hope, 1885* (Cape Town, 1886), pp. 404–09. For wages in Britain in the
nineteenth century see Gareth Stedman Jones, *Outcast London: A Study in the Relationship between Classes in Victorian Society* (Oxford, 1971), pp. 31n62, 216–17.

16. These were the prices charged in 1875. See the Blue Book MS return for
1875 (unprinted), GH 28/94 (enclosure 134).

17. This estimate is based on the cost of the diet that Rowntree and Bowley,
at the end of the nineteenth century, estimated was the absolute minimum needed
for an adult male workhouse inmate. For a description of this diet, and its use as a
poverty index in an English context, see John Foster, *Class Struggle and the Industrial
Revolution: Early Industrial Capitalism in Three English Towns* (London, 1974),
pp. 255–56.

18. This estimate is, if anything, on the low side. The *Griqualand West Investor's Guardian*, 30 June 1881, estimated the minimum living costs of a "gentleman"
with an official position at £4 per week; board and lodging: £2 10s., clothing: 10s.,
washing: 7s. 6d., doctor, church, etc.: 12s. 6d.

seer's wife, in a letter published in a newspaper in 1880, complained that the £5 per week her husband received was barely enough to pay for food and lodging. Both she and her children had to do various jobs to pay for "extras" such as clothing.[19] Another example of the difficulties of making a living is provided by the case of Elsa Smithers and her family. They had first come to Kimberley in the early 1870s but, unable to make ends meet, had moved to Pretoria. The return of the Transvaal to Boer rule in 1881 forced the Smithers back to Kimberley. Elsa's two brothers managed to find unskilled work in the mines, but she and her mother had to supplement the family income by sewing mealie sacks, darning socks and mending clothing for bachelor workers, and by taking in boarders.[20] As one commentator on working-class life in Kimberley pointed out, most white workers were paid "just enough to live on."[21]

Skilled workers, with their higher rates of pay, had greater financial security. The £2 to £3 more per week that they received allowed many of them to save some money. Evidence of this relatively small-scale accumulation exists in the balance sheets of the Good Templars Savings Bank, an institution that specifically aimed at encouraging the working man to save. In its first year of operation, 1878, the bank received deposits totaling £8,000, none of them in excess of £150, from 550 depositers.[22] During the following four years larger deposits were made: £13,800 in 1879, £25,000 in 1880, £38,000 in 1881, and £50,000 in 1882.[23] Although withdrawals almost equaled deposits in most years, the sums involved do indicate a small amount of capital in the working community. This capital provided the better paid with a limited measure of security against the possibility of unemployment and the probability of injury or disease.

The Good Templars Bank was just one of a number of organizations established in the later 1870s to ameliorate the harshest conditions of life for white workers. These organizations took two forms: those established by members of Kimberley's bourgeoisie,

19. *Daily Independent*, 16 July 1880.

20. Elsa Smithers, *March Hare* (London, 1935), pp. 132, 134.

21. See Theo Schreiner in the *Diamond News*, 20 July 1880.

22. George Bottomley and C. R. Gowie to Administrator Warren, 30 October 1879, GLW 143 (3016).

23. *Daily Independent*, 29 December 1882.

including a bank, an industrial school for the "wayward" children of workers, and a building society; and those established by the workers themselves—most of them so-called friendly societies.

Richard Southey had first proposed the establishment of a bank for people with limited means in 1874. Believing that the future of the diamond industry lay with small holdings, he considered that a bank, by paying interest even on very small deposits, would encourage people to save and provide for their future rather than leave everything to chance. He introduced legislation in 1874 to establish such a bank, with clauses limiting the maximum amount that could be deposited to no more than £150 and allowing deposits of sums as small as 1s. Because of the depression in that year, however, Southey's plan was not implemented.[24]

Four years later members of Kimberley's bourgeoisie took up the plan, but for reasons somewhat different to those of Southey. In 1878, the Good Templars, an antiliquor organization dominated by a number of merchants and large claim holders, set up a savings bank based on Southey's legislation. Deposits were limited in their amount and interest rates made relatively high to attract small savers; the bank itself paid 4 percent and the state added another 2 percent. The Templars, led by George Bottomley, a wealthy claim holder and later to be one of the founders of the Kimberley Central Company, intended that the bank should serve two purposes. First, they hoped that workingmen would save their "surplus earnings" rather than waste them, as members of the bourgeoisie commonly believed, on gambling and liquor. Second, the Templars hoped that the act of saving would give workingmen "the taste of getting property." They believed that workingmen would then be able to escape the worst vagaries of the labor market and not become a burden on the charity of men of property during periods of depression.[25] Thus the Good Templars Bank would encourage the growth of "small capitalists," eliminate the need to establish costly charitable institutions, and permit the "surplus" from workers' earnings to be recycled by means of bank investments back into the mining industry.[26]

24. See the report of the early scheme in the *Diamond News*, 26 February 1878; and for Southey's regulations, Ordinance 26 of 1874.

25. For the origins of the bank see reports in the *Diamond News*, 26 February 1878; and the *Daily Independent*, 3 January 1883. See also C. R. Gowie to Administrator Lanyon, 16 February 1878, GLW 115 (326).

26. *Diamond News*, 26 February 1878.

Much the same aims lay behind the establishment of an industrial school and a building society in 1879. Both institutions were set up by men of property—claim holders and merchants—and were aimed at individuals without property. The industrial school was to train "young lads beyond the control of their parents . . . [in] some useful employment": essentially it was a trade school for children from poorer working families.[27] The building society, requiring low weekly contributions and offering low-interest mortgages, was established to encourage people to save and invest their capital in houses.[28] These institutions would, therefore, in various ways increase the productivity of white workers' limited capital while reducing the welfare demands that they might make on capitalists and the state.

The friendly societies established by workingmen in the later 1870s aimed more specifically than did the organizations listed above at lessening the harsh impact of the conditions of labor. One of the first of these societies, the Star of Griqualand lodge of the Association of Foresters, was established by "working men who in their better times provided against sickness and death."[29] In 1876, on the occasion of its inaugural dinner, the lodge had fifty-nine financial members and funds amounting to £174.[30] By 1881, the number of societies had increased considerably, with two lodges of Odd Fellows, two of Foresters, and one Roman Catholic society for workingmen, their combined membership totaling between two hundred and three hundred persons. One contemporary observer noted that their members were largely the better paid workingmen, generally head overseers and skilled workers, who had joined together mainly to secure medical benefits.[31] His observations are partly confirmed by the rules and regulations of the Guiding Star lodge of the Independent Order of Scottish Mechanics, which contain extensive and detailed provisions for medical benefits and disablement pensions. The

27. *Ibid.*, 19 June 1879. See also the issues of 17 June and 16 December. Two future mining capitalists, C. D. Rudd and Francis Baring-Gould, were leading supporters of the school.

28. *Ibid.*, 17 April, 10 May 1879. For a further report on the society see the *Daily Independent*, 25 July 1881.

29. *Diamond News*, 25 March 1876.

30. *Ibid.*

31. See the evidence of Dr. J. W. Matthews in the "Report of the Select Committee Appointed to Consider the Report on Friendly Societies," *CGHPP*, A6 1881, pp. 1–6.

rules include no provision, though, for the payment of unemployment benefits.[32] Like overseers, skilled workers suffered frequently from injuries and disease; unlike overseers, however, their services were much in demand, and they faced little risk of unemployment.[33]

There were no organizations established specifically for overseers, nor did these men form any of their own. They identified themselves socially with claim holders and merchants, yet they could not afford the membership fees of the main social organization of the bourgeoisie, the Masons. They could not even afford the small weekly fees of the friendly societies, which were in any case branches of British working-class organizations and attracted as members men who had belonged to such lodges in their home communities. And overseers in the late 1870s did not regard themselves as members of the working class.

But in 1880 overseers were brought face to face with the fact that mining companies regarded them solely as part of labor and intended to treat them in much the same way as were black laborers. The attempt by mining capitalists to introduce searching as a new form of labor control over black and white workers is a case in point, and helps shed light on early worker consciousness. To recapitulate briefly the discussion in chapter 3 above, the state introduced legislation in 1880, after considerable pressure over several years from mining capitalists, that required black laborers and white overseers to submit to daily body searches upon leaving the mines. Managerial and most skilled workers were exempt from the provisions of the legislation; the former because they were deemed to be trustworthy, the latter because most of them worked with machinery on the margins of the mines and had little contact with diamondiferous ground.[34] The passage of this legislation marked the first time that black and white workers at the fields were to be treated in the same manner.

32. "Revised Rules and Regulations of the 'Guiding Star' Lodge, No. 3, of the Independent United Order of Scottish Mechanics' Friendly Society, Kimberley, South African Diamond Fields," (established 1881), AG 1745 (8690).

33. To some extent these organizations resembled the Masons (which appealed to men of property), particularly in their elaborate ritual and rules. Unlike the Masons, however, officers of the Friendly Societies were elected by a vote of all the members; they did not have to buy their positions.

34. Ordinance [11] to Provide for the Searching of Natives and Others Employed on the Various Diamond Mines and Diggings within the Province, and for the Maintenance of the Police and Detective Forces Thereof, and for Other Purposes, 1880.

The overseers protested vigorously. Three arguments dominated their public utterances. First, they rejected the idea that they could not be trusted. Letters to the newspaper signed with nom-de-plumes like An Old Claimholder, Once a Claimholder, A Sympathizing Wife of Once a Claimholder, and others forcefully reiterated the point that many overseers had recently been claim holders themselves.[35] Once a Claimholder argued that overseers were "upright, reliable, honest men, of equal standing, education, and refinement with the possessors of the claims, which in many instances were once theirs."[36] As former claim holders, the letter writers stated that they regarded the interests of their new employers as the same as their own. They equated their new position not with that of wage laborers but with that of a "confidential servant" or a "trusted and trustworthy custodian of their master's wealth."[37] The legislation, according to Once a Claimholder, would destroy this bond of trust, since by treating all overseers as suspected thieves it would have the negative result of subverting their "honesty, honour, and standing," and men treated as thieves would soon become thieves.[38]

The second argument of the overseers was that there was a basic difference between the work done by white overseers and that done by black laborers and that because of this the two groups should not be treated in the same manner. This view was presented most clearly in a letter written by An Old Claimholder:

> The labourers, whether white or black, who pick, carry, shovel up, and load up, and otherwise handle the diamondiferous soil, and the band of watchers, whether white or black, who are appointed to prevent thefts by the former . . . [are] two classes as distinct and even antagonistic in interests as can well be imagined, and it will be a bad day for the employers when these two classes are legislatively looked upon as one, even though it be only on paper.[39]

This distinction was also taken up by Once a Claimholder, who

35. *Daily Independent*, 10, 16 July 1880.
36. *Ibid.*, 10 July 1880.
37. *Diamond News*, 20, 29 July 1880.
38. *Daily Independent*, 10 July 1880. See also the petition, printed in the 14 July issue of the newspaper, presented by the overseers to the government.
39. *Ibid.*, 10 July 1880. As the quotation implies, there were some black overseers, but their numbers appear to have been very small.

suggested that whereas the aim of the overseer was "to find and preserve as much wealth for the claimholder as possible," the aim of the black laborer was "to filch as much as possible. . . ."[40]

The third argument of the overseers reflected their fears of degradation. Throughout their newspaper letters, and in public meetings, overseers argued that they did not want to be, in their words, "brought down to," "reduced to," or placed "in the same category as" the "Kafir." A Sympathizing Wife of Once a Claimholder expressed this view clearly in a letter to the newspaper:

> [I]t is more than I can bear (and I know I have a fellow sympathy in this respect), to think my husband—once a claimholder—should have to submit to such indignity ... (as searching). ... Only put it to yourself, the ill effects it would have on our children to see their father, who has always been held up to them as an example of honesty, to have him placed on a level with the natives, who, as a rule, do not consider stealing to be a sin—in fact their only sin in this respect is being found out. Then why place a white man on a level with a black?[41]

To be distrusted and to be submitted to daily body searches meant degradation to overseers, treatment that had been applied previously only to black workers. The heightened racism apparent in white public discourse during the conflict over the introduction of searching thus reflected not only preexisting racist attitudes but also a real fear that the already declining position of the overseer would become much worse. Considering how badly black workers were treated, no whites wanted to share their position.

The overseers did not organize their opposition to searching effectively. Apart from letter writing and some public meetings, their only other demonstration of unity was the sending of a petition to the Cape government protesting the legislation. And even then over half of the more than one thousand overseers in the mines did not sign.[42] This lack of unity reflected two factors. First, as dis-

40. *Ibid.*

41. *Daily Independent*, 16 July 1880, quoted in Smalberger, "I.D.B. and the Mining Compound System," p. 403. See also, e.g., letters from overseers and reports of meetings published in the *Diamond News*, 20 July 1880; and the issues of the *Daily Independent* referred to in the notes above.

42. The petition contained 539 signatures, 393 of them belonging to overseers and many of the remainder to merchants and shopkeepers, *Diamond News*, 22 July 1880.

cussed above, overseers did not conceive of themselves as having distinct interests opposed to those of their employers. Despite talk at the time of the antagonism between capital and labor, overseers did not believe in such a division except insofar as it applied to white capitalists and black laborers. Second, many overseers feared for their jobs, since there was considerable white unemployment at the time.

In the end, however, despite the weakness of the overseers, the searching law was not applied in 1880. The most important factor preventing its application was the shortage of black labor. Because it was well known that black workers would rather change employers than accept any form of searching, no employer was ready to risk his labor supply by enforcing the law. In addition, not all mining employers were united in their support of searching. The large mining capitalists were its main supporters, while most of the small employers opposed its application to white workers, believing it a degrading practice.[43] Moreover, the fact that white workers had the vote was particularly important. Some of the leading mining capitalists had political ambitions and recognized that the white mine workers' vote, if effectively mobilized, could be a crucial factor in any future election. For these reasons, black and white workers escaped for the moment the further degradation involved in searching.

In concluding this section, three points should be stressed. First, the rapidity of the transition of many whites from small claim holders to relatively unskilled proletarians worked against the development of a worker consciousness in this early period. Overseers, despite their subsistence living, nonetheless identified themselves with the bourgeoisie of which they had recently been part. Furthermore, their position as surrogate bosses supervising black labor reinforced their belief that they were still part of the managerial sector in capital-labor relations. Second, overseers were placed in an antagonistic relationship to black workers by the very nature of their job, while skilled whites considered themselves separate from both because of their skills (which provided greater financial benefits) and their limited contact with either in the workplace. Third, capitalists hoped to increase profits and cut costs by eliminating theft and reducing the expense of supervision. Searching would provide

43. For a discussion of the division see the *Diamond News*, 22, 29 July 1880.

these benefits by ensuring closer surveillance of black workers while, through the use of daily examinations at the mine entrances, eliminating the need for so many overseers throughout the mines. Although the mining capitalists did not succeed in attaining these goals in 1880, the prospect remained that they would try again to obtain greater profits at the expense of black and white workers.

## ECONOMIC STRUGGLE AND THE GROWTH OF LABOR CONSCIOUSNESS, 1882–84

The depression that afflicted the diamond industry in the early to mid-1880s had particularly severe effects on white workers. Unemployment increased with the demise of many companies and a reduction in the size of the work forces of most of those that remained in operation. Between the middle of 1882 and the end of 1883 the number of white men employed in the diamond mines declined by 30 percent.[44] Most of these unemployed whites remained in Kimberley, since the cost of transportation prevented those without money from leaving and there was little work elsewhere in South Africa at that time for the white unskilled.

Increasing use of machinery by the surviving companies further reduced the demand for unskilled white labor in Kimberley. The companies that survived the depression—generally the larger operations with greater financial resources such as the Kimberley Central and French companies—maintained high levels of production with a reduced labor force through a more intensive use of machinery and the introduction of new forms of mining technology, in particular the use of underground shafts to escape the growing problems of open working.

Indeed, the development of technology transformed the ratio of skilled mine workers to overseers in the Kimberley mine. Whereas in 1883 the skilled to overseer ratio was 1:1.4 (i.e., an average of 109 skilled workers to 143 overseers), by June 1884 this had changed to a ratio of 2:0.8 (205 skilled workers to 86 overseers). Even in the other mines, which were not so deep or so actively worked with machinery, the ratios changed considerably: in the Dutoitspan mine from 1:3 to 1:1.5; in the De Beers mine from 1:3 to 1:1; in the

---

44. See the table in the "Report of the Inspector of Diamond Mines for the Year 1889," *CGHPP,* G11 1890, p. 38.

Bultfontein mine from 1:2 to 1:1.[45] Thus, although the white work force was considerably reduced, this development had a much greater impact on overseers than on skilled workers.

To be unemployed in Kimberley was to risk destitution. Those who could afford to do so left Kimberley with the onset of the depression. The very large withdrawals made from the Good Templars Bank in the third and fourth quarters of 1882, which exceeded deposits by 50 percent, were attributed by the bank and others to people leaving for the eastern Transvaal gold fields.[46] Most workingmen, however, had no savings, especially if they were overseers and had a family to support as well as themselves. As early as the beginning of 1882, there had been reports of destitute white men in Kimberley.[47] In November 1882, the *Daily Independent* suggested that some form of civic relief should be provided for the many "respectable men" out of work and in an impoverished condition.[48] Little, if anything, appears to have been done. In December of the following year, the paper was still calling for a "display of public philanthropy" and stressed the need for a soup kitchen.[49] In March 1884, a letter writer to the paper using the pseudonym Humanitas again drew the attention of readers to the great amount of poverty in the community and stated that many people were near starvation.[50] The various organizations established in the later 1870s to protect the welfare of workers could not cope with the severity of the depression. Nor were members of the bourgeoisie ready, or perhaps even able, to assist the unemployed or destitute through the provision of private charity.

Even for those who remained in employment, earning a living became increasingly difficult. One severe problem was the heightened risk of injury or accidental death due to increased difficulties in mining. In the early 1880s mining accidents increased in number and in type, especially in the most actively worked mine, Kimber-

45. See the "Report of the Inspector of Diamond Mines for the Year 1883," *CGHPP,* G30 1884, pp. 7, 23, and his report for 1884, G28 1885, p. 17. See also, John Fry to assistant commissioner for Crown lands and public works, 10 July 1884, LND 1/160 (458).

46. See the report of the *Daily Independent,* 9 January 1883; and, for the movement to the gold fields, the letter of the Reverend C. F. Tobias to Miss Trench, published in the *Quarterly Paper of the Bloemfontein Mission,* no. 59, January 1883, USPG.

47. *Daily Independent,* 30 March 1882.

48. 8 November 1882.

49. 11 December 1883.

50. 11 March 1884. See also the issues of 16 June 1883 and 13 June 1884.

ley. In 1882, the combined death and accident rate for white workers in that mine amounted to 50 per thousand and the death rate to 24 per thousand.[51] Most of these deaths and injuries were caused by reef falls, but a growing number were due to new factors. In 1883, for example, fifty accidents were caused by or related to the use of machinery, half of them occurring in the Kimberley mine. The increased use of explosives was another factor in the high accident rate. An official report on explosive-related accidents in the Dutoitspan and Bultfontein mines in 1884 found that the majority were caused by managerial negligence.[52] Yet neither companies nor the state provided any form of accident compensation.

Comparison of Kimberley's accident rates with those in British mines clearly shows the exceptional risks faced by workers in the diamond diggings. In Britain before the establishment of government regulation in the notoriously dangerous coal mines, the death rate in that industry was considered appallingly high at 5 deaths per thousand men employed. By the 1870s, the establishment of a system of government regulation in the coal mines had reduced the death rate to an annual average of 2 per thousand, and the rate was further reduced in subsequent years.[53] In effect, therefore, mine workers in Kimberley and De Beers were twelve times as likely to die in the course of their work as their British peers.

The experiences of one member of Kimberley's white work force, Richard Richardson, illuminate the impact of these changes in the diamond industry. Richardson came to the Cape Colony from England with his wife and two children in the early 1880s. It appears from the evidence available that he was an unskilled laborer who had left England to escape poverty and was attracted to the Cape by the reports of high wages available. But he had the misfortune to arrive at a time of widespread depression throughout the country. His life in the Cape, far from the being an escape from poverty, turned into a desperate struggle to survive.

51. The percentages are based on statistics contained in the "Report of the Inspector of Diamond Mines for the Year 1882," *CGHPP,* G34 1883, p. 16. The accident rate in the other mines was much lower.

52. Inspector of machinery to inspector of mines, 17 May 1884, LND 1/220; inspector of mines to assistant commissioner of Crown lands and public works, 27 May 1884, LND 1/220.

53. See Oliver MacDonagh, "Coal Mines Regulation: the First Decade, 1842–1852," in Robert Robson (ed.), *Ideas and Institutions of Victorian Britain* (London, 1967), pp. 58–80.

In his first few years in the Cape, Richardson moved all over the colony. During the course of two to three years he worked in nine different towns, ending up in 1884 laboring on the Queenstown railway extension. By that time his wife and children had, because of illness, returned to England. Work on the extension provided, in Richardson's words, "bare wages," and he complained in letters to his wife that the contractor was "grinding . . . down" the workmen and preventing them from saving any money by charging outrageous sums for board and lodging. With work on the extension completed and unable to find any further employment in Queenstown, Richardson decided to move to Kimberley where, he had heard, there were well-paying jobs. He hoped to earn enough in Kimberley to send money home to support his family, pay for his own return passage, and have enough over so that they could move to Canada and buy a farm.

Richardson did not have much success in Kimberley. He was lucky enough to secure some laboring work with the Elma Diamond Mining Company in the De Beers mine. But his pay for loading trucks with debris to be removed from the mine was very low, and he could not send any money to his family. After a few months' work he was killed in a mining accident, probably caused by one of the trucks tipping over and crushing him. Richardson was thirty-seven when he died. He left nothing in his estate apart from a few shillings owed him by the Elma Company.[54]

Two aspects of Richardson's life have relevance for the general experience of white workingmen in the Cape. First, with depressed conditions throughout the colony, many men moved to the diamond fields in search of work. Despite the depression in Kimberley, the town still had the reputation of being a place of wealth. Yet the influx of newcomers such as Richardson only compounded the employment problems for unskilled white workers.[55] Second, Richardson's lack of property was typical of most members of the working class. An examination of the estates of 97 individuals who died in Kimberley in late 1885 and 1886 found 33 to be those of workingmen,

54. Details on Richardson's life are drawn from his letters to his wife, and those that she wrote to various officials in Kimberley in an attempt to locate any property he might have left. The letters are filed with Richardson's estate papers, Kimberley Estates, vol. 20, p. 2. For a discussion of the experiences of white workers on the Cape railway see Purkis, "The Politics of Railway-building," chapt. 8.
55. See the letter of Reverend Tobias referred to in note 46.

a number that corresponds to the approximate proportion of white workers in the general white population. Of these 33 men, 27 were overseers, engine drivers, or other mineworkers. The most significant common feature of these mineworkers' estates is the almost complete lack of property in them. Most of the men died, like Richardson, impoverished. Such men included Achilles Guidi, single, 43 years old, an Italian laborer for the Oriental Diamond Mining Company, who left some clothing, his bed, and a watch to his heirs; Thomas Johnson, married, 38, a mason from Yorkshire, who worked for the French Company and left nothing; Henry Loader, married, 37, and John Lee, single, 24, both miners from Cape Town, who also left nothing.

There were some exceptions to this general pattern of poverty, but they were restricted to skilled workers. The largest of the mineworkers' estates was that of an engine driver from Germany who, when he died at the age of 45 leaving a widow and four children, had a small iron house valued at £35 situated on leasehold land. The next-largest estate was that of a 22-year-old single miner from Devonshire, who left £10 in a post-office savings account. Their estates, self-evidently tiny, amounted to no more than the equivalent of two weeks' to a month's wages. And these estates containing some property were a small minority, amounting in total to no more than 5 of the 27 estates of mine workers.[56]

Economic pressures impinged severely on workers; equally oppressive, however, in the eyes of the workers themselves, were a number of policies adopted by the industrialists to secure the profitability of the industry. Unlike unemployment and poverty, which could always be attributed to the impersonal workings of economic forces, attempts by employers to institute greater controls over their workers and to cut the costs of labor in 1882, 1883, and 1884 made white mine workers increasingly aware of a sharp and contradictory division between their own interests and those of industrialists.

Attempts by industrialists to control what they believed to be a huge amount of diamond theft had important repercussions for white mine workers. In the early 1880s, in the face of declining profits, many leading company owners identified IDB as the most serious threat to the survival of the industry and demanded that the

56. Kimberley Estates, vol. 20.

state increase the punishments of those convicted of theft. They met with considerable success. More severe penalties were introduced in law, a special court was established to try illicit dealers, and the Kimberley detective department was expanded, made independent of the police force, and its costs subsidized by the mining companies.[57]

The detective department had a powerful impact on the white community, particularly through its use of entrapment procedures. Detectives, black and white, constantly attempted to trap people by offering to sell them obviously illicit stones at extremely low prices. In 1883, for example, the department spent £2,789 on diamonds for trapping purposes and paid another £559 to informers. All told, the expenses of the department in that year, including salaries, amounted to just under £40,000.[58] The attentions of the detectives were directed at black laborers, white mine workers, and members of the town's petty bourgeoisie—the owners of canteens, hotels, and "Kafir eating-houses." While the detectives and their employers considered black workers to be the actual thieves, they also believed that stolen diamonds entered the illicit market through the hands of otherwise respectable white middlemen.

Even with the knowledge that the detectives were trapping, many members of Kimberley's proletariat and petty bourgeoisie took the chance of making a quick profit. Most of the whites arrested for IDB were members of those two classes; of 47 men and women imprisoned in the Kimberley jail in 1882 for IDB offenses, 43 were either mine workers, small shopkeepers, or members of the non-mining working class (carpenters, laundresses, a policeman, and others).[59]

The use of the detective department was one method that mining capitalists experimented with to secure their profits; another method was lowering wages, which was more direct in its impact on all workers. Mining companies had tried to lower the wages of black workers in 1881 and 1882. Each time they had failed to secure their object due to a critical shortage of black workers. In November 1882, however, with the price of diamonds plummeting, the two largest companies in the Kimberley mine, the Kimberley Central

---

57. See chapt. 3.
58. "Statements of Revenue and Expenditure by the Detective Department ... for the Year 1883," *CGHPP,* G6 1884, pp. 3–4.
59. CO 6839A contains a list of the prisoners held in the Kimberley jail.

and the French, announced that they were lowering the wages of their white overseers.

The action taken by these two companies reflected the great importance of white labor costs to the larger and more mechanized companies. Although whites comprised only a small proportion of the mines' work force, they received a very large share of the total wage bill because of the size of their wages relative to those of blacks. And with increasing numbers of skilled men at work, the white share of the wage bill grew ever larger. In 1882, only 15 percent of the Kimberley Central Company's workers were white. Yet these men, one-third of whom were skilled workers, received 46 percent of the total wages paid by the company. By the following year their share had risen to 55 percent. In addition, the very size of the work force of the larger companies—the Kimberley Central had 1,124 employees in 1882—meant that these wages amounted to a great deal of money. The wage bill for the Central in 1882 was £40,877; in 1882-83 it rose to £62,561.[60] Large companies thus had much to gain by reducing the cost of their white labor.[61]

The overseers of the Kimberley and French companies reacted quickly to the wage-reduction proposal. They held a meeting of all overseers employed in the Kimberley mine on 16 November 1882, a few days after knowledge of the wage-reduction scheme first became public. Three men dominated the meeting. Mr. Figg, an overseer for the French Company, was in the chair. The two other major participants and speech makers were Frank Cusens, an overseer for the Kimberley Central Company, and Joseph Wearne, a miner also employed by the Central.[62]

The three men differed considerably in their approaches to the issue of wage reduction and how it should be dealt with. On two matters Figg and Wearne were in agreement; they felt that the conditions of labor were extremely bad, especially with the working

60. See the second annual report of the company published in the *Daily Independent*, 30 May 1882, and the third annual report published in the same paper, 2 June 1883. In 1884 and 1885 the amount of wages going to white workers ranged between 56 percent and 61 percent. See the reports of the company in the *Daily Independent*, 15 December 1884, 16 June 1885. See also the "Tabulated Costs of Sundry Working Expenses for the Three Months Ended 31 January 1885," KCDM, DBA.

61. The major saving in Rhodes' 1882 proposal to amalgamate the De Beers mine would have come from reduced white labor costs, not lower black labor costs. See chapt. 1.

62. There is an extensive report of the meeting in the *Daily Independent*, 18 November 1882.

day usually extending to thirteen hours, and they believed that workingmen could only succeed so long as they were united in their endeavors. With regard to the attitude that they should adopt toward their employers, though, Figg and Cusens, the overseers, held quite different views from those of Wearne, the miner. Figg, for example, in arguing that the workmen should be moderate in their actions and words, stated that he considered the interests of workers and employers to be identical: all were "strangers in a strange land" and all were working for "the betterment of mankind." He received Cusens' support in claiming that the men were banding together for protection only, not to oppose their employers but to defend their already shaky economic position. Such sentiments were much the same as those expressed by overseers at the time of the struggle over the introduction of searching in 1880.

Joseph Wearne, on the other hand, took a much more antagonistic approach toward capital. His participation in the meeting stemmed from a belief that the industrialists intended to lower the wages of all white workers and were starting with the overseers. In his speech to the meeting, Wearne argued that the Central and French companies were acting in a "tyrannical" manner by lowering wages, especially since they had recently made good profits. The Kimberley Central had, after all, made a profit of 53 percent on its invested capital in its second year of operations ending in April 1882 and had announced a quarterly dividend of 12 percent in May. Wearne accused the Central and French companies of trying to take advantage of the generally difficult times by lowering wages more than was necessary to support their previously inflated profit rates. He argued that they were trying "to grind down the working man and take every atom of manliness out of him."[63]

In his choice of language, his reference to "tyranny," and his idea that companies should only make "reasonable" profits, Wearne reflected his British working-class background. Another speaker at the same meeting, a Mr. Shapland, argued from a similar standpoint when he stated that he and other men had come to the diamond fields not just to make a subsistence living, for they had done that in England, but to make a good living. Shapland, in supporting Wearne's argument that the men should strike for an agreed rate of wages, also called for the establishment of a workingmen's associa-

63. *Ibid.*, 18, 24, 25 November 1882. On the Central's profits see the *Independent*'s issue of 30 May 1882.

tion to coordinate strike action. Such action, he continued, had been the "saving of the working man in England." Despite the lukewarm response of the two overseers, Figg and Cusens, to these proposals, the rest of the men at the meeting endorsed them enthusiastically.[64]

Other members of the community regarded this demonstration of worker unity with great concern. Industrialists saw it as a threat to their profits, while most merchants believed that their economic well-being and that of the community in general was dependent on the mining companies making large profits. The argument of those who opposed the overseers were expounded at length in an editorial in the *Daily Independent*. Stating that the depression affected everyone, the editorial writer argued that the only way to alleviate general distress was to allow the companies to make greater profits through a reduction of working expenses. The writer noted that the shareholders had a right to expect profits and that if they did not get any then they would force the companies to cease all work. Claiming that white workers were liberally paid, even if they did work long hours, the editorialist called on the workers to consider seriously the interests of employers and shareholders and to assist such people, and ultimately their own economic welfare, by voluntarily accepting a wage reduction. He concluded with an admonition to the overseers not to consider strike action, arguing that nothing would be "more regrettable than to see the old world struggle between capital and labour transplanted to the colonies."[65]

Before a worker's association was formed, however, a deputation from the overseers met with the directors of the two companies. The deputation's arguments must have been convincing, because the directors agreed to withdraw the wage-reduction proposal, even going so far as publicly to deny that they had ever considered unilaterally lowering wages.[66] Even though the exact reasons for the directors' change of heart are not known, two factors were probably important in influencing their decision. First, the extent of white worker unity evident at the meeting had come as something of a shock to them. There had been no previous case of white workers combining effectively, either within an occupational grouping such as that of the overseers, or across job divisions such as existed between skilled and supervisory labor. Industrialists in the past had,

64. *Ibid.*
65. 24 November 1882.
66. *Ibid.*, 25, 30 November 1882.

like the editorialist in the *Daily Independent*, publicly stressed their belief in the existence of a special relationship between white workers and employers, and they had eschewed the use of such pejorative terms as *labor* and *capital* with their connotations of class conflict. When employers had referred to labor in the past, they had restricted that term to black workers. With the mobilization of the overseers and their skilled worker allies, industrialists were faced for the first time with organized white workers threatening strike action and proposing to form a union.

The second factor to influence the directors was their recognition that the continued use of open-mining technology at great depths placed their mine in a very precarious position. Joseph Wearne made the point in one of his speeches that if the men went on strike for even as short a period as one week that would be enough to cripple the mines for months. With the pumping equipment left unattended and no work carried out on reef removal, the Kimberley mine would flood, which would in turn destabilize the margins of the mine and cause even greater subsidence.[67] The costs of bringing the mine back into operation after such a turn of events would be enormous.

The agreement of the directors of the Kimberley Central and French companies not to reduce wages, while an immediate victory for the overseers, removed the incentive to form a strong union along the lines envisaged by Wearne and Shapland. In early December 1882, however, one month after the agreement over wages had been reached, Figg established an organization along quite different lines. This new body was not a union but rather a form of mutual-benefit society much like the friendly societies established in the later 1870s. The Amalgamated Employees of Griqualand West Association, as it was called, required a weekly membership subscription that would be used for a fund to provide benefits to those who were injured in the mines or to the dependents of those killed. Described approvingly as a "mutual improvement society" by the *Daily Independent*, the organization received vocal support from Kimberley's bourgeoisie. George Goch, a prominent merchant who had been influential in the establishment of the Good Templars Savings Bank and the building society, heartily approved of its formation, believing that it would encourage men to save, keep them

67. *Ibid.*, 18 November 1882.

away from canteens, and, through self-policing of its members, prevent any "thieves" from getting jobs in the mines.[68]

Yet the organization attracted little support from workingmen; only thirty turned up at its inaugural meeting. Figg attributed this lack of support to fear on the part of the men that they would be sacked if their employers found out that they had joined. This might have been true, although the limited aims of the organization seem to have been a more important disincentive to membership. Those who could afford to pay weekly subscriptions already belonged to benefit societies, and those who could not afford them were more interested in trying to make ends meet.[69]

Having failed to reduce wages, the industrialists next attempted to introduce a system of searching their employees. In November 1882, the same month that the overseers won their fight over wages, a committee of mining company directors drew up a set of regulations based on the Searching Ordinance of 1880. These regulations, which included financial penalties recoverable through the courts, were given legal force by the governor of the Cape in January 1883.[70]

Searching was to be applied to black and white workers in all four mines, but with some exceptions and some differential applications. As was the case in 1880, managers and those who worked on the margins of the mines (where most of the engine drivers and mechanics were employed) were exempted from the provisions of the new regulations. Therefore, the men most affected by the new system were the white overseers and the black laborers. Not only were these men to be searched daily, but they were also to wear uniforms—pocketless in the case of overseers, mealie sacks in the case of laborers.[71]

The overseers objected to wearing a uniform, although their protests were somewhat muted.[72] The overseers of the Kimberley Central Company, for example, repeated the old arguments of 1880. They claimed that they occupied a special position of trust, that

68. *Ibid.*, 25 November 1882.

69. *Ibid.*, 25 November, 6 December 1882.

70. Proclamation No. 1, 1883, repr. in the *Daily Independent*, 10 January 1883. See also chapt. 3.

71. The searching regulations were put into force in early March, *Daily Independent*, 2 March 1883.

72. For the much stronger resistance of the black workers to the wearing of uniforms see chapt. 3.

they were really managers or submanagers, and that searching was degrading, especially as it put them on the same level as blacks. They did add one new objection to those originally made in 1880. They asked that if searching did have to be enforced they be allowed to examine one another and not have members of the detective department do the job. Having suffered the attention of detectives in the past, overseers did not trust such men, who they believed would try to work off old scores or boost arrest statistics by planting illicit stones on innocent men.[73]

The employers and their white employees reached a compromise. The overseers, threatened by a high unemployment rate, agreed to submit to searching by employees of the detective department, but only so long as it was done in a perfunctory manner and out of sight of black workers, and only so long as they did not have to wear uniforms. They believed that the basis of their authority over black workers would be severely weakened if it were seen that they were also distrusted by their employers. Both these conditions were agreed to by the employers. The compromise, though chipping away at the position of the overseers, did allow them to retain their jobs and some of their dignity.[74]

In late September 1883, however, after a rather rudimentary version of the searching system had been in force for seven months without having had any noticeable effect on the output of diamonds, industrialists led by George Bottomley and J. B. Robinson stated that they would extend searching to the margins of the mines and require all men to submit to close examinations of their bodies upon entering and exiting the mining areas.[75]

The mechanics and engine drivers strongly opposed the implementation of these new proposals. On the day that the regulations were to be enforced, they went on strike. They quickly transformed an interim strike committee into a fully fledged union, the first ever on the diamond fields. The Artisans' and Engine Drivers' Protection Society combined the features of a benefit society and a trade union. Like a benefit society, it had a membership fee and a weekly subscription, and payments were planned for men injured in the course of their work. But its main objects were those of a trade union: "to

73. *Ibid.*, 20, 21, 23 February 1883.
74. *Ibid.*, 23 February 1883. For a description of the system in practice see the issue of 6 April.
75. *Ibid.*, 27 September, 3 October 1883.

raise funds for the protection of the Society and its Members . . . to resist the laws relative to stripping and passing through the Searching Houses . . . [and] to raise funds for the purpose of material support of any Members should they be thrown out of employment."[76]

The engine drivers and mechanics, at a series of public meetings, sought the support of all other white workers in the mines. The men at these meetings, skilled workers and overseers alike, agreed that any form of strip searching was reprehensible and degrading, since it implied that those being searched were thieves. The men took up the old argument of the overseers that searching would "lower" white workers to the "level" of the black laborer. William Egglestone, one of the leaders of the skilled workers, stated that he did not want to be treated like a "nigger" or "Kafir" (the terms were used interchangeably).[77] The employers' argument that there was no reason for the men to object to searching, since dock laborers in Britain submitted willingly to the same practice, was countered by the proposition that the situation of dockers was equivalent to that of black laborers at the mines and therefore did not relate to men who held supervisory or skilled jobs.[78] The skilled workers did not, however, support the claim of the overseers that whites should be accorded managerial status. So far as the skilled men were concerned, they had certain rights as artisans and did not consider themselves on a par with either laborers or bosses.

The united white workers sought the support of black workers for their strike—and with considerable success. Most black workers stopped work and many attended the strike meetings of the whites, although only as observers. In gaining this support, white workers took advantage of the special position that they occupied in the organization of production. They could, as the most immediate and visible agents of management, use their company-endowed positions to persuade black workers to participate in anticompany actions. Black workers, for their part, were quite ready to assist anyone who would help them get rid of the searching system.

The strikers took a number of measures, some of them violent,

76. *Rules of the Artisans' and Engine Drivers' Protection Society* (Kimberley, 1883). It cost £1 1s. to join the society, followed by a weekly subscription of 2s. 6d.
77. For reports on the meetings see the *Dutoitspan Herald*, 16 October 1883; *Diamond Fields Advertiser,* 15, 16, 18, 19 October 1883; and the *Daily Independent,* 16, 18, 19 October 1883.
78. *Dutoitspan Herald,* 16 October 1883.

to ensure that no work was carried out in the mines. In the Dutoitspan mine, for example, companies that tried to continue work had their employees and machinery pelted with stones by a large group of black and white strikers.[79] In another case at the same mine, a scabbing engine driver was stripped naked and beaten up in the street by white strikers before being rescued by his employer.[80] Elsa Smithers' two brothers continued to work, but because of constant harassment by the strikers spent the duration of the struggle living, working, and sleeping in the French Company's shaft in the Kimberley mine.[81] Within a matter of days the strikers had brought work in the mines to a complete halt.[82]

The employers responded to these actions in a disorganized and ineffective manner. At first they cajoled and threatened the strikers. Mr. Moering, a director of the French Company, argued at a meeting with skilled employees that the employers were the "friends" of workingmen, not their enemies. He suggested that both industrialists and their employees were the victims of a surprise attempt by Cape Town and government interests to introduce searching and denied that either he or his fellow directors wanted to search workers. At the same meeting Moering, together with R. English, a director of the Kimberley Central Company, stressed that employers would never meet with skilled workers and overseers at the same time but would only negotiate with them separately. While expressing sympathy for the plight of skilled workers, Moering and English argued that overseers had no legitimate grievance whatsoever. With his "friendly" approach not having much impact on his audience, Moering next threatened the skilled workers with the loss of their jobs. He told them that since Kimberley was such a small society with limited white labor needs it would be very easy to break a strike, especially through the importation of scab labor. As he noted, "If they [employers] could not get British workers they would have to get somebody else," meaning by the latter black or foreign men. Yet despite such threats, the strikers refused to go back to work.[83]

79. *Ibid.*, 20 October 1883. See chapt. 3 for a description of the actions taken by black strikers.
80. *Ibid.*, 16 October 1883.
81. Smithers, *March Hare*, pp. 135–36.
82. *Dutoitspan Herald*, 16 October 1883; *Daily Independent*, 16, 17 October 1883; *Diamond Fields Advertiser*, 16 October 1883.
83. *Diamond Fields Advertiser*, 15 October 1883.

The actions of the employers were no more effective than the arguments of Moering and English. They could not find any scab labor in the town, since all white as well as most black workers supported the strike, and as the railway did not yet reach Kimberley it was no easy matter to bring in men from outside at short notice. And though the strikers were united the employers were not. Some argued for a hardline policy that would crush the strikers even if it took several months. Others considered that a self-defeating proposal, in that most companies could not afford to stop working for one week let alone six months. Nor did all employers have an antagonistic attitude toward their workers. One of them, a Mr. McFarland, expressed the view that it was unfair to force past claim holders, who he believed constituted a majority of the strikers, to undergo the degradation of body searches just because they had lost out in the quest for fortune.[84]

Eventually employers and white workers reached a compromise. White employees agreed to accept two of the searching regulations that were also applied to black workers; they would pass through the searching houses, although ones separate from those used by blacks, and they would wear a uniform—"Mechanics to wear a complete serge suit—Overseers to wear [a] serge coat with Bedford cord trousers" (not exactly what they had hoped for but certainly far better than the mealie sacks that blacks were meant to wear). For their part, the employers agreed that the searching of whites would be largely a formality, with no body examination of any kind.[85]

Neither side was particularly happy with the compromise. The two leaders of the white strikers, William Egglestone and Joseph Wearne, both skilled workers, argued that it was the best deal that could be won in a difficult situation. Egglestone claimed that he did not object to searching itself but only to "rough searching." Wearne noted that at least the men could have their uniforms made to measure.[86] On the other hand, at least one overseer expressed considerable bitterness at the deal that had been struck. In a letter to a newspaper he argued that the new regulations removed the over-

84. *Daily Independent*, 18 October 1883.

85. *Ibid.*, 18, 19 October 1883; reports of a meeting of employers and employees, 30 October 1883, 11 March 1884, minute book, September 1882–January 1890, KMB, DBA.

86. *Daily Independent*, 19 October 1883.

seers from a position of trust and placed them alongside the laborers. Overseers were, he noted, to be treated much as blacks already were: uniformed, assumed to be thieves, and to have these implications of criminality physically reinforced by a twice-daily examination.[87] For overseers, any form of searching meant a weakening of their position relative to black workers and to white employers.

Skilled workers did not take the suggestions of distrust quite so seriously. Their jobs depended on their mechanical skill, not on their reputation. So long as searching was cursory, and the uniform not degrading, they were prepared to accept the new regulations in the belief that enforcement would have little practical effect on their working lives.

These differences in attitude created a basic weakness for any form of white worker unity. Although both skilled workers and overseers had joined together in strike action, the dominant role had been played by the former, and the final compromise reflected their particular concerns. Also, neither skilled men nor overseers conceived of a white working class, much less one that included blacks. The only union established, the Artisans' and Engine Drivers' Protection Society, was for skilled workers alone; it did not make provision for overseers as members.

The employers were also dissatisfied with the compromise. Limited searching had not been very productive in the past, and they remained certain that theft was severely reducing profits. They had managed to extend the system in part to skilled workers and to get all workers to wear a uniform, and that was a mark of some success. Yet industrialists had assumed that, given the generally depressed condition of the white labor market, they should have been able to extract much greater concessions from their workers.

In many ways the key issue in this struggle, for white workers and industrialists alike, was the role of black labor. The success or failure of white strike action was largely dependent on the mobilization of black workers, for only with their support could all work in the mines be effectively brought to a halt. Yet this alliance of convenience reflected no identification of interests by whites with blacks. The latter could make or break the whites' strike, but they were not regarded as fellow workers.

87. *Ibid.*, 23 November 1883.

Industrialists feared the potential strength of an alliance of black and white workers. During the strike, one employer had pressed for the absolute crushing of the strikers on the grounds that if the whites won their demands then the blacks would be sure to push for the same conditions.[88] After the strike, a director of the De Beers Mining Company reported to his shareholders that the employers had been forced to stop short in their demands for fear that the black laborers, without work during an extended strike, would leave the diamond fields. Since it would have taken several months to rebuild the work force, production in the mines would have been halted for a financially crippling period.[89]

In short, the searching struggle raised two problems for industrialists beyond the immediate difficulties of limiting theft and cutting costs. First, they faced a white work force that, given basic internal weaknesses, was still much more united and conscious of having interests antagonistic to those of capitalists than had ever existed in the past. Second, the problem of controlling black labor, and preventing white workers from using blacks to further their own interests, had taken on compelling significance.

The growing concern of mining capitalists at the developing strength of white labor was reflected in the political platforms adopted by two of their number in the parliamentary election campaign of February 1884. C. D. Rudd of the De Beers Company and R. English of the Kimberley Central Company, standing for Parliament at a time when the searching issue was fresh in everyone's mind, publicly placed themselves on the side of white workers. Rudd spoke at campaign meetings of his personal experiences as an overseer and claimed that he had never allowed himself to be strip searched.[90] English, who stated in public that he was running as an independent candidate but was in fact supported by a secret grant of £1,500 from his company, also proclaimed his support for the position of white workingmen, emphasizing (much as Moering had done earlier) that employers and their white employees were essentially "friends" who had to remain allied for their mutual economic well-being against "Kafir thieves."[91] This was all quite a

88. *Ibid.*

89. F. S. P. Stow, quoted in the *De Beers Mining Company Annual Report for 1884*, p. 9, SAL.

90. *Dutoitspan Herald*, 31 January 1884. Rudd had not been employed as an overseer but had supervised blacks working on his claims.

91. *Daily Independent*, 5, 31 January, 2, 7, 9, 12 February 1884.

turnabout for these two men who, only five months previously, had been among the leaders of the industrialists in calling for the strict enforcement of the searching regulations. Yet, for Rudd at least, appealing for the support of white voters was a successful policy: he was elected to Parliament with the assistance of the Artisans' and Engine Drivers' Protection Society.[92]

One month after the election, however, Rudd and English along with their fellow industrialists adopted quite a different approach to labor relations. In early March the head of the detective department, John Fry, issued instructions to his searching officers that they examine the open mouths and boots of all white workers. These instructions were immediately enforced by the largest companies in the mines, the Kimberley Central (English's company), the De Beers (Rudd's), the French, and the Bultfontein.[93] Although Fry was a state servant, his immediate employers were the mining boards of the four mines that were controlled in turn by the representatives of these large companies. Therefore, while it appeared in public as though the state in the person of Fry was trying to enforce more stringent regulations, the mining companies were in fact responsible for the adoption of this new policy.

Skilled workers initially responded to this employer initiative by encouraging overseers to form a protection society of their own so that worker resistance could be strengthened and coordinated. At a mass meeting of white workers from the Dutoitspan and Bultfontein mines in early April, James Brown, the president of the Artisans' and Engine Drivers' Protection Society, called on the overseers to defend their rights and not permit employers to treat workingmen as "dogs" and "criminals." He appealed to their concern for their reputation, stating that every workingman on the diamond fields "had a character, and more than that, had a right to protect it. . . ." He added that no man could live or work in the mines without such a "character," yet some employers wished to treat the men "like fools, or thieves, more or less." Brown argued that only a strong union organized along the lines of the skilled workers' union could save the overseers from further degradation.[94]

William Egglestone supported Brown's argument. He added his

92. *Dutoitspan Herald*, 16 February 1884.

93. John Fry to Henry Tucker (secretary to the Board for the Protection of Mining Interests), 27 March 1884, letters received, LSAE, DBA.

94. *Dutoitspan Herald*, 5 April 1884.

belief that examination of the mouth and the boots was only the tip of the iceberg; later would come still more demands, until finally the men would have to strip naked like black laborers. Egglestone's speech to those assembled ended with a rhetorical flourish when he stated that he "would not submit to being searched, although he thought he was to be shot the next minute; he would rather say, 'Shoot me in my clothes' (loud and prolonged applause)."[95]

Six days later, on 8 April, a large meeting of overseers, after listening once again to James Brown, agreed to establish an Overseers' and Miners' Protection Association. It was modeled on the skilled workers' organization, with a weekly membership subscription, illness and unemployment benefits, and provision for the establishment of a strike fund.[96] Now all white workers in the mines had a union.

But just as the white workers organized their forces, so did the industrialists. In mid-April John Fry took steps in conjunction with his industrial employers to prepare for the eventuality of a strike and to determine what measures would be necessary to break it. Fry recommended that employers identify those workers, black and white, whom they regarded as "dependable" so that these men could be sworn in as special constables. On 19 April Fry, his preparations for a clash underway, brought matters to a head with the promulgation of new, and far stricter, searching regulations:

> 1. Instructions will be issued daily by the Searching Inspectors as to the proportion and rotation in which employees are to be searched.
> 2. Each employee selected shall at once fall out and remain in one position until the remainder have passed out of the house.
> 3. The search shall be conducted in the following manner:
>     (a). Hat or headgear, as well as hair to be examined.
>     (b). Mouth to be opened and examined.
>     (c). Coats and boots to be removed and laid on one side.
>     (d). The employee then being clothed in Trousers, Socks, Shirt, and under clothing, the Searcher shall proceed with flat hands to feel down the Shirt, Trousers, and Socks, making a thorough external search, and, should any protuberance, similar to that caused by a diamond, be felt, to remove that portion

95. *Ibid.*
96. *Daily Independent*, 9 April 1884.

of the clothes where it exists—Pocket of Trousers to be turned out.

(e). Coat and boots then to be carefully examined. Coats and Trousers not to contain more than one pocket each.

(f). Any motion, such as swallowing, or attempted concealment to be carefully noted—and reported to the Officer in charge who will act according to circumstances.

4. Searchers are warned that any remarks made by them to those they Search, or any behaviour of an aggravating or irritating nature, calculated to cause annoyance, will render them liable [to penalties]. . . .[97]

On 22 April members of the Artisans' and the Overseers' unions held a joint meeting to decide on a common program of action. They unanimously agreed to refuse to undergo any form of searching and to use the financial resources of their respective organizations to pay the legal costs of any of their members who might be prosecuted for resisting the searching law.[98] But although skilled workers and overseers were united in their opposition to the new regulations, they still retained their separate organizations.

When three days after this meeting the employees of the Kimberley Central, French, De Beers and Bultfontein companies refused to undergo the new searching procedures, they were dismissed by their employers. In response, the remaining white workers in the mines came out on strike. They were joined by most of the black mine workers. During the next few days, the white strikers held numerous meetings to coordinate their actions. In these meetings, largely organized by the skilled workers under the leadership of James Brown and William Egglestone, the strikers emphasized the need to oppose the degradation of their labor, to fight all attempts to reduce white workers to the level of blacks, and to make employers accept the position that all white workers occupied positions of trust and therefore should be treated as honest men.[99]

In addition to stating what they believed to be their rights (which were much the same as those that they had claimed in the past), speakers at these meetings for the first time clearly identified those whom they considered their enemies. Those identified as being

97. John Fry to Henry Tucker, 15 April 1884, with copy of regulations dated 19 April attached, letters received, LSAE, DBA.
98. *Daily Independent*, 23 April 1884.
99. *Ibid.*, 25, 29 April 1884.

particularly villainous included Cecil Rhodes of the De Beers Company and John X. Merriman, the Cape parliamentarian, who was involved in various mining enterprises. The strikers considered these men, along with some others, to be members of the "dynamite faction," a term that referred to those capitalists whose companies worked at great depths on a large-scale and thus had to do considerable blasting. All four companies enforcing the new regulations were members of that faction.[100]

One speaker at the strikers' meetings reversed the usual argument of employers that workers could not be trusted because they were all potential thieves and suggested that it was the capitalists who were the greatest thieves of all. Mr. Olsen, the speaker, explained his interpretation of the origins of the struggle between workers and their employers in the following words:

> [I]n the early days of the Fields a capitalist would arrive from Europe with a capital of £5, and after being here a little while would commence buying the claimholder's diamonds from the claimholder's boys [i.e., illegally]; in a year or two the capitalist would get the claimholder's claims out of him, when the unfortunate claimholder would be turned into an overseer. This had actually taken place, and now the grateful capitalist wanted to strip the overseer of his clothes as a wind up to the whole affair.[101]

In a further speech along the same lines, Olsen suggested that of the millions of pounds worth of diamonds supposedly stolen every year "Chairmen, Directors, and Secretaries of Companies got nine-tenths."[102]

Conflict between worker and employer finally erupted into violence on 29 April, when the strikers decided to force those companies that were still carrying on with limited work to halt all operations. Several hundred strikers, black and white, went first to the property of the Victoria Mining Company, the second-largest operation in the De Beers mine, and successfully demanded that all work stop. They next moved on to the Kimberley mine and approached the pumping gear of the Kimberley Central Company. This gear was on a site bounded by the properties of the Central

100. *Ibid.*, 24, 25, 29 April 1884.
101. *Ibid.*, 24 April 1884.
102. *Ibid.*, 29 April 1884.

and the French companies and was guarded by a strong force of police, detectives, and special constables, all of whom were armed. The strikers demanded that pumping of water from the mine cease. This demand was refused by the special constables, most of them members of the management of the mining companies, under the command of R. English. There are two versions of what happened next. The *Diamond Fields Advertiser,* which had taken a pro-employer position throughout the conflict, reported that the strikers, armed with pickhandles and other clubs, charged the men guarding the pumps and forced them to use their guns in self-defense. The *Daily Independent,* however, in an account that was largely corroborated by evidence given at a later inquest, claimed that two to five minutes after the strikers called for the pumping gear to cease operations the special constables fired without provocation into the assembled crowd. All reports did agree that neither the police nor the strikers fired any shots.[103]

Six of the strikers were killed and six injured by the firing. Philip Holmes, the leader of the crowd of strikers, was killed as he approached the pumping gear. The *Daily Independent* reported that he was shot through the head just after calling out "Don't fire on us. We are not come here to do any harm. Allow me to speak." Paul Roos, seventeen, was shot dead by a searcher. He was said to have been lying on the ground, looking for a stone to throw in self-defense, when he got a bullet in the head. Others killed included Alexander Vucinovich, a miner and blaster for the French Company, Frederick Pollett, an engine driver from the Dutoitspan mine, Joseph Sablach, an overseer for the French Company, and Louis Kettleson, who was identified neither by occupation nor nationality. William Egglestone's rhetoric of three weeks earlier had come true; at least the men were shot in their clothes.[104]

Initially, the shooting made the white strikers even more determined to continue their struggle. On the day following the incident there was a massive demonstration of worker solidarity when fifteen hundred to two thousand white workers marched through Kimber-

103. The report of the *Diamond Fields Advertiser* is used by Smalberger, "I.D.B. and the Mining Compound System," p. 409. See also the *Daily Independent,* 30 April 1884. For the evidence given at the inquest see 1/KIM 3/1/11 no. 105 1884, inquest into the death of Philip Henry Holmes.

104. *Daily Independent,* 30 April, 1 May 1884. See also the inquest evidence in 1/KIM 3/1/11 no. 105 1884.

ley in a funeral procession for their dead fellows.[105] During the following days the strikers held a number of meetings to plan further action. Brown and Egglestone once again dominated the proceedings, and in their speeches they expressed considerable bitterness toward their employers. Brown, for example, in calling for the continuation of the strike referred to the struggle as a "battle" and argued that victory was essential if workingmen did not want to have to "bow and cringe to a man simply because he was an employer of labour." Egglestone supported these sentiments further, arguing that if the white men did not stand up for their rights they would end up being treated as slaves.[106]

Yet worker unity soon crumbled, despite the provision of martyrs for the cause. Although the funeral procession had attracted the support of nearly all white mineworkers, the subsequent meetings had a steadily diminishing level of attendance; fifteen hundred men at a meeting on 3 May, only four hundred gathering three days later. By 7 May most of the strikers, black and white, had accepted the new searching provisions, returned to their jobs, and the mines were in full operation.[107]

Three factors accounted for this rapid breakdown in worker resistance. First, the industrialists identified themselves as the upholders of law and order, labeled their opponents thieves, and secured the full support of the state for their views. George Bottomley summed up the public position of his fellow industrialists when he claimed that the mining companies had no interest in enforcing the searching regulations and breaking the strike other than to ensure that "the law was maintained."[108] John X. Merriman applied much the same argument previously used against black workers—that they were all thieves—to white employees when he stated that the strike leaders were either IDBers themselves or the agents of such men. As he put it, the conflict represented not a legitimate labor dispute but rather "the final struggle of the IDB."[109] The Cape Pre-

105. *Daily Independent*, 1 May 1884.
106. *Ibid.*, 5 May 1884.
107. *Dutoitspan Herald*, 6, 8 May 1884.
108. *Daily Independent*, 8 May 1884. Compare this with the similar claims that had been made previously by Moering when the employers had tried to extend the searching regulation in September 1884.
109. Merriman to Captain C. Mills, 30 April 1884, in Phyllis Lewsen (ed.), *Selections from the Correspondence of J. X. Merriman* (Cape Town, 1960), I, p. 175. See also his speech to Parliament on the issue, *Debates*, 7: 1 (April, 1884): 38.

mier, Thomas Scanlen, had accepted this interpretation of the issues involved, believing even before the conflict had broken out that only "a thorough enforcement of these [searching] regulations" would eliminate the problem of theft in the diamond industry.[110]

Indeed, because of the official acceptance of such views, the state took a number of measures to quell the lawbreakers. Before the shootings of 30 April local officials led by E. A. Judge, who was civil commissioner and the senior civil servant in Kimberley, banded together to form a quasi–local government and assist the industrialists in keeping the mines working. Fearing the strength of the strikers, Judge telegraphed to Cape Town for troops.[111] Soldiers were not needed after the brutality of the shooting, however. Armed police, detectives, and special constables patrolled the town, breaking up any attempts at protest action taken by the strikers and protecting the properties of those companies that had restarted operations.[112] The police arrested a number of the strike leaders, including William Egglestone, and charged them with "riot and public violence."[113] By contrast, none of the special constables who had fired the fatal shots were charged with any crime. In fact, the court of inquest into the death of Holmes found that he and his fellow marchers had been killed while engaged in unlawful and riotous behavior.[114] By such measures, the strikers were effectively placed outside the law.[115]

The industrialists took additional measures of their own to break the strike. In the aftermath of the shooting they announced that those men who did not immediately return to work would never be rehired. They also forbade any of their employees from belonging to unions and blacklisted the strike leaders.[116] Such mea-

110. Minute from the prime minister to the governor, 26 April 1884, PMO 286 (87).

111. For the actions of the local administration see E. A. Judge, "An Autobiographical Account of His Life in South Africa by Edward Arthur Judge," unpublished MS, pp. 421–25, Judge Family Papers BC500 B67, UCT.

112. *Dutoitspan Herald*, 8 May 1884.

113. *Ibid.*, 8, 15 May 1884.

114. *Ibid.*, 8 May 1884.

115. At the conclusion of the strike the Kimberley Mining Board passed a resolution of thanks to the government "for its prompt and cordial assistance during the 'strike,' its protection of life and property, and the firm position taken up by it with regard to the Searching Rules and Regulations." See the "Resolution of the Kimberley Mining Board," 6 May 1884, minute book, KMB, DBA.

116. *Dutoitspan Herald*, 8 May 1884.

sures could be successfully enforced, since the Kimberley Central and French companies between them controlled over two-thirds of the jobs available to whites in the Kimberley mine, while the De Beers and Bultfontein companies each controlled half the jobs in their respective mines.[117] Furthermore, there was a surplus of whites in Kimberley—men such as Richard Richardson, who had come to the town in a desperate search for work and who would accept whatever terms the employers offered. As a result of these pressures the former strike leaders had to leave Kimberley if they were to have work, while neither the Artisans' nor the Overseers' associations survived beyond the end of May.

Yet the most important factor in the breaking of the strike was not the pressure of external forces but rather the lack of internal unity among the strikers. In part this lack of unity reflected the limited aims of the men. They were, after all, on the defensive, trying to prevent the imposition of new controls at a time when, with the industry still depressed and few jobs available, their economic position was very weak. Their defensive posture was clearly reflected in the last words uttered by Holmes—"We are not come here to do any harm"—and reiterated at almost the very same moment by James Brown, who, meeting elsewhere in the town with a group of employers, pleaded that "the masters would only help instead of trying to crush the men."[118]

But the crucial weakness was the continuing division between white and black workers. Overseers, concerned with such issues as "trust," "levelling," and "managerial status," and skilled workers, also determined to defend their particular job-related "rights," saw blacks as a weapon to be used against employers but not as an ally in a class struggle between capital and labor. They considered blacks as both different from and less than themselves, both racially and in terms of their respective places in production; blacks were neither managers nor skilled workers but laborers only. The white strike leaders believed that the blacks on strike had to be carefully and strictly controlled lest they carry the struggle farther than desirable. At demonstrations at the property of the Ne Plus Ultra Company, for example, when black strikers started to destroy buildings and machinery white strikers persuaded them to desist. Then again,

117. For a statistical breakdown by employer of the white work force in the mines see the *Daily Independent*, 16 October 1883.
118. *Daily Independent*, 30 April 1884.

when Holmes led his band of marchers to the Kimberley Central Company he asked one of his fellow white strikers, "Tell the niggers not to do anything. Keep them back, don't let them do any damage." Later in the day the blacks were told, "*Voetsak* [push off], we don't want you."[119] Such division in the work force ensured that the strike would fail in the face of the determined unity of employers and the state.

Paradoxically, Cecil Rhodes, soon to be the preeminent industrialist at the diamond fields, conjured up the image of a powerful black-white worker alliance and used it as a further weapon against the strikers. Appealing to his parliamentary colleagues not to investigate the shooting affray, he argued that the struggle in Kimberley was not between capital and labor, or among white men only, but rather "white men [and IDBers at that] supported by natives in a struggle against whites."[120] Rhodes' labeling of the white strikers as betrayers of their race, and his linking them with blacks as thieves, was clearly successful at the time; Parliament voted by a wide margin not to investigate. But his associations had long-term implications. Industrialists thereafter not only identified all opposition to their wishes as being criminally inspired, much as they had done in the past, but also portrayed any alliance between whites and blacks as a betrayal of racial responsibilities. Thus the work force was conscious of itself as divided by job and by race, and employers ensured that for whites this division was sanctioned by an ideology that equated respect for law and order with obeisance to industrialists and an acceptance of racial exclusiveness.

---

119. *Dutoitspan Herald*, 15 May 1884; *Daily Independent*, 1 May 1884.
120. *Debates* 7:1 (April, 1884): 36, 37. See also Rudd's speech along much the same lines to the House.

# Part Two: 1885–95

CHAPTER FIVE

# Economic Competition, Political Conflict and the Origins of Monopoly, 1885–88

From the beginning of diamond digging, people in Kimberley had struggled and competed against one another to make a profit. Their efforts led to increasing production, which rather than boosting gains had the opposite effect: in general, the more diamonds mined, the lower carat prices fell, and the more ephemeral profit became. During the 1870s smaller operations, unable to survive lowered profit margins, gave way to ever-larger businesses, as small claim holders were replaced by large individual capitalists, who were succeeded in turn by private companies and then by public joint stock operations. But these shakeouts failed to put the industry on a sound footing. Instead, the early 1880s saw perhaps the gravest crisis of all when in 1882 depression in the European diamond market nearly halved carat prices and sent one-third of Kimberley's companies to the wall. The 1882 crisis prompted a new round of competitive production, as each of the remaining large companies introduced measures to ensure its own survival. The companies instituted stricter and stricter controls over mine workers, further mechanized the labor process, and sought to consolidate operations into fewer and larger enterprises.

In the short term such innovations reduced real wages, increased productivity, and, assisted by technological difficulties in some of the mines, brought relative stability to the diamond market. In the long term, however, none of the companies achieved predominance in the market, leading to an escalating cycle of mutually destructive competition. By 1885 the industry was deep in crisis.

The innovations instituted in the workplace exacerbated conflict not only between capitalists and workers in the mines but also between industrialists and merchants in Kimberley and the Cape. Carat prices were at their lowest level ever, and profits meager. Continued competition in a situation in which the leading companies were all adopting the same measures with regard to the organization of labor and of mining threatened the industry with ever-present crises of overproduction. As one observer of the diamond industry, John X. Merriman, put matters in September 1885, "they [the mining companies] are collectively rushing on to ruin ... each one imagin[ing] that he will have the field to himself and will be the fittest that survives. . . ."[1]

But within three years of Merriman's dire warning the diamond industry had been consolidated into a single operation under the control of a giant corporation. The same men who ran this corporation exercised a commanding role in Kimberley and Cape politics, and profits poured from the mines into the pockets of these diamond magnates. This chapter examines the process by which the acceleration of competitive production resulted not in ruin but in the transformation of the diamond industry into a monopoly enterprise.

## COMPETITIVE PRODUCTION IN CRISIS: 1885-86

By 1885, the diamond-mining companies were striving frantically against one another to make a profit and to achieve predominance within the industry.[2] The three largest companies in the Kimberley mine—the Central, French, and Standard—were engaged in the costly procedure of changing to underground operations due to crippling problems with open-cast mining. Development work on shafts and tunnels, often poorly planned and executed, absorbed huge amounts of their capital and shifted labor from the more profitable digging of diamonds. The result in the short term was that the carat production of these companies fell precipitously, reaching its nadir in June 1885, when the Kimberley mine provided only one-fifth of the industry's total diamond output, compared with one-quarter at the beginning of the year and nearly one-half three years

1. Merriman to J. B. Currey, 4 September 1885, Lewsen, *The Correspondence of J. X. Merriman*, I, p. 200.
2. See also chapt. 1 for an introduction to the issues raised in this section.

earlier.[3] This decline in the Kimberley mine's output was offset at the industry level, however, by expanding production in the other mines. Ever mindful of the fact that if the companies in the Kimberley mine succeeded in putting their underground workings into full operation the rest of the mines would be put out of business, industrialists in De Beers, Dutoitspan, and Bultfontein sought to build up the value of their properties as quickly as possible. Such a strategy aimed at providing immediate profits at the expense of the Kimberley mine's difficulties and at ensuring that if an industrywide amalgamation scheme was floated (as many at the time expected) then the weaker mines would be incorporated with higher valuations for their properties than would have been the case earlier.

But rising output coupled with heavy working costs had a harsh impact on the industry's overall financial condition. Carat prices dropped to their lowest level ever, pulling down total revenues in turn. The Kimberley mine suffered most: without expanded output to compensate for lower prices, its revenue loss exceeded that of the other three mines combined.[4] The government, at the urging of the Standard Bank, introduced legislation imposing levies on all the companies in the Kimberley mine in order to resolve the £500,000 debt of the Kimberley Mining Board.[5] As a result of these developments, the Central Company ran at a loss for the first time in its history and (not for the first time) failed to pay a dividend, as did the French Company.[6] Financial matters in the other mines were little better, with the Dutoitspan companies producing diamonds at less than cost, and some of the largest companies in Bultfontein suspending operations in the latter half of 1885.[7]

Practically the only exception to this generally dismal picture was provided by the balance sheets of the De Beers Mining Company. De Beers doubled its output between 1884 and 1885, and this

3. For output figures see the Board for the Protection of Mining Interests, *Returns of Diamonds September 1st, 1882, to December 31st, 1885*, pp. 21–24.

4. *Ibid.*, pp. 20, 25.

5. Half-yearly report, general manager, Standard Bank, to London, 8 August 1885, pp. 49–50, GMO 3/1/18, SBA.

6. The Central Company had not paid a dividend since April 1883. See the Standard Bank's inspector's report, 22 December 1885, p. 92, INSP 1/1/86, SBA. On the French Company see the *Daily Independent*, 10 August 1886.

7. Half-yearly report, general manager, Standard Bank, to London, 8 August 1885, pp. 46–47, GMO 3/1/18, SBA.

increase, combined with a lowering of working costs and a rise in the number of carats found in each load excavated, enabled the company to pay a 12 percent dividend on 1885's operations.[8] De Beers' success did not, though, compensate for the weakness of the rest of the industry in the eyes of the investing public. Share prices, the clearest barometer of investor confidence, bottomed out in 1885 with, for example, Central scrip, which had a face value of £100 (and selling for upwards of £260 just a few years earlier), being quoted at £35, Griqualand West Mining Company (Dutoitspan mine) £10 scrip quoted at £1 10s., and even De Beers £10 shares going for £4.[9] Clearly, investors held the diamond industry in low esteem.

Lack of investor confidence had important ramifications for amalgamation, generally agreed upon as providing the only long-term solution for ever-decreasing profits. If local companies—whether in the Kimberley mine alone or throughout the diamond fields—were to combine into one business venture, they needed foreign capital to fund the takeovers (since the money markets of the Cape had been exhausted in the early 1880s), and that would be difficult to attract given the poor returns being posted.[10] Alternatively, the low value of the industry prevailing in 1885 meant it was quite possible that overseas speculators might step in and try to pick up mining properties at bargain prices. And that is exactly what happened in the final quarter of the year.[11]

C. J. Posno, a London-based speculator with large interests in the Dutoitspan and Bultfontein mines, in partnership with diamond merchants and Parisian bankers floated a scheme in Paris and London to take over the mines. Posno and his partners proposed the

8. See the table of statistics in Mitchell, *Diamonds and Gold*, p. 8.

9. James Henry, *The First Hundred Years of the Standard Bank* (London, 1963), p. 74n2. The share quotations are for December 1885.

10. On the need for foreign capital see Merriman to Lewis Mitchell (general manager of the Standard Bank), 18 January 1886, Merriman Papers, 1886/18a; on the decline in investments by local banks in the diamond industry see the *Daily Independent*, 6 July 1886; and on the desire of the largest of these banks to cut all financial ties with the industry see the report of the Standard Bank's inspector, 22 December 1885, p. 196, INSP 1/1/86, SBA, which included the line: "I cannot help thinking it will be a fortunate day when this Bank is quite clear of direct interests in the four diamond mines."

11. See the "Returns of Transfers of Shares," 1884–86, DOK 2/6, 2/7, 2/8, for evidence of the increasing interest that overseas speculators took in the industry in the mid-1880s.

formation of a new company, the Unified Diamond Mines Limited, that would acquire ownership of all the mines and work them as a single unit.[12] In return for handing over their properties, Kimberley's industrialists would receive scrip in the new company—with the £10,000,000 paper capital of the Unified (less 8 percent commission for the Paris bankers) allotted in equal portions among the four mines—but no cash.[13] For Posno and his partners the scheme promised, if successful, control of the industry at minimal cost. For his local supporters (Kimberley's banks and others with large sums of money tied up—often because of bad debts—in the three poorer mines, especially Dutoitspan and Bultfontein), it offered a realization of their assets before developments in the Kimberley mine could make them worthless. For the industry at large the scheme guaranteed, in Posno's words, termination of "the commercial crime of over-production. . . ."[14] But for those in Kimberley who considered their own properties and the entire industry much more valuable than Posno's offer suggested (primarily people with investments in the Kimberley and De Beers mines), and who wanted to keep control in their own hands, the Unified scheme was an unmitigated evil to be opposed at all costs.

Industrialists, whether for or against the Unified scheme, continued to pursue similar strategies in trying to shore up their financial position. The largest companies in the Kimberley mine, followed by the largest in the De Beers, increased the mechaniza-

12. On the origins of the scheme see the letters of Posno to Merriman, 11, 25 June 1885, Merriman Papers, 1885/194, 1885/200; Merriman to Currey, 4, 24 September 1885, and Merriman to Posno, 23 December 1885, Lewsen, *The Correspondence of J. X. Merriman*, I, pp. 199–202; and the *Daily Independent*, 2, 23, 28, 30 September, 14, 20 October 1885, 11 January 1886 (this issue includes a list of the Unified's directors).

13. For details on how the scheme was meant to work see the "Note upon the Scheme for the Purchase of the Diamond Mines of the Cape, which is the Object of the Company Called the Unified Diamond Mines Limited," London, 7 August 1885, and the "Report of the Committee of Valuation, Formed to Apportion £2,200,000 amongst the Proprietors of the Dutoitspan Mine," London, 7 August 1885, Merriman Papers, 1885/222a, 1885/237b.

14. Although supporting the Unified scheme, the Standard Bank's officers remained skeptical as to its chances of success. On these matters see the reports of the general manager, Standard Bank, to London, 6 February 1885, p. 40, GMO 3/1/17, and 8 February 1886, p. 50, GMO 3/1/19, that of the bank's inspector, 22 December 1885, pp. 211, 216, INSP 1/1/86, SBA; and also the *Daily Independent*, 20 February 1886. For Posno's statement see his letter to C. D. Rudd, 12 November 1885, Merriman Papers, 1885/250b.

tion of production as they concentrated operations underground and applied ever-stricter controls over mine workers with the widespread institution of closed compounding for blacks and the threat of "barracking" for whites.[15] Such measures enabled these companies to increase productivity and reduce working costs; developments that were reinforced by the opening in November of the Cape to Kimberley railway, which significantly lowered food and fuel prices.[16] The Central Company, in particular, had by December 1885 overcome many of the problems first encountered in changing to underground digging, and largely because of the Central's increased activities, monthly carat production in the Kimberley mine doubled between the middle and end of the year, productivity per man employed rose by one-third, and working costs per load excavated moved closer to 10s. than 20s.[17] Continued production difficulties and a large burden of debt prevented the Central from getting out of the red immediately, unlike the De Beers Mining and a number of other companies that reduced costs and increased output sufficiently to offset low carat prices and to report growing profits by the end of the year. But the Standard Bank's inspector believed that once underground operations could be worked at full steam the Central's success was "assured."[18]

15. On the expansion of deep-level digging and of compounding (introduced at the beginning of 1885 by the French and Central companies) see the "Report of the Inspector of Diamond Mines for the Year 1885," *CGHPP,* G40 1886, pp. 3–5, 9, 12–14; and on plans (initiated by the Central) to put all white workers into barracks see the minute book (directors' meetings), 3 November 1884–26 February 1885, pp. 68, 147, and the minute book (finance committee meetings), 6 February 1885–24 November 1885, 19 June 1885, KCDM, DBA.

16. On the impact of the railway see the reports of the inspector of diamond mines, *CGHPP,* G40 1886, p. 30; and of the general manager, Standard Bank, to London, 8 February 1886, pp. 46–47, GMO 3/1/19, 2 August 1886, p. 65, GMO 3/1/20, SBA.

17. For an overview of the Central's position, and that of other Kimberley mine companies, see the report of the general manager, Standard Bank, to London, 8 February 1886, pp. 47–48, GMO 3/1/19, SBA. For production statistics see the Board for the Protection of Mining Interests, *Returns of Diamonds September 1st, 1882, to December 31st, 1885,* p. 21; and the report of the inspector of diamond mines, *CGHPP,* G11 1890, pp. 36, 38.

18. The inspector did, however, remain somewhat skeptical as to the ability of the Central's management to succeed fully in implementing underground operations. See his report, 22 December 1885, pp. 92, 194–96, 209–11, 216, INSP 1/1/86, SBA. On the profits of De Beers Mining and other companies see, e.g., the *Daily Independent,* 3 October, 15 December 1885, 30 January 1886; and Mitchell, *Diamonds and Gold,* p. 8. The majority of companies on the diamond fields, however, did not pay dividends.

The improving returns encouraged the directors of the Kimberley Central and De Beers companies to undo the Unified scheme. The promoters of the Unified had stated that they would go ahead with their plans only if within six months of the scheme's public announcement they had received support from the owners of two-thirds in value of the properties in the four mines. The Kimberley Central's directors, convinced of the superiority of their own property, rejected the idea that the four mines were of equal value and refused to go along with the scheme. Cecil Rhodes and the directors of the De Beers Mining Company likewise repudiated the concept of equal value and rebuffed the Unified's local agents. With no hope of gaining the required two-thirds support, the Unified's promoters withdrew their offer at the end of February 1886.[19]

Although the measures adopted by the companies initially boosted the financial health of the industry and staved off an outside takeover, they had a deleterious effect on mine workers. Jobs remained few, with only half as many people at work in 1885 as at the beginning of the decade. Wages declined, for black and white employees alike. The rapid adoption of closed compounding throughout the diamond fields made white workers fear that similar controls would be extended to them. Worst of all, accident rates soared with the introduction of deep-level digging. In the Kimberley mine the death rate per thousand men employed rose from 4.4 in 1884 to 13.3 in 1885; in the De Beers mine (slower to go underground) it rose from 1.9 in 1885 to 17.7 in 1886.[20] Such conditions led one white mine worker to describe his position and that of his peers as no better than that of "slaves" and "beasts of burden."[21]

The same measures that had a harsh impact on the lives of mine workers also impinged on the business of Kimberley's merchants and shopkeepers. A contraction in the profits won and in the number of people employed by the mines from 1882 on caused commercial life to dwindle "down to very small figures" by the end of 1885. Closed compounding exacerbated matters by removing black work-

19. On local objections to the Unified scheme and its ultimate failure see the *Daily Independent*, 30 September, 10 October 1885, 12, 26 February 1886; the letters of Merriman to his wife in January and February 1886, reprinted in Lewsen, *The Correspondence of J. X. Merriman*, I, pp. 206–09; and the minutes of a meeting of De Beers' directors, 5 February 1886, xerox copy in the Smalberger Papers, UCT.

20. *CGHPP,* G11 1890, pp. 38, 39, 42.

21. See the letters of G. T. Greenwood in the *Diamond Fields Advertiser,* 20 October, 5 November 1885.

ers from the reach of shopkeepers (since company stores supplied the needs of compound inmates), while barracking threatened to do the same with white customers. Moreover, the prospect of eventual amalgamation promised an even more dismal future with the likelihood of a reduced work force, a smaller urban population, and the monopolizing of trade by company stores (which were supplied directly by overseas wholesalers).[22]

Merchants and shopkeepers had responded to earlier actions of the industrialists that they felt harmed local commerce by holding public protest meetings, petitioning government, forming "protection associations," and running candidates for political office.[23] Indeed, Kimberley's four parliamentary seats had gone in the 1884 election to men who claimed to represent the "commercial interest." One of the successful candidates, C. D. Rudd, adopted a rather ambivalent platform and later claimed that he had stood for Parliament in 1884 solely to protect the industry's interests with regard to compounding, liquor prohibition, and the strict enforcement of the trapping law. But the others unequivocally espoused such anti-industry policies as repeal of the Diamond Trade Act and a return to free trade in diamonds, prohibition of closed compounding, accident compensation for injured mine workers, introduction of taxation on the industry, and (a minority view) government purchase of the mines so that they could be worked to the advantage of the whole community and not just a few industrialists.[24] These candidates had won with the electoral support of white mine workers. Because practically all white mine workers, of whom there were twelve hundred in 1884 and fifteen hundred in 1886, met the minimum franchise qualifications—to be a male British subject, resident at the diamond fields for at least six months, and to be either a claim

22. On dwindling trade see the reports of the general manager, Standard Bank, to London, 6 February 1884, p. 26, GMO 3/1/16, 9 August 1884, p. 41, GMO 3/1/17, and that of the Standard Bank's inspector, 22 December 1885, pp. 207, 215, 217, INSP 1/1/86, SBA. One local Anglican missionary, the Reverend George Mitchell, noted in his quarterly report to his superiors that Kimberley as a whole was "contracting," its population "diminishing," and a "gloom generally gathering." See his "Report for the Quarter Ending 31 March 1886," *Annual Reports, 1886*, p. 302, USPG.

23. The merchants objected in particular to the prohibition of free trade in diamonds, which they felt excluded them from sharing in the profits of the industry, and to any attempt to compound mine workers and thus limit their access to their main customers.

24. For details on the early political activities of merchants and on Rudd's ambivalence, see my dissertation, "The Making of a Monopoly," pp. 248–51.

holder or in possession of immovable property worth £25 or in receipt of at least £100 per annum in wages—and made up the largest
block of voters in Kimberley, they could determine local political
success or failure.[25]

The decline of conditions in the workplace and in business
pushed mine workers and commercial people closer together and
intensified their criticisms of the mining industry. At a public meeting in January 1886, for example, speakers condemned the Unified
scheme (at the time not yet undone) because it would lead to a
takeover of the mines by foreign capitalists, to the institution of
measures to produce "the greatest amount of profit at the smallest
possible expense," and, inevitably, to fewer jobs and less trade. The
only solution, argued one speaker, was for government intervention
to force working of the mines and to enact accident compensation
legislation because industrialists could not be trusted to work in
the community's interest.[26]

Such criticism could have been shrugged off by Kimberley's
industrialists had significant changes not already taken place in the
distribution of political power in the Cape. Before 1884's election,
industrialists had exercised considerable political influence in Kimberley and in the Cape. Cecil Rhodes and J. B. Robinson (the latter
being one of the largest holders of mining scrip on the diamond
fields) had won two of Griqualand West's three parliamentary seats
in 1881 and thereafter strongly argued the case of the diamond
industry in Cape Town.[27] They had been extremely successful in
getting legislative support to limit participation in diamond trading (the Diamond Trade Act), and government help in disciplining
mine workers (through the pass laws, searching regulations, and
the breaking of the 1884 white workers' strike). They had also persuaded their parliamentary colleagues not to tax the diamond industry, despite the fact that it was easily the largest business in the
colony and despite massive government deficits. In early 1884, for
example, with a £675,000 deficit looming and total debts of
£20,000,000, the Cape Parliament (in which Rhodes held the posi-

25. Since less than half of the nearly five thousand people on the electoral
register voted in 1884, mine workers had a dominant role to play. For the numbers
voting in 1884 see the *Blue Book for the Colony of the Cape of Good Hope, 1885*, p. 282.

26. *Daily Independent*, 30 January 1886.

27. Two of Griqualand West's seats were in Kimberley (Robinson held one of
these until 1884), and one at Barkly West (the river diggings, held by Rhodes). In
1884, Kimberley's seats were doubled, giving Griqualand West five in all.

tion of treasurer from March to May 1884) levied additional taxes on brandy and wine farmers (the people suffering the most from a colonywide depression) and on the miniscule copper-mining industry but left the diamond industry untouched.[28]

The March 1884 election changed the balance of power. Candidates claiming to represent the interests of merchants and mine workers swept the board in Kimberley, although Rhodes kept his seat in Barkly West. Dutch-speaking farmers in the Cape, who had been hit the hardest by the depression that afflicted the colony throughout the early 1880s, turned to political action for solutions to their economic difficulties and won just under half the seats in the new Parliament.[29] Although not a majority in the House, these Boer parliamentarians, organized into the Cape's first political party, the Afrikaner Bond, under the leadership of Jan Hofmeyr, were strong enough to put the Cape merchant-dominated ministry of Thomas Scanlen out of office in May 1884 when it did not abide by the wishes of the brandy farmers on an agricultural issue, and they formed a new administration with their own candidate, Thomas Upington, as premier.[30]

Upington had little sympathy for Kimberley's industrialists. As a prominent member of the Cape liberal establishment, he had long criticized the inhuman ways in which mining employers treated their black workers and had strongly opposed government support for the shooting of white strikers in April 1884.[31] As a lawyer he had condemned the Diamond Trade Act for its overthrow of such tenets of British legal practice as the presumption of innocence until guilt

28. For Rhodes' views on taxation see his parliamentary speeches of 1 August 1883 and 9 June 1884, reprinted in "Vindex" (F. Vershoyle), *Cecil Rhodes: His Political Life and Speeches, 1881–1900* (London, 1900), pp. 53–59, 75–91. See also the speech of Gordon Sprigg, *Debates*, 7:1 (May, 1884): 65–76; and J. H. Hofmeyr, *The Life of Jan Hendrik Hofmeyr (Onze Jan)* (Cape Town, 1913), pp. 263–64, 280.

29. On economic problems in the agricultural districts of the Cape see T. R. H. Davenport, *The Afrikaner Bond: The History of a South African Political Party, 1880–1911* (Cape Town, 1966), pp. 95–98.

30. On the rise of the *bond* see Hofmeyr, *The Life of Hofmeyr*, pp. 210, 243, 245, 247; Davenport, *The Afrikaner Bond*, pp. 89–90; Phyllis Lewsen, *John X. Merriman: Paradoxical South African Statesman* (New Haven, 1982), p. 110. Hofmeyr did not take the premiership himself on the grounds of ill health and the fear that a Boer as head of government would exacerbate unnecessarily the existing antagonism between Dutch and English speakers.

31. For Upington's view on the shooting see the *Debates*, 7:1 (May, 1884): 37–38.

was proven and the right to trial by a jury of one's peers. As a member of Parliament for an agricultural district in the eastern Cape and dependent on the support of the *bond* for his ministry's retention of power, he believed that the state should aid farmers and others in the colony by extracting more revenue from the single relatively prosperous sector of the economy—diamond mining.[32]

Once in power, Upington gave practical effect to his objections to Kimberley's industrialists. He refused their constant requests that the provisions of the Diamond Trade Act be extended to the entire Cape Colony rather than be restricted to Griqualand West. He declared that the industry's supposedly representative body, the Board for the Protection of Mining Interests, was in reality the tool of J. B. Robinson and suggested that its members should be chosen by Parliament and not elected by claim holders and company directors. And in order to augment government revenues in 1886 he raised railage rates and thereby put back up the price of fuel and foodstuffs in Kimberley. Most threatening of all, he proposed the introduction of workers' compensation legislation and considered imposing some form of direct taxation on the industry. John X. Merriman believed that Upington was trying to draw "a distinction between the mercantile [Merriman included the mining industry in this sector] & the farming community and to be trying to teach the latter that their advantage lies in crushing the former as far as possible."[33]

By the beginning of 1886, competition within the diamond industry—and the stakes involved—were rising, while relations among industrialists, mine workers, Kimberley's merchants, the Cape government, and overseas speculators were worsening. The specter of overproduction remained ever-present, although diamond prices were going up (buoyed by an improving European economy), shares were attracting more buyers (expecting to make

32. Upington only took up the latter position—taxation of the diamond industry—in 1885. Although he represented Caledon, an important grain-producing area, he did not believe that the farming community should be exempted from taxation. For biographical details see W. J. de Kock and D. W. Kruger (eds.), *Dictionary of South African Biography* (Cape Town, 1972), II, pp. 758–59; and for a critical assessment of his ministry, Lewsen, *John X. Merriman*, pp. 121–22.

33. Merriman to Currey, 24 March 1886, Merriman Papers, Letters to J. B. Currey. See also the *Debates*, 7:2 (May, 1885): 32–33; "Report of the Inspector of Diamond Mines for the Year 1885," *CGHPP*, G40 1886, p. 30; *Daily Independent*, 30 March, 3 April 1886. The Board for the Protection of Mining Interests had been formed in 1882 in reaction to merchant criticisms of the industry.

a quick profit if some amalgamation scheme went through), and dividends were increasing.[34] Cecil Rhodes, whose De Beers Mining Company had proven itself the most profitable operation on the diamond fields, proposed in mid-February 1886 an amalgamation scheme that would incorporate all the mines and would place control of the industry in his own hands.[35] Yet at the same time the Kimberley Central's underground operations were expanding, and as soon as they were worked to full capacity (possibly a matter of months) the impact on De Beers, Dutoitspan, and Bultfontein alike would be "disastrous."[36] Regardless of which company achieved control, however, political power had fallen into the hands of men unsympathetic to the pleading of industrialists for special treatment, suggesting that even if De Beers amalgamated the mines or the Kimberley Central triumphed, government intervention might make the whole exercise unprofitable.[37]

But amalgamation in some form clearly offered the only solution to the problems of competition. What was required of anyone who sought to be the amalgamator was the ability to deal not only with the economic issues involved but also with the political aspects. And few thus far had demonstrated that ability. Though George Bottomley, chairman of the Kimberley Central, had been politically active early in the 1880s, by 1885 he was an elderly man whose speculations in Central shares had practically bankrupted him, so that he was, in the words of the Standard Bank's inspector, "not capable of doing much."[38] J. B. Robinson had taken a leading role in politics, but by the end of 1885 he too was in serious financial

34. On diamond prices see the *Daily Independent*, 22 February 1886; on dividends, *ibid.*, 15 December 1885, 27 February 1886; and on shares, *ibid.*, 13 March 1886; and the half-yearly report of the general manager, Standard Bank, to London, 8 February 1886, p. 50, GMO 3/1/19, SBA.

35. For Rhodes' proposal see the minutes of a meeting of De Beers' directors, 5 February 1886, xerox copy in the Smalberger Papers, UCT; and the *Daily Independent*, 12 February 1886.

36. "Disastrous" is from the report of the Standard Bank's inspector, 22 December 1885, p. 209, INSP 1/1/86, SBA.

37. The *Daily Independent* editorialized that just at the very moment that "prosperity after a long eclipse . . . [was] again dawning on the Diamond Fields . . . [it was] already threatened by the Government. . . ." 1 April 1886.

38. See the inspector's reports, 31 December 1884, pp. 45, 287, and 22 December 1885, p. 41, INSP 1/1/86, SBA. Bottomley lost the chairmanship to Francis Baring-Gould in 1886.

difficulties.[39] Cecil Rhodes was the only major industrialist prominent in politics who was not mired in personal monetary problems.
In addition, he alone of his peers had come to the conclusion that
"the key to Cape politics" lay with the Afrikaner Bond and that it
was only by working with this organization that he could attain his
objectives in Kimberley.[40]

## THE POLITICAL CHALLENGE OF MERCHANTS
## AND MINE WORKERS: 1886

It was J. B. Robinson, however, who championed the cause of the
"mining interest" against that of the "commercial interest" (in the
terminology of the time) in a by-election fought in May 1886. The
most prominent of Kimberley's merchant parliamentarians (and
the most scathing of the industry's critics), George Garcia Wolf, had
died, and the contest for his seat provided an opportunity for industrialists to vie for political support. Robinson spoke out against
free trade in diamonds, arguing that a return to such a policy would
bankrupt half the companies in the mines and ensure foreign domination of the industry. On the issue of closed compounding he
struck a more conciliatory note, suggesting that industrialists had
no desire to harm merchants and were ready both to allow compound inmates out once a week to shop in the town and to pay
wages solely in cash and never in kind ("truck" as it was then
termed).[41] But he emphasized that by any reckoning Kimberley's
future depended on the prosperity of diamond mining, and this
meant that industrialists should decide what was good for the town.

Robinson's "commercial" opponent disagreed. J. J. O'Leary
was a shopkeeper who earlier had been a small claim holder and
one of the leaders of the 1875 Black Flag uprising. An outspoken
critic of the acquisition of the mining industry by large capitalists,

39. See Merriman's listing of Robinson's liabilities, quoted in Roberts, *The
Diamond Magnates*, p. 176.
40. The quotation, from a conversation between Rhodes and James Rose Innes
in 1885, is cited in Lewsen, *John X. Merriman*, p. 127. On Rhodes' early approaches
to the *bond* see *ibid.*, pp. 117, 126–27; Merriman to Currey, 24 September 1885, and
Merriman to Aggie (his wife), 16 January 1886, in Lewsen, *The Correspondence of
J. X. Merriman*, I, pp. 202, 205–06; Hofmeyr, *The Life of Jan Hofmeyr*, pp. 249–61;
Davenport, *The Afrikaner Bond*, pp. 89–94.
41. *Daily Independent*, 1 May 1886.

O'Leary disputed Robinson on every point. He supported free trade in diamonds as a measure essential to the rejuvenation of the urban economy. He opposed all forms of closed compounding, rejecting Robinson's proposed compromise as an unacceptable intrusion on the right of merchants to have free access to their customers. Furthermore, he argued that the consolidation of the mining companies into ever-larger combinations, and ultimately into a monopoly, was the worst fate that could befall Kimberley, since it would cut the work force and cripple mercantile trade while benefiting only a small number of local capitalists and foreign speculators. And he criticized the appalling death rates suffered by workers in the deep-level mines. To the consternation of Robinson and his supporters, O'Leary called for state intervention in the mining industry to prevent the takeover of the mines by foreigners and to enact laws holding employers responsible for mine safety and for the payment of accident compensation.[42]

O'Leary won the election easily, with the support of merchants and mine workers. The mercantile community was solidly behind him, and his candidacy was endorsed at public meetings by members of all three trade associations—the Chamber of Commerce (composed of wholesalers and large retail merchants), the Shopkeepers' Association (small retailers), and the Licensed Victuallers' Association (liquor dealers). The liquor dealers, who did much of their business with blacks, were particularly vehement in their opposition to the industrialists' policies of compounding and prohibition, and they called on all business people to join together in political action and so destroy the ability of mining companies to "rule . . . the roost" and "crush" the commercial sector, which they felt had been the case in the past. White mine workers, fearful of blacklisting, did not speak out openly, but they did give their votes to the candidate who spoke to their pressing concerns about mine safety. The election clearly sharpened the language of politics and demonstrated the ability of opponents of mining capital to retain electoral support in Kimberley.[43]

42. *Ibid.* Employers were not held responsible for safety in the workplace nor required by law to pay compensation to accident victims. Moreover, as the inspector of mines noted, the "majority of employers of labour in these mines look upon regulations for safety as mere harassing restrictions, and in some cases . . . consider such requirements as arbitrary and despotic and . . . unnecessary." W. T. Erskine to secretary for lands and mines, 9 April 1886, LND 1/220 (35/86).

43. *Daily Independent,* 4, 5, 7 May.

Kimberley's industrialists failed to exhibit the same unity of purpose as their opponents. Robinson himself was not a popular candidate. Widely disliked personally, he had also thrown himself wholeheartedly behind the Unified scheme and thereby alienated those people, such as the directors of the Kimberley Central and the De Beers Mining companies, who wished to keep control of the mines in Kimberley.[44] Yet, as Merriman noted, such division worked to the detriment of the industry as a whole, since by failing to unite behind Robinson Kimberley's mining capitalists lost any chance at winning political power.[45]

At much the same time that Robinson was going down to defeat in Kimberley, Cecil Rhodes was forging a political alliance with the Afrikaner Bond in Cape Town. Having courted the *bond* throughout 1885 over such issues as the acquisition of Bechuanaland and the limitation of the black franchise in the Cape, Rhodes redoubled his efforts in 1886 as the weakness of the industrialists' political position in Kimberley became apparent.[46] In early May (when O'Leary won the by-election), Rhodes along with just one other English-speaking member of Parliament provided the crucial votes that enabled the *bond* to repeal an economically crippling excise tax imposed two years earlier (at Rhodes' urging) on wine and brandy farmers. Jan Hofmeyr responded by calling on all members of the *bond* "not [to] forget, that they had been helped by . . . Mr Rhodes" and to regard such a man who reconciled the interests of English- and Dutch-speakers as their benefactor.[47]

The political contest shifted to Cape Town with O'Leary's arrival there after his Kimberley victory. O'Leary found that he and Upington agreed on the need for workmen's-compensation legislation. In the first session of Parliament following the Kimberley by-

44. Robinson's obituary in the *Cape Times*, 7 November 1929, quoted in Alan Jeeves, "The Control of Migratory Labour in the South African Gold Mines in the Era of Kruger and Milner," *Journal of Southern African Studies*, 2:1 (1975): 22, referred to "the loathsomeness of the thing that is the memory of Sir Joseph Robinson."

45. See Merriman to Currey, 24 March 1886, Merriman Papers, Letters to J. B. Currey. Merriman was somewhat biased in that he and Robinson had been close allies in the Unified scheme.

46. On Rhodes' early courting of the *bond* see Merriman's letters to Currey, 25 February 1885, and to his wife, 16 January 1886, in Lewsen, *The Correspondence of J. X. Merriman*, I, pp. 192–93, 205.

47. See Hofmeyr, *The Life of Hofmeyr*, pp. 280–81; and Lewsen, *John X. Merriman*, pp. 127–28.

election, Upington (with O'Leary's support) introduced a bill to hold diamond-mining employers responsible for all injuries caused by deficient equipment and negligent techniques, and to provide workmen's compensation ranging up to a maximum of three years of a man's wages. This was the first legislative measure ever introduced in the Cape Parliament that placed the responsibility for work safety and employee compensation squarely on the shoulders of the employer.[48]

Two of Kimberley's parliamentarians, C. D. Rudd and Cecil Rhodes, strongly criticized this proposal for state intervention. Rudd, who earlier had supported the idea of voluntary welfare societies paid for equally by workers and employers, totally rejected the idea that the state should in any way adjudicate relations between employers and their employees or that companies should be at all responsible for the negligent actions of their managerial staff.[49] In attacking the Upington-O'Leary bill, Rudd claimed that the proposed legislation would worsen the relations between men and their masters, since the latter, instead of voluntarily treating the injured "as they did at present . . . with generosity," would under compulsion adopt a strict interpretation of the law and pay the lowest possible benefits to accident victims. Rhodes, who argued against the bill with vehemence equal to that of his fellow De Beers Mining director, tried to secure the support of *bond* members by suggesting that farmers too would be held liable for all injuries suffered by their workers. The *bond* members, however, were not yet solidly allied with Rhodes, nor were they ready to abandon their premier on this issue, particularly after Upington assured Parliament that the legislation would only be enforced in Kimberley. Rhodes and Rudd lost the debate, and the bill passed all three parliamentary readings by overwhelming margins.[50]

Having defeated the industrialists on an issue of major concern to white mine workers, O'Leary next turned to one critical to com-

48. See the copy of the bill attached to Erskine to secretary for lands and mines, 9 April 1886, LND 1/220 (35/86).

49. White mine workers had established numerous mutual benefit societies to care for those of their number who were sick or injured. For details on these societies, see the *Daily Independent*, 20 August, 30 September, 25 October 1885; and the appendices to the "Report of the Select Committee on the Friendly Societies Act," *CGHPP*, A9 1889.

50. *Debates*, 7:3 (June, 1886): 348–49, 434–36, 441–43.

mercial people—closed compounding. In early June he proposed a legislative measure, the Labourers' Wages Regulation Bill, to prohibit the payment of "truck" wages in the mines and to stop the operation of company stores in the compounds. This bill challenged the very foundation of closed compounding, because without company stores the mining employers would have to release their black workers on a weekly if not daily basis to purchase foodstuffs and other goods, a practice that, despite Robinson's earlier promises to the contrary, had the support of none of the largest companies.[51]

Debate over the proposed legislation unleashed powerful emotions in Kimberley. At a Town Council meeting in Beaconsfield (a dormitory suburb of Kimberley located near the Dutoitspan and Bultfontein mines) held to discuss O'Leary's anti-compounding proposals, one councilor (a shopkeeper and small claim holder) blamed the ills of the community on "the Directors and those foreigners" who had "worked out the old diggers, and not satisfied with having taken their shares [in the mining companies] . . . wanted also to take away the living of the people" by using the truck system and closed compounds to destroy the commercial sector. Another councilor, also a shopkeeper, similarly identified foreign capitalists as the real enemy and argued that it was wrong that so few men should monopolize so much wealth; he suggested that some of the profits of the industry should be redistributed more widely in the local community. The council as a whole followed the lead of these two men in proclaiming its readiness to support the passage of any legislation limiting truck and compounding.[52]

In the course of the next few weeks division over the bill grew in Kimberley. Shopkeepers held several public meetings to explain their position and generate support. At one of these meetings in Beaconsfield, several speakers took up the earlier line of the liquor dealers and argued that the industrialists wanted to "crush" the commercial sector of the economy through, initially, closed compounding, and ultimately by the establishment of one giant "Syndicate." Speakers at other meetings emphasized the common interests that commercial people and white mine workers shared in opposing compounding. Graphic evidence of the success of the speakers in getting across their message came when one large

51. *Daily Independent*, 12 June 1886.
52. *Ibid.*, 27, 28 May, 3 June 1886.

crowd, including shopkeepers, white mine workers, and "coloured boys," burned J. B. Robinson in effigy.[53]

Yet the commercial sector was not completely united in support of O'Leary's bill. Members of the Chamber of Commerce announced that they accepted the argument of the mining companies that the "sole object" of closed compounding was "the better prevention of theft," and they agreed that only the elimination of IDB would return the diamond industry to profitability and thereby improve their own business. The chamber, which included in its membership men with financial interests in diamond mining and diamond-marketing firms, called on the government not to intervene in the regulation of the industry.[54]

Among mining employers, J. B. Robinson again took the lead in trying to coordinate their actions. At one meeting in early June of representatives of the mining companies, Robinson urged those assembled to form a strong organization to protect the interests of the industry. While denying that any employer paid his workers in truck, he asserted that those who supported O'Leary's bill were not legitimate businessmen but were either IDBers or supporters of the illegal trade, men whom he and other speakers dismissed as "unscrupulous dealers in liquor" and "evil disposed." Having labeled their mercantile opponents as criminals, much as they had done with black workers before, those at the meeting agreed to petition Parliament to reject O'Leary's bill and to send a deputation to Cape Town to argue their case, although they did not yet agree on the need to establish a formal organization as Robinson urged.[55]

At the same time that Robinson was marshaling support in Kimberley, Rhodes in Cape Town continued to strengthen his alliance with agricultural interests. He followed up his vote in support of Hofmeyr on the excise-tax issue with additional votes for *bond* causes: the stopping of Sunday trains; required religious teaching

53. *Ibid.*, 8, 10, 16 June 1886. The "coloured boys" were most likely Malays, Coloureds, and Indians who owned numerous small retail establishments in Kimberley.

54. *Ibid.*, 5 June 1886. See the issue of 8 June for the shopkeepers' argument that members of the chamber had large sums of money invested in the mining industry.

55. *Ibid.*, 12 June 1886. Besides Robinson, other prominent speakers at this meeting included Hinrichsen of the Victoria Company and Baring-Gould of the Kimberley Central. The Board for the Protection of Mining Interests still existed at this time but functioned more as an administrative body overseeing the operations of the detective department rather than as a lobbying organization.

in schools; increased irrigation measures; and, most important of all, support for import duties to protect Cape agricultural producers. As with the farmers, Rhodes' and the mining industry's economic interests lay in exports, not imports. And Rhodes, like Hofmeyr, believed that the consumer rather than the producer should be taxed. Therefore, he believed that diamond capitalists and farmers could find common cause in opposing export levies and taxation on production and should instead put the burden for generating state revenue on the merchants (the importers) and the workers (who made up the bulk of the consumers).[56]

Despite the heightened language of Kimberley politics, with its numerous references to "crushing," "foreigners," and "IDBers," representatives of the mercantile community and of the diamond industry met in Cape Town in mid-June and worked out a compromise on O'Leary's anticompounding bill. O'Leary, together with his fellow Kimberley parliamentarians, Moses Cornwall (a retailer and deputy sheriff) and George Goch (a large merchant with investments in mining companies), agreed to drop the original wording of the bill's clause prohibiting all company shops and to substitute a regulation allowing such shops, so long as they sold only "essential items" and so long as the profits from compound operations were spent on municipal or other public purposes. Rhodes, leading a delegation of mining-company directors, agreed in turn to a clause prohibiting the compounding of white men (unless the latter agreed voluntarily to the practice) and the sale of any goods to white employees.[57]

O'Leary and Rhodes justified their compromise in terms of political expedience. O'Leary, speaking to his supporters back in Kimberley, argued that the anticompound bill could not be enacted in a single parliamentary session and that in the meantime mining employers might well place all their workers in compounds and open company stores supplied with goods imported directly from overseas wholesalers, thereby destroying Kimberley's mercantile community in one blow and making the whole question of state intervention moot. He also pointed out that lack of unity among commercial men necessitated compromise. Rhodes, for his part, stressed the need for industrialists to show their readiness to give

56. See Michell, *The Life and Times of Rhodes,* I, pp. 99–100, 225–32, 237; Hofmeyr, *The Life of Hofmeyr,* pp. 279, 380–82; and Lewsen, *John X. Merriman,* p. 128.
57. *Daily Independent,* 19 June 1886.

ground on nonessential issues if they were not to alienate the members of the Cape Parliament.[58]

Compromises made in the give-and-take atmosphere of the Cape Parliament, however, had little appeal in sharply divided Kimberley. Shopkeepers were incensed that control of the compound trade should remain in the hands of the mining companies. As one of their number put matters, once the practice of company stores was legalized "for the nigger . . . [it] would [soon] become law for the white man" as well. Moreover, who was to decide which were essential items and which not? They wanted all compound shops prohibited. Many industrialists, some not doing so well out of mining as Rhodes, others claiming to be morally opposed to state intervention, were equally adamant in decrying the deal. In general, they felt that Rhodes had made an unnecessary and "ridiculous compromise" in renouncing projected compound profits for the public good, and stated that they would not accept, whether in principle or in practice, any legislative restriction on what they could sell to employees on company property.[59]

In the face of such discontent—their own and that of the merchants—industrialists in Kimberley, especially J. B. Robinson and a number of directors of the Kimberley Central, took steps to unify their forces and to disarm those of their commercial opponents. First, they established an organization to "protect and further all interests concerned with Diamond Mining," the Griqualand West Miners' Union. Having appropriated the terminology of workingmen's organizations, the industrialists next sought the parliamentary seat of the man most closely identified with the interests of white mine workers and small business people. In late June they brought a high-court action against O'Leary for having engaged in the common, but illegal, practice of "treating" prospective voters to drinks in hotel bars and succeeded in having his election overturned.[60]

58. On O'Leary's arguments see *ibid.*, 19 June, 2 July 1886. With regard to the lack of unity in the commercial sector, O'Leary felt that he could not count on such people as George Goch and other members of the Chamber of Commerce who apart from being merchants also had financial investments in mining companies. On Rhodes' maneuverings and the political credit that he won in the House see Merriman to Currey, 18 June 1886, Merriman Papers, Letters to J. B. Currey; and Upington's speech opposing government acquisition of the mines, *Debates*, 7:3 (June, 1886): 438.

59. *Daily Independent*, 19, 21 June, 24 July 1886; Merriman to Currey, 18 June 1886, Merriman Papers, Letters to J. B. Currey.

60. *Daily Independent*, 2, 3, 10 July, 5 August 1886.

Third, in preparation for the coming by-election, the Miners' Union arranged a series of meetings with the various commercial organizations and the two municipal councils on the diamond fields with the aim of reaching a new agreement with regard to compounding. The initial meeting took place between the Miners' Union and the Kimberley Chamber of Commerce. The Miners' Union representatives, including Rhodes (attracted perhaps by the newfound resolution of his peers) but not Robinson (who, faced by impending bankruptcy, had suddenly moved north to try his luck in the Rand gold fields), put forward an alternative to the O'Leary-Rhodes compromise (which Rhodes now repudiated): there should be no compounding of white men, and all supplies for company stores would have to be bought in Kimberley; in return there should be no restrictions on what goods could be sold in the compounds. Such a compromise was intended to appeal to the wholesalers and large retailers (who made up most of the chamber's membership), since they could bid for compound supply contracts and thus retain the bulk of their business.

While appealing to the economic sense of the members of the chamber, the union representatives were not loath to use the mailed fist to put across their points. Rhodes, for example, stated that the "mining interest" now had considerable parliamentary support and that O'Leary's bill had no chance of passage in its unmodified form. R. Hinrichsen and A. W. Davis, directors of two of the larger companies in the De Beers and Bultfontein mines (the Victoria and the Griqualand West respectively), were even more blunt. Hinrichsen pointed out that if the chamber did not agree to the union's proposals then the mining companies would cease buying goods locally and would, in addition, speed up the amalgamation process, eliminate all the smaller firms, and thus thoroughly and irreversibly deplete the population and the trade of the town. Davis stated that he would be "robbed of thousands of pounds" by IDBers if not allowed to compound his workers and, taking up some old arguments, described those attacking closed compounding as just "a few unprincipled vagabonds, and apologies for shopkeepers in the form of coolie shopkeepers."[61]

The Miners' Union's combination of economic carrots and sticks had its desired effect. The members of the chamber agreed

61. *Ibid.*, 15 July 1886.

to the new proposal, with the added proviso that no black labor contracts last for more than two months (so that there would be some regularity in men coming out of the compounds and shopping for additional goods in the town), and that no goods be sold to white workers by the company stores. Although one merchant claimed that he had been won over to the proposal because the "Mining Companies had right and justice on their side," the real attraction was that the large merchants would be able to retain much of their trade by supplying the compounds direct at the expense of the smaller shopkeepers, the liquor dealers, and the eating-house keepers.[62]

Representatives of the Miners' Union next held separate meetings with the Shopkeepers' Association, the Kimberley and Beaconsfield municipal councils, and the Licensed Victuallers' Association. Although they made much the same arguments as they had to the large merchants, the union representatives had considerably less success with these groups. The small shopkeepers felt that the Miners' Union–Chamber of Commerce compromise was not in the "small man's interest" and would lead to the monopolization of trade and the demise of the retailer. They continued to insist that black workers be permitted to leave the compounds to purchase basic living supplies on a regular, preferably weekly, basis. The councilors, most of whom were also small retailers or liquor dealers, made similar objections to the new proposal, as did the licensed victuallers, who in addition repudiated the claims of the industrialists that they sold adulterated alcohol and in turn charged the mining companies with attempting to establish liquor monopolies in the compounds.[63]

Still, there was considerable division among the small retailers and liquor dealers as to how they should deal with the industrialists. They were torn particularly between a recognition that their long-term survival depended on the continuing profitability of the mining industry and a desire for immediate alleviation of their economic ills. Most commercial men counseled caution in dealing with the industrialists, in the hope of securing a better compromise. A minority, however, posed the conflict in more rigid terms. C. A. Austen, a Beaconsfield councilor and a shopkeeper, blamed the industrialists for all the problems facing his community. In meeting

62. *Ibid.*, 17 July 1886.
63. *Ibid.*, 28 July 1886.

after meeting between the union and various groups of commercial men, Austen denounced the industrialists as nascent monopolists, callous manipulators of the IDB issue, and enemies of merchants and mine workers alike. But for the moment Austen swung few people to support his point of view. Although the shopkeepers and others did not accept the Miners' Union proposals, they did not reject them outright either. No immediate decision was necessary, however, since the House of Assembly held over a final decision on O'Leary's bill until the 1887 session.[64]

By late July 1886, with the conclusion of this series of meetings, a tentative realignment of forces had taken place. On one side were the industrialists, now allied with the wholesalers and large merchants. On the other side, and in a state of some disarray, were the small businessmen.

This realignment of forces was clearly demonstrated in the by-election held in late July. J. J. O'Leary stood again for the seat that he had been forced to vacate. He was supported, as before, by the shopkeepers, the liquor dealers, most of the Beaconsfield councilors (including Austen), the mayor of Kimberley and some of his councilors, and those parliamentarians who represented the "commercial interest." The preferred candidate of the Miners' Union was W. S. Lord, a Kimberley lawyer. Lord's published list of supporters included the names of the foremost industrialists and merchants of the town, a combination that Lord laid stress on when he stated that he was standing not to represent the Miners' Union alone but "to unite Mining and Mercantile Interests, to destroy antagonism between English and Dutch, and to raise and civilize the Native Races. . . ."[65]

Lord's stated desire for social unity meant support for policies dear to the hearts of industrialists. He believed that IDB was a real threat to the profitability of the industry and should be stamped out by whatever means were necessary; closed compounding seemed to him the best means to achieve that end. He believed that drunkenness was rampant among blacks and that prohibition should be introduced for Kimberley's black population. Yet he also recognized that if he was to be elected he needed the votes of white mine

64. *Ibid.*, 21 June, 10, 22, 23, 27 July 1886.

65. For O'Leary's list of supporters see the *Daily Independent*, 5 August 1886, and for Lord's supporters and his political views see the issues of 5, 7, 12 August 1886.

workers. Thus he too lined himself up alongside those who had already announced their opposition to the compulsory compounding of white men.[66]

O'Leary waged a bitter campaign against Lord and the Miners' Union, extending his criticism of the diamond industry to issues well beyond closed compounding. He attacked the pass laws, the very basis of black labor control, as a "great disgrace to a civilized community." He argued that most IDB was a figment of the imagination of industrialists and the detective department, a ruse to permit them to oppress commercial men and white mine workers. He opposed amalgamation and supported government purchase of the mines and the working of the industry in the interests of the wider community rather than in those of large capitalists and foreigners. And he recommended the imposition of taxation on the industry. Moreover, O'Leary and his supporters called on white mine workers to rally behind his candidacy. Austen raised the specter of closed compounding and the replacement of white men by black if workers did not stand united, pointing out that one company already employed Zulu overseers in place of white. O'Leary, Austen, and others also took up the issue of the ballot, arguing that if elected O'Leary would ensure that a secret ballot was introduced in Kimberley, since with the public ballot there had been too much influence exerted by mining employers over the political choices of their workers.[67]

O'Leary's representation of himself as the candidate of the small merchant and the mine worker produced victory. He beat Lord by a slightly smaller margin than that which he had secured over Robinson in May. Although more than half of O'Leary's votes came from electors in Kimberley itself, he was proportionately strongest in Beaconsfield (with 63 percent of the vote) and weakest in the De Beers ward (with only 30 percent), localities dominated respectively by small businessmen and industrialists. Despite political organization and the securing of merchant allies, Kimberley's industrialists had failed to make any significant gains in terms of voter support. With O'Leary back in Parliament and proclaiming that he intended to reintroduce the original uncompromised version of his compound legislation, the *Daily Independent* bitterly re-

66. *Ibid.*, 7 August 1886.
67. *Ibid.*, 10, 22, 27 July, 5, 10, 12, 16, 17 August 1886.

flected the industrialists' disappointment when it editorialized that the "forces of extremism" had triumphed.[68]

The key to electoral success in Kimberley lay with white mine workers. Indeed, mining employers had recognized that fact and had tried to win the allegiance of their men before the by-election defeats confirmed matters. Rudd, for example, in mid-July 1886, announced De Beers' intention to establish a voluntary sickness and accident benefit society and stressed that employer and employee shared a special relationship that should remain free from state interference. Rudd's ideas were taken further by W. T. Gaul, Kimberley's leading Anglican clergyman and a beneficiary of the industrialists' charity, who applauded the concept of voluntary association—because by emphasizing *"mutual respect, mutual responsibility, and mutual trust"* it harmonized "the relations between capital and labor" and ensured that all men learned "the principle of responsibility—the worker to his work, the employer to his workmen, and all to one another." Gaul denounced compulsory compensation legislation for setting "class against class" and as being better suited to the harsh factory environments of England and America. Mine workers, however, demonstrated their skepticism of such views at the polling booth.[69]

After the election, R. Hinrichsen followed up the arguments of Rudd and Gaul. Speaking at a ceremonial dinner of the Austrian Benefit and Protection Society (all of whose members were mine workers and many of them the Victoria Company's employees) held two days after O'Leary's victory, Hinrichsen alluded to the good feelings that he felt had always existed between mining employers and their white workers. He argued that the boss and the workers were all "working men together," the only difference being that he as a company director received his "wages" monthly while they received theirs weekly. Linking the future prosperity of the men with the profitability of the mining companies, he argued that the interests of labor would best be served by the success of industrial capital. And that success, he stressed, depended on the industrialists not being opposed in the policies they wanted to institute.[70]

Other industrialists and clergymen in Kimberley affirmed Rudd's, Gaul's, and Hinrichsen's emphasis on the need for employ-

68. *Ibid.*, 18 August 1886.
69. *Ibid.*, 16, 19, 24 July 1886.
70. *Ibid.*, 20 August 1886.

ees to work hard, stay away from sinful and expensive pleasures, and be loyal to employers. Numbers of them argued, in the weeks and months after O'Leary's reelection, that workingmen were degraded and led into vice by drink and impure thoughts, especially in a community with a distinct shortage of women, and were in need of uplifting. Supporters of the Salvation Army, for example, a body originally established in Kimberley by J. B. Robinson, sought to save women from prostitution by emphasizing the need for "purity" among white workingmen. In the same vein, members of the Diamond Fields Association for the Elevation of Manhood and Morality, an organization formed in late August 1886 by Kimberley clergymen with the encouragement of George Bottomley, directed their attentions at young white males with the aim of making them "think purely," "read purely," "talk purely," and "guard the honour of women." One member of the association suggested that young men could acquire this purity by marrying early, so as to save themselves from temptation, but added that in order to take such an expensive step they would have to practice thrift and economy. For those who could not afford marriage, the same speaker counseled that they make their jobs their "constant passion."[71]

Yet while employers voiced concern for their workers' welfare, they were instituting new policies in the deep-level mines that seriously threatened both the position of white miners and the safety of all employees. Competition between the mining companies, particularly the Kimberley Central and De Beers Mining, intensified throughout 1886 as each company sought to produce as many diamonds as possible. By the end of the year the Central had so expanded operations that it alone excavated more stones than either the Dutoitspan or the Bultfontein mines and nearly as many as the entire De Beers mine, an effort that boosted the Central's revenue but kept carat prices low. Rhodes, determined not to be put out of business by the Central, responded by reducing his complement of white workers and increasing that of black, working the De Beers Company's claims to the fullest extent possible, and practically doubling the amount of ground excavated from the mine. Mine workers paid a heavy toll for such returns, particularly in the De Beers mine where, according to the Standard Bank's inspector, operations were carried out with a "reckless disregard for human

71. *Ibid.*, 27 August, 16, 27 September, 1, 18 October, 11 November 1886.

life. . . ." By January 1887, with De Beers' black compounds grossly overcrowded and accidents multiplying, the death rate in the mine had risen to 150 per thousand men employed.[72]

Conditions also declined in the two poorest mines, where some companies began replacing their white employees with cheaper men, either blacks or imported workers. The Bultfontein Mining Company (the largest company in the Bultfontein mine), for example, employed whites in 1886 as managers, skilled workers, and head overseers only. The remainder of the company's work force, 850 out of a total of approximately 900 men, were black, including 60 Zulu guards (replacing white overseers) and sorters.[73] In March 1887, the *Daily Independent* reported a "new departure" even more ominous for white labor: one mining company was hiring "natives . . . to watch the white 'boss' [meaning the white employees], instead of the 'boss' watching the nigger." Later in the same year, the *Independent* reported that Joseph Mylchreest, the largest private claim holder in the Dutoitspan mine, had imported men from the Isle of Man to replace his regular white employees. The paper described the Manxmen as "very honest, hardworking, and very cheap."[74]

At the same time, control of Parliament fell into the hands of men apparently unsympathetic to mine workers, foreclosing any chance of legislative remedies for the workers' problems. An old friend and political ally of Rhodes, Gordon Sprigg, became premier when Upington, plagued by illness and debts, resigned in November 1886.[75] Rhodes cemented his alliance with Jan Hofmeyr by continuing to speak out in support of such *bond* causes as restriction of the black franchise. Hofmeyr rejected calls for the imposition of

72. For the quotation see the Standard Bank's inspector's report, 12 February 1887, p. 174, INSP 1/1/87, SBA. For output statistics see the Board for the Protection of Mining Interests, *Returns Showing Import of Diamonds into and Exports from Kimberley . . . for Year Ended December 31st, 1887* (Kimberley, 1888); and Mitchell, *Diamonds and Gold*, p. 8. For the changing ratio of white workers to black, from 1:5 in 1885 to 1:12 in 1886, see the reports of the inspector of diamond mines, *CGHPP*, G40, 1886, p. 40, G26 1887, p. 6, and G11 1890, p. 38. On the rising death rate, especially of black workers, see the reports of the protector of natives, *NABB*, G5 1886, p. 28, G6 1888, p. 16; and the *Daily Independent*, 10 February 1887.

73. See the *Daily Independent*, 10 July 1886, 3 June 1887; and the evidence of A. W. Davis, manager of the Bultfontein Mining Company Limited, printed in the "Report of the Commissioners Appointed to Inquire into and Report upon the Diamond Trade Act," *CGHPP*, G3 1888, pp. 130–31.

74. 23 March, 8 June 1887.

75. Hofmeyr, *The Life of Hofmeyr*, pp. 284–85.

taxation on diamond mining and on the issue of whether a secret ballot should be introduced for elections came down firmly on the side of the public ballot, arguing that farmers, like all employers, should be able to count on the votes of their employees.[76] The most striking example of Rhodes' parliamentary influence came in June 1887 when O'Leary reintroduced the Labourers' Wages Regulation Bill in its original uncompromised form. Unlike the 1886 debates on the bill, when Rhodes and Rudd spoke alone in opposition, large numbers of House members, many of whom had visited Kimberley at Rhodes' invitation and toured the compounds, argued against O'Leary. The legislation that the House finally passed at the end of July bore little relation to that introduced in early June. Gone were the prohibitions on company shops and the compounding of white workers. In their place were the provisions agreed upon in 1886 by the Miners' Union and the Kimberley Chamber of Commerce: all goods for the compound stores to be purchased from Kimberley wholesalers; all wages to be paid in cash; and an unwritten agreement to be undertaken that black contracts should not last for more than two months and that whites should not be compounded. Parliament also agreed in July, at the request of Rhodes, Baring-Gould, and others, to establish a commission to investigate the diamond industry and to determine the need for compounding. The membership of the commission was then packed with supporters of compounding.[77]

Unwritten agreements, however, offered no protection to white mine workers. Within a month of the passage of the new legislation, the De Beers Mining and Kimberley Central companies announced publicly their support for the introduction of some form of compounding for white workers. C. D. Rudd and William McHardy (the Kimberley Central's manager) argued that white miners should be "isolated" from the general population, with Rudd suggesting that they be placed in a "cantonment" (he did not like the word "com-

76. *Ibid.*, 314-15, 373-86. See also Rhodes' speech of June 1887 on the black franchise, published in "Vindex," *Cecil Rhodes*, p. 159. In this speech Rhodes said: "Treat the natives as a subject people as long as they continue in a state of barbarism and communal tenure; be the lords over them, and let them be a subject race, and keep the liquor from them."

77. See the *Debates*, 7:4 (June–July 1887): 27, 126–31, 146, 264–65, 285; *Daily Independent*, 30 June, 10, 23, 25 July, 24, 25 August 1887; "Vindex," *Cecil Rhodes*, pp. 167, 170; and Act 23 of 1887, Act to Prohibit the Payment of Wages of Artificers and Labourers in Goods, or Otherwise Than in the Current Coin of the Country.

pound" for whites) where the men would have "ample society and intercourse amongst themselves." Such isolation would then remove men from the temptations offered by IDBers as well as ensure that employers could keep an eye on their employees twenty-four hours a day.[78]

Despite Rhodes' success in Parliament in overcoming the political opposition of white mine workers, these men could still exercise some choice in the workplace, at least so long as mining companies competed against one another. Mine workers who feared death or compounding in the deep-level mines could always attempt to find a job in the open-cast mines; the pay was lower, but so too was the accident rate.[79] In addition, men could move north and try their luck on the newly developing gold fields of the Rand.

## IN PURSUIT OF AMALGAMATION: 1886–87

The answer to the industry's problems—workers who were not completely subordinate to their employers, and diamond prices that stayed low—lay as always in amalgamation, a fact recognized more clearly than ever in 1886–87 by the directors of the De Beers Mining and Kimberley Central companies. With regard to the problem of labor, C. D. Rudd and Francis Baring-Gould (chairman of the Central) argued that "the great object in amalgamating the mines" was to be able "to control the white employes." On the matter of prices, Rhodes believed that amalgamation would enable him to "place the diamond mining industry in the position it ought to occupy, that is, not at the mercy of the buyers, but the buyers under the control of the producers. . . ."[80]

Throughout 1886 and 1887, therefore, the De Beers and Kimberley Central companies raced to amalgamate their adjacent mines. The De Beers Company, in a relatively strong financial condition as a result of Rhodes' intensive digging operations, took an early lead, absorbing most of its smaller competitors by the final

78. For the views of Rudd, McHardy, and others on the issue of white compounding (for and against) see *CGHPP*, G3 1888, pp. 39, 40, 41, 42, 86, 90–91, 100–03, 107, 108, 132, 133.

79. For statistics on wage and accident rates see the "Report of the Inspector of Diamond Mines for the Year 1890," *CGHPP*, G11 1890, pp. 39, 42.

80. For the agreement of Rudd and Baring-Gould see their exchange in *CGHPP*, G3 1888, p. 102; for Rhodes' statement see the report of De Beers' annual meeting printed in the *Daily Independent*, 7 May 1887.

quarter of 1886.[81] Only one major competitor remained, Hinrichsen's Victoria Company, but speculation in the share market kept
pushing its price higher. To avoid paying more than he considered
the company worth, Rhodes drew on the financial assistance of the
London diamond merchant Jules Porges (and his local associate,
Alfred Beit) to buy up secretly in European share markets a majority holding in the Victoria. The success of this maneuver ensured
that by May 1887 Rhodes had practical control of the entire De
Beers mine.[82] Although a heavy burden of past debt retarded the
Kimberley Central's acquisition plans, this company too met with
considerable success.[83] Its chairman, Francis Baring-Gould, stated
in early June 1887 that negotiations were well underway for the
acquisition of a number of small competitors, while later in the
same month he announced that the Standard Company, the third-
largest operation in the mine, had agreed to amalgamate, thereby
giving the Central control of all but the French Company.[84]

Thus, by the middle of 1887 the future course of the diamond
industry hinged on the fate of the French Company. If the Kimberley
Central acquired the French as Baring-Gould hoped, then it could
expand output, push carat prices down to a level at which no other
company could make a profit, and thereby force the De Beers, Dutoitspan, and Bultfontein mines to close. But if De Beers got the
French, as Cecil Rhodes planned, then the Central's scheme for control of the entire Kimberley mine could be thwarted, an amalgamation of the four mines brought about, and all investments in the
diamond fields protected. As Rhodes later put matters, in determining what to do about the French he "had to choose between the

81. De Beers made a working profit of £310,596 and out of this paid dividends
amounting to £199,350 in the twelve months ending 30 March 1887. See the report
of the general manager, Standard Bank, to London, 2 August 1886, p. 65, GMO 3/1/
20, SBA; and the *Daily Independent*, 17 May 1887. On the company's acquisitions
see its amended articles of association, DOK 3/2.

82. Because of widespread speculation in Victoria shares, the bulk of which
were held in Europe, Rhodes still ended up paying more than he wanted to. See
Stow to Rhodes, 15 September 1887, Stow letter book, 26 September 1885–
12 October 1887, p. 437, Stow Papers; and the *Daily Independent*, 7 April, 3, 7 May
1887.

83. In June 1887, the Central reported a working profit (the first since the beginning of 1885) of £206,939 for the previous twelve months, only two-thirds that of
De Beers. Moreover, the Central, unlike De Beers, had several hundred thousand
pounds of debt. See the *Daily Independent*, 10 June 1887.

84. *Ibid.*, 25 February, 28 May, 10, 18 June 1887. See also the company's
amended articles of association, DOK 3/5.

ruin of the diamond industry [essentially meaning his mine] or the control of the Kimberley mine."[85]

Even before the final contest between the Kimberley Central and De Beers took place, however, the changing structure of financial holdings in the diamond share market tipped the balance of forces in Rhodes' favor. Heavy speculation in diamond shares, locally and overseas, had been fueled by the payment of large and regular dividends from early 1886 onward, as well as by heightened expectations of imminent amalgamation. These speculators bought not only into the stronger companies but also into the weaker ones, in anticipation of cleaning up when the former inevitably absorbed the latter.[86] Jules Porges, for example, primarily a diamond merchant and the founder and leading shareholder of the French Company, had large financial interests in Dutoitspan and Bultfontein companies, as did his local partner, Julius Wernher.[87] Such speculation could be very profitable in the booming share market of late 1886 and early 1887. Alfred Beit, a diamond merchant in Kimberley since the 1870s, doubled his own wealth when he cleared a profit of £100,000 on speculative purchases of Victoria shares while ostensibly aiding De Beers in its takeover of that company.[88] Barney Barnato, another long-time diamond merchant with investments in mining companies, made thousands of pounds when the Standard Company absorbed his largely defunct but potentially valuable Barnato Diamond Mining Company in early 1887 and even more when the Central took over the Standard soon after. Having acquired a huge shareholding in the Central as a result of this series of takeovers, Barnato speculated further in other companies and other mines, becoming one of the largest holders of mining scrip on the

85. For the quotation see the *Daily Independent*, 2 April 1888, and for earlier statements of Rhodes' plans see the issues of 10 April 1886, 7 May 1887.

86. On rising dividends see, e.g., the report of the general manager, Standard Bank, to London, 9 February 1887, p. 45, GMO 3/1/20, SBA. On the increasing amount of speculation see the *Daily Independent*, 7 May 1887; and the voluminous "Returns of Transfers of Shares," 1886–87, DOK 2/8, 2/9, 2/10, 2/11, 2/12, 2/13, 2/14, 2/15.

87. See the Standard Bank's inspector's reports, 29 September 1883, pp. 514, 548, 31 December 1884, p. 162, INSP 1/1/86, 12 February 1887, p. 92, INSP 1/1/87, SBA.

88. By January 1888, Beit was worth a quarter of a million pounds, quite an improvement on the £35,000 he had considered himself worth in December 1884. See *ibid.*, 31 December 1884, pp. 41, 162, INSP 1/1/86, 12 February 1887, p. 27, 21 January 1888, pp. 23, 25, INSP 1/1/87, SBA.

diamond fields.[89] By the latter half of 1887 local and foreign speculators held the bulk of Kimberley's shares.[90]

While potential amalgamation fueled share speculation, the
implementation of the Kimberley Central's plans would render
much diamond scrip valueless. The Central planned to buy up companies only in the Kimberley mine and to force the rest into bankruptcy. Baring-Gould had announced at his company's annual
meeting in June 1887 that he expected that in the future the Central
would make a working profit of 4 percent, enough to please the chairman but hardly satisfactory to speculators.[91] Rhodes' plans promised far better returns for the speculators, with the opportunity to
make money playing the market not only in Kimberley and De
Beers' shares but also in those of Dutoitspan and Bultfontein, which
could be picked up very cheaply.[92]

Rhodes made the first move, offering £950,000 (four-fifths in cash)
for the French Company at the beginning of August 1887.[93] Since
De Beers lacked the funds to make such an offer, Rhodes had visited
London in July and, with Beit's assistance, had secured the financial
backing of N. M. Rothschild and Sons. Rothschild's, a firm that had
attempted unsuccessfully to carry out an amalgamation scheme of
its own based on large holdings in the Dutoitspan and Bultfontein
mines in 1882, and an active speculator in diamond shares in 1886–
87, expected to make a quick profit of several hundred thousand
pounds on Rhodes' deal.[94] With the French Company's directors
apparently amenable to the deal, F. S. P. Stow, one of Rhodes' closest associates and a member of De Beers' Board, exulted that with
the company "practically in our hands" and having "the almighty

89. On Barnato's improving fortunes see the reports of the Standard Bank's
inspector, 31 December 1884, p. 37, 22 December 1885, p. 33, INSP 1/1/86,
12 February 1887, p. 26, 21 January 1888, p. 21, INSP 1/1/87, SBA.

90. See the "Returns of Transfers of Shares" referred to in note 86.

91. *Daily Independent*, 10 June 1887.

92. Dutoitspan and Bultfontein shares sold for a fraction of the price of shares
in the other mines. For some quotations see, e.g., the following reports of the general
manager, Standard Bank, to London, 2 August 1886, p. 62, 9 February 1887, p. 44,
GMO 3/1/20, 8 August 1887, p. 48, GMO 3/1/21, SBA.

93. See the letters of the general manager, Standard Bank, to London, 10, 17
August 1887, pp. 650, 667, GMO 3/1/21, SBA; and the copy of the agreement filed with
De Beers' articles of association, DOK 3/2.

94. On Rothschild's earlier activities in Kimberley see chapt. 1 and DOK
2/9, 2/13. On the 1887 deal for the financing of the French purchase, which guaranteed
Rothschild's at least £100,000 and promised much more, see the copy of the agreement in DOK 3/2.

Kimberley crowd by the throat . . . amalgamation of the two mines [was assured] as the Central is now bound *to come to us.*"[95]

Matters did not go quite as simply as Stow expected, however. Barnato, more interested in share speculation than in amalgamation, denounced Rhodes' offer at a public meeting and urged the owners of French shares to hold out for better terms.[96] Baring-Gould, refusing to accept defeat, began buying as many French shares as possible and in early September made a counteroffer of £1,300,000 for the company.[97] These moves propelled prices upward to such an extent that Rothschild's grew uneasy and advised Rhodes that they could not hope to purchase enough French shares to prevent a Central takeover.[98] Rhodes in turn feared that Rothschild's, having "a speculator's view . . . [rather than] an investor's," might decide to abandon him and "make half a million" profit by selling the shares already purchased on behalf of De Beers to the Central instead.[99] With so much uncertain, Rhodes' closest advisers counseled him throughout September to negotiate a settlement with the Central rather than enter a bidding war that De Beers might well win, though only at a huge cost. Rothschild's, for example, telegramed him: "If amalgamation not concluded now irritation will be so great that it will be put off indefinitely meanwhile diamond market ruined. French pretensions increased."[100]

Rhodes reached an agreement with the Central in early October, but on terms largely of his own making. The Central had hoped to raise the money for its French counteroffer by borrowing £1,500,000 from the Standard Bank. In the final week of September, however, the Standard's head office in London, believing that the Central had inadequate collateral, and going against the advice of

95. Stow to K. S. Caldecott, 4 August 1887, Stow letter book, 1885–87, p. 400, Stow Papers. The emphasis is in the original.

96. *Daily Independent*, 22 September 1887.

97. Stow to Caldecott, 18, 30 August 1887, Stow letter book, 1885–87, pp. 411, 419, Stow Papers; general manager, Standard Bank, to London, 14 September 1887, pp. 776–77, GMO 3/1/21, SBA.

98. Stow to Rhodes, 8, 15 September 1887, Stow letter book, 1885–87, pp. 427, 434; Rhodes to Stow, telegram, 22 September 1887; "Stow Memoir," typescript, p. 37, Stow Papers.

99. Rhodes to Stow, undated memorandum (c. mid-September 1887), Stow Papers, vol. 2.

100. Stow Papers, vol. 2. See also Stow to Rhodes, 8, 22, 27 September 1887, Stow letter book, 1885–87, pp. 427, 434, 439, 450–51; Carl Meyer to Stow, 8 September 1887, and Donald Currie to Stow, 9 September 1887, Stow Papers, vol. 2.

its Cape Town manager, refused to make the loan.[101] The tide quickly turned against the Central. Within a few days of the Standard's decision, Sir Donald Currie, the holder of a large block of shares in the Central, threw in his lot with De Beers.[102] By the first week of October, Stow was again in good form, writing that the "Central people have been very chirpy all along . . . [but now] find themselves . . . cornered." Since the Central clearly could not hope to take over the French, and any bidding war would be costly, Rhodes offered Baring-Gould a compromise settlement. De Beers would resell the French Company to the Central for £300,000 cash and 35,600 Central £10 shares—then quoted at three to five times their face value— thereby reinforcing public perceptions of the latter company's financial strength and making sure its share prices stayed high, if in return the Central would agree to amalgamate with De Beers on terms to be arranged in the future. Baring-Gould agreed verbally to the deal, as did Barnato and Beit, who were now the largest holders of Central and De Beers and very wealthy men because of their share speculations. Under the terms of this deal, amalgamation would be achieved without a drop in any company's share value, satisfying the industrialists and speculators alike. By the middle of October, with his immediate goal reached, Rhodes was ordering his overseas agents to buy up shares in Dutoitspan and Bultfontein as quickly as possible, to ensure that "no foreign vulture" stepped in and prevented him from obtaining control of all four mines.[103]

101. General manager, Standard Bank, to London, 14, 28 September 1887, pp. 777, 834–35, GMO 3/1/21, SBA.

102. Meyer to Stow, 3 October 1887, Stow Papers, vol. 2.

103. The general manager of the Standard Bank noted that the resale deal meant that the Central paid De Beers £950,000, the price De Beers had paid for the French, plus a bonus of £425,000 in cash and shares, making a total of £1,375,000. The final amount of the deal depended on the quoted price of Central shares; at three times face value, the lowest figure quoted in late 1887, the 35,600 shares De Beers received were worth more than £1,000,000. See the general manager's report to London, 5 October 1887, p. 860, GMO 3/1/21, SBA. On the Central's agreement to amalgamate and Barnato's willingness to work with Rhodes see also Stow to Caldecott, 3 October 1887. Stow letter book, 1885–87, p. 457, Stow Papers (quoted in the text); Rhodes to Stow, 22 October 1887, Stow Papers, vol. 2; Louis Goldschmidt to Merriman, 3 October 1887, Merriman Papers, 1887/203; Barnato to the directors of De Beers, 14 March 1888, Stow Papers, vol. 1; minutes of a meeting of De Beers' directors, 20 February 1889, "De Beers Extracts from Minutes," November 1888– December 1891, Stow Papers, vol. 1; "Stow Memoir," pp. 39–44, Stow Papers. For an attempt to demythologize the whole Barnato–Rhodes struggle see Robert Turrell, "Rhodes, De Beers, and Monopoly," *Journal of Imperial and Commonwealth History,* 10:3 (1982): 326–34.

But the October agreement did not bring about a complete amalgamation of the Kimberley and De Beers mines. Baring-Gould and Rhodes still needed to reach an accord as to the relative values of their respective mines, and that did not prove easy. Baring-Gould thought the Kimberley mine easily the most valuable and demanded that this be reflected in any settlement whereby shares in an expanded De Beers would be given in exchange for those in the Central. When Rhodes demurred and suggested that the shares be exchanged at par, Baring-Gould sailed to England in a vain attempt to persuade the Standard Bank to loan him money so that he could try to take over De Beers.[104] A share battle ensued, but for the Central rather than De Beers. Barnato and Beit, working on behalf of De Beers and for their own personal profit, joined with Rhodes in buying up Central stock, pushing share prices to record levels late in 1887 and early in the following year. By early March 1888 Rhodes, having spent £1,000,000 (most of it borrowed from Cape banks and from Beit and Porges), had acquired sufficient Central shares when added to those held by Barnato (who finally put in writing in mid-March his readiness to back Rhodes) to give De Beers control of the Kimberley mine.[105] Amalgamation, at least of the Kimberley and De Beers mines, was practically accomplished.

## COMBINING WEALTH AND POWER: 1888

In March 1888 Rhodes, together with Barnato, Beit, and Stow, incorporated a new company, De Beers Consolidated Mines Limited. Rhodes took this step because he considered the De Beers Mining Company's Trust Deed—which limited the activities of the company to the mining of diamonds—too restrictive. He wanted to reconstruct the diamond industry, to become involved in all manner of business ventures, and to expand northward beyond the borders of the Cape, and such activities could face legal challenge from discontented shareholders. The Trust Deed that Rhodes drew up for De Beers Consolidated permitted the new company to engage in any business enterprise, to annex land in any part of Africa, to gov-

104. General manager, Standard Bank, to London, 30 November 1887, p. 40, GMO 3/1/22, SBA.
105. See the letters of the general manager, Standard Bank, to London, 30 November 1887, p. 40, 18 January 1888, p. 191, 8 February 1888, p. 363, 7 March 1888, p. 475, GMO 3/1/22, SBA; the "Stow Memoir," pp. 60–62, 91, Stow Papers; and Rhodes' speech of 31 March 1887, reprinted in "Vindex," *Cecil Rhodes*, pp. 748–56.

ern foreign territories, and, if so desired, to maintain a standing
army in those territories. This new company would absorb all others on the diamond fields, account for two-thirds by value of the Cape
Colony's exports, and be the largest corporation on the continent.[106]

Rhodes believed that the control of a company "worth as much
as the balance of Africa" should be in the hands of four or five
wealthy men appointed to their positions for life; indeed, they
would be termed "Life Governors."[107] These people, he argued, having the biggest financial stakes in the industry, would be the most
determined in securing the greatest profits possible for the company
and thus for themselves. Being wealthy, they would not be so concerned with trying to gain short-term profits and would be more
likely to look to the long-term interests of the diamond industry.
And as prominent members of society they were likely to have the
political skills so necessary for running an industry in which profit
depended as much on government policies as on the organization
of production and marketing. As he put matters to the last annual
meeting of the De Beers Mining Company (before its absorption by
the Consolidated) in May 1888:

> We [mining men] have to deal with the political aspect of the
> question [of running an extractive industry], and the disposal
> and regulation of three or four millions [pounds] per annum.
> It [the company] might fall into the hands of Directors with
> small qualifications, who whilst nominally being in charge of
> the interests of the Company would only be looking out for their
> own personal advantage. I believe, for the protection of the in-
> dustry, that the number of four or five [life governors] with an
> enormous capital in it who are not allowed to speculate outside
> of it, except for the benefit of the Company, will be the best safe-
> guard we can get.[108]

Yet even wealthy men could not always be counted on to work
in the best interests of the firm, and for that reason Rhodes proposed
a generous package of financial benefits for those appointed to the
governorships. He had the trust deed of the Consolidated stipulate
that after the distribution of a 36-percent dividend (upped from 30
percent after objections from Rothschild's and other overseas inves-

106. See Rhodes' speech of 31 March 1887 reprinted in "Vindex," *Cecil Rhodes*,
pp. 778–79; and Williams, *Cecil Rhodes*, p. 104.
107. Rhodes to Stow, 19 April 1888, Stow Papers, vol. 2.
108. *Daily Independent*, 14 May 1888.

tors) the life governors together would be entitled to a quarter share of the remaining net profits.[109] Since the Kimberley Central had paid a dividend of 37 percent in 1887–88, and De Beers at the same time had paid out dividends and issued bonus shares equivalent in value to nearly 45 percent of its capital, Rhodes had good reason to expect that the life governors would do very well financially.[110]

As to who should be the life governors, Rhodes did not need to look beyond the founders of the Consolidated Company. He was clearly a very wealthy man himself and in his own eyes certainly the person most devoted to the interests of the company.[111] Barnato too was an obvious choice, being the largest shareholder on the diamond fields and claiming to be worth two million pounds.[112] Beit held large numbers of De Beers' shares, owned considerable investments in the Rand gold fields, and had just become a partner in Jules Porges' firm, thereby cementing his access to European money markets. Stow also was a large shareholder in De Beers, as well as being Rhodes' closest aide and his London representative in business dealings.[113] All became life governors of De Beers Consolidated in May 1888.

With wealthy men controlling the company, Rhodes next considered the question of political power. He expressed his views most clearly in a parliamentary speech in July objecting to O'Leary's introduction of a bill proposing the use of a secret ballot in Kimberley elections. Rhodes decried the bill as being unfair and "directed purely and simply against the mining community," and he

109. Rothschild's also objected to the concept of life governors, on the grounds that the scheme would unduly benefit a small number of people. Rhodes tried to eliminate this opposition by offering Lord Rothschild a life governorship; the offer was declined, although Rothschild did finally agree to the implementation of the scheme. See the considerable correspondence on this matter contained in the Stow Papers.

110. On the dividends of the Central and De Beers see the *Daily Independent*, 7 January, 31 March, 14 May 1888.

111. On Rhodes' investments see the report of the Standard Bank's inspector, 21 January 1888, p. 120, INSP 1/1/87, SBA.

112. On Barnato's claims and for listings of his shareholdings, see the reports of the Standard Bank's inspector (who thought a truer figure was £1,000,000), 21 January 1887, p. 21, INSP 1/1/87, 4 October 1890, p. 26, 3 October 1891, p. 22, INSP 1/1/88, and that of the general manager to London, 14 March 1888, p. 492, GMO 3/1/22, SBA.

113. On Beit's finances see *ibid.*, 27 July 1889, p. 28, INSP 1/1/87, SBA. Beit moved to London from 1889 onward. Stow's relations with Rhodes are well documented in the Stow Papers.

argued that it had no local support. Moreover, he stated that he would never dismiss an employee on the basis of the man's vote. At the same time, however, he stressed that three out of four of Kimberley's parliamentarians were merchants, that wine farmers had twenty-two members in the House, general farmers another twenty-two, and commercial men twenty-two or twenty-three, while the diamond mining industry had just one, Rudd. (Rhodes argued that he himself represented a farming district.) And yet the mining industry, Rhodes went on, accounted for two-thirds of the Cape's exports. "[W]ould . . . [it] be an unfair thing," he suggested, "if four men were to represent £4,000,000 [the annual value of diamond exports] when sixty-eight members of the House represent £2,000,000?" and added that he felt Parliament "require[d] the instruction and knowledge of members specially connected with the mining industry."[114] Clearly Rhodes had plans for the general election that year, when all four of Kimberley's parliamentary seats would be up for grabs.

Such a speech sounded particularly ominous in Kimberley, where matters were going from bad to worse for the industrialists' political opponents. By 1888, practically all black mine workers were housed in closed compounds and supplied by company stores.[115] This practice, the result of the previous year's compromise between the Miners' Union and the Chamber of Commerce, effectively cut out small retailers from much of Kimberley's commercial trade. While wholesalers and large retailers (often the same people) were doing quite well, small businessmen found it increasingly difficult to make ends meet.[116] And the completion of amalgamation promised worse times ahead.

The economic condition of white mine workers was also getting more difficult. The number of men employed in the mines dropped 13 percent between 1887 and 1888. Given that the size of the work force was already declining, Rhodes' proposal, made in his March 1888 speech, that the unprofitable mines be closed was particularly ominous. In 1888, Dutoitspan and Bultfontein employed 38 percent

114. *Daily Independent*, 25 July 1888; "Vindex," *Cecil Rhodes*, pp. 175–79.

115. "Report of the Inspector of Diamond Mines for the Year 1889," *CGHPP*, G11 1890, p. 26.

116. See the reports made by the Standard Bank's inspector, 12 February 1887, p. 175, 21 January 1888, p. 185, INSP 1/1/87, and the report of the general manager, 6 February 1888, pp. 54–55, GMO 3/1/22, SBA.

of the men working in the mines. Since Rhodes hoped to limit production and increase the level of mechanization in the Kimberley and De Beers mines, there would be no alternative employment for those who lost their jobs. Indeed, unemployment had already become serious by early June, when Rhodes put work in the Kimberley and De Beers mines on a half-time basis in an attempt to reduce the output of diamonds. Between eight hundred and one thousand mine workers, black and white, lost their jobs.[117]

Tensions arising from this combination of commercial decline and increasing unemployment, in the face of the wealth and power of industrial capital, erupted in a number of public demonstrations in Kimberley and Beaconsfield. On 4 June, just two days after the mass dismissal of mine workers, a twilight procession of the white unemployed, at the head of whom were some "coloured" men playing guitars, marched the half mile from Dutoitspan to Kimberley. The marchers pushed a cart containing an effigy of Rhodes. Coming to a halt outside the head office of the Consolidated Company, they ceremoniously burned the effigy with the following dedication:

> We will now commit to the flames the last mortal remains of Cecil John Rhodes, Amalgamator General, Diamond King and Monarch of De Beers but not of the Pan [Dutoitspan]. Thank God! And in doing so let us not forget to give three cheers for a traitor to his adopted country, a panderer to the selfish greed of a few purse-proud speculators, and a public pest. May the Lord perish him. Amen.[118]

A few days later another group of unemployed men marched through Dutoitspan and, in the market square, burned effigies of Rhodes' fellow directors, Barney Barnato, Alfred Beit, and C. E. Nind.[119] The protestors then posted a manifesto attacking the actions of those whom they identified as "speculative millionaires" in "shouldering out" the workingman from the mines. Apparently those at the meeting feared retribution, for they wore masks. At one stage some in the crowd reportedly called out, "Go it Jones" and,

117. General manager, Standard Bank, to London, 13 June 1888, p. 830, GMO 3/1/22, SBA; "Report of the Inspector of Diamond Mines for the Year 1889," *CGHPP,* G11 1890, p. 38. De Beers claimed the number was closer to 500. See William Pickering (acting secretary, De Beers) to Rhodes, 4 June 1888, Stow Papers, vol. 2.

118. *Daily Independent,* 5 June 1888.

119. The Consolidated Company had a board of directors of which the life governors were ex officio members.

"Go it Oddfellows Arms," suggesting that prominent roles were played by E. H. Jones, the mayor of Kimberley, a prominent critic of De Beers who owned considerable amounts of now vacant rental property and at least one of the friendly societies that white workers had first formed in the late 1870s to protect their interests.[120] Although not repeated in subsequent months, these demonstrations signaled heightened levels of antipathy toward Kimberley's wealthy industrialists among shopkeepers and the unemployed.

Yet this tension did not produce conflict between industrialists and white mine workers, largely because the latter were so dependent on the former for their livelihood. The extent of this dependency was clearly exhibited in early July 1888, when a fire of horrendous proportions broke out in the De Beers mine. Nearly one-third of the mine's work force was killed, most by asphyxiation, in a disaster that an official commission of enquiry determined had been caused largely by employer negligence.[121] Quite apart from the tragic consequences for those killed and for their dependents, the fire also exacerbated the economic pressures on all mine workers. Production was halted in the De Beers mine for at least two months, putting four hundred white employees and two thousand black temporarily out of work. There were no unemployment benefits for these men. In addition, within a few weeks of the De Beers fire the company stopped work on its properties in the Dutoitspan mine because of problems caused by the continued use of open-cast digging techniques. Another 380 white men and 2,500 black lost their jobs.[122]

Few of these men had the financial resources to survive long in Kimberley without work. The estates of the twenty-seven white men who died in the fire, most of them miners and thus the best-paid workers, clearly show the generally impoverished state of the white

120. *Daily Independent*, 12 June 1888. Jones, a member of the Chamber of Commerce, had been a strong opponent of the compromise reached between the chamber and the Miners' Union. Most of his capital was tied up in rental properties, and therefore he needed prosperous times to make a profit.

121. Two hundred and two men died in the fire. Such a high death toll was caused by a lack of emergency exits, large amounts of combustible materials left lying in the underground tunnels, and a refusal by De Beers' management to cease mining operations until eight hours after the fire started. See the "Report of the Commission of Inquiry into the Recent Disaster in De Beers' Mine," *CGHPP*, G66 1888.

122. *Diamond Fields Mail and Mining and Commercial Advertiser*, 15 August 1888. Operations also stopped temporarily in the Kimberley mine at approximately the same time due to a huge fall of reef.

work force. Only four of the men left any property, and that only amounted to a combined total of £337. The dependents of the remaining victims had to rely on De Beers' charity to tide them over. With such limited financial resources, and with no means of alternative employment in Kimberley, white mine workers had to rely for their very survival on the good offices of their employers.[123]

With the fire and the closing of two of the mines exacerbating the problems of commercial decline and high unemployment, Rhodes' political opponents were in a weakened state by the time of the Cape's general election in November 1888. Kimberley's Chamber of Commerce had largely faded from the scene, its members either securing relatively profitable compound supply contracts or having shifted much of their energies to the more promising markets emerging on the Witwatersrand.[124] The Shopkeepers' Association had disbanded after the Miners' Union and the Chamber of Commerce had reached their compromise. In the case of the white mine workers, not only did they face a future in which the absolute number of jobs was sure to decline, but they also had the immediate problem of keeping their jobs at a time when employers could draw at will from a large pool of unemployed within the town.

The contrast between the political strengths of industrialists, merchants, and mine workers was clearly displayed in the election campaign. J. J. O'Leary stood again but without any of the well-organized commercial support that he had received in his successful candidacies in 1886. And even he was not ready to stand on a platform of total opposition to the industrialists, stating that he now regarded himself as a representative of commercial and mining interests. Some of the smaller business people did establish a new body, the Citizens' Political Association, but its members appear to have been much more vehemently anti-Barnato than opposed to the industrialists in general. In fact, the association's manifesto stated that there was a "complete community of interest between all the different industrial and trade interests on the

123. For details on the estates of the mine workers see the "De Beers Mine Fire, 1888," file 82, De Beers reel 44A, DBA.

124. *Daily Independent*, 27 September, 24, 25, 31 October 1888. On the movement of business to the Rand see, e.g., the comments of the manager of the Kimberley branch of the Standard Bank quoted in the general manager's report to London, 6 February 1889, pp. 50–51, GMO 3/1/23, SBA; and Hermann Eckstein to J. B. Taylor, 19 October 1888, HE 125, pp. 491–92, BRA.

Fields. . . ."[125] At a time of depression and unemployment there was little point in attacking head-on the town's sole provider of trade and jobs.

The Miners' Union, now an organ of the Consolidated Company, ran a much more aggressive campaign. It supported a number of men whom its members considered sympathetic to the industry. The candidates, who included Barney Barnato, J. H. Lange (a barrister and formerly the Crown prosecutor of those charged with IDB crimes), W. S. Lord (the solicitor standing once again), and Thomas Lynch (a long-time mining entrepreneur), stated in their campaign speeches that to oppose the industry in any way was a sure road to ruin for the entire community. All spoke against any form of taxation on the industry, whether at the point of production, on exports, or on dividends. Nor did they want any legislative limits placed on closed compounding or any reduction in the penalties provided by the Diamond Trade Act for IDBers. They did address themselves to some of the concerns of white mine workers by declaring their opposition to the compounding of white men (although none supported legislative prohibitions), and they did announce their support for the introduction, at some unspecified time in the future, of a secret ballot. In addition, Barnato addressed a pressing concern of the Consolidated's employees when he expressed support for the introduction of a three-shift system in the mines, since this would permit men to work an eight-hour day rather than the existing twelve-hour shift.[126]

Barnato went much further than his fellow candidates in articulating his political philosophy. He did this largely in the pages of a newspaper, the *Critic* (later called the *Wasp*), which he and his brother published for the duration of the election. The *Critic* pursued two themes. The first, purveyed through a series of biographical sketches of Kimberley's most successful men, was that hard and honest work was enough to guarantee any man economic well-being. Of Joseph Mylchreest, for example, the large claim holder who had sacked his white employees and replaced them with Manxmen, the *Critic* argued that his great wealth was a product of "Years and years of honest . . . [and] sheer hard work. . . ." The paper further praised Mylchreest for his "generous disposition and his ac-

125. *Daily Independent*, 11 September, 8 October 1888.
126. See, e.g., *ibid.*, 24, 25, 31 October 1888.

knowledged kindliness of heart," and his charity: "The struggling working man, the parson bent upon expanding his good work, the widow or the orphan have never appealed [to him] in vain for assistance. . . ." The second theme was that business success was a prime qualification for participation in politics, an argument much like that enunciated earlier by Rhodes. Thus, the paper praised Edward Peach, a wholesale merchant engaged in the compound supply trade and a prominent supporter of Barnato, for his business acumen and hoped that he would soon put it to work for the benefit of society at large by engaging in "the politics of the colony."[127]

But the most lavish praise of all was reserved for Barney Barnato himself. As with that of the other subjects of the *Critic*'s attention, his business success was attributed to honest hard work: "There has never been a stumble or a fall in his steady march, and he can look back with satisfaction and reflect that he has reached his splendid elevation by the diligent exercise of economy, integrity and industry. Barney I. Barnato has been the architect of his own fortune." With regard to the second theme, Barnato's election advertisement made much of his wealth and how his possession of it qualified him to be the best representative of the voters' interests. The advertisement informed the voters that Barnato was a candidate "whose Wealth is invested in your behalf and has been sunk for your benefit; who is willing to use his influence and marvellous intellectual endowments to brighten your existence and ameliorate your lot." It added that by supporting Barnato Kimberley's voters would be electing a man who could "cement the bond of friendship between Capital and Labour" and bring "prosperity" and "happiness" to all. The advertisement ended with a ringing call to those men who formed the largest block of the voting population: "Miners! If you wish your working hours lessened, your labours lightened, your pay increased, and your homes made happy, VOTE FOR BARNATO."[128]

Barnato and his allies backed up in practical fashion these calls for the support of white mine workers. Largely because of pressures exerted by mining employers on their employees to get on the electoral roll, mine workers registered in record numbers and accounted for nearly half the town's voters by the time of the 1888

127. The *Critic*, 13 October, 6, 10 November 1888.
128. *Ibid.*, 13 November 1888.

election.[129] Having such a large block of voters available, the controllers of the Consolidated made sure that the men understood the political preferences of their employers:

> Since visiting the De Beers Compound [on the occasion that Rhodes spoke to his workers], we have had a private Smoking Concert in the Kimberley Mining Board Office to which the employes of the Central Company were brought; the Manager of the Company was in the chair, and then entered Mr Barnato accompanied as always by the Chairman of the Board of Directors [Rhodes], then . . . Mr. Barnato was eulogized, and with all due modesty eulogized himself. . . . The employes are told this is the nominee of the Miners' Union, this is a large owner in the mines the working of which affords you employment, this is the man we want you to vote for; but, recollect, vote which way you like, here is the Chairman of Directors and there is perhaps another Director present, but vote which way you like, no harm will come to you. At the Griqualand West Company's Compound . . . the employes were brought together, and again there appeared on the scene the bear [Barnato], the bear leader [Rhodes], two other candidates, an extra Director and a few speculators. The now familiar play was again rehearsed, the characters taking their parts in due order . . . many men are cowed and frightened by being called to pass a vote of confidence in a candidate in the presence of the Directors. . . .[130]

Given the public nature of the ballot, white mine workers could do little to resist such pressure, especially if the employers—and by the end of 1888 there was really only the Consolidated—organized effectively. The *Daily Independent* reported the following barroom dialogue between two overseers:

> 'How are they [the employers] to know how yer going to vote? What's to prevent me from going to the polling place at the dinner hour by myself?'
> 'Why, what's to prevent yer?' asked the other with a derisive laugh. 'Nothink if yer a bally idiot, but if yer a wise man yer will find a good deal to prevent yer.' 'Supposing,' he continued with a sneer, 'supposing on the polling day the floors is barred

129. See the *Daily Independent*, 14 November 1888, with regard to employers pushing their employees to get on the electoral roll. For the composition of the electorate see the *List of Persons Residing in the Electoral Division of Kimberley Whose Names Have Been Registered in the Year 1887* (Cape Town, 1888).

130. *Daily Independent*, 26 October 1888.

to all carts [which would take the men to the polling booth from their place of work] except Barney's carts, what man is there who will be fool enough to say he don't want a ride? Same way at the mine. When the fellers come out at tiffin time [lunch] there will be cabs of all the candidates, but yer bosses will be there, and so will lots of others who have got eyes and tongues. How many do you think is there who will dare to get in a cab wot hasn't got Barnie's colors a flying?'

'Even then,' said the obstinate one, 'you need not vote for him at the polling place, and no one need know it.'

'What when there's no Ballot Act, and when yer 'ave to yell out who yer vote for before a regler crowd,' shouted the De Beers man, 'Well, you *are* a green 'un.'[131]

There were few green 'uns in Kimberley. Barnato and his fellow Miners' Union candidates all won election to Parliament. Barnato easily headed the poll, with over fifteen hundred votes—one-and-a-half times the number cast for O'Leary, who finished well behind Lange and Lynch and in a disputed draw with Lord that he later lost.[132] Instead of having three parliamentarians representing merchants and only one the diamond industry, Kimberley now had all four of its parliamentarians committed, in varying degrees, to supporting the policies of the Consolidated Company.

But Barnato's political victory, and that of the other Miners' Union candidates, was really something of an anticlimax, not much more than a symbolic confirmation of the fact that political power rested in the hands of the same people who had already established their control over the diamond industry. For the economic and social transformations that permitted the diamond magnates to win political power in Kimberley had been quite fundamental. The mining industry itself had been rationalized and consolidated through the introduction of deep-level digging and the pursuit of amalgamation. Merchant capital had been forced to submit to the overwhelming power of industrial capital, with those commercial men who remained in Kimberley split between wholesalers dependent for their profits on supplying De Beers' compounds and small retailers equally dependent on the company's favor in granting them periodic access to black mine workers (when the latter ended their

131. *Ibid.*, 8 November 1888.
132. *Ibid.*, 14 November 1888. Moses Cornwall also stood again but lost his seat. George Goch had moved north to the Rand, where he made a considerable fortune in gold mining and became mayor of Johannesburg in 1904.

contracts) and continued access to white mine workers. All black workers had been locked up, their movement to, from, and within Kimberley was under the control of state and company officials working together with rural authorities (both colonial officials and chiefs). And white mine workers were made aware that if they wished to live and work in Kimberley, they would have to give complete support to whatever policies—economic or political—their employers pursued. The dominance of industrial capital in Kimberley appeared complete.

# CHAPTER SIX

# Completing the Monopoly, 1888–95

The establishment of De Beers Consolidated Mines in 1888 marked the practical advent of a monopoly in the diamond industry, but it did not immediately transform Kimberley's economy into that of a company town. It was only in the half decade following amalgamation that the structure of the diamond industry and of Kimberley's economy took final shape, as De Beers' directors sought to extend the company's monopoly horizontally, by acquiring complete control of all the mines, and vertically, by regulating marketing as well as production. They hoped to increase the rate of profit by further cutting working costs and to reinvest their considerable financial returns in ventures outside the industry, Kimberley, and, oftentimes, southern Africa. The implementation of such policies was by no means a straightforward or painless process. Diamond merchants, producers, and overseas financiers often had opposing views on pricing and output policies and on how profits should be disbursed, while the attempts made to reduce working costs impinged still more on the already difficult lives of mine workers, merchants, and others in Kimberley's urban community. The conflict produced by the working out of these various contradictions and tensions among financiers, producers, merchants, and workers, no less intense in the early 1890s than it had been in the 1880s, determined the exact form that monopoly capitalism would take in Kimberley.[1]

1. For a discussion of the main features of monopoly capitalism see Maurice Dobb, *Studies in the Development of Capitalism* (New York, 1963 [1st ed. 1947]), pp. 320–34.

## MONOPOLY AND ITS CONTRADICTIONS

Rhodes and his fellow directors needed to control the marketing as well as the production of diamonds if they were to ensure the profitability of their enterprise. Competition and crises of over-production in the 1880s had caused carat prices to decline by nearly one-third between 1882 and 1887–88.[2] Attempts by producers at horizontal combination to restrict output and regulate prices had proved abortive. In December 1887, for example, the De Beers Mining, Kimberley Central, and a number of other companies agreed to pool their monthly output of diamonds and sell the stones to whichever merchant, generally Barney Barnato or Alfred Beit, bid the highest price. This arrangement, and an associated agreement between the producers to restrict their output of diamonds, broke down in the middle of 1888 because the mining companies, although formally committed to amalgamation, were not yet integrated into a single operation. In order to protect their separate financial interests, they continued with competitive production policies, secretly evaded the reduced-output policy, and kept producing more stones than the market could bear, with the result that prices fell and diamond stockpiles grew.[3] The only solution to such problems lay in the completion of horizontal integration and the institution of vertical integration; that is, the extension of monopoly control over the production and marketing of diamonds to ensure that supply and demand could be regulated by De Beers and not fought over by a number of competing interests.[4]

Yet the implementation of vertical integration had its complications, not the least of which was the division between diamond merchants and producers that, far from being eliminated with the completion of amalgamation, thereafter entered the Consolidated's boardroom. Amalgamation had only been brought about with the support of men (such as Barnato and Beit) more interested in marketing than in production and those (such as N. M. Rothschild and

2. On carat prices see the "Report of the Inspector of Diamond Mines for the Year 1889," *CGHPP,* G11 1890, p. 37.

3. On the establishment of the pooling arrangement see the letters of the general manager, Standard Bank, to London, 21 December 1887, 29 February, 14 March 1888, pp. 101, 441–42, 493, GMO 3/1/22, SBA. On its breakdown see below.

4. For an illuminating discussion of the turn from competitive to monopoly production in American business from the 1870s onward see Alfred Chandler, *The Visible Hand: The Managerial Revolution in American Business* (Cambridge, Mass., 1977), chapt. 10, especially pp. 315–20.

other overseas financiers) more interested in speculation than industrial development. In exchange for their financial assistance, these men received considerable representation on De Beers' board, accounting for half the directors in Kimberley and a majority of those who met in London (where a separate board had been set up in 1888 to represent the interests of De Beers' majority overseas shareholders).[5]

Though it was to the financial advantage of the merchants as shareholders (and as speculators on the share market) that the company should be profitable, it was to their even greater advantage as marketeers that the highest rate of profit be earned in the sphere of exchange (where profit was the difference between wholesale and retail prices), rather than in that of production (where profits derived from the difference between wholesale prices and working costs). If they could get diamonds cheaply from De Beers, then the merchants, who as directors helped set the company's wholesale prices, could reap huge profits, secure in the knowledge that through the company's horizontal monopoly they also regulated the number of stones reaching the market. Financiers, always ready to take their profit from whichever sphere seemed most promising, already had close links with the diamond merchants and appeared likely to ally themselves with them in the establishment of pricing and marketing policies. For Rhodes and others whose investments were in production and who, as Rhodes liked to put it, "devote their lives to work for the Company," manipulation of the market by "selfish interests" and "speculators" was anathema. Yet the need for vertical integration was obvious—the problem was how this could be achieved without the merchants and the financiers despoiling the producers of the lion's share of the profits.[6]

Two constraints on the upward mobility of diamond prices further complicated matters. First, if carat prices rose considerably, a large number of abandoned or partially worked diggings could be mined at a profit, resulting in another cycle of overproduction and falling prices. De Beers would either have to buy up these compet-

5. Approximately two-thirds of De Beers' shares were held by overseas investors in the early 1890s. See the half-yearly report of the general manager, Standard Bank, to London, 10 August 1892, p. 36, GMO 3/2/1/1, SBA; and Reunert, *Diamonds and Gold*, p. 73.
6. For Rhodes' views see his letters to F. S. P. Stow, 19 April 1888 and July 1890, Stow Papers, vol. 2.

ing operations at great cost or see its production monopoly disappear. Second, a large price rise would affect demand adversely. The market for diamonds had expanded enormously in the 1880s as lower carat prices and smaller stones made it possible for large numbers of people in England, Europe, and, increasingly, America, to possess an item that had been restricted previously to the very wealthy. Contraction was sure to follow expansion if diamond prices again soared, and people would likely turn to other less expensive gems.[7] Having embarked on supplying a mass market, the diamond industry could hardly turn back the clock. Thus, in moving toward vertical integration, merchants and producers had to ensure that in a competitive search for profit they did not destroy their market.

Disputes over pricing had considerable implications for the company's labor policies. De Beers made its money from the difference between working costs and wholesale prices; if the latter fell then so too would the rate of profit. Amalgamation and the full institution of deep-level mining operations would increase the fixed costs of working, since a sizable proportion of earnings would have to be earmarked for debt payments (on loans used to acquire mining properties to secure the horizontal monopoly), and large amounts of capital would be tied up in depreciating machinery. With the rate of profit squeezed from both ends, it would become imperative that the company reduce those working costs over which it retained significant control by cutting the price and increasing the productivity of labor.

But De Beers could not reduce labor costs with impunity. The use of coercion and force, whether by compound guards or Kimberley police, were certainly readily available strategies—and ones long employed against black workers and white. But De Beers had to ensure that the costs of repression not exceed the savings of reduced labor charges. Black mine workers could always resist increased demands through go-slows, sabotage, strikes, riots, or, once their contracts were up, abandonment of the diamond fields for the alternative job markets of the Rand. White mine workers, if conditions became unbearably bad, could likewise attempt a return to their earlier tactics of union organization and political agitation or also move to the Rand. In sum, the company had to accomplish the

7. R. Hinrichsen (a director of De Beers) to Rhodes, 11 July 1890, Rhodes Papers 7A, Rhodes House.

difficult task of lowering labor costs enough to increase the rate of profit yet not so much as to breed outright defiance in its workers.

Just as the merchants' and producers' conflict over pricing had considerable ramifications for labor, so too did their agreement on the need to reduce production have great significance for Kimberley and its inhabitants. If the institution of horizontal and vertical monopoly were successful, considerable profits would accrue. There was no point, however, in reinvesting these profits in the diamond industry, since the logic of monopoly, whether in the short term or the long, was contraction, not expansion. Such a process would have a twofold impact on Kimberley. On the one hand, contraction promised fewer jobs to working people, a smaller market for merchants, and less prosperity for the urban market. On the other, Kimberley had no economic ventures outside diamond mining to attract investors. Therefore, the large profits to be won by monopolists would surely go elsewhere.

Yet, as with labor, De Beers could not just trample on the town. If conditions became too harsh, if the company were seen solely as an exploitative concern operated in the interests of foreign capital, if a sharp division were perceived between the interests of the town and those of the industry, then popular opposition to De Beers would likely grow. Such opposition could be costly, because the company's profitability rested in large part on state and local policies—sanctioned by public support—with regard to labor control especially, and the industry's continuing freedom from direct taxation. If this support eroded, the company's political strength would decline. Thus, the final contradiction: how could monopoly be instituted fully in the mining industry without turning Kimberley against De Beers?

## INSTITUTING MONOPOLY, 1888–90

Cecil Rhodes, addressing his shareholders on 31 March 1888 at a meeting to incorporate the De Beers Mining Company and its properties into the newly established De Beers Consolidated Mines, stated his intention to make the Consolidated "the richest, the greatest, and the most powerful Company the world has ever seen."[8] Flushed by his success in acquiring a majority shareholding in the

8. Rhodes' speech is reprinted in "Vindex," *Cecil Rhodes*, pp. 748–79. The quotation is taken from p. 779.

Kimberley Central Company, with control of the De Beers mine already in hand, and with large financial interests in Dutoitspan and Bultfontein, Rhodes expected that the Consolidated's complete takeover of the mines could be accomplished in a relatively straightforward manner. To the remaining Kimberley Central stockholders he offered one Consolidated share for every two of their Centrals, arguing (in opposition to popular opinion but with specific reference to production statistics) that rather than the Kimberley mine being worth three times De Beers, the latter was in fact worth twice the former.[9] To investors in Dutoitspan and Bultfontein he offered leasing arrangements instead of shares, since, believing that the mines were "too poor to pay and too rich to leave," he did not want to exchange valuable company scrip for their worthless holdings but did want to ensure company control of their diamond output.[10]

If such offers were accepted, Rhodes argued, De Beers would acquire complete control of diamond mining without having to increase its capital beyond £3,400,000 and without increasing its liabilities much beyond the £1,500,000 debt already incurred in financing amalgamation.[11] If the offers were rejected, Rhodes warned, he had the power to force submission. His two-thirds shareholding in the Kimberley Central made resistance there ultimately pointless. With regard to Dutoitspan and Bultfontein, he threatened to expand the Consolidated's output of diamonds until carat prices fell to a level at which neither mine could be worked economically but at which the deep-level mines (with their much greater concentrations of diamonds) would still turn a profit.[12] Yet Rhodes did not really expect to have to go to such lengths. After all, with so much economic power, and assuming that there should be no rational opposition to his belief that monopoly was "the whole essence of diamond mining," he considered his arguments for peaceful conquest persuasive enough.[13]

9. *Ibid.*, pp. 757–60.
10. *Ibid.*, pp. 761–70, 774. During the period 1882–87 companies in Dutoitspan paid an average annual dividend of one-half of 1 percent and those in Bultfontein one-third of 1 percent. See the *Daily Independent*, 13 June 1888.
11. "Vindex," *Cecil Rhodes*, pp. 774–77.
12. *Ibid.*, pp. 755–56, 773, 774, 775, 766–70. Dutoitspan produced one-fifth of a carat of diamonds for every sixteen cubic feet of ground excavated, Bultfontein one-third of a carat. De Beers, by contrast, produced one-and-a-quarter carats.
13. See Rhodes' speech quoted in the *Daily Independent*, 2 April 1888.

But few were won over. The Kimberley Central shareholders (led by the company's chairman, Francis Baring-Gould) pointed out that the market value of Central shares matched that of De Beers, disputed Rhodes' low valuation of their mine, and rejected his offer out of hand.[14] A collapse in the diamond stock market confirmed them in their opposition. Share prices plummeted in April, forced down by a loss of investor confidence caused by Rhodes' threat to flood the diamond market and by an apparent attempt by some diamond merchants and financiers "to bear" the Consolidated's stock in the hope of earning a quick profit and later increasing their holdings when the share market bottomed out.[15] By June De Beers' shares had fallen 30 percent in value and were being quoted at a significantly lower figure than Kimberley Central's.[16] Companies in Dutoitspan and Bultfontein also rejected Rhodes' terms, believing that he could not make good on his threat to lower prices without doing unacceptable damage to De Beers' profits and certain that ultimately they could get a better offer for their properties.[17]

By early August prospects for Rhodes' takeovers looked dismal. Numerous companies continued with their independent operations in Dutoitspan and Bultfontein, while a minority band of Kimberley Central shareholders, rejecting overtures from Rhodes and in defiance of their own directors' wishes, pursued court action to block any absorption of the Central by De Beers on the grounds that these were not similar companies (as the trust deed of the Central re-

14. Shares in the Kimberley Central (face value £10) and De Beers (face value £5) sold at £50 each in March, *Economist*, 2 June 1888, p. 695. Baring-Gould had earlier supported amalgamation. His apparent turnabout caused much bitter feeling among De Beers' directors and ultimately cost him a life governorship. On the latter issue see the extensive correspondence between Rhodes and Stow in the Stow Papers.

15. See the letter of the general manager, Standard Bank, to London, 11 April 1888, p. 585, GMO 3/1/22, and his half-yearly report, 8 August 1888, pp. 54–55, GMO 3/1/23, SBA; Rhodes to Stow, 19 April 1888, Stow Papers, vol. 2. One Johannesburg speculator, Hermann Eckstein, wrote privately in April that the drop in share prices was "probably chiefly due to the bad health of the Emperor of Germany," and he thought that shares unloaded immediately could be repurchased later at a profit. See his letters to J. B. Taylor, 19 and 20 April 1888, HE 50, pp. 174, 189, BRA.

16. De Beers' shares were selling at £34 5s., Kimberley Central's at £38. On share prices see the *Economist*, 2 June 1888, p. 695, which referred to the trading in diamond scrip as "a gamble of the most pronounced type." For De Beers' management's view of matters see Neville Pickering (acting secretary of De Beers) to Rhodes, 4 June 1888, Stow Papers, vol. 2.

17. *Economist*, 2 June 1888, p. 695.

quired).[18] De Beers, after all, was not just a diamond mining company but, according to the Central litigators, an operation whose trust deed permitted it to engage in any economic activity, raise armies, and annex and govern foreign territories.[19] The final straw came in late August when the Cape Supreme Court upheld the dissidents' argument; Rhodes concluded that "amalgamation [had] failed...."[20]

Rhodes' failure was costly. Prior to the end of March 1888, with competitive production still in full swing, the European diamond market was already glutted and prices falling.[21] Rhodes' speech exacerbated these problems of overproduction and price decline. On the one hand, diamond merchants, fearful that Rhodes would carry out his threat to flood the market, largely ceased buying. On the other, mining companies, particularly those in Dutoitspan and Bultfontein, either maintained or stepped up diamond production, attempting to prevent their receipts from falling and to demonstrate the productivity of their properties. As a result, prices kept falling. Rhodes sought to ameliorate the situation by cutting in half output from the De Beers mine—a far cry from his previous threats of dumping—but to no avail. By June, Kimberley's mining companies had several hundred thousand carats of diamonds on hand, all of them largely "unsaleable," while the financial condition of the Consolidated itself, with little revenue and high fixed costs, had become "precarious."[22]

Rhodes tried once more to fix matters by getting all the mining companies to agree to reduce their monthly output to two-thirds the average level ruling during the first half of the year, but again without success. None abided by this unwieldy agreement, the ear-

18. Rhodes concluded an interim agreement with the Kimberley Central's board in May 1888 to get control of the Central's property. See the *Economist*, 2 June 1888, p. 694. De Beers' acquired practical control of the Kimberley mine on 31 July 1888, even though the legal dispute over ownership continued long afterward. See the half-yearly report of the general manager, Standard Bank, to London, 8 August 1888, p. 50, GMO 3/1/23, SBA.

19. For the litigants' arguments see Williams, *Cecil Rhodes*, pp. 102–03. For a discussion of the De Beers Trust Deed see Michell, *The Life and Times of Rhodes*, I, pp. 192–94.

20. Rhodes to Stow, 25 August 1888, Stow Papers, vol. 2. For the Supreme Court's judgment see Williams, *Cecil Rhodes*, p. 104; and Michell, *The Life and Times of Rhodes*, I, p. 194.

21. *Economist*, 10 March 1888, p. 310.

22. C. Nind (a director of De Beers) to Rhodes, 4 June 1888, Stow Papers, vol. 2.

lier "pooling" arrangement for the sale of stones fell apart, and all returned to the old system of each selling, or at least trying to, their output on a daily basis.[23] Overall, the financial return for 1888 (Rhodes' hoped-for year of monopoly) was poor indeed compared to that of 1887 (the zenith of competitive production); unregulated output and market disarray resulted in a 10 percent drop in receipts.[24]

While receipts fell, working costs rose when disaster struck the deep-level mines in the latter half of 1888. Fire in the De Beers mine on 11 July, discussed earlier in terms of its human costs, added considerably to the financial burdens of the company. The underground workings were destroyed, remained nonproducing for three months, and were only brought back into operation at a cost of a quarter million pounds.[25] The "crushing in of the underground roofs and pillars" of the Kimberley mine on 7 November, caused by the adoption of an inherently defective mode of excavation, led to the total destruction of deep-level operations, leaving every shaft and tunnel filled with debris. Before production could resume, "the mine had to be reopened from top to bottom," a task that consumed several hundred thousand pounds and took more than three months of work.[26]

With production and marketing in disarray and working costs getting out of control, Rhodes realized that he had to obtain complete ownership of the mines if De Beers' monopoly was to be secured. His first target was the Kimberley mine. The Supreme Court in its decision on the Kimberley Central had left open a loophole: anyone who acquired legal ownership of at least three-quarters of the Central's shares could liquidate the company and purchase its property at public auction.[27] Therefore Rhodes, with the financial

23. See the letters of the general manager, Standard Bank, to London, 23 May, 13, 20, 27 June 1888, pp. 758–59, 831, 849, 864, GMO 3/1/22, and his half-yearly report, 8 August 1888, p. 55, GMO 3/1/23, SBA.

24. See the returns published in the Cape of Good Hope, *Statistical Register, 1895* (Cape Town, 1896), p. 236.

25. *First Annual Report, De Beers Consolidated Mines Limited, July 1889*, p. 2; "Report of the Inspector of Diamond Mines for the Year 1888," *CGHPP*, G22 1889, p. 7.

26. For the "crushing" quotation see the inspector of diamond mines' report, *CGHPP*, G22 1889, p. 4 (and pp. 12–13, 14 for discussion of equally critical problems in the open-cast mines). The other quotation is from Williams, *The Diamond Mines*, I, pp. 307–08.

27. Rhodes to Stow, 25 August 1888, Stow Papers, vol. 2.

backing of Rothschild's, pursued the necessary proportion of shares, negotiating for the holdings of Baring-Gould and other directors of the Central and tendering for those of the "dissentients" who had brought the legal action. He soon met with success. Baring-Gould and the Central directors agreed in mid-October to exchange their shares for De Beers' scrip (on terms considerably more favorable than those that Rhodes had demanded in March), while the dissentients sold out in February 1889, also at considerable personal profit. Now that De Beers held well over three-quarters of the Central's stock, Rhodes immediately liquidated the Central. Moreover, when the Central's property went on the auction block, De Beers tendered the highest bid (£5,338,650, of which over 95 percent went back to De Beers as the majority shareholder) and thereby acquired legal ownership of the Kimberley mine in July 1889.[28]

Rhodes pursued control of Dutoitspan and Bultfontein with equal success. Slips and reef falls in both of these open-cast mines in the latter half of 1888 speeded up the acquisition process, since most companies, already in financially dire straits, had to devote capital and labor in the first half of 1889 to clearing their properties of debris rather than to mining diamonds.[29] Rhodes offered these companies two means by which they could escape their financial predicament. With regard to the largest and most productive companies, the Griqualand West in the Dutoitspan mine and the Bultfontein Consolidated in the Bultfontein, he suggested a leasing arrangement by which De Beers would take control in perpetuity of all mining operations and in turn guarantee to pay the lessors a fixed annual return on their capital (4 percent in the case of the Griqualand West, 7.5 percent in that of the Bultfontein Consolidated). With regard to the smaller companies, those least able to work at a profit, Rhodes proposed outright purchase, although for sums considerably less than their shareholders had anticipated receiving before the worsening of the reef problems. Neither leasing nor purchase arrangements were financially appealing, but the alternative was much less so—continued independent operations in

28. Stow to Rhodes, 2, 30 August, 4, 10, 19, 22 October 1888, Rhodes to Stow, 9 November 1888, Stow Papers, vol. 2; half-yearly report of the general manager, Standard Bank, to London, 6 February 1889, p. 47, GMO 3/1/23, SBA; Williams, *The Diamond Mines*, I, p. 295 (for a facsimile of the check dated 18 July 1889) and p. 314; Hedley Chilvers, *The Story of De Beers* (London, 1939), pp. 263–64.

29. See the annual reports of the inspector of diamond mines, *CGHPP,* G22 1889, pp. 12, 13, 14, and G11 1890, pp. 25, 31, 32.

the face of the increasing difficulties and expenses of open-cast mining, and competition from De Beers' deep-level operations. The Griqualand West and Bultfontein Consolidated entered into leases in perpetuity on Rhodes' terms, while another seven companies sold their properties to De Beers. By the beginning of September 1889 Rhodes had achieved his horizontal monopoly, with all four mines in the possession of the Consolidated. He then stopped all digging operations in the open-cast mines and concentrated company activities in the deep-level mines.[30]

Such a monopoly did not come cheaply. By the latter half of 1888 the high price that Rhodes had to pay in De Beers' scrip and in cash for the Kimberley Central's shares had forced him to raise the Consolidated's capital to £3,950,000 (£550,000 more than he had wanted) and to increase its borrowings to £2,250,000 (£750,000 more than anticipated). By the end of 1889 the added cost of acquiring Dutoitspan and Bultfontein had more than doubled De Beers' indebtedness. Interest payments alone on the almost £5,000,000 owing amounted to at least £330,000 annually, and the addition from 1890 onward of repayments of the principal pushed the amount going to debt servicing closer to £600,000. These charges accounted for one-third of the company's operating costs, a heavy financial burden indeed.[31]

Still, Rhodes had claimed in March 1888 that any increase in De Beers' debts could "be wiped out by our savings [made] in cost of working" through reorganizing mining, increasing mechanization, and "diminution in the cost of labour."[32] That claim, however, had been made when Rhodes anticipated annual interest payments

30. Rhodes to Stow, 9 November 1888, Stow Papers, vol. 2; general manager, Standard Bank, to London, 7 August 1889, pp. 42–43, GMO 3/1/24, SBA; "Report of the Inspector of Diamond Mines for the Year 1889," CGHPP, G11 1890, pp. 31, 32; Second Annual Report, De Beers Consolidated Mines Limited, 30 March 1890, pp. 4, 10. Rhodes had publicly claimed only a few months earlier that he had no intention of closing the two mines, and a few small companies continued operations in them.
31. For cost breakdowns see the balance sheets printed in the company's annual reports. See also Barnato's speech printed in the First Annual Report, De Beers, July 1889, pp. 5–6; Lionel Phillip's estimate of working costs published in the Daily Independent, 25 March 1890; Rhodes' speech to the 1893 De Beers' shareholders' meeting, printed in "Vindex," Cecil Rhodes, pp. 789–90, 803; Reunert, Diamonds and Gold, pp. 46–47; Williams, The Diamond Mines, I, p. 306; and Chilvers, The Story of De Beers, pp. 264–65. On having to increase the company's capital more than he had intended Rhodes wrote to Stow, 9 November 1888, "It is so harrowing to my feelings that I hate to think of it," Stow Papers, vol. 2.
32. "Vindex," Cecil Rhodes, p. 775.

of no more than £75,000, rather than nearly five times that amount, and before disaster struck in the deep-level mines. Consequently, increased debts and production expenses in 1889 made it more imperative than ever that Rhodes reduce working costs if his newly won monopoly was to be financially successful.

The problem of cost could be dealt with in part by making mining more efficient. To this end the Consolidated's general manager, Gardner Williams, sought to systematize operations in the De Beers mine, and to a lesser extent in the Kimberley mine, and to substitute whenever possible "mechanical for manual or animal labour." Under his direction the company sank several new vertical shafts (reaching deeper and permitting greater haulage than did the incline shafts that they largely replaced), put into operation increasingly powerful hauling, pumping, and washing machines, and illuminated much of the underground diggings with electricity rather than candles (which had caused the De Beers fire).[33] In addition, Williams completely reorganized tunneling operations in both mines during the first half of 1889, replacing the previous system of block caving with one of terrace caving which he described as follows:

> The system which I have laid out is to work the levels back from the surrounding hard rock, in sections or levels thirty feet apart, forming as it were terraces, each upper level being worked back in advance of the one below it. By this method there can be no danger of a general collapse of the underground works, as all the levels remain solid, with the exceptions of the tunnels. Only a few galleries at a time will be driven on each level, and the pillars between them will rest upon the solid blue [ground] below.[34]

(See figure 6.1.) He believed the new system to be much safer and, without further modification, able to be carried out at any depth. Such measures raised considerably the productive capacity of the deep-level mines. In the De Beers mine, for example, the company

33. Williams was quoted by the inspector of diamond mines, *CGHPP,* G22 1889, p. 3. See also that report in its entirety and the inspector's report for 1889, G11 1890, for detailed descriptions of the process of mechanization. Williams later wrote about "systematic mining" in *The Diamond Mines,* I, chapt. 11.

34. *First Annual Report, De Beers, July 1889,* p. 10. See also the report of the inspector of diamond mines, *CGHPP,* G11 1890, p. 47; and Williams, *The Diamond Mines,* chapt. 11.

hauled nearly one-and-a-half times as much ground in 1889 as it had the previous year, despite employing fewer mine workers.[35] But these measures also put new strains on the cost structure of mining. In the short term, development work and the purchase of new machinery necessitated considerable capital expenditures. In the long term, the company's continuing investment in machinery, on top of its heavy financial liabilities, swelled fixed costs to well over half the total operating expenses.[36]

With fixed charges on the rise, Rhodes sought to diminish the cost of labor. By expanding machine operations in the deep-level mines and ceasing work in the open-cast mines in 1889, he cut the number of men employed in the diamond industry by one-third within the year.[37] At much the same time he restructured the work force, particularly in the De Beers mine, where the Consolidated concentrated its activities. A new contract entered into with the Cape administration in November 1889 gave the company twice the number of black convicts it had formerly employed—men whom Gardner Williams considered did double the work for half the cost of free labor—and these provided practically all the surface workers required by the De Beers mine.[38] Underground, subcontracting and piecework largely replaced wage labor. White miners tendered on an individual basis to excavate diamond-bearing ground at a set price per sixteen-cubic-foot load. These miners then subcontracted informally with black laborers who, in return for their daily wage, had to meet certain production targets (generally in terms of feet of holes drilled for blasting or number of trucks loaded).[39] There was much less room in this new system for the overseers formerly used by the company. Below ground overseers' skills were largely

35. See the *First Annual Report, De Beers, July 1889*, p. 10, and the *Second Annual Report, De Beers, 31 March 1890*, p. 6.

36. See De Beers' balance sheets.

37. *CGHPP,* G11 1890, p. 38; *NABB,* G4 1890, p. 57.

38. By the end of 1889 De Beers had 650 convicts at work. On their terms of employment see the "Memorandum of Agreement . . . between . . . Cape of Good Hope . . . and De Beers," 18 November 1889, enclosed in secretary, De Beers, to under colonial secretary, 19 May 1903, CO 1903, folio 157; and the "Reports on the Management and Discipline of Convict Stations and Prisons for the Year 1889," *CGHPP,* G38 1890, p. 7. For Williams' preference for convict over free labor see his annual report for 1888, printed in the *Daily Independent,* 14 May 1888, and his evidence given to the Select Committee on Griqualand West Trade and Business, *CGHPP,* A7 1891, pp. 425–26.

39. *CGHPP,* G22 1889, p. 9; Williams, *The Diamond Mines,* II, p. 61.

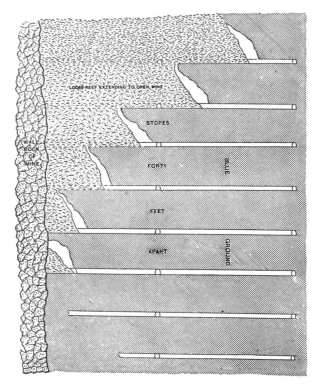

FIGURE 6.1   Terrace caving in the diamond mines, c. 1889 (Williams,
*The Diamond Mines of South Africa*, vol. 1, p. 320)

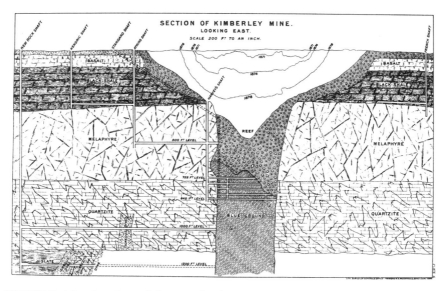

FIGURE 6.2   Section of the Kimberley mine, c. 1891 ("Report of the
Inspector of Diamond Mines for the Year 1891," *CGHPP*
G 27 1892)

unnecessary, while above ground De Beers took advantage of an influx of British immigrants in 1889 to hire new men for supervisory tasks, such as guarding convicts, at wages significantly less than those paid previously. Company officials expressed considerable pleasure at being able to hire this "new class of people" in place of the old overseers, whom they now considered "nigger drivers" who had "never done a day's work in their lives...."[40]

Having wrought considerable changes in the workplace Rhodes, in continuing pursuit of more efficient and ever-cheaper labor, extended further the Consolidated's control over the lives of its workers. The problem with free black employees, according to De Beers' management, was that they were not "always at hand"—they got drunk, they malingered, they arrived late for work—and machine operations required above all a constantly available and punctual work force. Moreover, as Williams complained, if free workers attempted to escape, the company could "not shoot them" as it could the convicts.[41] The solution lay in restructuring and tightening up the operation of the existing labor compounds. Instituting on an industry-wide basis in 1888–89 measures that he had already tried successfully in the De Beers mine, Rhodes first enlarged the compounds for the deep-level mines. The five expanded compounds (two for underground workers and three for surface workers) housed not only the forty-five hundred or so blacks employed daily in the two mines but also an additional few hundred men, so that a surplus of labor over and above immediate needs was always available.[42] Furthermore, these compounds were made entirely self-sufficient, with company stores selling food and clothing (but not liquor), and company hospitals providing medical care, all done in order that no

40. On the "influx" see the *First Annual Report, De Beers, July 1889*, p. 11; and Chilvers, *The Story of De Beers*, p. 263. On the drop in wages see below. For management's contempt for overseers see the evidence given by Williams and W. H. Craven (De Beers' secretary) to the Select Committee on Griqualand West Trade and Business, *CHGPP*, A7 1891, pp. 103, 115, 117, 433.

41. *CGHPP*, A7 1891, p. 426.

42. On the number of compounds and the size of their complements see the annual reports of the inspector of diamond mines, *CGHPP*, G22 1889, p. 9, G11 1890, p. 38, G24 1891, pp. 4, 6; *NABB*, G4 1890, p. 57, G4 1891, p. 15; and the *Second Annual Report, De Beers, 31 March 1890*, p. 10. Francis R. Thompson, a former manager of De Beers' compounds, noted that because conditions were so harsh in the mines "to work 900 men we want 1,400 or 1,500 men, for natives won't stay the whole week with the white miner." See his evidence printed in the "Report of the Commissioners Appointed to Inquire into and Report upon the Diamond Trade Act," *CGHPP*, G3 1888, p. 12.

inmate would have any reason to leave during the course of his employment contract of two or three months.[43] Finally Rhodes, "so as to prevent any communication between outsiders and mining employes going to or returning from work," constructed covered ways connecting the compounds directly with the mines and along which Zulu guards armed with clubs marched their charges.[44] Such measures succeeded, at least by 1890, in providing the mines with "a constant supply of efficient labour."[45]

White workers were not exempt from the extension of company control beyond the workplace. Early in 1889 De Beers began construction of Kenilworth, a "cantonment," or model village, for its white employees. Kenilworth was essential to the final implementation of the compound system, a parallel institution for whites where, like blacks, they would be dependent on De Beers for their entire livelihood and thus be more easily subjected to the demands of industrial discipline. The village was sited two miles out of town, distance to be the barrier to intercourse with the rest of Kimberley's inhabitants, which corrugated iron walls provided in the case of compounded blacks. A tram line was built to ensure that De Beers' employees got to work on time. Many of the necessities of daily life were provided, including a mess hall, kitchen, library, and billiard room. All activities were monitored, not by uniformed guards as in the compounds and convict station but by undercover officers of the detective department.[46] Construction of the town was, however, a sizable and expensive undertaking, and by the end of the year fewer than 10 percent of De Beers' white employees had been accommodated.[47]

All the same, expanded machine production and more efficient

43. For descriptions of the compounds see the *Daily Independent,* 27 March 1888; the reports of the inspector of diamond mines, *CGHPP,* G22 1889, p. 9, G11 1890, p. 26; *Second Annual Report, De Beers, 31 March 1890,* pp. 10, 23; *NABB,* G4 1891, p. 15; and Williams, *The Diamond Mines,* II, pp. 53-57.

44. *CGHPP,* G11 1890, p. 29.

45. The statement is Barnato's, quoted in the *Third Annual Report, De Beers Consolidated Mines Limited, 31 March 1891,* p. 27. For other comments along the same lines see Williams quoted in the *Daily Independent,* 14 May 1888; and the testimony of various compound managers printed in the "Report of the Liquor Laws Commission, 1889-90," *CGHPP,* G1 1890, pp. 1039-43.

46. *Second Annual Report, De Beers, 31 March 1890,* p. 10; *Third Annual Report, De Beers, 31 March 1891,* pp. 5, 21; Williams, *The Diamond Mines,* II, pp. 111-18; Chilvers, *The Story of De Beers,* p. 262.

47. *Second Annual Report, De Beers, 31 March 1890,* p. 10.

and cheaper labor did indeed yield the result that Rhodes had promised—lowered working costs. De Beers spent, depending on the mine, between 10 and 14 percent less to excavate and process each load of ground removed from the mines in 1889 than it had the previous year. And the price kept going down as the company put ever-larger machinery into operation and employed fewer workers.[48]

Yet reduced operating costs could not alone solve the financial difficulties of the company. The savings made were not always enough to offset the growing burden of fixed charges. Also, as excavations went deeper, diamond finds declined (by 15 percent per load between 1888 and 1889 alone), further limiting the benefits of lowered production expenses.[49] Only a considerable rise in diamond prices promised to strengthen De Beers' finances, a solution Rhodes strove for throughout 1889 as he used the company's growing control over production to manipulate supply and demand in the diamond market. Once he had full possession of both Kimberley and De Beers, he cut their output of stones. With reef difficulties simultaneously curtailing operations in the still-independent open-cast mines, the total number of diamonds entering the market in the second quarter of the year fell and prices shot up. Stones that averaged 20s. per carat in 1888 fetched 30s. by the middle of 1889.[50] Rhodes' acquisition and closure of Dutoitspan and Bultfontein in September enabled him to cut total output still further. In October diamond sales amounted to 163,660 carats, half the monthly average of the previous year, while the carat price hit 38s. 3d., a 90 percent increase on 1888's average return.[51]

But Rhodes had overreached. With prices forced so high, demand began to fall off in the final two months of 1889. At the same time, competing mining companies on the Kimberley diamond fields and in the Orange Free State (their operations made suddenly profitable by the price rise), stepped up production and threatened to undercut De Beers' newly won monopoly. And, as the London *Economist* noted, continued high prices would be sure to aggravate mat-

48. See *ibid.*, pp. 6, 7; and the table of statistics printed in Williams, *The Diamond Mines*, II, p. 320.

49. *Second Annual Report, De Beers, 31 March 1890*, p. 1; *Third Annual Report, De Beers, 31 March 1891*, p. 4; Williams, *The Diamond Mines*, II, p. 320.

50. *Daily Independent*, 20 July 1889.

51. *Statistical Register, 1895*, pp. 236–37.

ters by permitting the largely worked-out mines of India to be brought back into operation.[52]

Such developments benefited neither Rhodes nor those diamond merchants (the largest in the trade) who were shareholders and directors of the Consolidated. All stood to lose financially so long as the market remained in flux. A possible solution existed in the creation of a marketing monopoly to match that of production, and the setting by the monopolists of mutually beneficial output quotas and price schedules. Producer and merchant could together manipulate the market and maintain the most profitable balance between supply and demand. After a number of abortive attempts, four of the largest diamond merchants—Wernher Beit & Company, Barnato Brothers, Mosenthal Sons & Company, and A. Dunkelsbuhler—succeeded in February 1891 in putting together a group of dealers ready to act in concert. The Syndicate (as this group was later known) offered to purchase De Beers' entire production from February to April, with output not to exceed two hundred thousand carats monthly, and payments to be made on a sliding scale ranging from 37s. per carat for February's diamonds to 39s. for April's.[53] To ensure that neither competing diamond merchants nor the public got wind of this price-fixing venture, all negotiations and the very existence of the Syndicate were kept secret. Rhodes and the De Beers Board (one-quarter of whose members belonged to the Syndicate) accepted the offer. Thus, by the beginning of 1890, a practical monopoly extended from the workplace to the marketplace with company and syndicate recognizing that their financial interests were inextricably tied, and agreement reached that production "be regulated by demand" and prices "not be put up excessively."[54]

The combination of lowered production costs and increased carat prices caused De Beers' profits to soar. Whereas the company

52. *Economist*, 9 November 1889, p. 1427, 28 December 1889, p. 1669.

53. On an early and abortive attempt to form a diamond syndicate see the *Daily Independent*, 11 March 1889. On the Syndicate and its composition see Chilvers, *The Story of De Beers*, p. 265; Alpheus Williams, *Some Dreams Come True* (Cape Town, n. d. [1948]), p. 327; Theodore Gregory, *Ernest Oppenheimer and the Economic Development of Southern Africa* (Cape Town, 1962), pp. 54–55; and Lenzen, *The History of Diamond Production*, pp. 165–66. Each member of the Syndicate agreed to take a set percentage of the total number of stones purchased. Wernher, Beit & Co. took 23 percent, Barnato Bros. 20 percent, Mosenthal Son & Co. 15 percent, and another seven dealers had smaller shares ranging from 10 percent down to 2 percent.

54. The words are Barnato's, from his chairman's speech printed in the *Second Annual Report, De Beers, 31 March 1890*, p. 32.

had an operating profit of £310,409 for the twelve months ending 31 March 1889, in the following year it reported £1,209,780. In part this quadrupling reflected the increased size of the company. More important, it was a result of the operating margin of profit having jumped from the already respectable figure of 34 percent in 1888 to almost 52 percent in 1889. In short, De Beers made a profit of more than ten shillings on every pound's worth of diamonds sold in 1889—more than sufficient to pay a 20-percent dividend that year.[55]

Yet few of these profits made their way into Kimberley's economy or into that of the Cape. With foreign investors holding two-thirds of De Beers' stock by the beginning of the 1890s and nearly all debenture holders likewise overseas, close to three-quarters of the company's financial disbursements went outside Africa.[56] And with monopoly leading to contraction, there was little incentive to reinvest in the diamond industry. Even the company itself was not a particularly attractive long-term prospect, since, with the selling price of the shares generally four times their face value, the actual dividend return on invested capital was little more than 5 percent. Those, such as Rhodes, Barnato, Beit, Rothschild's, and others who made money from diamonds, often by speculating in De Beers' shares, invested their profits elsewhere: in speculation in Rand gold-mining shares, in the floating of the British South Africa Company to exploit concessions in Mashonaland and Matabeleland, and back in Europe.[57]

55. The operating margin of profit reflects the working profit (i.e., before allowance was made for debt servicing, depreciation, etc.) as a percentage of income from diamond sales (i.e., not including income from other investments, etc.). *First Annual Report, De Beers, July 1889,* pp. 2, 5; *Second Annual Report, De Beers, 31 March 1890,* p. 3.

56. In January 1888 less than 50 percent of De Beers' dividends had been paid to overseas shareholders; by 1892, 74 percent of total disbursements (dividend and debenture payments) went overseas. See the report of the inspector, Standard Bank, 21 January 1888, p. 185, INSP 1/1/87, and the half-yearly report of the bank's general manager, 10 August 1892, p. 36, GMO 3/2/1/1, SBA; and Reunert, *Diamonds and Gold,* p. 73.

57. On the poor return of diamond shares as investments see the *Economist,* 25 January 1890, p. 110. Barnato later agreed that De Beers' shares paid a low return but stressed that they were of blue-chip quality—"the mining consols of the world," *Third Annual Report, De Beers, 31 March 1891,* p. 22. On the speculation elsewhere of the diamond magnates see the half-yearly report of the general manager, Standard Bank, to London, 7 August 1889, p. 41, GMO 3/1/24, SBA; J. S. Galbraith, *Crown and Charter: The Early Years of the British South Africa Company* (Berkeley, 1974), pp. 85–86, 122–25; and Colin Newbury, "Out of the Pit: The Capital Accumulation of Cecil Rhodes," *Journal of Imperial and Commonwealth History* 10:1 (1981): 30–35.

Political power in Kimberley and the Cape was, however, essential to the protection of De Beers' profits and to the pursuit of speculation in southern Africa. The company's high rate (at least on paper) of dividends drew increasing public attention to the fact that the diamond industry, the most profitable enterprise in the subcontinent, remained free from direct taxation. Calls for taxation and higher tariffs on the industry had to be forestalled.[58] Moreover, Rhodes needed support from the Cape government in implementing successfully his plans for Mashonaland: to help convince the British government to assist his vast concessionary empire; to remind the Transvaal government, rather averse to Rhodes' encircling moves, that the British South Africa Company had powerful allies; and, in immediately practical terms, to ensure that the Kimberley railway was extended northward in order to supply the BSA's expeditionary forces.[59]

Rhodes secured this political power in 1890. De Beers already had a lock on Kimberley's parliamentary seats. Rhodes added national office to his local power base in July 1890 when, with the assistance of parliamentary allies, he helped bring down the administration of J. G. Sprigg and, after successful negotiations for the continued backing of the Afrikaner Bond, became premier himself.[60] Refusing to give up any of his business positions, he combined the premiership with the chairmanships of De Beers and the BSA, arguing that "the three would work for each other, and the whole for the benefit of all."[61]

Chairman of the wealthiest company in Africa, chairman of a chartered concern expected to rival the past glories of the British East India Company, and leading politician in his adopted country, Rhodes appeared to be at the pinnacle of success in 1890. Other enterprises in Great Britain and the United States might have been more profitable, yet others larger, but none could match Rhodes'

58. For an expression of company fears that the public might call for increased taxation see Barnato's speech reprinted in the *Third Annual Report, De Beers, 31 March 1891*, p. 22; and for a later example see the letter of Rhodes to the secretary of De Beers' London transfer office, 16 April 1893, Stow Papers, vol. 2.

59. For Rhodes' machinations with regard to Mashonaland and Matabeleland see Galbraith, *Crown and Charter*, pp. 85–86, 89–90, 123–25, and in general chapts. 3 and 4. See also Lewsen, *John X. Merriman*, pp. 137, 139.

60. J. G. Lockhart and C. M. Woodhouse, *Rhodes* (London, 1963), p. 183; Lewsen, *John X. Merriman*, p. 139.

61. Rhodes made this statement in the first speech he gave in Kimberley after having become premier, *Daily Independent*, 5 September 1890.

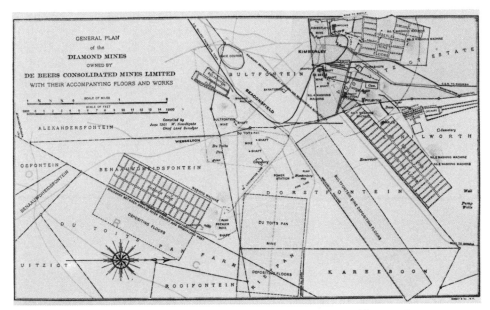

FIGURE 6.3   General plan of the diamond mines owned by De Beers
Consolidated Mines, 1901 (Williams, *The Diamond Mines of
South Africa*, vol. 1, between pp. 316 and 317)

combination of economic and political strength. He might well have
claimed that he had fulfilled his prophecy and made De Beers, within
two years of its formation, "the richest, the greatest and the most
powerful Company" in the world.[62]

## YEAR OF DISCONTENT, 1890–91

But, as the *Economist* pointed out, it was "much easier" for De
Beers "to bring about a monopoly than to render it permanently

62. Dividends from the diamond industry exceeded those of the gold industry
up until 1893–94. See Witwatersrand Chamber of Mines, *Seventh Annual Report for
the Year Ending 31st December 1895* (Johannesburg, 1896), pp. 174, 178; Reunert,
*Diamonds and Gold*, p. 227; Williams, *The Diamond Mines*, II, p. 320; and S. H.
Frankel, *Capital Investment in Africa: Its Course and Effects* (Oxford, 1938), p. 95. For
comparative material on big business in America, where giant combines arose from
the 1870s onward, and Britain, where the process of amalgamation did not take off
until the end of the 1890s, see Alfred Chandler, "The Beginnings of 'Big Business' in
American Industry," *Business History Review* 33:1 (1959): 1–31; and P. L. Payne, "The
Emergence of the Large-Scale Company in Great Britain, 1870–1914," *Economic
History Review* 20:3 (1967): 519–42.

PLATE 6.1    Cecil John Rhodes (Williams, *The Diamond Mines of South Africa*, vol. 1, p. 272)

PLATE 6.2    Mine workers, 1893 (Johannesburg Public Library)

remunerative."[63] No sooner had Rhodes acquired the Kimberley mines and reached agreement with the Syndicate than the foundations of his new edifice began to crumble. Merchants and producers differed over the control of diamond output, carat pricing, and the distribution of profits. Company employees struggled against the increasingly onerous conditions to which they were subjected in the workplace, and the onset of depression in Kimberley fueled widespread protest against the "tyranny" of "organized Capital and Monopoly." The discovery of yet more diamonds in Griqualand West "knocked on the head the doctrine that the Almighty had put diamonds in payable quantities in only four holes," thereby undermining the entire structure.[64] By mid-1891 De Beers' future looked bleak.

PLATE 6.3   Kimberley and the "big hole," 1899 (Cape Archives, AG 6229)

63. *Economist*, 15 August 1891, p. 1050.

64. The reference to "organized Capital" is from the *Manifesto of the Knights of Labour of South Africa* (Kimberley, 1892); the allusion to the Almighty was made by Davis Allen, manager of the Kimberley Diamond Mining Company Limited, in his evidence to the Select Committee on Griqualand West Trade and Business, *CGHPP*, A7 1891, p. 351.

The first challenge came late in 1889 when two diamond merchants, both of them members of De Beers' board and within a matter of months of the Syndicate as well, sought to undercut the company's production monopoly. Woolf Joel (a nephew and business partner of Barnato) and Harry Mosenthal (of Mosenthal Sons & Company) secretly made heavy investments in newly developed mines in the Orange Free State, Joel in the Koffiefontein mine, Mosenthal in the Jagersfontein. With access to their own supply of diamonds, albeit one much smaller than that produced by the Kimberley mines, these men would then be able to bargain down De Beers' wholesale prices.[65]

Rhodes, who soon learned of these share transactions, acted quickly. First, without the knowledge of his own board (and its merchant members), he had De Beers purchase claims in Koffiefontein sufficient in number to prevent the mine from being worked profitably as a single unit. Next he negotiated, also secretly, to acquire the shareholdings of the local directors of the Jagersfontein Mining Company. Having purchased their stock, he had these men remain on the Jagersfontein board as "dummy-holders" for De Beers and adopt drastic output reduction policies for "their" mine.[66] The Consolidated's production monopoly thus remained in place, at least for the moment.

A more serious conflict arose over pricing and output policies. Since diamonds, as a luxury commodity, immediately felt the slightest shift downward in the world economy, merchants tried to minimize their risk of loss by buying cheaply, keeping as few stones on hand as possible, and limiting the total number of carats entering the market. Members of the Syndicate pursued these strategies in 1890 by setting among themselves maximum prices that they would pay diamond producers; by using their position on De Beers' board to establish wholesale prices that, in the eyes of the other

65. The Orange Free State mines had been worked in the 1870s and 1880s but in a very limited way, since they were not rich in diamonds. On the purchases see Rhodes to Stow, 22 November 1890, Stow Papers, vol. 2; and the half-yearly report of the general manager, Standard Bank, to London, 10 August 1892, p. 38, GMO 3/2/1/1, SBA. See also Gregory, *Ernest Oppenheimer*, p. 53.

66. Rhodes to Stow, 22 November 1890, Stow Papers, vol. 2; Gregory, *Ernest Oppenheimer*, p. 53. Rhodes' dealings in Koffiefontein were something of an open secret. See, e.g., Barnato's coy refusal to answer questions on the matter at the company's annual meeting, noted in the *Second Annual Report, De Beers, 31 March 1890*, p. 33.

directors at least, worked to the merchants' "interest first & then the Company's"; and by allying themselves with Rothschild's to direct management to cut diamond production to no more than one hundred thousand carats per month, a level of output at which De Beers would have had difficulty making a profit.[67]

Such actions were anathema to Rhodes. As he noted later, he "look[ed] on De Beers as an investment and not a speculation, and wish[ed] to make the property as safe as possible, and able to face all contingencies."[68] In addition, he anticipated using funds generated by De Beers to finance his new ventures elsewhere in southern Africa. Depressed wholesale prices and the "natural greed" of shareholders in demanding the immediate disbursement of all profits as dividends clearly obstructed such goals.[69] The solution, Rhodes believed, lay in the establishment of a large cash reserve, of at least one million pounds, invested in blue chip stocks. Such a fund would enable the company to institute a strong price-support scheme. Whenever the merchants refused to pay De Beers' prices (to be set in the future by a committee consisting only of directors with no financial interests in the trade) or the market softened, then the company could borrow money using its investments as collateral and so "continue our work independent of an immediate sale of diamonds."[70]

Fearing, however, that the diamond merchants would be sure to oppose plans so inimical to their interests, and that shareholders would inevitably loot the reserve for higher dividends, Rhodes chose to institute his scheme in secret. With the connivance of De Beers' management, but without informing his fellow directors, Rhodes maintained diamond output at two hundred thousand carats per month throughout the latter half of 1890, twice the amount

67. The quotation is from a letter by C. E. Atkinson (a director of De Beers) to Stow, 14 March 1892, Stow Papers, vol. 1. For similar views expressed by other members of De Beers' board and management see Stow to Rhodes, 13 November 1890, 13 March 1891, Rhodes Papers 7A (14, 30), Rhodes House; Craven to Stow, 22 December 1890, and Stow to Craven, 29 January 1892, Stow Papers, vol. 1. For the directive to lower diamond output see Rhodes to Stow, 19 May and 19 July 1890, Stow Papers, vol. 2.

68. Rhodes to secretary, De Beers' London transfer office, 6 April 1893, Stow Papers, vol. 2.

69. For the reference to greed see Rhodes to Stow, 19 July 1890, Stow Papers, vol. 2. This letter has been misdated 1891 by someone other than Rhodes.

70. Rhodes to Stow, 28 August 1891, Stow Papers, vol. 2. For an earlier expression of the same idea see idem, 19 July 1890, Stow Papers, vol. 2.

set by his board.[71] Once a large number of diamonds had been accumulated, Rhodes arranged in 1891 for their surreptitious shipment to Europe. There a non-Syndicate dealer, working on commission, sold the stones in small, widely dispersed lots. The proceeds of these sales, over £500,000 in 1891, were then invested in low interest bearing but highly secure British Consols.[72]

These activities could not remain secret for long. The Syndicate members, particularly those on De Beers' board, generally "stop[ped] at nothing to obtain information" about the company, and all had their spies in Kimberley, especially in the detective department, where production was rigorously monitored in the course of the war against IDB. Indeed, leaks from the department were the likely reason that Beit found out about Rhodes' stockpiling of diamonds almost from the inception of the practice.[73] And Beit and other members of the Syndicate, ever alert to any stones whose provenance they did not know entering the European market, also learned of Rhodes' diamond shipments as soon as they began.[74] In response to these discoveries Carl Meyer, Rothschild's representative on De Beers' board and a close associate of Beit, protested in March 1891 to the board Rhodes' "immoral and unfair" conduct and called for the cessation of the "reserve" policy.[75]

But Rhodes was intransigent. He refused to end either surplus production or overseas sales unless the board in its entirety agreed to the establishment of a price-support scheme. His opponents had no immediate recourse. If they made their complaints public then other merchants would learn of the existence of the Syndicate (this at least was still a secret well kept from small dealers and the public) and no doubt discover that its members got diamonds from De Beers at a discount. If the public also heard of how diamond prices were being manipulated, the market was sure to weaken.

71. Rhodes to Stow, 19 May and 19 July 1890, Stow Papers, vol. 2; Stow to Rhodes, 17 September 1890, Rhodes Papers 7A (5), Rhodes House.

72. The details of these transactions can be followed in the correspondence passing between Rhodes, Stow and F. T. Gervers (the diamond dealer involved) collected in the Stow Papers, vols. 1–3. In all, Rhodes took only three of his fellow directors, out of nineteen on the board, into his confidence.

73. For the quotation see Stow to Rhodes, 13 November 1890, Rhodes Papers 7A (14), Rhodes House. See also Rhodes to Stow, 19 July 1890, Stow Papers, vol. 2.

74. Stow to Rhodes, 13 March, 14, 24 April, 22 May 1891, Rhodes Papers 7A (30, 27, 37, 48), Rhodes House.

75. Meyer's views are referred to in Stow to Rhodes, 13 March 1891, Rhodes Papers 7A (30), Rhodes House.

The result of such internecine conflict was a serious decline in De Beers' fortunes. The sale of Rhodes' diamonds, in an international market already weakened by the collapse of the Argentinian economy (in which European financiers had sunk much of their investment capital) and by a widespread feeling that carat prices had been pushed too high too fast, produced a drop in demand and prices. By the middle of 1891 diamonds fetched 30 percent less per carat than they had averaged the previous year. Company stock values more than matched this downward tumble, with De Beers' shares registering a 50 percent fall in the same period. Since the company had to earn a net profit of over £330,000 per annum (to service its debts) "before the ordinary shareholders receive[d] anything," the *Economist* in August considered it a very poor investment.[76]

These problems with the market had a considerable impact on the workplace because the only immediate solution available was to tackle costs yet again. Rhodes and De Beers' management raised the cost efficiency of deep-level digging by further concentrating operations in the De Beers mine, by doubling the horsepower of the mine's machinery, and by replacing English coal with cheaper local supplies.[77] They also lowered labor costs by increasing the number of convicts at work, by implementing stricter forms of control in the compounds, and by cutting the wages of black workers and white.[78]

Such measures took a heavy toll on De Beers' employees. The accelerated expansion of deep-level digging had many dangers: the roofs of tunnels collapsed because of the "soapiness" and friability

76. *Economist*, 15 August 1891, p. 1049. On the fall in diamond prices see the table of monthly returns in the *Statistical Register, 1895*, p. 237. On the collapse of the Argentinian economy and its reverberations in Europe see Atmore and Marks, "The Imperial Factor," pp. 130–31; and P. L. Cottrell, *British Overseas Investment in the Nineteenth-Century* (London, 1975), pp. 38–39.

77. On the concentration of operations see the *Third Annual Report, De Beers, 31 March 1891*, pp. 5, 6. On the increase in horsepower see the annual reports of the inspector of diamond mines, *CGHPP,* G11 1890, p. 48, and G24 1891, p. 15. On coal see De Beers' third annual report, p. 8; and the reports of the inspector of diamond mines, G27 1892, p. 13, G26 1893, p. 13, G38 1894, p. 6. Although colonial coal was not of the same high quality as imported coal, the fact that it cost only one-third as much more than offset any difference in fuel efficiency.

78. On the increasing use of convict labor see the annual reports of the department of prisons and convict stations, *CGHPP,* G38 1890, p. 7, G35 1891, p. 4, G50 1892, p. 4. On the substitution of convict for free labor see the *Daily Independent* and the *Diamond Fields Advertiser,* 16 July 1891.

of the blue ground being excavated; men fell down shafts, black workers occasionally slipped to their deaths from the primitive ladders that were their only means of access to the mining levels seven hundred to eight hundred feet below the surface (whites traveled in elevator "cages"); and "mudrushes" posed a new "peril to life."[79] Mudrushes occurred when water, collecting on the surface of the mines (a catchment area of 30 acres in the case of Kimberley, 19 acres in that of De Beers), percolated through the vast amounts of accumulated debris, formed a sludge, and burst with enormous force into the underground workings (comprising 3 acres in Kimberley and 6 in De Beers) below. These rushes could fill up thousands of feet of tunnels within a matter of minutes, allowing little opportunity for escape.[80] The cumulative effect of the new dangers was a death rate from accidents in the early 1890s averaging six to seven fatalities per thousand men employed overall in the mines and double that range underground.[81] Although something of an improvement on returns in the early and mid-1880s, De Beers' accident death rate was still far in excess of that current in British mines, a difference which Gardner Williams preferred to attribute to the "carelessness" and "stupidity" of his black workers rather than to any inherent defects in the mode of operations.[82] Whatever the causes, the practical effect (for De Beers' white employees at least) was that mining accidents accounted for approximately one-third of the total deaths (including natural) that they suffered annually.[83]

79. The quotation is from Williams, *The Diamond Mines*, II, p. 40. For detailed descriptions and statistical breakdowns of the increasing number of accidents occurring in the mines see the annual reports of the inspector of diamond mines.

80. Mudrushes are described in detail by the inspector of diamond mines, *CGHPP*, G27 1892, pp. 5–6; and by Williams, *The Diamond Mines*, II, pp. 40–44. The solution to mudrushes was better drainage, but this work was not fully undertaken until the end of the 1890s. See Williams, *ibid.*, I, pp. 317–18, 334–37, II, p. 44.

81. For death-rate statistics see the annual reports of the inspector of diamond mines—which from 1891 onward give a breakdown between surface and underground rates—and the *Statistical Register, 1895*, p. 238.

82. Gardner Williams was quoted by the inspector of diamond mines, *CGHPP*, G22 1889, p. 10. For contemporary references to the lower British rates (averaging no more than 2/1,000) see the inspector of diamond mines' report, *CGHPP*, G38 1897, p. 14; and Williams, *The Diamond Mines*, II, pp. 44–45. For official comment on Williams' generally poor record on safety precautions see the correspondence in the file "Rules for Safety in the Mines, 1889," LND 1/285 L1863.

83. See the annual reports of the De Beers Benefit Society, 31 March 1891 and 31 March 1893, enclosed in portfolio 32 (De Beers Benefit Fund), uninventoried records, Cape Archives.

Accidents were not, though, the prime cause of death for black mine workers; pneumonia was. The increasing prevalence of this disease—much less evident in the early to mid-1880s, when the major causes of death were due to poor sanitation—was a product of expanded deep-level digging with very poor ventilation underground (where the air was full of detritus and temperatures ranged anywhere from 56°F near the surface to 93°F at the work face), and overcrowded accommodation in the compounds.[84] Pneumonia accounted for two-thirds of the fatalities recorded by De Beers' two compound hospitals in the early 1890s and was primarily responsible for the fact that Kimberley's black death rate (forty-one per thousand in 1891 and fifty-five per thousand in 1892) averaged one-and-a-half times the town's white rate and was double that of other urban black communities in the Cape Colony.[85]

Pressures in the compounds and in the workplace to make blacks work harder for less money also increased. Men employed underground (70 percent of De Beers' black work force in 1890–91) were in a particularly difficult position.[86] On the one hand, basic living conditions were determined by the compound managers, company employees with whom the blacks had initially signed contracts that stated the duration of the period of labor and the supposed rate of pay. The compound managers' prime responsibility was to keep up the supply of labor to the underground works. They did this by permitting men surplus to immediate needs to remain,

84. On the increase in pneumonia-related deaths see the annual reports of the district surgeon, *CGHPP*, G13 1888, pp. 23–24, G17 1890, p. 31, G15 1891, p. 40; and especially the letters of Dr. A. H. Watkins reprinted in the "Report of the Liquor Laws Commission, 1889–90," *CGHPP*, G1 1890, pp. 1057–58. On poor ventilation and extremes of temperature see the *Second Annual Report, De Beers, 31 March 1890*, p. 21. With regard to the compounds see the annual reports of the civil commissioner and of the registrar and protector of natives, printed in *NABB*, G6 1888, p. 16, and G3 1889, p. 17. For official recognition that overcrowding was the prime cause of pneumonia see the report of the 1901 commission of inquiry into the compounds, pp. 6, 7, NA 800/429.

85. The death rate in the Kimberley mine hospital averaged 31.75/1,000 between 1891 and 1899, and that in the De Beers mine hospital averaged 50.25/1,000 during the same period. See the "Compound Hospital Returns," file 276, De Beers reel 36A, DBA. For Kimberley's death rate and the death rates of other communities in the Cape see the "Reports on Public Health for the Year 1892," *CGHPP*, G14 1893, pp. xv–xvi. The district surgeon thought that, because of the difficulty of collecting complete records on the town's migratory population, Kimberley's death rate was probably higher than that shown by the published figures.

86. For statistical breakdowns of the work force see the reports of the inspector of diamond mines, *CGHPP*, G24 1891, pp. 4, 5, and G27 1892, pp. 4, 7.

uncontracted and unpaid, in the compounds until required (in contravention of the law), and by persuading men to recontract without leaving the compounds (and thereby ignoring the legal requirement that all servants enter contracts "willingly" and in public at the government registrar of servants' office). The opportunities for bringing undue pressures on their charges in such a situation were endless: men were fined, beaten, and otherwise punished for transgressing compound rules. Moreover, government officials did not inspect the compounds or monitor the actions of the white managers.[87] On the other hand, the actual conditions of employment in the workplace and the real daily wages received were determined by De Beers' white mining subcontractors. In order to fulfill their own contractual obligations, the subcontractors set daily job targets and penalized financially those of their black workers (with whom they had no separate written contract) who did not meet these.[88] With compound managers and subcontractors working to cheapen the price of labor, black wages were pushed down 25 percent between 1890 and 1891.[89]

Although wages fell, the cost of living did not. Compound inmates were not charged for accommodation or medical care (except for a hospital tax of 1s. per month that went to the government), but they did have to purchase food, and this took a large share of their wages. De Beers refused to ration men, on the grounds that free supplies would only encourage malingering whereas having to make purchases from company stores meant that men had to "work to eat."[90] The prices charged in these stores were at least as high

87. On the ill treatment of compound inmates see, e.g., J. Leary (protector of natives) to under secretary, native affairs, 7 October 1889, NA 455; Leary to general manager, De Beers, 12 February 1891, enclosed in E. A. Judge (civil commissioner) to under secretary, native affairs, 6 May 1895, NA 455; S. B. Liefeldt (protector of natives) to under secretary, native affairs, 1 April 1891, NA 455; *idem*, 1 September 1891, NA 407. On the lack of registration in the compounds see the statement of the registrar of natives, 9 September 1889, and correspondence between the registrar and the under secretary, native affairs, all contained in NA 320.

88. See Williams' description of the system reprinted in *CGHPP*, G22 1889, p. 9.

89. See the *Statistical Register, 1891* (Cape Town, 1892), p. 239; *Second Annual Report, De Beers, 31 March 1890*, p. 21; and Williams' evidence to the Select Committee on Griqualand West Trade and Business, *CGHPP*, A7 1891, p. 425. The figures published in the *Statistical Register* generally reflected the maximum rather than the average wage paid.

90. The statement was made by F. R. Thompson, De Beers' compound manager, in evidence reprinted in the "Report of the Commissioners . . . upon the Dia-

as those ruling in Kimberley's retail establishments, since the Labourers' Wages Regulation Act stipulated that the town's merchants should not be undercut, and often considerably higher,
because the more that was spent on daily living expenses the longer
men would have to stay in the compounds to save money to take
back to their rural homes. De Beers made a profit of £10,000 per
annum on its compound operations, all of it deriving from the sale
of foodstuffs and other items to black workers. Compound inmates
tried to economize by establishing their own "eating clubs," with
each member contributing a set sum for food each week and either
sharing cooking responsibilities or paying someone else (usually
one of the crippled men who remained in the compounds long after
they could no longer work in the mines) to cook for them. Still, with
at least one-third, and sometimes more than half, of their wages
going to purchase food, most of De Beers' black employees recon-
tracted for periods of up to nine months at a stretch.[91]

Living costs absorbed an even greater proportion of the shrunk-
en wage packets of white workers. In 1890–91 De Beers paid skilled
white employees an average of £5 per week and unskilled men (overseers, convict guards, talleymen, and so forth) between £3 and £4
per week. This was quite a drop from the mid-1880s, when skilled
wages ranged between £6 and £7, and unskilled averaged £5.[92] Yet
Barney Barnato, in giving evidence in 1889 to a royal commission
in support of a pay raise for Kimberley's police officers, had argued

---

mond Trade Act," *CGHPP*, G3 1888, p. 12. The company did provide food for its
convict workers but not in generous quantities. Indeed, De Beers had the lowest
ration scale of any convict station, and this no doubt accounted for the prevalence
of scurvy in its station. See the letter of the medical officer to secretary of the law
department, 27 June 1891, CO 6443; and the letter of the superintendent (De Beers
convict station) to attorney general, 8 June 1892, CO 6470.

91. For some examples of the amount spent on food see the statements of
Charlie, Charlie Lura, Lepolo, and Daniel Mshavavu given in 1893 to the Cape Labour Commission, *CGHPP*, G3 1894, pp. 366–68. On the length of time men spent in
the compounds see the report of the inspector of diamond mines, *CGHPP*, G22 1889,
pp. 6, 9; and on the amounts of money saved and the time taken to do so—an average
of perhaps £2 to £3 per month for the higher-paid workers—see the statements of
Charlie et al. referred to above and the comments of various compound managers
reprinted in *CGHPP*, G1 1890, pp. 1039–43.

92. See the reports of the inspector of diamond mines, *CGHPP*, G24 1891,
pp. 4, 6, and G27 1892, p. 4; *Second Annual Report, De Beers, 31 March 1890*, p. 21;
the evidence of Williams in *CGHPP*, A7 1891, pp. 442–43; and the *Statistical Register,
1891*, p. 239.

that a white single male needed to earn at least £5 per week for a "bare living."[93]

Whether or not a man made a bare living depended to a considerable extent on the state of race relations in the workplace. White subcontractors, talleymen, and overseers, not company management, decided if black laborers had worked hard enough and fixed the exact amount written in on daily wage tickets. Blacks for their part had less direct but no less potent means to manipulate white pay packets. If dissatisfied with work conditions, blacks underground could engage in wage disputes, go-slows, contrive "accidents" and other forms of sabotage, and thereby prevent white subcontractors from meeting their obligations to the company. White wage earners such as overseers and convict guards were no less dependent financially on black labor. De Beers paid a commission to each employee, white and black, free and convict, who found a diamond; whites received 1s. 6d. per carat, blacks 3d. Since whites had no physical contact with excavated ground, they depended on their black charges to pass on any diamonds found. If blacks were discontented, they could leave the diamonds in the ground or sweep them off the sorting tables along with the rest of the debris, thus depriving their overseers of the commissions.[94] Yet these commissions accounted for a third of the white wage earners' income at the end of the 1880s and permitted men who received a base pay of approximately £3 from the company to take home a weekly sum closer to £5.[95] In short, supplemental income generated by black cooperation or compliance made the difference for white workers between barely surviving and not surviving at all.

In 1890-91 racial noncooperation and violence became the order of the day in the workplace. The combination of a high cost of living, falling wages, and a rise in accident and mortality rates produced enormous strains, as men struggled to last out their thir-

93. "Report of the Select Committee on Cape Town and Kimberley Police Forces," *CGHPP,* A11 1889, p. 66.

94. Employees underground, who were less likely to find diamonds in the hard ground, received twice the commission of floor workers. See the *Second Annual Report, De Beers, 31 March 1890,* p. 20; and the letter of the superintendent (De Beers convict station) to secretary of the law department, 22 April 1889, CO 6427.

95. On the proportion of take-home pay accounted for by commissions see the evidence given by Barnato and by James Lawrence (mayor of Kimberley) to the Select Committee on Cape Town and Kimberley Police Forces, *CGHPP,* A11 1889, pp. 37, 66.

teen-hour work days.[96] Disputes broke out constantly about wages, safety, and what constituted adequate work. Furthermore, there were no readily available means by which these could be settled other than by confrontation between the disputants. Neither whites nor blacks relied on company officials for impartial arbitration. Nor did they turn to the courts, except infrequently, since almost without exception witnesses gave evidence along racial lines, whites for whites, blacks for their "brothers," thus negating each others' testimony, while with time being money no one wanted to waste it in lengthy litigation away from the workplace.[97] The result was that men turned more and more to violence to achieve their ends. Blacks underground extinguished the lights in the tunnels and attacked whites with boring drills, stones, and other implements; whites assaulted blacks with feet, fists, and *sjamboks* and on occasion hurled them to their deaths down mine shafts. Race relations had so deteriorated by the middle of 1890 that the inspector of diamond mines warned Rhodes of the likelihood of "the Kaffirs rising against . . . the white men and murdering . . . them."[98]

Such racial violence threatened the very basis of diamond mining. The inspector of diamond mines concluded in his annual report for 1890 that unless measures ("legal or otherwise") were taken to discipline black workers, "one of two results must follow . . . the industry of underground working in diamond mines must cease; or the employment of the greater part of Kaffir labour in such workings be abandoned."[99] De Beers could survive neither of those two eventualities.

96. Men worked a twelve-hour shift, with at least another hour spent getting to and from the work face.

97. On problems with the legal system, and the reference to blacks regarding fellow workers as "brothers," see C. C. Erskine (inspector of mines) to the chairman, De Beers, 29 May 1890, enclosed in Erskine to assistant commissioner of Crown lands, 29 May 1890, LND 1/346 L4323; and Erskine's annual report for 1890, *CGHPP*, G24 1891, p. 3.

98. Erskine to Rhodes, 29 May 1890, LND 1/346 L4323. For reports of blacks using violence against whites see Erskine's annual report for 1890, *CGHPP*, G24 1891, pp. 3–6. For white violence see, e.g., the case of Richard Leggo, a subcontractor charged with having thrown a black employee to his death, reported in the *Daily Independent*, 29 January 1891; the police commissioner's report for 1890, 18 February 1891, CO 3685; and the inspector of diamond mines' report for 1891, *CGHPP*, G27 1892, pp. 11–12. Leggo was eventually acquitted, largely on the basis that the only witnesses against him were black.

99. *CGHPP*, G24 1891, p. 4; and see in general pp. 3–6. In 1890–91 De Beers had acquired a bad name as an employer of labor among many blacks. On this point

While marketing was in disarray and racial conflict endemic in the workplace, conditions in the town were even more difficult as a result of the policies pursued by Rhodes. Consolidation, mine closings, and output reduction all had a profoundly depressing effect, given the importance of the industry in providing jobs and in underpinning Kimberley's mercantile and financial establishments. Yet the onset of a severe depression did not come as a surprise. The inspector of the town's largest bank, the Standard, had reported to his superiors in 1889 that "when we reach the completion of Mr Rhodes' work it seems to me that Kimberley may as well get a large wall built around it. The demand for labour must largely decrease and the population must largely drift away as there will no longer be an outlet for their abilities."[100]

The implementation of Rhodes' policies put thousands of men out of work, with little over half as many employed in the mines in 1890–91 as had been in 1887, the final year of competitive operations.[101] The sale of practically all diamonds to members of the Syndicate, most based in London, excluded local dealers (who according to the Standard Bank were the "money spenders and mainstay of the place [Kimberley]") and local banks from the trade. As a result of this change in marketing, by the beginning of 1891 most of Kimberley's several hundred diamond dealers had closed up shop and moved to the Rand, while the banks had lost their most profitable business.[102] Then also the extension of the railway northward

see the letter of the resident magistrate, Fort Beaufort, Cape Colony, to under secretary, native affairs, 6 April 1890, NA 793/167, reporting that none of the men in his district would go to work for De Beers; and the letter of the protector of natives (Leary) to Gardner Williams, 12 February 1891, enclosed in E. A. Judge to under secretary, native affairs, 6 May 1895, NA 455.

100. See the report of the Standard Bank's inspector, 27 July 1889, pp. 223–24, INSP 1/1/87. For a description of the decline that had already taken place in the mid to later 1880s see the inspector's report of 12 February 1887, p. 172, INSP 1/1/87, SBA.

101. *Statistical Register, 1895*, p. 238. De Beers employed 11,300 blacks in 1887 but only 6,772 in 1890; the number of whites fell from 1,920 to 1,592.

102. For the quotation see the report of the Standard Bank's inspector, 21 January 1888, pp. 185–86, INSP 1/1/87, SBA. On the spending power of the diamond dealers see also Barnato quoted in the *Third Annual Report, De Beers, 31 March 1891*, p. 27. The profits made by the banks from the local diamond trade are summarized in the half-yearly reports of the general manager, Standard Bank, GMO 3/1/23, 3/1/24, 3/2/1/1, SBA. On the decline in the diamond trade and the departure of both profits and dealers see the reports of the Standard Bank's inspector, 27 July 1889, pp. 223–24, INSP 1/1/87, 30 October 1891, p. 198, INSP 1/1/88, and those of the general manager, 10 February 1890, p. 30, 5 August 1891, p. 37, GMO 3/2/1/1, SBA. See also the *Third Annual Report, De Beers, 31 March 1891*, p. 27; and the Kimberley Stock Exchange, *No. 2 Register of Members, 1890–92*, JPL.

in 1890 ended Kimberley's position as the northern terminus for the Cape rail system and largely eliminated the town's merchants from the only major sector of commercial business not completely dependent on the diamond industry—the transshipment and supply of goods to the Rand, British Bechuanaland, and Mashonaland. Thereafter northern traders, instead of coming to Kimberley to obtain supplies, purchased direct from agents of Cape Town and Port Elizabeth wholesale houses and loaded up their wagons one hundred miles north at Vryburg.[103] Kimberley even lost access to the personal wealth of the diamond magnates. As noted above, these men preferred to speculate in gold-mining shares in the late 1880s, while after the recovery of the Rand from its depression of 1889–90, most moved north to settle and spend their money in Johannesburg rather than Kimberley.[104]

As a result of these developments, Kimberley's economy went into a severe slump. The local manager of the Standard Bank reported to his Cape Town superiors in June 1890 that "a shrinkage and tendency towards contraction" was clearly evident among all business in the town. His own balance sheets and those of his competitors showed that bank deposits had fallen 44 percent between 1889 and 1890 alone and were continuing to drop.[105] Property values also fell, by at least 50 percent, during the same period. Rents in general had to be reduced (except in Beaconsfield, where the town's absentee landlord, the London and South Africa Exploration Company—known sometimes as the "Exploitation Company"—refused to countenance any cut), but even then, with so many people out of work and commerce declining, few could pay on time if at

103. On the earlier importance of the rail trade see the report of the Standard Bank's inspector, 12 February 1887, p. 172, INSP 1/1/87, and of the general manager, 7 August 1889, pp. 41, 44, GMO 3/1/24. On the decline of the trade see the inspector's report of 4 October 1890, p. 178, INSP 1/1/88, and the reports of the general manager, 10 February 1890, p. 30, 10 February 1891, p. 48, 5 August 1891, p. 36, 17 February 1892, p. 41, 10 August 1892, p. 36, GMO 3/1/1/1, SBA. Railway development in general is discussed by van der Poel, *Railway and Customs Policies*.

104. See the report of the Standard Bank's inspector, 4 October 1890, p. 179, INSP 1/1/88, and the reports of the general manager, 7 August 1889, p. 41, GMO 3/1/24, 10 February 1891, pp. 1, 3, 5 August 1891, pp. 35–36, 10 August 1892, p. 37, GMO 3/2/1/1, SBA.

105. See the general manager's report to London, 6 July 1890, p. 29, GMO 3/2/1/1, SBA. For the bank's balance sheets see the half-yearly reports bound in the same volume. Kimberley shopkeepers estimated that they had lost as much as three-quarters of their trade. See the evidence of Albert Holt (merchant) to the Select Committee on Griqualand West Trade and Business, *CGHPP*, A7 1891, pp. 299–300.

all.[106] And the future promised no likelihood of any change for the better.

By the end of 1890 poverty had become widespread on the diamond fields. Conditions were at their worst in Beaconsfield, where a majority of the sacked mine workers lived. Without alternative sources of employment, many of the town's inhabitants were almost destitute, subsisting on occasional odd jobs, charitable handouts, and begging in the streets. A. P. Kriel, Beaconsfield's Dutch Reformed minister, stated in evidence to a parliamentary select committee investigating distress in Griqualand West in 1891 that every family, white as well as black, with which he had contact lived in poverty.[107] By April of that year thousands of the town's inhabitants had gone, leaving the place with half the population that it had had in 1888 and giving it the appearance of a ghost town. Kimberley was somewhat better off, if only because the deep-level mines remained in operation and renters did not have to deal with any octopuslike equivalent of the so-called Exploitation Company. Yet hundreds of white men, many of them former overseers, remained without work while trying to eke out a living for themselves and their dependents.[108]

106. See the reports of the Standard Bank's inspector, 27 July 1889, p. 223, INSP 1/1/87, 4 October 1890, p. 179, INSP 1/1/88, and of the general manager, 10 February 1890, p. 29, 5 August 1891, p. 37, GMO 3/2/1/1, SBA; and the evidence of E. H. Jones (mayor of Kimberley), CGHPP, A7 1891, pp. 40–42, 57–58, 76, and app. K. For the use of the term "Exploitation Company" see F. R. Statham's muckraking novel, Mr Magnus (London, 1896), p. 164.

107. For Kriel's evidence see CGHPP, A7 1891, pp. 183–203. See also the evidence of John Cowie (acting mayor of Beaconsfield) confirming Kriel's description, and that of J. B. Currey (local manager of the Exploitation Company) in dissent, ibid., pp. 139–40, 142–80, 267–68, 272–74, 276, 279; the Daily Independent, 21 October 1890, 10 June, 16 December 1891; and "The Petition of the Mayor, Members of the Town Council, Ratepayers and Inhabitants of the Town of Beaconsfield and Others . . . to His Excellency Sir Henry Loch," 1890, LND 1/347 L4410.

108. Many people who wanted to leave the diamond fields could not do so because whatever capital they had was tied up in devalued property in Kimberley and Beaconsfield. See "The Petition of the Mayor of Beaconsfield," 1890, LND 1/347 L4410; the evidence of Arthur Stead (a former mayor of Kimberley), CGHPP, A7 1891, p. 368; and a letter from the Exploitation Company's tenants published in the Daily Independent, 28 December 1891. On Beaconsfield's ghost-town appearance see CGHPP, A7 1891, pp. vii, 67, 255, and apps. K and N.

Some charitable institutions tried to help these people, but to little effect. One private organization provided a soup kitchen and temporary accommodation for the totally down and out. Another spent £104 17s., two-thirds of its annual income, assisting fifty-six needy people in 1890. And the Kimberley Hospital Board applied in 1890 for a government grant so that it could look after seventy white and black poor in addition to the fifty paupers it already housed.[109] De Beers for its part sent sixty or so ex-employees north in March 1891 to work for the BSA and offered laboring jobs in the mines at less than subsistence rates of pay to a few dozen more, but it provided no relief work for former overseers, nor did it support the giving of free handouts by any agency, for fear that undesirables from the rest of South Africa would flock to the diamond fields.[110] Such was the full extent of charity in Kimberley.

With no jobs and little public relief available, there were only two ways by which Kimberley's unemployed and poor could attempt to make a living. They could move to Barkly West, thirty miles away, and try their luck at the original alluvial diggings on the Vaal River. These diggings had been largely abandoned in the 1870s and early 1880s, but by the end of the latter decade more and more people were moving to the river. By the beginning of 1890 the river diggers numbered approximately 1,200 (200 of them Coloured, the rest white), and they employed between 2,500 and 3,000 black laborers. These were large numbers, accounting for 40 percent of the whites and 30 percent of the blacks employed by the diamond industry as a whole in Griqualand West.[111] The second way to make some money was to work the discarded ground of the Kimberley mining companies in the hope of finding diamonds missed in the original sorting process—debris washing as it was called at the time. Large heaps of debris lay about the town, all of them on land owned either by De Beers, the government, or, in the case of Bea-

109. *Daily Independent*, 9 July, 23 September 1889, 15 February, 26 July 1890, 19 July 1892.
110. *Ibid.*, 19 March 1891; *Third Annual Report, De Beers, 31 March 1891*, pp. 20, 24–27. See also the evidence of Craven and Williams in *CGHPP*, A7 1891, pp. 101, 102, 103, 115, 117, 119, 431, 432.
111. See the reports of the inspector of diamond mines, *CGHPP*, G26 1887, p. 12, G24 1891, pp. 16–23, G27 1892, pp. 15–20, G26 1893, p. 18.

consfield, by the Exploitation Company. Before 1890 the landowners
had prohibited public working of the debris, claiming that it was
private property. Clear evidence of the need for some form of relief
and public pressure exerted in that year, however, forced the landowners to give way: the Exploitation Company allowed one hundred
whites to wash debris on the depositing floors of the Dutoitspan and
Bultfontein mines; De Beers gave permission for another one
hundred whites, all of them former employees (but no ex-overseers),
to work the De Beers mine floors; while the Kimberley Borough
Council, taking over the government's property, licensed at least six
hundred people (again all whites who had to prove that they had
absolutely "no property or means of support") to work on the Kimberley floors.[112] According to the *Daily Independent*, in November
1890 these debris washers, along with the thousand or so black
laborers they employed, did "as much to keep [commercial] trade
alive as all the rest of the community [including De Beers] put
together."[113]

Yet neither river digging nor debris washing provided much of
an income for those directly involved. In 1890, for example, the river
diggers found only 28,122 carats, little over 1 percent of the diamond industry's total output that year. The mean return on the sale
of these diamonds, when divided by the number of diggers at work
and allowance made for black wages, was well under 5s. per digger
per day, not enough to live on.[114] Debris washers did little better.
Although they produced over 5 percent of the industry's diamond
output, the stones were of very poor quality (selling for one-third
the average price of De Beers' diamonds), and the financial returns
low; most people could not make a living.[115]

In such depressed times the discovery of a new mine, some four
miles from Kimberley, excited public speculation that salvation was
at hand. Wesselton, named after J. J. Wessels, the Boer on whose
land it was located, had been discovered in September 1890 but

112. Debris washing is discussed at length in my dissertation, "The Making of
a Monopoly," pp. 326–34.

113. 3 November 1890. See also the issue of 19 January 1891.

114. See the report of the inspector of diamond mines, *CGHPP*, G24 1891, p. 17;
and the *Statistical Register, 1895*, pp. 236–37.

115. See the evidence of Cowie, Jones, and Stead, *CGHPP*, A7 1891, pp. 45, 161–
62, 376, and apps. J. and N; and also the *Third Annual Report, De Beers, 31 March
1891*, p. 7.

the find kept secret for fear that the public would "rush" the farm.[116] Yet word of the discovery and of the covert mining operations being carried out by a lessee of Wessels (H. A. Ward) soon leaked out, and on 5 February 1891 approximately six hundred of Kimberley's residents, many of them debris washers, marched to the farm. The rushers promptly pegged out claims and settled in to dig, ignoring the appeals of Ward that the sanctity of private property be respected and likewise repudiating the leaseholder's assertion that, since the farm was held under an Orange Free State title, neither the state nor the public had any right (as provided for by Cape law) to minerals found on the land. Recalling the earliest days of diamond mining, when many of those who were now debris washers had once been claim holders in the Kimberley mines, the first rushers and others who later joined them established an organization—the Wessels' Mine Claimholders and Protection Association—to regulate the new diggings. And they petitioned the governor of the Cape to grant them legal title to their claims.[117]

Public working of the new mine, argued the petitioners (1,042 of them), would permit people previously under the thumb of absentee "moneyed monopolists" and "on the verge of starvation" to "be again occupied in winning those glittering gems, as in the past good old days. . . ." Adversity was to be a thing of the past, for now "every honest man would have an opportunity of making a living for himself and [his] family," while a renewed emphasis on individual enterprise rather than company production (the latter controlled by men "in whose hearts the welfare of the Colony as a whole finds little or no echo") would benefit the entire country.[118] Prosperity, in short, rested on breaking De Beers' monopoly.

Rhodes did not agree. So far as he was concerned, just finding another mine was "bad luck" for De Beers; that it be proclaimed a public digging would be catastrophic.[119] Yet with the richness of Wesselton still undetermined, he did not want to part with a significant amount of the company's capital buying up property that

116. For a brief history of Wesselton see Williams, *The Diamond Mines*, I, pp. 344–57. Diamonds had been found on the property in the 1870s but not in payable quantities.

117. *Daily Independent*, 5 February 1891. See also the "Papers and Correspondence Relating to . . . the Proclamation of . . . Wessels' Farm . . . as a Public Digging or Mine," *CGHPP,* A1 1891.

118. *CGHPP,* A1 1891, p. 13.

119. Rhodes to Stow, 29 November 1891, Stow Papers, vol. 2.

might later turn out to be worthless. As it happened, most of the first rushers soon abandoned their claims because of the paucity of diamond finds.[120] Therefore, Rhodes secretly negotiated an option to purchase, for a relatively small sum, half of Ward's interest in the mine while soliciting reports on the likely yield of future finds. Publicly his administration declined for the moment to proclaim Wesselton a public digging or to grant the rushers legal title to their claims. The future of the mine was thus placed in limbo.[121]

Government inaction fueled impassioned denunciations of Rhodes and De Beers in Kimberley. On 23 February more than two thousand people gathered in Beaconsfield and then marched to the center of Kimberley to demand that Wesselton be thrown open to the public. Two further meetings in early March drew equally large crowds. Speakers at these meetings made it quite clear what they thought was to blame for the grinding poverty on the diamond fields: the "down-right, hard-fisted, solid-crushing monopoly" held by De Beers, "one of the cruellest monopolies that ever oppressed mankind." Not only was the company's economic power denounced but its political leverage too. Speakers warned that so long as Kimberley had no secret ballot company employees would remain "born slaves," and they suggested that little trust could be placed in a government that was essentially a tool of Rhodes.[122] A few weeks later, in mid-April, a letter writer to the *Daily Independent* signing himself Americus described the "De Beers Monopoly" as "the South African contribution to the modern system of aggregating huge capital and creating Trusts and Monopolies" and warned that "this heartless combination of capital" accentuated "the struggle between capital and labour." Such struggle, Americus wrote, would "eventually lead to revolution."[123] The language of class had finally emerged in Kimberley.

Action soon followed. On 22 April several hundred people led by J. H. Wilson, by turn a pioneer claim holder, diamond-company manager, overseer, and latterly debris washer, marched from Kimberley to Wesselton behind banners proclaiming, "Down with Mo-

120. For opposed views within the company concerning the likely value of Wesselton see Stow (who thought the mine likely to turn out to be a fraud) to Rhodes, 10 March 1891, and Beit (who disagreed) to Rhodes, 27 May 1891, Rhodes Papers 7A (24, 18), Rhodes House. On the number of men digging at Wesselton see the correspondence contained in *CGHPP,* A1 1891.

121. See *CGHPP,* A1 1891; and Williams, *The Diamond Mines,* I, p. 347.

122. *Daily Independent,* 24 February, 4, 13 March 1891.

123. *Ibid.,* 15 April 1891.

nopoly" and, "No Starvation amidst Plenty." Once at the farm the marchers staked out new claims and began digging. They publicly reestablished a Diggers' Association and secretly founded a society based on the American Knights of Labor, with both these organizations controlling operations in the mine. Within two weeks of this second rush an estimated fifteen hundred to two thousand white diggers employing an equal number of black laborers were at work, their actions receiving considerable support from many of Kimberley's influential citizens (at least those not directly connected to De Beers). Local and state authorities gave no such support—but then, as Wilson noted, there was no reason to respect agents of a government that in essence amounted to "none other than the De Beers Consolidated Mines Limited."[124]

Rhodes struck back. Within a week of the second rush his administration upheld officially the legal standing of Wessels' Free State title. All minerals now belonged to the property holder to dispose of as he wished, and the public had no legal right of access to the land. Wessels took advantage of this decision to pursue successfully court action for trespass against the rushers. When the latter refused to abide by the court's ruling the police moved in, arrested the leaders of the Diggers' Association, and forced the remaining people to abandon Wesselton.[125] Rhodes' control of state agencies made his power in Kimberley seem insuperable.

Yet Rhodes' very success in Kimberley weakened his position in Parliament. Political opponents, Thomas Upington (a former premier) chief among them, took the offensive, charging Rhodes with abuse of office and blaming De Beers for the existence of poverty in Kimberley. Upington's marshaling of the evidence documenting poverty—particularly that of Kimberley's Boer population—was so compelling that a majority of his colleagues, including J. H. Hofmeyr, leader of the Afrikaner Bond and usually Rhodes' chief ally, joined together in calling for a parliamentary investigation into the causes of distress on the diamond fields.[126] Assertions by Rhodes and

124. *Ibid.*, 22, 23, 27, 28, 29 April, 1, 21 May 1891.
125. *Ibid.*, 23, 27, 28 April 1891; *CGHPP*, A1 1891; report of the police commissioner, 28 July 1891, CO 3865; speech of Upington, *Debates* 8:3 (16 June 1891): 81–83.
126. For Upington's speech see *Debates* 8:3 (16 June 1891): 79–83. For Hofmeyr's stand see *ibid.*, pp. 82–83. See also the continuation of the debate on 22 June 1891, pp. 110–16. For reference to the widespread poverty afflicting Kimberley's Dutch-speaking population see Kriel's evidence, *CGHPP*, A7 1891, pp. 183–202, and app. Q; and the letter from the Rev. A. V. Lyttelton, 28 May 1891, repr. in the *Quarterly Paper of the Bloemfontein Mission*, no. 93 (15 July 1891), p. 120.

his associates that matters in Kimberley "had better be left to the natural state of things" were swept aside in the face of a widespread feeling that state intervention might be necessary to improve conditions in Kimberley.[127]

But Rhodes stopped affairs from getting completely out of hand. After agreeing to the appointment of a select committee so long as its membership consisted of "gentlemen who had not in any way expressed their views on the question [of Kimberley's distress]," he proceeded to ensure, through juggling of votes in the House, that a majority of the members were his business associates and political allies, among them the very men who had been the most vociferous opponents of the establishment of the committee.[128] Moreover, Rhodes' nominees then decided that the committee should hear evidence in Cape Town only, thus effectively excluding those witnesses who could not afford to travel south. At the same time (late June) as this political gerrymandering was going on, Rhodes acted in concert with the Exploitation Company to prohibit the working of debris from the De Beers, Dutoitspan, and Bultfontein mines—putting several hundred people out of work—and pursued court action to establish once and for all that only the claim holder (meaning De Beers) had legal title to excavated ground, including that from the Kimberley mine. If this court action succeeded, all debris would be placed off limits to the public.[129] Rhodes might compromise with his parliamentary colleagues in Cape Town, but he had no intention of giving succor to his opponents in Kimberley.

Such actions invited confrontation. The acting mayor of Beaconsfield, John Cowie (once a shopkeeper, later a debris washer), in

127. The words are Merriman's, *Debates* 8:3 (16 June 1891): 84. On the appeal of state intervention to Kimberley's residents see the editorial in the *Daily Independent*, 13 May 1891, calling for government purchase of the mines. Privately, Rhodes wrote to Stow, 20 June 1891, that he was "fighting the socialists at Kimberley now in the Cape Parliament." Stow Papers, vol. 2.

128. For Rhodes' statement see the *Debates* 8:3 (22 June 1891): 114. The committee included seven parliamentarians who were members or supporters of Rhodes' ministry (including Merriman and Barnato) and only two members of the opposition (Upington and Sprigg).

129. Barnato stated that De Beers opposed debris washing because the increased output of low quality stones caused prices for such diamonds to fall, and since De Beers itself produced a certain number of poor-quality stones, company revenues suffered from this competing production, *Third Annual Report, De Beers, 31 March 1891*, pp. 24–26. See also the *Daily Independent*, 30 June 1891; and the *Diamond Fields Advertiser*, 10 February 1892.

giving evidence to the select committee in early July, described amalgamation as a "gigantic swindle" perpetrated on the community by a few greedy industrialists. The mayor of Kimberley, E. H. Jones (the town's largest private landlord), attacked De Beers in the same forum as a "vast trading institution" that robbed merchants and workingmen alike of their livelihood, all for the profit of "English shareholders," and he called for state intervention to force the reopening of Dutoitspan and Bultfontein as well as the public working of Wesselton and the debris heaps.[130] But the clearest and most threatening demonstration of antipathy for De Beers came with the dynamiting of the company's head office on the night of 9 July, a week-and-a-half after the close down of debris washing and on the heels of the mayor's appearance before the select committee.[131]

In sum, De Beers' monopoly had come under severe attack by the middle of 1891. Diamond merchants and producers bickered over output quotas and price schedules to the detriment of company profits. Racial antagonisms in the workplace threatened to bring underground operations to a halt. Furthermore, the decline in Kimberley's commercial fortunes and the spread of poverty raised the possibility of class warfare breaking out between all the people not directly employed by De Beers who were allied against the company (whether shopkeepers, debris washers, or the unemployed) and those who were deemed the company's foreign bosses. Considering the way things were going, Rhodes could hardly continue to claim that he held effective control over the richest and most powerful company in the world.

## RESOLVING THE CONTRADICTIONS, 1891–95

One key to resolving De Beers' predicament lay in control of the market. In the past the company had maximized profits by restricting output and securing high carat prices. During economically depressed times, when the overall demand for diamonds was sure

130. See *CGHPP,* A7 1891, pp. 62, 73, 91, 172.

131. *Daily Independent,* 10 July 1891. The bombing was more symbolic than practical, since it only caused £100 worth of damage. See Williams to Rhodes, 11 July 1891, Rhodes Papers 7A (55), Rhodes House. For Barnato's publicly stated fears of the likelihood of subversion, with the Knights of Labour as the source of all evil, see his parliamentary speeches printed in *Debates* 8:3 (13 July 1891): 210, 14 July 1891: 219–20.

to fall, this high rate of profit could be sustained by cutting output rather than price, with savings in production costs making up for any drop in receipts. To perpetuate such a policy, however, required that the company have complete control of the number of stones entering the market and the financial strength to stockpile diamonds without the expectation of an immediate sale—two attributes that De Beers lacked by the middle of 1891.

But Rhodes took a number of steps in the final quarter of 1891 and the first quarter of 1892 to regain control of diamond supply. First of all, he arranged to purchase the new mine, since in August the parliamentary select committee concluded that De Beers' policies had nothing to do with Kimberley's problems and that therefore the government should not intervene to require public working of the mines, and an internal company report in the same month had indicated that Wesselton might turn out to be very rich. By November 1891, after the expenditure of £450,000, Wesselton belonged to De Beers. De Beers did not immediately take over the mine but as part of its purchase agreement permitted Ward to operate the mine on a five-year lease.[132] Three months later, in February 1892, Rhodes won his court case for ownership of mine debris. The Cape Supreme Court ruled that all excavated ground belonged to the claim holder from whose property it had been taken; in effect, either De Beers or the Exploitation Company. Thereafter, with both companies generally opposed to debris washing, fewer than fifty white men—"deserving" ex-employees of De Beers—were permitted to continue with the practice, while the police patrolled the mine properties to ensure that no one was engaged in illicit washing of the ground.[133] Later in February De Beers used its dominant po-

132. See the report of the inspector of diamond mines, *CGHPP,* G49 1896, pp. 7–8. For the select committee's report see *CGHPP,* A7 1891, pp. v–xii. On the acquisition of the mine see Francis Oats (a director of De Beers) to Sir Donald Currie (chairman of De Beers' London board), 3 August 1891, Miscellaneous Reports file 265, De Beers reel 113, DBA; Rhodes to Stow, 29 November 1891, Stow Papers, vol. 2; *Diamond Fields Advertiser,* 11 February 1892; half-yearly report of the general manager, Standard Bank, to London, 17 February 1892, pp. 40–41, GMO 3/2/1/1, SBA; *Fourth Annual Report, De Beers Consolidated Mines Limited, 30 June 1892,* balance sheets and p. 24; Williams, *The Diamond Mines,* I, p. 347; and Chilvers, *The Story of De Beers,* p. 267.

133. On the number of debris washers at work see the annual reports of the inspector of diamond mines, *CGHPP,* G27 1892, p. 6, and G26 1893, p. 4. On the company's cessation of debris washing and the policing of the debris heaps see the *Diamond Fields Advertiser,* 11 February, 30 March, 30 April, 3 May 1892.

sition on the Dutoitspan Mining Board (a body composed of claim-holder representatives and nominally in charge of keeping the mine in working order) to deny a request by the few remaining independent operators that the mine be pumped clear of water. With flooding reaching critical proportions, practically all excavations came to a halt.[134]

Having taken care of the Kimberley diamond fields, Rhodes also did what he could to keep diamond yields from the Orange Free State mines at a minimum. The Jagersfontein Company, at De Beers' direction, produced only a few stones, while in Koffiefontein De Beers simply abandoned its thousand-odd claims when the Free State government in early 1892 ordered compulsory working of the mine as a means to assist a growing number of poor whites. Excavations in the mine fell largely into abeyance, since finds were poor and few people could make any money from small-scale open-cast operations.[135] By the middle of 1892 Rhodes again controlled southern Africa's diamond output.

He also succeeded finally in getting the diamond merchants on the De Beers' Board to consent to the establishment of a price-support system. Although some of the merchants had agreed grudgingly in mid-1891 to Rhodes' proposal to build up a reserve fund, they had suggested that the money be used to pay off company debts rather than to prop up wholesale prices.[136] Because Rhodes considered such a suggestion quite contrary to his aims, he continued with the "secret" sale of diamonds well into 1892, despite the vociferous objections of Syndicate members.[137] Left "holding large stocks" of devalued stones, some of the smaller merchants had concluded by February 1892 that there was little point staying in the

134. See the *Diamond Fields Advertiser*, 16 February 1892; and the inspector of diamond mines' report for 1892, *CGHPP,* G26 1893, p. 8.

135. *Diamond Fields Advertiser,* 8 January, 19 May 1892; Williams, *The Diamond Mines,* II, p. 323 (for production figures in the Jagersfontein mine); and McGill, *A History of Koffiefontein,* p. 12. Rhodes also bought up huge amounts of land in Griqualand West, which he turned into horse farms, in order to prevent the discovery of yet more diamond mines. See Chilvers, *The Story of De Beers,* pp. 270–71.

136. See Rhodes' comment ridiculing Julius Wernher's suggestion about debt payments: "We are not making this reserve to reduce our obligations but in order to maintain our position with the diamond buyers," Rhodes to Stow, 28 August 1891, Stow Papers, vol. 2. See also Barnato's speech to the annual meeting of the company, *Third Annual Report, De Beers, 31 March 1891,* pp. 23, 28.

137. Rhodes to Stow, 29 November 1891, Stow Papers, vol. 2; E. Bernheim (a member of the Syndicate) to Stow, 7 March 1892, Stow Papers, vol. 1; Craven to Stow, 4 April 1892, Stow Papers, vol. 1.

diamond business if they had to engage in the impossible task of "competing directly against the producer. . . ."[138] Still, Rhodes could not easily force all the merchants into submission so long as they remained large holders of the company's scrip and so long as they could (and did) make up some of their losses by manipulating stock prices to their advantage and the producers' disadvantage.[139] However, publication in March and April 1892 in South African and English newspapers of stories documenting the existence of the Syndicate and unmasking Rhodes' sales undermined public confidence in the diamond market (demonstrated by an 18 percent fall in carat prices in March), threatening the financial interests of merchants and producers alike.[140] Therefore, the De Beers Board agreed on 20 April 1892, at the instigation of Rhodes and Alfred Beit, to establish a reserve fund, amounting at the time to £650,000, solely "to support the Diamond Market."[141]

This agreement marked the beginning of a long-term balancing act between merchant and producer interests. Syndicate members who were also on the De Beers' Board were henceforth excluded from the directors' subcommittee that set wholesale diamond prices; Rhodes and the company's management kept output at levels that merchants and producers regarded as returning the maximum price possible given the state of the market.[142] In May and June 1892, for example, De Beers cut production drastically in order to force up prices. After a brief initial slump carat prices began

138. Dunkelsbuhler & Co., Abrahams, V. A. Litkie & Co., and Joseph Brothers to the directors of De Beers, 24 February 1892, Stow Papers, vol. 1.

139. For evidence of earlier stock manipulation by Rothschild see Stow to Rhodes, 17 and 19 September 1890, Rhodes Papers 7A (5, 7), Rhodes House; and with regard to further manipulation in 1893 see the half-yearly report of the general manager, Standard Bank, to London, 9 August 1893, p. 42, GMO 3/2/1/1, SBA.

140. See the joint letter of non-Syndicate diamond buyers to Rhodes, 19 February 1892, Stow Papers, vol. 2; the *Diamond Fields Advertiser*, 26 March 1892; and the letter of Stow to secretary of De Beers' London board, 25 April 1892, Stow Papers, vol. 2, referring to publication of an article in the periodical *South Africa*. On the fall in carat prices see the *Statistical Register, 1895*, p. 237.

141. See the minutes of the meeting of De Beers' board, 20 April 1892, Stow Papers, vol. 2. The fund consisted of the proceeds of Rhodes' secret sales. See the letter of Messrs. Deloitte & Co. (auditors), to the directors of De Beers, 4 July 1892, Stow Papers, vol. 1. The existence of the fund was publicly announced so as to reassure the market. See the speech of Francis Oats, *Fourth Annual Report, De Beers, 30 June 1892*, pp. 23-24.

142. See Oats' speech in De Beers' fourth annual report, pp. 23-25; and the comments of Rhodes in the *Fifth Annual Report, De Beers Consolidated Mines Limited, 30 June 1893*, p. 22.

to move progressively upward, reaching a peak of 31s. 8d. in April 1893, 32 percent higher than twelve months previously.[143]

Moreover, the new arrangement survived a severe test in 1893. Early that year America, where De Beers sold one-third of its diamonds, entered a deep depression that lasted eighteen months.[144] With the demand for diamonds way down, De Beers reduced its output, refused to sell stones at cut prices, and drew on its reserve fund to pay for operating expenses. Resulting financial tensions strained relations between merchants and producers. The former argued that market conditions were so bad, and chances of improvement so remote, that De Beers should lower its wholesale prices. When the company refused, the merchants resorted to old practices and "beared" De Beers' shares in order "to recoup themselves for whatever loss . . . [they] sustained on their . . . [diamond] shipments."[145] Rhodes found that after a few months of no diamond sales the company's reserve had become "overburdened."[146] Rather than such struggle resulting in deadlock, though, a compromise was reached, with Barnato and a group of Syndicate merchants agreeing late in 1893 to purchase De Beers' entire diamond stockpile, albeit for a carat price (averaging 25s.) lower than that ruling at the beginning of the year.[147] As Rhodes noted in a speech to his shareholders at the end of the year, merchants and producers alike benefited ultimately from higher retail diamond prices, and none wanted to see the market in disarray.[148]

Improving conditions in the American and European economies, evident from mid-1894 onward, led to a cementing of the relationship between merchants and producers. Rhodes reported to his shareholders in October 1894 that the "market . . . looked brighter and better" and that diamond stockpiles were being depleted rapidly.[149] Although he considered diamond prices unlikely

143. *Statistical Register, 1895*, p. 237.

144. See Rhodes' speech in the *Fifth Annual Report, De Beers, 30 June 1893*, p. 22.

145. See the half-yearly report of the general manager, Standard Bank, to London, 9 August 1893, p. 42, GMO 3/2/1/1, SBA.

146. See the *Fifth Annual Report, De Beers, 30 June 1893*, p. 24; and the *Sixth Annual Report, De Beers Consolidated Mines Limited, 30 June 1894*, p. 27.

147. See Rhodes' speech, made in November 1893, printed in De Beers' fifth annual report, pp. 22, 24, 26.

148. *Ibid.*, p. 22.

149. *Sixth Annual Report, De Beers, 30 June 1894*, p. 27.

to climb to 30s. per carat in the near future, he did forecast a continuing upward trend. He stated that De Beers did everything necessary to keep prices high by reducing diamond output "to the lowest limit possible," even if this meant utilizing only one-quarter of the company's productive capacity, and by selling "just what the world requires."[150] As a result of such policies Syndicate members, reassured by Rhodes' apparent commitment to output regulation and optimistic about future economic prospects, took a major step in 1895 to consolidate marketing. Prior to that year no merchant had had enough confidence in the market to buy diamonds for more than a month or two in advance at a time. In July 1895, however, the Syndicate contracted to purchase, for £5,400,000, De Beers' entire output for the following eighteen months and thereby instituted what would become a continuing pattern of long-term contracts.[151] Regulation by a monopoly producer and a merchant combine working in concord was at last established in the marketplace.

This subordination of the market to De Beers' regulation proved an essential factor in enabling the company to overcome the near anarchy that had prevailed in the mines in 1891 and that threatened to bring underground work to a halt. This anarchy was itself a direct product of the coercive measures that, because of fluctuating market demands, De Beers had used against its employees in order to lower costs. With a growing measure of control acquired over diamond supply and demand, and a resulting elimination in large part of fears about the company's financial health, De Beers tempered the worst excesses of employer despotism and sought to win a greater degree of worker acceptance of their conditions of employment.[152] Underpinning this emphasis on having workers understand that what was good for De Beers was good for them was the hard fact that cheap labor remained essential to the company's profitability and that in the last resort coercion would not be dispensed with.

150. *Ibid.*, p. 29.

151. *Seventh Annual Report, De Beers Consolidated Mines Limited, 30 June 1895*, p. 10; half-yearly report of the general manager, Standard Bank, to London, 7 August 1895, p. 55, GMO 3/2/1/1, SBA; *Eighth Annual Report, De Beers Consolidated Mines Limited, 30 June 1896*, pp. 12–13.

152. Michael Burawoy has devised a useful aphorism with regard to this process: "Anarchy in the market leads to despotism in the factory. . . . Subordination of the market leads to hegemony in the factory." See his *Manufacturing Consent: Changes in the Labor Process under Monopoly Capitalism* (Chicago, 1979), p. 194.

From 1892 onward the government protector of natives and the company compound managers played increasingly major roles in alleviating discontent in the workplace and the compounds. The protector, with the encouragement of his superiors, carried out much more rigorously than he had in the past the letter of the law in regard to his duty to inspect "from time to time all compounds . . . for the purpose of protecting generally the rights of . . . [com-pounded] natives."[153] He visited the compounds daily, listened to the inmates' complaints—most of these relating to the nonfulfillment of contractual obligations and to the use of physical force by white overseers and subcontractors—sought to resolve all disputes, and whenever he did not succeed brought an action on behalf of the black complainants before the magistrate's court.[154] The compound managers also took a large role in settling disputes. As one of them noted, all the inmates of his institution were contracted to him personally and therefore he was "their master."[155] According to De Beers' policy, blacks were "encouraged to bring all their complaints and grievances to the compound manager, who should, at all times, be willing to listen patiently . . . and take steps to remedy them, if real." In addition, the company instructed its managers to ensure that wages were paid regularly and that no white man should strike a black.[156] Although the protector found that compound managers' practices did not always meet the company's ideal of behavior, blacks did at least acquire a means of making known their griev-

153. The quotation is from Act 34 1888, clause 6. With regard to the expansion of the protector's duties see S. B. Liefeldt (protector) to under secretary of native affairs, 1 April 1891, NA 455; *idem*, 1 September 1891, NA 407; J. Rose Innes (under secretary of native affairs) to Liefeldt, 25 March 1892, NA 320; Liefeldt to Rose Innes, 8 April 1892, NA 320; and the annual report of the protector, 9 January 1892, enclosed in civil commissioner to secretary of native affairs, 16 January 1892, NA 210.

154. Descriptions of the protector's activities can be found in his monthly reports. These documents are filed in the following archival volumes: NA 231, 236, 242, 247, 254, 259, 320, 334. See also the protector's annual reports published in the *NABB*.

155. The quoted statement was made by Seymour Dallas in his evidence to the Cape Labour Commission, *CGHPP,* G3 1894, p. 392.

156. For the source of the quotation see the memorandum on the organization of De Beers' compounds prepared by Frank Mandy (one of the company's compound managers), 30 April 1895, NA 775/161. See also Dallas' evidence to the Cape Labour Commission, *CGHPP,* G3 1894, p. 392; the protector's annual report for 1895, *NABB,* G5 1896, p. 34; and Williams, *The Diamond Mines,* II, p. 56.

ances and saw some possibility of obtaining redress without having to take matters into their own hands underground.[157]

De Beers also took a number of other measures to instill obedience and alleviate tensions among its black workers. British and German missionaries, with encouragement and financial aid from the company, regularly entered the compounds to teach daily classes and to preach Sunday services. In the course of doing God's work these men stressed to their pupils the importance of temperance, punctuality, and respect for those in authority.[158] On occasion they also pointed out that men who had been injured or who had died as a result of mining accidents were likely sinners who had tempted "the Almighty" and been punished for their fall into evil. The missionaries' monopoly on education through the printed word was reinforced by a company order banning from the compounds all literature other than bibles and hymn books.[159] Alongside these endeavors the compound managers fostered games, dancing, singing, and other recreational activities in the belief that with a combination of "constant work, good wages, plenty of amusements, good food, and fairplay, the natives in . . . [the] compounds [would] have neither time nor inclination for riots and insubordination."[160]

Yet coercion remained an integral part of De Beers' practices. The compound managers used a variety of means to compel obedience: they lodged men from "the various tribes" in separate accommodations within the compounds in an effort to make it "difficult for the natives to form riotous combinations"; they imposed fines; they placed men in compound detention houses; and those they considered persistently "troublesome or turbulent" they expelled after first taking photographs (which were then "pasted in

157. Mandy argued that the effectiveness of the compound system largely rested in the hands of the compound manager: "If the manager is readily accessible, is just, firm, and kind, 'boys' will prefer to settle their quarrels under his arbitration [rather] than fight them out." NA 775/161.

158. On the origins of missionary visits to De Beers' closed compounds see the report of the founding of the Kimberley Mission Association, formed jointly by pastors and compound managers, *Quarterly Paper of the Bloemfontein Mission*, no. 79 (15 January 1888), pp. 12–13. The USPG Archive contains regular reports from the missionaries concerning their compound activities. See also the Wesleyan Methodist Church of South Africa, *Eleventh Report of the South African Missionary Society* (Cape Town, 1893), pp. 105–06.

159. See the quarterly report of the Rev. George Mitchell, 30 June 1892, pp. 55–56, USPG Reports 1892, no. 7. See also Williams, *The Diamond Mines*, II, p. 72, for the point that De Beers supplied all its compound inmates with bibles.

160. The words are Frank Mandy's, NA 775/161.

a book kept at the [compound] entrance") so that a blacklist could be enforced.[161] To ensure that there was always a plentiful supply of laborers readily available to replace any men who were injured in accidents or who objected to working conditions, De Beers continued to keep up to twice as many blacks in the compounds as were needed in the workplace.[162]

But coercion had its practical limits. In 1894 the Wesselton mine produced a clear example of what could happen if compound inmates had "no . . . means of making known their complaints."[163] Wesselton at that time was operated by H. A. Ward under a lease from De Beers. With the American depression reducing the demand for diamonds in 1893 and early 1894, Ward and several of his partners chose to accelerate production, in the hope that by increasing the number of diamonds sold they could make up for the drop in carat prices, and lowered costs by cutting wages and by lengthening the working hours of their black employees. The result was considerable discontent among the workers and widespread demands for better conditions. When these demands were not met, and Ward in addition refused to allow any of his black employees to leave the Wesselton compound and seek better terms elsewhere or to take their complaints to the protector of natives, violent conflict broke out. At dawn on Monday 6 March the compound inmates—some eight hundred to nine hundred of them—gathered together and insisted that they be permitted to leave. The compound manager rejected this demand, called in the Kimberley mounted police and, when the men refused to go to work, ordered the police and the compound guards to fire. Three blacks died, seven were injured, and thirty arrested and charged with intent to murder their white employers.

161. *Ibid.*; Dallas, *CGHPP,* G3 1894, p. 392; and, with regard to the existence of the compound lockup, see the correspondence contained in the file NA 775/161. Much harsher measures were adopted in the convict station, where recalcitrant workers were put in chains, placed in stocks (a punishment not permitted in any of the Cape Colony's other convict stations), and flogged with a cat-o'-nine-tails.

162. Most of these men were uncontracted, a practice that was illegal and that defrauded the government of the revenue it normally derived from the registration of contracts. For voluminous correspondence on this problem see, e.g., the letters of the registrar to under secretary, native affairs, 12 June 1894, NA 320; protector to civil commissioner, 18 May 1895, NA 581; Seymour Dallas to registrar of natives, 12 September 1895, NA 231; and protector to under secretary, native affairs, 14 February 1896, NA 236.

163. E. A. Judge (civil commissioner) reported in *NABB*, G8 1895, p. 26.

The courts, though, did not find Ward's case convincing. The judge-president of the Griqualand West High Court announced from the bench his sympathy for men whom he considered had "legitimate . . . grievances" yet had been treated like "prisoners"—especially by having been kept uncontracted in the compounds, so that they had no legal rights, and by having been refused access to the protector of natives. The judge stated that it was only the means chosen by the strikers (he believing that they had attacked the police and not vice versa) that he thought abhorrent.[164] He found eighteen of those charged innocent of any wrongdoing and the remaining twelve guilty only of common assault. In short, outright coercion was costly. It alienated black workers, who thereafter avoided the mine, and it angered officials, whose support was so necessary to the working of the pass-law system.

De Beers' compounds stood in marked contrast to the situation at Wesselton. The protector of natives did note in his annual report for 1895 that there was still far too much hitting of "natives . . . for the most trivial offences," a practice he felt was sure "to injure the labour supply," and he pointed out that men were often lured to De Beers' compounds by labor agents' false promises of free tobacco and liquor, only to find out once incarcerated that they got "nothing for nothing, and very little for their money" at the company stores.[165] And Kimberley's civil commissioner, the protector's immediate superior, did argue that the compound system required continued monitoring by "an independent public official" in order to ensure that black workers were treated fairly by their employers.[166] The protector, however, considered that all in all De Beers' compound managers carried out their responsibilities in a conscientious manner and "guard[ed] the interests of the natives."

164. The incident and the resulting court case are reported in considerable depth in the *Diamond Fields Advertiser*, 6, 10, 13, 14, 17, 20, 22 March, 10, 12 April, 10, 11 May 1894; and *NABB*, G8 1895, p. 26.

165. See his annual report, *NABB*, G5 1896, pp. 34–35. For further references to the connection between mistreatment of workers and declining supplies of men see the company's seventh annual report, p. 4, and its eighth annual report, p. 4.

166. *NABB*, G8 1895, p. 26. See also De Beers' response to the civil commissioner's criticisms, contained in Craven to Judge, 16 April 1895, NA 455. For references to the difficulties that government officials sometimes had in getting compound managers to abide by compound regulations see, e.g., the letters of the protector to under secretary, native affairs, 30 September 1890, NA 231, 31 January 1895, NA 231, 24 July 1895, NA 775/197, 31 August 1895, NA 231. See also the annual reports published in the *NABB*, G9 1894, pp. 24–25, G5 1896, p. 34.

This behavior, he felt, accounted for the general lack of complaints about ill treatment or the nonpayment of wages.[167] Though the protector's idea of good treatment might have been relative—pneumonia continued to kill hundreds of men annually, mining accidents tens more, and wages were lower than they had been at any time since the early 1870s—and men might not have wanted to risk blacklisting by complaining about their treatment, there was little question that the violent racial conflict that had racked the mines in 1891 had in large part been alleviated.[168]

De Beers' white employees also made few complaints, even though their working and living conditions remained onerous. In the mid-1890s white wages, like black, were the lowest since the beginning of mining.[169] Single men could generally get by on their weekly wage, but married men with families found it almost impossible to make ends meet and had to seek out additional sources of income. The women of the household sewed and put their daughters into domestic service, while boarders were often taken into homes already crowded with family members. In one case indicative of many, the South African novelist Sarah Gertrude Millin boarded in the house of a company employee while attending school. There she "learnt what it means not to have enough for one's needs, how things are stretched . . . and missed and yielded because there isn't the money to hold or maintain them." Always hungry, Millin also found little physical comfort, since the house was crowded with the mine worker, his wife, daughters, and grandchildren. There was so little room available that she had to share the mine worker's bed on a shift system, occupying it at night while he was at work and moving out at dawn when he returned home.[170]

Such conditions were borne largely because Kimberley offered no alternative means of employment. Men who lost their jobs because they complained or because De Beers decided to cut back on production found themselves competing for work in an urban labor market still glutted with those who had been sacked at the begin-

167. *NABB*, G5 1896, p. 34.
168. De Beers did on occasion sack men who complained to the protector and who, because they were uncontracted, could not be legally helped by that official. See the letter of the protector to under secretary, native affairs, 1 July 1895, NA 775/197.
169. *Statistical Register, 1901* (Cape Town, 1902), p. 264; *CGHPP,* G11 1890, p. 39.
170. See Millin's autobiography, *The Night Is Long* (London, 1941), especially pp. 73–75.

ning of the decade. The only means of escape from that situation was to scratch out a living at the river diggings or to move to the Rand, where conditions and wage rates in the gold mines were no better (and often much worse) than those in Kimberley.[171]

But coercion was not the only factor securing the submissiveness of De Beers' white employees. The company was ready to ameliorate the working conditions of its employees so long as any measures taken did not impinge on profits. In March 1892, for example, the mining subcontractors called on De Beers to introduce an eight-hour shift in place of the then current twelve-hour shift. The company ultimately agreed to this request after a delay of six months but limited its application solely to the underground operations, where payments were made on the basis of piecework. The eight-hour shift was not introduced in the surface operations, where most of the people were wage employees or convicts, because De Beers did not have any means of strictly monitoring the amount of work done and in any case considered that these men did not work as hard as those underground.[172]

Rhodes emphasized to his white employees the special relationship that he felt existed between them and the company. He argued that their supervisory abilities and "attention to duty"—he made no mention of their mining skills—"amply" repaid the company for the "extra cost" of employing white labor and ensured that De Beers would never move to a system of employing blacks only.[173] And in calling on the men to vote for company-sponsored candidates in Kimberley's parliamentary elections, he stressed that at the diamond fields, unlike other parts of the world, the interests of "capital and labour . . . [were] unanimous," since the financial well-being of all depended on De Beers' maximizing its profits.[174]

White employees, in turn, accorded Rhodes and De Beers considerable deference. When the miners first approached Gardner Williams with regard to the introduction of eight-hour shifts, and he

171. On the high cost of living and the general inability of most white mine workers in South Africa to make a comfortable living see the "Report on the Trade, Commerce, and Gold Mining Industry of the South African Republic for the Year 1897," *BPP,* C9093 (1899), LXIV, 1, p. 39.

172. See the *Diamond Fields Advertiser,* 30 March, 4 April 1892; *Daily Independent,* 3 January, 4 February 1893; and the *Fifth Annual Report, De Beers, 30 June 1893,* p. 6. The duration of the mechanics' working week was later reduced as well, from 57.5 hours to 54, on the grounds that their work was particularly onerous.

173. *Sixth Annual Report, De Beers, 30 June 1894,* p. 29.

174. *Daily Independent,* 26 September 1892. See also the issues of 1 August and 10 November for similar exhortations.

put off making an immediate decision on the matter, their leaders argued that there should be no agitation because the general manager could be "trust[ed]," and as they "did not understand much about the wants of the top men and even if they did it would be out of place as far as they were concerned to interfere."[175] Williams vindicated that trust. They cheered Rhodes when he noted the unanimity of capital and labor and, when called upon to cast their public ballots, voted almost without exception for De Beers' candidates.[176] Rhodes supplied in return, if not safe jobs or high wages, at least the basis of a living.

De Beers held much the same stranglehold, albeit one tempered by frequent expressions of company paternalism, over the town as it did over its employees. With the purchase of Wesselton and the cessation of debris washing, De Beers eliminated the only practical means by which men previously displaced by mine closings and the implementation of output reduction policies could eke out a living. Thereafter neither jobs nor welfare were available to the unemployed and the poor in Kimberley. The Knights of Labour, for example, set up an employment bureau in early 1892 and found just eight jobs, none of them in Kimberley, for the two hundred men whom it registered.[177] The Kimberley Borough Council employed a few whites to break stones for the town's roads, but had no more than £700 available annually for this work and so paid the men a less than subsistence wage of 5s. per day.[178]

The Cape government, abiding by the conclusion of the Select Committee on Griqualand West Trade and Business that "as the distress and poverty in Kimberley have arisen from natural causes, so they must be left to natural remedies," refused to take any action to help the community.[179] The law did provide that all profits—av-

175. *Diamond Fields Advertiser,* 30 March, 4 April 1892.

176. *Daily Independent,* 26 September 1892, 21 June 1893; civil commissioner to under colonial secretary (enclosing an election return showing the number of votes cast and for whom in each polling station), 29 January 1894, CO 3773.

177. *Daily Independent,* 2, 11 July 1892.

178. *Ibid.,* 20 February, 8 June 1892; "Mayor's Minutes [Kimberley Borough Council] for the Year 1892," p. 24, for 1893, p. 11, for 1894, p. 9, for 1895, p. 13, KPL.

179. For the quotation see *CGHPP,* A7 1891, p. x. The phrasing was remarkably similar to that used by John X. Merriman in his original objection (quoted above) to the establishment of the committee. The similarity is hardly surprising, since Merriman drafted the committee's majority report. On the government's refusal to act see especially the letter from J. Smuts (acting private secretary to the governor) to town clerk, Beaconsfield, 20 February 1893, repr. in the *Daily Independent,* 28 February 1893.

eraging £10,000 per annum—made by De Beers from its compound operations (largely by overcharging in the compound stores) go to charitable purposes, but Rhodes personally decided what these monies should be spent on, and he had some rather idiosyncratic ideas. In the three years 1893–95 he donated £17,000 to build a sanatorium for the well-off ("a bit of a hobby of mine," Rhodes called it), £2,203 to pay off the accumulated debts of a commercial exhibition held in 1892, £2,125 to Kimberley schools, £1,200 to the Griqualand West Turf Club ("that saved the stand," in Rhodes' view), £1,000 each to the Kimberley Rifles and the Griqualand West Brigade, £750 to assist the establishment of a school of mines, and just £150 to the Poor Whites' School Building Fund.[180] In the face of such charity, most of those unable to earn a living in Kimberley moved elsewhere, to the river diggings, the Free State mines, and the Rand.[181]

Commercial life withered. Shopkeepers found it increasingly difficult to stay in business with fewer people in the town and most of those having little money to spend. Indeed, the Standard Bank's inspector reported in October 1891 that most of the town's merchants considered Kimberley "done for."[182] De Beers' financing of a railway line through to Johannesburg in 1892 exacerbated matters by eliminating what little remained of Kimberley's forwarding trade. A decline in 1892 alone of 200–300 percent in the value of the town's fixed property clearly demonstrated the pervading sense of crisis.[183] To an ever-increasing extent business in the town was, in the words of the manager of the Standard Bank, "virtually reduced to [supplying] the requirements of the employees of the mines."[184]

Because three-quarters of these employees were black laborers

180. *Eighth Annual Report, De Beers, 30 June 1896*, p. 13.

181. See the *Daily Independent*, 10 April 1893; Reunert, *Diamonds and Gold*, p. 77; the annual reports of the inspector of diamond mines, *CGHPP*; and for the experiences of a person whose family made the move to the river, Sarah Gertrude Millin's autobiography, *The Night Is Long*, and her novel *The Dark River* (London, 1919), especially pp. 14–15.

182. See his report of 3 October 1891, p. 198, INSP 1/1/88, SBA.

183. On the railway line see the *Fourth Annual Report, De Beers, 30 June 1892*, p. 23; and on property values see the report of the Standard Bank's inspector, 31 December 1892, p. 49, INSP 1/1/88, SBA.

184. Quoted in the general manager's report to London, 7 August 1894, p. 61, GMO 3/2/1/1, SBA. See also his report of 13 February 1895, p. 41, GMO 3/2/1/1, for a similar statement.

locked up in closed compounds, De Beers could determine which merchants had access to this market. Small shopkeepers hardly entered the commercial picture, since with the closing of the compounds in the late 1880s they had been excluded from that trade altogether. For those who did get access, the compound trade was a mixed blessing because De Beers used its massive buying power to get supplies at the lowest possible price, either by forcing Kimberley's merchants to compete against one another for the contracts available or by secretly evading the Labourers' Wages Regulation Act and importing goods direct from outside wholesalers.[185] When a group of Kimberley's merchants in 1894 challenged the company to prove that it did not buy from outside suppliers and that it only supplied the basic necessities of life to its compounded employees, De Beers responded that if the complainants were not ready to accept the word of the company's English auditors on these matters, then it considered "no good can result by continuing discussion."[186] One of De Beers' directors counseled the merchants to show moderation and to recognize that "what is in the interest of the Company is to the interest of the town, and of the whole Colony."[187]

Merchants could respond to these terms in two ways. They could close down their businesses and join the exodus to the Rand— and this they did in increasing numbers, with most of the town's largest merchants having moved north by the middle of the 1890s.[188] Alternatively, they could remain in Kimberley—operating on a retail level and, in exchange for their economic survival, giving De Beers their full political support. As R. H. Henderson, a Kimberley merchant and mayor of the town in the late 1880s and again in the

185. For the provisions of the Act see chapt. 5. For merchants' concerns about the compound trade and their complaints about the way in which the company treated them see the *Diamond Fields Advertiser,* 10, 14, 17 March, 2, 5, 21, 25 April, 1, 2, 3, 4, 8, 11, 15, 19, 23, 24 May, 15, 22 June 1894; and the *Verbatim Report of the Meeting [between Kimberley and Beaconsfield town councillors and merchants] . . . and De Beers . . . Re the Compound System* (Kimberley, 22 May 1894), bound in with the *Regulations of the Borough of Kimberley* (Kimberley, 1893), KPL.

186. See the *Verbatim Report* (referred to in the previous note) of the meeting between the merchants and representatives of De Beers. For the quotation see the letter from William Pickering (acting secretary of De Beers) to secretary of the Committee Re the Compound System, 5 June 1894, repr. on p. 24 of *ibid.*

187. See the *Verbatim Report,* p. 12, for the comment by Henry Robinow.

188. For the origins and continuation of this exodus see the reports of the Standard Bank's inspector, 31 December 1892, p. 49, 31 December 1894, pp. 41–42, INSP 1/1/88; and those of the general manager, 10 August 1892, p. 37, 2 February 1893, p. 26, 7 February 1894, p. 46, GMO 3/2/1/1, SBA.

late 1890s, noted in his memoirs, compound-supply contracts went to those people who publicly supported and voted for the full ticket of four parliamentary candidates that De Beers put forward in each election.[189] Though recognizing the extent of manipulation that went on, Henderson still considered De Beers' monopoly of the diamond industry "essential for . . . the general welfare" and believed that the company used its enormous power "profitably and wisely."[190]

When Sarah Gertrude Millin moved from the mine worker's house to board with a Kimberley grain merchant ("who had the distinction of sometimes selling his produce to de Beers Company"), the first lesson she was taught was "to honour de Beers Company." But that was just the beginning. She soon learned that "de Beers was not a business, it was a religion. One had to believe in de Beers. One was blasphemous if one didn't. Benefits, commandments, the place to which one was called, one's daily bread, life and death, flowed from de Beers." In short, deference to De Beers was the means to survival in Kimberley.[191]

CONCLUSION

By the middle of the 1890s De Beers' monopoly had been fully secured: marketing was under control, working costs falling, the company's employees co-opted and coerced, and Kimberley's residents deferring to the dictates of the diamond magnates. Rhodes proclaimed at the company's eighth annual general meeting on 28 December 1896 that Kimberley's diamond industry was "one of those cases where a monopoly is judicious and justified by the results," and he announced himself much pleased by the results of his endeavors. Yet, he added, to the amusement of his audience, things were going so well, just "like clockwork" in fact, that dia-

---

189. *An Ulsterman in Africa* (Cape Town, 1944), pp. 58–59.
190. *Ibid.*, pp. 48, 50.
191. *The Night Is Long*, p. 45. See also Statham's *Mr Magnus*; S. C. Cronwright-Schreiner, *Some Vital Facts about Kimberley and Johannesburg for Working-men and Friends of the Native* (n. p., n. d. [Johannesburg, 1900]); and, for a discussion of the deferential attitudes adopted by members of Kimberley's black petty bourgeoisie, Brian Willan, *Sol Plaatje: South African Nationalist, 1876–1932* (Berkeley, 1984), chapt. 2.

mond mining had become "a matter of course and uninteresting."[192] Such were the discontents of the "Great Amalgamator."[193]

De Beers' financial returns justified Rhodes' good humor. The company made a profit of £1,712,854 during the twelve months ending 30 June 1896, the highest since its formation, on sales totaling £3,165,382 and paid out £1,500,000 in dividends.[194] The large gap between the cost of producing diamonds (kept low by the depressed share of income going to pay wages) and the price De Beers received for them was the cornerstone of the company's successful implementation of its monopoly. The second key factor accounting for De Beers' profitability—one that allowed the company to make money in economically depressed years as well as in boom times—was Rhodes' adherence to the policy of manipulating output in order to maintain the highest possible carat price. Throughout the early 1890s the company made profits averaging over one million pounds annually, even during the difficult times in 1891 and 1893–94, since by keeping output down Rhodes ensured that prices remained high and that the difference between cost of production and market return did not shrink but remained at the maximum level possible.[195]

In developing such control over output, De Beers displayed several other features characteristic of monopoly capitalism. The company greatly underutilized its plant. In 1894, for example, Rhodes claimed that De Beers could produce at will three to four times the then current level of output.[196] It maintained a large reserve of labor, men whom it could call upon and dismiss at will in accord with the demands of output schedules and sufficient in number to ensure that wage rates (and thus costs) could be kept at a minimum.[197] Moreover, De Beers neither expanded itself nor permitted others to enter diamond production. And it did not generate economic development in Kimberley. As a monopoly enterprise De Beers had reached the limits of its growth almost from the moment of inception in 1888. In order to protect the company's monopoly, its directors sought to eliminate rival enterprises either by pur-

192. *Eighth Annual Report, De Beers, 30 June 1896*, pp. 12, 14.
193. See Williams, *Cecil Rhodes*, p. 115.
194. *Eighth Annual Report, De Beers, 30 June 1896*, p. 1.
195. For statistics on profits see the company's annual reports; and also Williams, *The Diamond Mines*, II, p. 320.
196. *Sixth Annual Report, De Beers, 30 June 1894*, p. 29.
197. The lowering of costs is documented in the company's annual reports and shown also in a table in Williams, *The Diamond Mines*, II, p. 320.

chasing and closing down existing mines or by acquiring those areas in which future diamond finds seemed likely and prohibiting prospecting.

Without expansion—which would have been counterproductive for profitability—the industry did not attract new investors in the mid-1890s, apart from those who assumed that De Beers was a blue-chip stock, because the returns paid to those who had not got in on the ground floor or who were not interested in playing the market were low by any contemporary standard. Rather, Kimberley's magnates went in seach of better investment opportunities elsewhere, largely on the Rand, and left the "city of diamonds" largely bereft of people and of capital, no more than "a small stagnant town" servicing the needs of the "big hole."[198]

---

198. James Bryce used the term "city of diamonds" to refer to Kimberley, which he visited on his travels in South Africa in 1895. See his *Impressions of South Africa* (London, 1897), pp. 245-52. On Kimberley as a small stagnant town see Sarah Gertrude Millin's semiautobiographical novel *The Dark River,* p. 166. The "big hole" is the name by which the Kimberley mine was, and is, familiarly known.

# Epilogue: 1905

The ten years between 1895 and 1905 were tumultuous ones indeed. In December 1895 Leander Starr Jameson, at the instigation of his employer Rhodes and bankrolled by De Beers and the British South Africa Company, led a band of armed BSA police into the Transvaal with the aim of overthrowing Paul Kruger's Boer government and replacing it with one more amenable to the demands of mining capitalists. The failure of Jameson's raiders, disarmed without a struggle on the last day of 1895 as they entered the Transvaal, left their nominal leader in prison, four of Rhodes' fellow plotters (including his brother) under sentence of death by Kruger for treason, and Rhodes himself politically disgraced and out of office in the Cape.[1]

Just a few months later the Ndebele and Shona in Rhodesia rose up against the oppressive rule of the BSA and fought a bitter war of independence. The uprising was finally put down in 1897, with the Shona dynamited into submission, but not before blacks had shown their hatred of the gold industry by casting the bodies of white miners down mine shafts and not before BSA shares had fallen to a quarter of their prewar value.[2] That same year Rhodes' fellow life governor Barney Barnato fell, threw himself, or was pushed to

1. Geoffrey Blainey, "Lost Causes of the Jameson Raid," *Economic History Review* 18 (1965): 350–66; Richard Mendelsohn, "Blainey and the Jameson Raid: The Debate Renewed," *Journal of Southern African Studies* 6:2 (1980): 157–70.

2. Terence Ranger, *Revolt in Southern Rhodesia* (London, 1967); Charles van Onselen, *Chibaro* (London, 1976), pp. 14–15.

a death by drowning while sailing to England. Two years later, in 1899, war broke out between the British and the Boer republics. The Anglo-Boer war lasted three years, devastated much of South Africa, and produced thousands of casualties.[3] Kimberley and the diamond industry were hit badly, with the town under siege for four months and the mines idle during that time.[4] Rhodes did not live to see final victory, dying at the beginning of 1902. The following year the sole surviving original life governor, Alfred Beit, suffered a stroke on receiving news of the development of a new diamond mine near Pretoria in the Transvaal.[5]

Yet De Beers continued to flourish. Every year between 1895 and 1901 (with the sole exception of war-torn 1900) the company paid a 40-percent dividend amounting to just over one-and-a-half million pounds annually, while from 1902 to 1904 the yearly payout averaged more than two million pounds.[6] The returns for mining operations during the twelve months ending 30 June 1905 demonstrated De Beers' strong financial condition. The company reported an operating profit of £1,865,335 (10 percent higher than that of 1895) on diamond sales of £4,802,844 (one-and-a-half times that of 1895), even though the weight of diamonds found in each load of excavated ground averaged only .38 carats (down from .85 in 1895), and the total number of carats sold numbered 1,960,313 (four-fifths of 1895's sales). Increased diamond prices, with stones from the Kimberley and De Beers mines fetching 52s. 10d. per carat, twice what they had sold for a decade earlier, accounted for the rise in profits. This price increase, in turn, was largely the result of a new marketing arrangement worked out in 1901 with the Syndicate,

3. Among many studies see in particular, Atmore and Marks, "The Imperial Factor," pp. 105–39; Shula Marks and Stanley Trapido, "Lord Milner and the South African State," *History Workshop* 8 (1979): 50–80; Thomas Pakenham, *The Boer War* (London, 1979); Peter Warwick (ed.), *The South African War: The Anglo-Boer War 1899–1902* (London, 1980).

4. For a discussion of the war's impact on Kimberley and the diamond industry see the eleventh and twelfth annual reports of De Beers; and Roberts, *Kimberley: Turbulent City,* chapt. 20.

5. Roberts, *Kimberley: Turbulent City,* pp. 334–36, 344. The first major diamond finds at the mine had been made in 1902. F. S. P. Stow had resigned his life governorship in 1898.

6. De Beers also made payments to its life governors over and above these dividends; such payments ranged from an average of £150,000 in the late 1890s to £316,000 in 1901. The life-governor scheme was wound up in 1901 and the life governors paid off with extra shares. See De Beers' annual reports, particularly that of 1901.

whereby the latter agreed to pay De Beers £356,875 wholesale for 165,000 carats each month and to split evenly all profits made on the resale of the stones. This agreement meant that finally neither would benefit from undercutting the other, which had often been the case in the past.[7] Moreover, despite the discovery of the Premier mine in the Transvaal, De Beer's production monopoly remained largely in force. Whereas the company's sales amounted to near £5,000,000 in 1905, those of the Premier mine (which produced diamonds of a much lower quality than those from the Kimberley mines—"rubbish" goods according to one of De Beers' directors) came to £900,000. Brazil's exports were worth £800,000, and India's only £5,000.[8] Confident about future prospects, De Beers' directors paid out £1,800,000 in dividends in 1905.

The directors' confidence rested in part on the continuing political influence exercised by their company. Although Rhodes had lost the premiership of the Cape in 1896 and had fallen out with Hofmeyr's Afrikaner Bond, he kept his parliamentary seat and remained a powerful force in Cape and British politics until his death. And Kimberley elected to parliament, with dependable regularity, De Beers' nominees. Perhaps most pleasing to the company's directors was that one of their own number, Dr. Jameson, having rehabilitated his political fortunes, won the premiership of the Cape in 1904. In this new role Jameson worked as ever on De Beers' behalf. In 1905, for example, when legislation to provide a greater level of compensation for people injured during the course of their work came before the House, Jameson amended the draft bill so that it favored employers (and De Beers in particular) at the expense of their employees, rather than the other way round as the bill's pro-

7. See the *Thirteenth Annual Report, De Beers Consolidated Mines Limited, June 1901*, p. 2; and the "Memorandum of Agreement made the Second Day of December, 1901, between De Beers Consolidated Mines, Limited . . . [and] 'the Syndicate,'" Rhodes Papers, Rhodes House. For a discussion of some of the antagonisms affecting relations between syndicate and company in the later 1890s see Newbury, "Out of the Pit," pp. 36–39.

8. De Beers made most of its profits on higher-quality stones, and the price of these goods was not affected by competition from the low-quality output of the Premier mine. In 1905, for example, when De Beers earned an average of 52s. 10d. for each carat it sold, the Premier earned only 23s. See the *Seventeenth Annual Report, De Beers Consolidated Mines Limited, June 1905*, p. 35; and Percy Wagner, *The Diamond Fields of Southern Africa* (Cape Town, 1971 [1st ed. 1914]), p. 339. On the Indian and Brazilian returns see William Crookes, *Diamonds* (London, 1909), pp. 4, 5. The mines in the Orange Free State were controlled either by De Beers or by members of the Syndicate.

ponents had originally intended. Under the terms of Jameson's legislation, men injured would receive up to a maximum of 50 percent
of their wages while off work, rather than 50 percent as of right,
and only the dependents of those black miners who had been married in a Christian ceremony (a tiny minority of mine workers)
could receive any compensation for work-related deaths.[9] Political
leverage of this sort also accounted for the fact that the diamond
industry still remained largely free of any form of direct taxation,
despite widespread public calls for its imposition.[10]

The financial benefits accruing from political influence were more
than matched by those secured through De Beers' continued reliance on the employment of cheap black labor. In 1905 approximately fifty thousand blacks, 40 percent of them recruited, the rest
having come to Kimberley under their own steam, contracted to
work in the mines for periods of three, six, or twelve months, with
an average of between fifteen thousand and twenty thousand employed at any one time.[11] Jameson's Cape government supplied another twelve hundred convicts, approximately two-thirds of them
sentenced for stock theft, collected from every part of the colony
and sent to work on the floors of the De Beers mine.[12] All these mine

9. On Jameson's actions see the letter from his private secretary to the secretary of De Beers, 31 March 1905, contained in De Beers reel 161, file 368 (Workmen's
Compensation Act, 1905–1935), DBA. Jameson had already shown a callous disregard for the interests of mine workers when, in 1883–84, he had been one of the
doctors who had refused to diagnose the infection killing hundreds of people as
smallpox but had instead pretended that it was a nonlethal disease that afflicted
blacks only. On this matter see chapt. 2.

10. The £1,800,000 in dividends issued by the company in 1905 were paid free
of any Cape income tax, while those paid in 1904 had incurred a tax bill of £140,000.
Francis Oats, the chairman of the annual meeting in 1905, feared that if economic
conditions in the colony as a whole took a dive the public demand for major taxation
of the diamond industry might become too strong to resist. See the *Seventeenth
Annual Report, De Beers, June 1905*, pp. 32–35, and the balance sheets included in
the report.

11. Those who were recruited had to stay for the longer periods. On this matter
see the letter from the registrar of contracted servants to secretary of native affairs,
31 December 1902, NA 419. On the numbers at work in the mines see the registrar's
annual report published in *NABB*, G46 1906, pp. 67–68; and the *Eighteenth Annual
Report, De Beers Consolidated Mines Limited, June 1906*, pp. 25, 46. On recruitment
see De Beers' annual reports of June 1905, pp. 21, 31, and of June 1906, p. 25.

12. On the numbers of men in De Beers' convict station and the reasons for
their conviction see the annual report of the prisons service, *CGHPP*, G19 1906,
pp. xx, xxi. On the readiness of the Cape administration to supply as many men as
possible see the letters from the under colonial secretary to secretary of De Beers,
3 July 1905, 23 May 1906, De Beers reel 42, file 417 (convict station, 1905–06), DBA.

workers lived behind walls and fences for the duration of their contract or sentence, the free men in eighteen closed compounds, the prisoners in what was "by far" the largest convict station in the Cape.[13] De Beers got these men cheaply, contracting to pay an average of 24s. per week to free workers and between 2d. and 3d. per day to the government for each convict. The company sometimes paid free workers less than their contract tickets required, as for example when there was not enough work to occupy all those in the compounds. When this happened, as it did in 1905 (with some workers getting no more than 5d. per day), the protector of natives took official steps to rectify the situation if it came to his notice.[14]

Company and state actions ensured that the cost of black labor stayed low. When black mine workers engaged in a number of strikes in 1905 in attempts to push wage and piecework rates higher, De Beers reacted as always: it called in the police, discharged those men who refused to return to work, and had the ringleaders convicted in the magistrate's court under the provisions of the Masters' and Servants' Act.[15] Attempts by convicts to ameliorate their conditions of service, by working slower (officially termed "laziness" or "idleness") or by acquiring "forbidden articles" (generally tobacco), were dealt with more harshly. Indeed, inmates of the De Beers convict station were punished twice as frequently as men in any other prison in the Cape, with most transgressors of station regulations placed in a set of stocks (the only ones permitted in the colony), usually for three hours a day for two to three days at a time.[16]

13. See De Beers' annual report of June 1906, p. 25, for a listing of the company's compounds. On the convict station see the annual report of the prisons service, *CGHPP*, G19 1906, p. xx.

14. On free workers see the letter of the protector to registrar of contracted servants, 31 August 1905, and that of the registrar to secretary of native affairs, 1 September 1905, NA 658 (2407). With regard to the convicts, De Beers paid 2d. per day for the first four hundred men and 3d. per day for each man in excess of that number. See the letter of the under colonial secretary to secretary of De Beers, 3 July 1905, De Beers reel 42, file 417, DBA.

15. See, e.g., the breaking of a strike by drill boys in June and July 1905 described in the correspondence passing between the protector, registrar, and secretary of native affairs, 1 July, 30 June 1905, NA 658 (2407). On the prevalence of strikes that year see the *Seventeenth Annual Report, De Beers, June 1905*, p. 13.

16. The punishment statistics were published in the annual reports on prisons and gaols. See, e.g., that of 1905, *CGHPP*, G19 1906, p. xxiii. For the punishment records of individual prisoners see, e.g., that of Funde Bonga contained in CO 1950 folio 222 vol. 3, and that of Klaas Witbooi in CO 1952 folio 222 vol. 5.

Company concern to keep up a regular supply of cheap labor to the mines led also to strict control being exercised over the lives of blacks residing outside the compounds in the town. De Beers' directors wanted mine workers, once their contracts were up, either to return immediately to their rural homes or else spend just a brief period resting in Kimberley before reengaging for another period of labor. They did not want the men to remain in town for lengthy periods and become "idlers" or, worse still, IDBers. Therefore, company officials pushed throughout the late 1890s and the early 1900s for a reduction in the number of locations in Kimberley and the removal of all blacks (many of whom still dwelt outside the existing locations) to a few centralized institutions, where the only legal residents would be mine workers resting between contracts (and their immediate dependents), and those people employed in the town either as domestic servants or in other sectors of the urban economy.[17] The removal process was complete well before 1905, with every black resident in the town living in one of three municipal locations. The inhabitants of these urban compounds (for that is what in essence the locations most resembled) were constantly harassed as council officials checked daily to ensure that every person had a permit to reside in Kimberley, that all were gainfully employed, that each head of household had paid the location hut tax, and that there were no idlers, no IDBers, and no brewers of "Kaffir beer."

One black who grew up in Kimberley's Location No. 2 in the early 1900s, Z. K. Matthews, the son of a mine worker, long remembered the location superintendent, Mr. Bird, "the first white man I ever saw . . . mounted on a white horse and [with] . . . a white uniform, with brass buttons down the centre of the tunic, a white hel-

17. For a description of the black urban populations of Kimberley and Beaconsfield in the 1890s see the letter of the town clerk, Beaconsfield, to resident magistrate, Kimberley, 4 February 1894, and that of the resident magistrate to under colonial secretary, 31 January 1894, CO 7070. On the municipal requirement that all blacks should live in a location see the revised regulations of the borough of Kimberley, dated 3 February 1898, a copy of which can be found in CO 7147. This regulation was later declared ultra vires by the Cape attorney general, although that did not prevent its being put into practical effect. With regard to De Beers' support for removals of the black population and the centralization of locations see the letters passing in 1900 between the company and Kimberley's municipal officers contained in De Beers reel 8, general letter books, book 12 (3 July 1899 to 26 February 1900), and reel 14, general letters (1898–1900), DBA; and the letter from De Beers' secretary to Rhodes, 15 September 1900, Rhodes Papers 7B (258), Rhodes House.

met cupped over his red face, and a pistol in a holster that hung from his belt. From where I peered up at him, through the wire fence around our small yard, he looked like a giant, a fearsome giant who came from that dangerous world beyond the 'Location,' bringing pain and panic with him to our family and to all the people among whom we lived."[18] Still, life in the world beyond, the streets of Kimberley, could be much worse, for there Matthews and his fellow blacks not only faced constant racial discrimination but were forever at the mercy of the police checking as always that every black had a pass and was out and about only with the express permission of his or her white master.[19]

White employees of De Beers did not suffer from such overt harassment, but they still remained dependent on company paternalism for their survival in Kimberley. The mines employed an average of twenty-seven hundred whites in 1905, nearly twice as many as a decade earlier, and paid them £3 to £5 10s. per week.[20] In return for this bare living wage, the company expected the complete support of the men, especially in political campaigns, and pressured employees to register and vote in municipal and parliamentary elections.[21] Just to make sure of the men's loyalty, the company and the detective department took extra precautions—with the result that Kimberley in 1905 was, according to the report of a visiting organizer for the Amalgamated Society of Engineers, "honeycombed by a service of spies, touts, and pimps" in the employ, more or less, of De Beers.[22]

But the very success of the company in exercising such control over Kimberley and in so dominating the diamond industry lulled De Beers' directors into a false sense of their own omnipotence. They were supremely confident that the enormous profits of the early 1900s would continue forever, that the company's monopoly was unassailable, and that their own ability to run everything could not

18. Matthews, *Freedom for My People*, p. 1.
19. See *ibid.*, chapt. 1, for a description of life in Kimberley for a black youth during the first decade of this century.
20. See the *Seventeenth Annual Report, De Beers, June 1905*, p. 12; and the annual report of the inspector of diamond mines, *CGHPP,* G65 1906.
21. For the measures taken to get men onto the voting rolls see the letter from the secretary of the De Beers Benefit Society to secretary of De Beers, 26 April 1905, De Beers reel 123, file 321 (Parliamentary Voters Roll, 1903–38), DBA.
22. The organizer's report, published in the *Amalgamated Society of Mining Engineers Journal*, July 1905, is cited in David Ticktin, "The Origins of the South African Labour Party, 1888–1910" (PhD, University of Cape Town, 1973), p. 29.

be challenged. Indeed, the chairman of De Beers' annual meeting in 1905 advised his stockholders to look to the future with "complacency."[23]

That attitude proved De Beers' undoing. Rhodes had long recognized that to prevail in diamond mining the company had to maintain its monopoly in the production and marketing of stones, a lesson that his successors soon forgot. When the first diamond finds were made at the new Premier mine in 1902, De Beers' directors, fearful initially that the discovery would turn out to be a fraud and sure later that the stones were only of a mediocre quality, chose not to try to acquire the mine. The foolishness of that decision was clearly brought home to them in January 1905 with the unearthing in the new mine of the Cullinan, an enormous and almost flawless stone of 3,025.75 carats, the largest diamond ever found, thirty-six times the size of the gem that had set off the original rush to the Griqualand West mines in 1869.[24]

From 1905 onward De Beers' monopoly was steadily undermined. The directors of the Premier Mining Company chose to establish their own marketing organization rather than try to come to some agreement with the Syndicate. They adopted a policy of producing and selling as many diamonds as possible in order to turn a profit, even though in the process they cut by half the price received for low-quality stones, rather than by restricting output as De Beers continued to do.[25] At first this policy did not impinge on the price De Beers received for its stones, since the world demand for diamonds was strong, but widespread depression in America and Europe in 1907 soon caused the bottom to fall out of the diamond market. The Syndicate stopped buying, De Beers stopped producing, and two thousand white mine workers and sixteen thousand black in Kimberley were dismissed.[26]

23. *Seventeenth Annual Report, De Beers, June 1905*, p. 35.

24. The Cullinan diamond (named after Thomas Cullinan, the mine's discoverer), was more impressive still in that it was believed to be a fragment of an even larger stone. On the diamond itself see Crookes, *Diamonds*, pp. 77–79; for a rather disparaging description of the Premier mine written by the general manager of De Beers before the discovery of the Cullinan see Williams, *The Diamond Mines*, II, pp. 330–32; and on De Beers' early relations with the Premier see Gregory, *Ernest Oppenheimer*, pp. 59–60.

25. See Gregory, *Ernest Oppenheimer*, p. 60.

26. Despite the downturn in carat prices De Beers still made a profit even in the midst of depression. See the *Twentieth Annual Report, De Beers Consolidated Mines Limited, June 1908*, pp. 4, 25, 27; and Gregory, *Ernest Oppenheimer*, pp. 60–62.

The depression had barely receded, and the market was only just on the mend, when in 1908 new diamond finds were made in German South West Africa. With its finances in a somewhat straitened condition, De Beers could not afford to invest heavily in the companies floated to work these new alluvial deposits. That too was a mistake, for over the next half decade the South West African mines proved extraordinarily rich and further undercut De Beers' faltering monopoly. Competition between De Beers, the Premier Company, and the Diamond Regie (a marketing operation that sold the diamonds produced in the South West mines) had become so intense by the beginning of the twentieth century's second decade that the organizations sought to come to some sort of working arrangement. Negotiations finally produced a compromise agreement on 30 July 1914. De Beers, the Premier, and the Regie agreed to establish a diamond pool, to split the market into shares of 48 percent, 38 percent, and 21 percent each respectively, and to market all their output through the Syndicate. A few days later, however, the outbreak of World War I rendered the agreement null and void.[27]

It was only after the war that De Beers' monopoly was finally destroyed, and then by a diamond merchant who proceeded to build a far stronger new monopoly enterprise on the foundations of the old. Ernest Oppenheimer had first arrived in Kimberley in 1902, a representative of the family firm of Dunkelsbuhler and Son (one of the founding members of the Syndicate). He remained in the town for the next decade-and-a-half, looking after Dunkelsbuhler's business while also taking a closer interest in De Beers' activities. He played an increasingly prominent role in municipal politics, becoming a town councilor in 1908 and being elected mayor for three consecutive terms in 1912–14, until the sinking of the *Lusitania* produced a wave of anti-German feeling that drove him from office.

In 1917 Oppenheimer, with the financial backing of J. P. Morgan and other American investors, formed the Anglo American Corporation in order to take over a number of gold-mining companies on the Rand. At much the same time that he expanded Anglo's gold-mining interests, Oppenheimer also sought to acquire diamond-producing properties. In 1920 he purchased from the Union government the South West mines confiscated from the Germans after the war. In 1922 Anglo agreed to purchase the diamond output of newly

27. See Gregory, *Ernest Oppenheimer*, pp. 62–70, 73–74.

developed mines in the Congo and in Angola. Later in the decade Oppenheimer won control of other newly discovered South African diamond fields in Lichtenburg and Namaqualand, successfully beating out De Beers at every step along the way in this series of acquisitions. Finally, in December 1929, with Anglo American having a stranglehold on world diamond production, De Beers' directors succumbed to an ultimatum from their archrival (whom they had already had to accept as a fellow director) and appointed him chairman of their board.

Thereupon Oppenheimer, leaving Anglo American in charge of his gold mines, put all his diamond interests under the aegis of De Beers, once again placing production in the hands of a single company. He cemented this monopoly into a form stronger even than Rhodes had ever achieved by creating a new marketing body, the Diamond Corporation Limited, which incorporated the old Syndicate members but which was controlled by the De Beers' Board and thus by the diamond producers rather than the diamond sellers. By March 1930, having had himself appointed chairman of the Diamond Corporation as well as of De Beers, Ernest Oppenheimer was truly "in charge of the diamond world," a position that he maintained until his death in 1957, one that his son, Harry Oppenheimer, occupied until 1984, and one that Ernest's grandson, Nicholas Oppenheimer, will take over in the future.[28]

28. *Ibid.*, introduction and chapters 1–4 in particular. Gregory's book was commissioned by Anglo American and thus bears the hallmarks of an in-house history, but it is nonetheless a remarkably thorough and insightful study. For a more critical study of De Beers and Anglo American, but one that relies to a very great extent on Gregory for much of its source material on the early history of the two companies, see Duncan Innes, *Anglo American and the Rise of Modern South Africa* (New York, 1984). For a contentious examination of the contemporary diamond industry see Edward Epstein, *The Diamond Invention* (London, 1982).

# Select Bibliography

GOVERNMENT ARCHIVES

*Cape Archives Depot, Cape Town (CA)*

| | |
|---|---|
| ACC 540 | Papers of Sir Lewis Michell |
| AG | Attorney-General's Archives |
| CO | Colonial Office Archives |
| COSC | Colonial Office Sundry Committees Archives |
| CR | Company Records found in the Griqualand West High Court |
| DOK | Deeds Office, Kimberley Archives |
| EC | Executive Committee Archives |
| GH | Government House Archives |
| GLW | Griqualand West Archives |
| HA | House of Assembly Archives |
| 1/KIM | Kimberley Magistrates' Archives |
| 3/KIM | Kimberley Municipal Archives |
| | Kimberley Estates Archives |
| LC | Limited Liability Companies Archives |
| LND | Lands Department Archives |
| | Uninventoried Lands and Mines Archives |
| NA | Native Affairs Archives |
| PMO | Prime Minister's Office Archives |
| PWD | Public Works Department Archives |
| | Portfolio 32: De Beers Benefit Society |
| SGGLW | Surveyor-General Griqualand West Archives |
| Theal | Basutoland Records, vol. 5, 1869–70, vol. 6, 1871–72 |
| VC | Verbatim Copies |

ZC          "RJD on the Diamond Fields" (microfilm)
ZT          Sir W. O. Lanyon Papers (microfilm)

*Natal Archives Depot, Pietermaritzburg (NAD)*

CSO         Colonial Secretary's Archives
SNA         Secretary of Native Affairs Archives

*Transvaal Archives Depot, Pretoria (TA)*

A596        Sir W. O. Lanyon Papers
ATC         Administrator of the Transvaal Colony Archives,
            1877–81
SN          Superintendent of Natives Archives


OTHER ARCHIVES

*Barlow Rand Limited, Johannesburg (BRA)*

HE          H. E. Eckstein Archives

*De Beers Consolidated Mines Limited, Kimberley (DBA)*

BMB         Bultfontein Mining Board Archives
DB Reel     Secretary of De Beers Consolidated Mines Archives
            (microfilm)
DTMB        Dutoitspan Mining Board Archives
KCDM        Kimberley Central Diamond Mining Company
            Limited Archives
KDM         Kimberley Diamond Mining Company Limited
            Archives
KMB         Kimberley Mining Board Archives
KMBS        Kimberley Mine Benefit Society Archives
LSAE        London and South Africa Exploration Company
            Limited Archives
            R. M. Roberts, private letter book, 1879

*J. A. Henry, Cape Town (Henry Papers)*

GM/LO       Extracts from the correspondence of the general
            manager of the Standard Bank to the London Office,
            1867–83

*Johannesburg Public Library, Johannesburg (JPL)*

Kimberley Stock Exchange, No. 2, Register of Members, 1890–92

*Kimberley Public Library, Kimberley (KPL)*

George Beet MSS
S. C. J. Hawthorne MSS
International Diamond Mining Company Limited, Insolvency Papers, 1883
Kimberley Debris Washers Association, Minute Book, 1890–91
Kimberley Debris Washers Association, Rules, 1891
W. S. Lockhart *v.* De Beers Mining Company Limited (record of the high court case), 1886
Mayors' Minutes, 1885–95

*Alexander McGregor Museum, Kimberley*

C. D. Rudd Papers
F. S. P. Stow Papers

*Rhodes House Library, Oxford*

Afr.mss. s.228 C. J. Rhodes Papers

*Royal Commonwealth Society Library, London*

Index to the General Plan of Kimberley Stands, 1882

*South African Library, Cape Town (SAL)*

J. B. Currey Papers
De Villiers Papers
J. H. Hofmeyr Papers
J. X. Merriman Papers
J. Rose Innes Papers
R. J. Roth, "Concerning the State of the Diamond Diggings in South Africa," MS
Olive Schreiner Papers

*Standard Bank Limited, Johannesburg (SBA)*

GMO        Half-yearly reports, general manager, Cape Town, to London office, 1880–96

GMO          Private official correspondence, branch manager, Kim-
             berley, to general manager, Cape Town
INSP         Half-yearly reports of the inspector of the Standard
             Bank, 1873–98

*United Society for the Propagation of the Gospel, London (USPG)*

Quarterly and Annual Reports, 1870–84
Letters and Papers Received, Diocese of Bloemfontein, 1867–90
*Quarterly Paper of the Orange Free State Mission* (renamed the *Quar-
terly Paper of the Bloemfontein Mission* in 1878), 1871–97

*University of Cape Town Library, Cape Town (UCT)*

BC127        Jacob Dirk Barry Papers
BC500        Judge Family Papers
             John Smalberger Papers

*University of the Witwatersrand Library, Johannesburg*

A22          L. Cohen Papers
A77          E. A. Maund Papers
A249f        A. Boggie, "Second Trip to the Diamond Fields," 1878,
             MS
A881         J. H. Pim Papers
AB751f       R. R. Langham-Carter MSS

*Yale University Library, New Haven*

CO107        Griqualand West Records, 1875–80 (microfilm)


OFFICIAL PUBLICATIONS

*Cape of Good Hope Parliamentary Papers (CGHPP)*
Annual Reports on the Management of Convict Stations and Pris-
ons, 1880–1910
Annual Reports of the District Surgeons, 1883–1906
Annual Reports by the Superintendent-General of Education, 1882–
1905
Annual Reports by the Inspectors of Diamond Mines, 1882–1910
Annual Reports by the Commissioners of Police, 1874–1910
Annual Reports by the Manager of the Vooruitzigt Estate, 1883–95
Blue Books on Native Affairs, 1873–1910

*Miscellaneous Papers, and Reports of Select Committees*

1871: G21, G33
1872: G15, G16, G34
1875: A16
1877: A4, A14, G8, G63
1878: A47
1879: A10, A26
1880: G71
1881: A6, A10, A63, A68, A71, C8
1882: A9, A28, A66, A73, A84, A87, A100, G11, G77, G82, G86
1883: A15, A38, A41, A42, A53, A66, G93, G101, G107, G120
1884: A11, A15, A27, G5
1885: A9, A11, A12, G50, G53
1886: A11
1888: A1, A8, A8a, C4, G2, G3, G66
1889: A3, A9, A11, A17
1890: A12, G1
1891: A1, A7, C1
1892: C2, G3
1893: C1, G39
1894: A13, G3, G6
1896: G6
1899: A19, G67
1906: A4, A4a, A10, C3, C9, G73
*Evidence taken at Bloemhof before the Commission appointed to investigate the claims of the South African Republic ... to ... the diamond fields* (Cape Town, 1871)
*Cape of Good Hope, Blue Book, 1870–85*
*Griqualand West Government Gazette, 1876–80*
*Statute Law of Griqualand West* (Cape Town, 1882)
*Report of the Government Commission on Native Laws and Customs* (Cape Town, 1883)
*Cape of Good Hope Government Gazette, 1883, 1889*
*Cape of Good Hope Parliamentary Debates, 1884–96*
*Cape of Good Hope, Statistical Register, 1886–1905*

*Union of South Africa Parliamentary Papers*

1913: UG39
1914: UG12, UG37

*British Parliamentary Papers (BPP)*

1871: C459
1872: C508
1873: C732
1875: C1342, C1348
1876: C1399, C1401, C1631
1877: C1681, C1732, C1748, C1814
1879: C2220, C2252, C2260, C2367, C2374, C2454
1880: C2584
1883: C3635
1885: C4587, C4588
1886: C4839, C4889, C4890
1887: C4956, C5238
1888: C5363, C5524
1889: C5620–2
1890: C5897–27, C6200, C6269
1891: C6495
1892: C6829–2
1893–94: C6857–50
1899: C9093
1903: Cd1506
1904: Cd1894, Cd1896, Cd1897
1905: Cd2399, Cd2600
1907: Cd3566
1912–16: Cd6515, Cd7505, Cd7706, Cd7707, Cd8156


NEWSPAPERS

*The Comet and Local Advertiser,* 1897
*The Critic,* 1888
*Daily Independent,* 1880–93
*Diamond Field,* 1870–77
*Diamond Fields Advertiser,* 1878, 1883–85, 1891–94
*The Diamond Fields Express and Griqualand West Mercantile Gazette,*
    1888
*Diamond Fields Herald,* 1885
*The Diamond Fields Mail and Mining and Commercial Advertiser,*
    1888
*The Diamond Fields Mining News,* 1896–97
*The Diamond Fields Times,* 1884–85
*Diamond News,* 1872–80
*The Dutoitspan Herald,* 1882–84

*Economist*, 1888–95

*The Griqualand West Investor's Guardian and Commercial Register,*
  1881

*Independent*, 1875, 1876, 1878

*The Kaffir Express*, August 1874

*Kimberley Colonist and Griqualand Gazette*, 1897

*Kimberley Free Press*, 1897–1907

*Mining Gazette*, 1875

*The South African Citizen*, 1897–98

*The Standard and Diggers News*, 1898

*Tsala Ea Becoana*, 1910


OTHER PUBLICATIONS
(Restricted to items cited in the text or notes.)

Algar, F., *The Diamond Fields with Notes on the Cape Colony and
  Natal* (London, 1872).

Angove, John, *In the Early Days: The Reminiscences of Pioneer Life
  on the South African Diamond Fields* (Kimberley, 1910).

Anon., *The South African Diamond Fields . . . by a Colonist* (London,
  1870).

———, "Two Days at the Diamond-fields: A Social Portrait," *Cape
  Monthly Magazine*, 2d series, 1 (July–Dec. 1870): 239–48.

——— [An Officer of the Royal Engineers], *A Story of a Four-months
  Sojourn in the Diamond Fields of South Africa* (Rangoon, n.d.
  [1871]).

———, "Among the Diamonds: By One Who Has Visited the Fields,"
  *Cape Monthly Magazine*, 2d series, 2 (Jan.–June 1871): 112–27.

———, "The Diamond-fields from a Commercial Point of View," *Cape
  Monthly Magazine*, 2d series, 3 (July–Dec. 1871): 308–10.

——— [W. B. Philip], "The Griquas and Their Exodus," *Cape
  Monthly Magazine*, 2d series, 5 (July–Dec. 1872): 321–37.

———, *Pamphlet Relative to the Concession of the Government of the
  South African Republic in Favour of Messrs Munnick, Posno & Webb
  for the Exclusive Right of Mining for Diamonds and Other Minerals,
  Between the Hart and Vaal Rivers* (Kimberley, 1875).

———, *Prospectuses of the Diamond Mining and Other Companies of
  Kimberley, Du Toit's Pan, Old De Beers, Bultfontein, Jagersfontein,
  and Koffyfontein, etc.* (Kimberley, 1881).

Arnot, David, and F. H. S. Orpen, *The Land Question of Griqualand
  West: An Inquiry into the Various Claims to Land in That Territory,
  Together with a Brief History of the Griqua Nation* (Cape Town,
  1875).

Atmore, Anthony, and Shula Marks, "The Imperial Factor in South Africa in the Nineteenth Century: Towards a Reassessment," *The Journal of Imperial and Commonwealth History*, 3:1 (1974): 105–39.

Babe, Jerome, *The South African Diamond Fields* (facsimile ed., Kimberley, 1976 [1st ed., New York, 1872]).

Barton, D. B., *A History of Tin Mining and Smelting in Cornwall* (Truro, 1967).

———, *Essays in Cornish Mining History* (Truro, 1968), vol. 1.

Beinart, William, "Production and the Material Basis of Chieftainship: Pondoland, c. 1830–1880," in Shula Marks and Anthony Atmore (eds.), *Economy and Society in Pre-Industrial South Africa* (London, 1980), pp. 120–47.

Blainey, Geoffrey, "Lost Causes of the Jameson Raid," *Economic History Review* 18 (1965): 350–66.

Board for the Protection of Mining Interests, *Our Diamond Industry* (Kimberley, 1885).

———, *Returns, Showing Imports into and Exports [of diamonds] from Kimberley . . . [and] Summary for Period September 1st, 1882, to December 31st, 1885* (Kimberley, 1886).

———, *Returns . . . for Year Ended December 31st, 1887, and Summary of Production . . . September 1st, 1882 to December 31st, 1887* (Kimberley, 1888).

———, *Returns . . . for Year Ended December 31st, 1888, with Summary of Production* (Kimberley, 1889).

Boyle, Frederick, *To the Cape for Diamonds: A Story of Digging Experiences in South Africa* (London, 1873).

Bryce, James, *Impressions of South Africa* (London, 1897).

Bundy, Colin, *The Rise and Fall of the South African Peasantry* (Berkeley, 1979).

———, "Peasants in Herschel: A Case Study of a South African Frontier District," in Shula Marks and Anthony Atmore (eds.), *Economy and Society in Pre-industrial South Africa* (London, 1980), pp. 208–25.

Burawoy, Michael, *Manufacturing Consent: Changes in the Labor Process under Monopoly Capitalism* (Chicago, 1979).

Burton, Richard, *Explorations of the Highlands of the Brazil . . .* (London, 1869), 2 vols.

Chandler, Alfred, "The Beginnings of 'Big Business' in American Industry," *Business History Review* 33:1 (1959): 1–31.

———, *The Visible Hand: The Managerial Revolution in American Business* (Cambridge, 1977).

Chapman, Charles, *A Voyage from Southampton to Cape Town . . .*

*Also a Description and Illustration of the Diamond Fields . . .* (London, 1872).

Chilvers, Hedley, *The Story of De Beers* (London, 1939).

Cohen, Louis, *Reminiscences of Kimberley* (London, 1911).

Collins, Wilkie, *The Moonstone* (Oxford, 1982 [1st ed., London, 1868]).

Cope, R. L., "Strategic and Socio-economic Explanations for Carnarvon's South African Confederation Policy: The Historiography and the Evidence," *History in Africa*, 13 (1986): 13–34.

Cottrell, P. L., *British Overseas Investment in the Nineteenth Century* (London, 1975).

Cronwright-Schreiner, S. C., *Some Vital Facts about Kimberley and Johannesburg for Working-men and Friends of the Native* (n. p., n. d. [Johannesburg, 1900]).

Crookes, William, *Diamonds* (London, 1909).

Currey, J. B., "The Diamond Fields of Griqualand West and Their Probable Influence on the Native Races of South Africa," *Journal of the Society of Arts* 24 (17 March 1876): 372–81.

Davenport, T. R. H., *The Afrikaner Bond: The History of a South African Political Party, 1880–1911* (Cape Town, 1966).

De Beers Consolidated Mines Limited, *Annual Reports*, 1889–1910.

De Kiewiet, C. W., *British Colonial Policy and the South African Republics, 1848–1872* (London, 1929).

———, *The Imperial Factor in South Africa: A Study in Politics and Economics* (London, 1941).

De Kock, W. J. (ed.), *Dictionary of South African Biography* (Cape Town, 1972), vol. 2.

Delius, Peter, "Migrant Labour and the Pedi before 1869," *Societies of Southern Africa* 7 (1977): 41–47.

———, "Migrant Labour and the Pedi, 1840–80," in Shula Marks and Anthony Atmore (eds.), *Economy and Society in Pre-Industrial South Africa* (London, 1980), pp. 293–312.

———, *The Land Belongs to Us: The Pedi Polity, the Boers and the British in the Nineteenth-Century Transvaal* (Johannesburg, 1983).

De Launay, Louis, *Les diamants du Cap* (Paris, 1897).

Dobb, Maurice, *Studies in the Development of Capitalism* (New York, 1963 [1st ed., London, 1947]).

Epstein, Edward, *The Diamond Invention* (London, 1982).

Etherington, Norman, *Preachers, Peasants and Politics: Southeast Africa, 1835–1880: African Christian Communities in Natal, Pondoland and Zululand* (London, 1878).

———, "Labour Supply and the Genesis of South African Confederation in the 1870s," *Journal of African History* 20:2 (1979): 235–53.

Farini, Gilarmi, *Through the Kalahari Desert* (London, 1886).

"Fossor," *Twelve Months at the South African Diamond Fields* (London, 1872).

Foster, John, *Class Struggle and the Industrial Revolution: Early Industrial Capitalism in Three English Towns* (London, 1974).

Frankel, S. H., *Capital Investment in Africa: Its Course and Effects* (London, 1938).

Galbraith, J. S., *Crown and Charter: The Early Years of the British South Africa Company* (Berkeley, 1974).

Germond, Robert, *Chronicles of Basutoland* (Morija, 1967).

Gregory, Theodore, *Ernest Oppenheimer and the Economic Development of Southern Africa* (Cape Town, 1962).

Guy, J. J., *The Destruction of the Zulu Kingdom: The Civil War in Zululand, 1879–1884* (London, 1980).

Harries, Patrick, "Labour Migration from the Delagoa Bay Hinterland to South Africa," *Societies of Southern Africa* (London, 1977), vol. 7, 61–76.

————, "Slavery, Social Incorporation and Surplus Extraction: The Nature of Free and Unfree Labour in South-east Africa," *Journal of African History* 22:3 (1981): 309–30.

————, "Kinship, Ideology and the Nature of Pre-colonial Labour Migration from the Delagoa Bay Hinterland to South Africa up to 1895," in Shula Marks and Richard Rathbone (eds.), *Industrialization and Social Change in South Africa. . . .* (London, 1982), pp. 142–66.

Harris, Marvin, "Labour Emigration among the Mocambique Thonga: Cultural and Political Factors," *Africa* 29:1 (1959): 50–65.

Hay, Douglas, et al. (eds.), *Albion's Fatal Tree: Crime and Society in Eighteenth-Century England* (New York, 1975).

Henderson, R. H., *An Ulsterman in Africa* (Cape Town, 1944).

Henry, James, *The First Hundred Years of the Standard Bank* (London, 1963).

Hofmeyr, J. H., *The Life of Jan Hendrik Hofmeyr (Onze Jan)* (Cape Town, 1913).

Hornsby, A. H., *The South African Diamond Fields* (Chicago, 1874).

Houghton, D. H., "Economic Development, 1865–1965," in Monica Wilson and Leonard Thompson (eds.), *The Oxford History of South Africa* (New York, 1969), vol. 1, pp. 1–48.

Hunt, D. R., "An Account of the Bapedi," *Bantu Studies* 5 (1931): 275–326.

Innes, Duncan, *Anglo American and the Rise of Modern South Africa* (New York, 1984).

Jeeves, Alan, "The Control of Migratory Labour on the South African Gold Mines in the Era of Kruger and Milner," *Journal of Southern African Studies* 2:1 (1975): 3–29.

Johnstone, Frederick, *Class, Race and Gold: A Study of Class Relations and Race Discrimination in South Africa* (London, 1976).

Jones, Gareth Stedman, *Outcast London: A Study in the Relationship Between Classes in Victorian Society* (Oxford, 1971).

Kallaway, Peter, "Labour in the Kimberley Diamond Fields," *South African Labour Bulletin* 1:7 (November 1974): 52–61.

Kimble, Judith, "Labour Migration in Basutoland, c. 1870–1885," in Shula Marks and Richard Rathbone (eds.), *Industrialization and Social Change in South Africa.* . . . (London, 1982), pp. 119–41.

King, C. W., *The Natural History of Precious Stones and of the Precious Metals* (London, 1870 [1st ed., 1867]).

Knights of Labour, *Manifesto of the Knights of Labour of South Africa* (Kimberley, 1892).

Lenzen, Godehard, *The History of Diamond Production and the Diamond Trade* (London, 1970).

Leslie, David, *Among the Zulus and Amatongas* (Edinburgh, 1875).

Lewsen, Phyllis (ed.), *Selections from the Correspondence of J. X. Merriman* (Cape Town, 1960, 1963, 1966, 1969), 4 vols.

———, *John X. Merriman: Paradoxical South African Statesman* (New Haven, 1982).

*List of Persons Residing in the Electoral Division of Kimberley Whose Names Have Been Registered in the Year 1887.* . . . (Cape Town, 1888).

Lockhart, J. G., and C. M. Woodhouse, *Rhodes* (London, 1963).

Macdonagh, Oliver, "Coal Mines Regulation: The First Decade, 1842–1852," in Robert Robson (ed.), *Ideas and Institutions of Victorian Britain: Essays in Honour of George Kitson Clark* (London, 1967), pp. 58–86.

McGill, Douglas, *A History of Koffiefontein: Town and Mine, 1870 to 1902* (privately printed, 1976).

Marais, J. S., *The Cape Coloured People, 1652–1937* (Johannesburg, 1957 [1st ed., 1939]).

Marks, Shula, and Stanley Trapido, "Lord Milner and the South African State," *History Workshop* 8 (1979): 50–80.

———, and Anthony Atmore (eds.), *Economy and Society in Pre-Industrial South Africa* (London, 1980).

———, and Richard Rathbone (eds.), *Industrialization and Social Change in South Africa: African Class Formation, Culture and Consciousness 1870–1930* (London, 1982).

Matthews, J. W., *Incwadi Yami; Or, Twenty Years' Personal Experience in South Africa* (London, 1887).

Matthews, Z. K., *Freedom for My People: The Autobiography of Z. K. Matthews: Southern Africa, 1901 to 1968* (London, 1981).

Mawe, John, *Travels in the Interior of Brazil* (Boston, 1816).

*Men of the Times: Transvaal* (Johannesburg, 1905).

Mendelsohn, Richard, "Blainey and the Jameson Raid: The Debate Renewed," *Journal of Southern African Studies* 6:2 (1980): 157–70.

Michell, Lewis, *The Life and Times of the Right Honourable Cecil John Rhodes, 1853–1902* (New York, 1910).

Millin, Sarah Gertrude, *The Dark River* (London, 1919).

——, *The Night Is Long* (London, 1941).

Mitchell, Henry, *Diamonds and Gold of South Africa* (London, 1888).

Mönnig, H. O., *The Pedi* (Pretoria, 1967).

Morton, William, *South African Diamond Fields, and the Journey to the Mines* (New York, 1877).

Moulle, M. A., *Mémoir sur la géologie générale et sur les mines de diamants de l'Afrique du Sud* (Paris, 1886).

Murray, Colin, *Families Divided: The Impact of Migrant Labour in Lesotho* (Cambridge, 1981).

Myburgh, A. C., *Native Names of Industrial Addresses* (Pretoria, 1948).

Newbury, Colin, "Out of the Pit: The Capital Accumulation of Cecil Rhodes," *The Journal of Imperial and Commonwealth History* 10:1 (1981): 25–49.

Newitt, Malyn, "Migrant Labour and the Development of Mozambique," *Societies of Southern Africa* 4 (1974): 67–76.

Palmer, Robin, and Neil Parsons (eds.), *The Roots of Rural Poverty in Central and Southern Africa* (London, 1977).

Parsons, Neil, "The Economic History of Khama's Country in Botswana, 1844–1930," in Robin Palmer and Neil Parsons (eds.), *The Roots of Rural Poverty in Central and Southern Africa* (London, 1977), pp. 113–43.

Payne, P. L., "The Emergence of the Large-scale Company in Great Britain, 1870–1914," *Economic History Review* 20:3 (1967): 519–42.

Payton, C. A., *The Diamond Diggings of South Africa* (London, 1872).

Ranger, Terence, *Revolt in Southern Rhodesia* (London, 1967).

*Regulations of the Borough of Kimberley* (Kimberley, 1893).

Reunert, Theodore, *Diamonds and Gold in South Africa* (London, 1893).

Roberts, Brian, *The Diamond Magnates* (New York, 1972).

————, *Kimberley: Turbulent City* (Cape Town, 1976).

Robertson, Marian, *Diamond Fever: South African Diamond History, 1866–69, from Primary Sources* (Cape Town, 1974).

Robinson, John (ed.), *Notes on Natal: An Old Colonist's Book for New Settlers* (London, 1872).

Ross, Robert, *Adam Kok's Griquas: A Study in the Development of Stratification in South Africa* (Cambridge, 1978).

Rouillard, Nancy (ed.), *Matabele Thompson: An Autobiography* (London, 1936).

*Rules and Regulations Framed by the Committee of Management of the Jagersfontein Diggings* (Bloemfontein, 1879).

*Rules of the Artisans' and Engine Drivers' Protection Society* (Kimberley, 1883).

Samuel, Raphael (ed.), *Miners, Quarrymen and Saltworkers* (London, 1977).

Sauer, Hans, *Ex Africa* (London, 1937).

Shillington, Kevin, "The Impact of the Diamond Discoveries on the Kimberley Hinterland: Class Formation, Colonialism and Resistance among the Tlhaping of Griqualand West in the 1870s," in Shula Marks and Richard Rathbone (eds.), *Industrialization and Social Change in South Africa. . . .* (London, 1982), pp. 99–118.

Silver, S. W. & Co., *Handbook to South Africa. . . .* (London, 1872, 1880, 1891 eds.).

Smalberger, John, "I.D.B. and the Mining Compound System in the 1880s," *The South African Journal of Economics* 42:4 (1974): 398–414.

————, "The Role of the Diamond-mining Industry in the Development of the Pass-law System in South Africa," *International Journal of African Historical Studies* 9:3 (1976): 419–34.

Smithers, Elsa, *March Hare* (London, 1935).

Statham, F. R., *Mr Magnus* (London, 1896).

Steytler, J. G., *The Diamond-fields of South Africa . . . the Immigrant's Guide* (Cape Town, 1870).

Stow, George, "Griqualand West," *Cape Monthly Magazine*, 2d series, 5 (July–Dec. 1872): 65–78.

Strauss, Teresa, *War along the Orange: The Korana and the Northern Border Wars of 1868–69 and 1878–79* (Cape Town, 1979).

Streeter, E. W., *The Great Diamonds of the World* (London, 1882).

Sutton, I. B., "The Diggers' Revolt in Griqualand West, 1875," *International Journal of African Historical Studies* 12:1 (1979): 40–61.

Tavernier, Jean B., *Travels in India by Jean Baptiste Tavernier*, trans. from French ed. 1676 by V. Ball (London, 1889), 2 vols.

Thompson, Leonard, "Cooperation and Conflict: The Zulu Kingdom and Natal," and "Cooperation and Conflict: The High Veld," in Monica Wilson and Leonard Thompson (eds.), *The Oxford History of South Africa* (Oxford, 1969), vol. 1, pp. 334–90, 391–446.

————, "The Subjugation of the African Chiefdoms, 1870–1898," and "Great Britain and the Afrikaner Republics, 1870–1899," in *The Oxford History of South Africa* (Oxford, 1971), vol. 2, pp. 245–86, 289–324.

————, *Survival in Two Worlds: Moshoeshoe of Lesotho, 1786–1870* (Oxford, 1975).

Trollope, Anthony, *South Africa* (London, 1878), 2 vols.

*Turner's Kimberley, Old De Beers, Dutoitspan, Bultfontein and Barkly Directory and Guide* (Kimberley, 1878).

Turrell, Robert, "The 1875 Black Flag Revolt on the Kimberley Diamond Fields," *Journal of Southern African Studies* 7:2 (1981): 194–235.

————, "Rhodes, De Beers and Monopoly," *The Journal of Imperial and Commonwealth History* 10:3 (1982): 310–43.

————, "Kimberley: Labour and Compounds, 1871–1888," in Shula Marks and Richard Rathbone (eds.), *Industrialization and Social Change in South Africa*. . . . (London, 1982), pp. 45–76.

————, "Kimberley's Model Compounds," *Journal of African History* 25:1 (1984): 59–75.

Tyamzashe, Gwayi, "Life at the Diamond Fields, August 1874" (orig. pub. in the *Kaffir Express*, 1 August 1874), repr. in Frances Wilson and Dominique Perrot (eds.), *Outlook on a Century* (Lovedale, 1972), pp. 19–21.

Van der Horst, Sheila, *Native Labour in South Africa* (London, 1942).

Van der Poel, Jean, *Railway and Customs Policies in South Africa, 1885–1910* (London, 1933).

Van Onselen, Charles, *Chibaro: African Mine Labour in Southern Rhodesia, 1900–1933* (London, 1976).

————, *Studies in the Social and Economic History of the Witwatersrand: New Ninevah, New Babylon* (London, 1982), 2 vols.

Vickers, H. J., *Griqualand West: Its Area, Population, Commerce and General Statistics* (Kimberley, 1879).

"Vindex" [F. Vershoyle], *Cecil Rhodes: His Political Life and Speeches, 1881–1900* (London, 1900).

Wagner, Percy, *The Diamond Fields of Southern Africa* (Johannesburg, 1914).

Wagner, Roger, "Zoutpansberg: The Dynamics of a Hunting Frontier, 1848–67," in Shula Marks and Anthony Atmore (eds.), *Economy and Society in Pre-Industrial South Africa* (London, 1980), pp. 293–312.

Warwick, Peter (ed.), *The South African War: The Anglo-Boer War, 1899–1902* (London, 1980).

Weakley, George, *The Diamond Discovery in South Africa* (Colesberg, 1869).

Wesleyan Methodist Church of South Africa, *Eleventh Report of the South African Missionary Society* (Cape Town, 1893).

Wheatcroft, Geoffrey, *The Randlords: The Exploits and Exploitations of South Africa's Mining Magnates* (New York, 1986).

Willan, Brian, "Sol Plaatje, De Beers and an Old Tram Shed: Class Relations and Social Control in a South African Town, 1918–1919," *Journal of Southern African Studies* 4:2 (1978): 195–215.

———, "An African in Kimberley: Sol T. Plaatje, 1894–1898," in Shula Marks and Richard Rathbone (eds.), *Industrialization and Social Change in South Africa. . . .* (London, 1982), pp. 238–58.

———, *Sol Plaatje: South African Nationalist, 1876–1932* (Berkeley, 1984).

Williams, Alpheus, *Some Dreams Come True* (Wynberg, n. d. [1948]).

———, *The Genesis of the Diamond* (London, 1932).

Williams, Basil, *Cecil Rhodes* (London, 1921).

Williams, Gardner, *The Diamond Mines of South Africa* (New York, 1905 [1st ed. 1902]), 2 vols.

Wilson, Francis, *Labour in the South African Gold Mines, 1911–1969* (Cambridge, 1972).

Witwatersrand Chamber of Mines, *First Annual Report [for 1889]* (Johannesburg, 1890).

———, *Seventh Annual Report for the Year Ending 31st December 1895* (Johannesburg, 1896).

Worger, William, "Workers as Criminals: The Rule of Law in Early Kimberley, 1870–1885," in Frederick Cooper (ed.), *Struggle for the City: Migrant Labor, Capital and the State in Urban Africa* (Beverly Hills, 1983), pp. 51–90.

Young, Sherilynn, "Fertility and Famine: Women's Agriculture in Southern Mozambique," in Robin Palmer and Neil Parsons (eds.), *The Roots of Rural Poverty in Central and Southern Africa* (London, 1977), pp. 66–81.


UNPUBLISHED DISSERTATIONS AND MANUSCRIPTS

Ginsberg, David, "The Formation of an African Migrant Labour Force on the Diamond Fields, 1867–1900" (Oxford University workshop, 1974).

Kallaway, Peter, "Preliminary Notes towards a Study of Labour on the Diamond Fields of Griqualand West" (MS, 1974).

————, "Black Responses to an Industrializing Economy: 'Labour Shortage' and 'Native Policy' in Griqualand West 1870–1900" (MS, 1976).

————, "Class Formation, Culture and Consciousness: The Making of Modern South Africa" (MS, 1980).

Minott, L., "Sir Richard Southey, Lieutenant-Governor of Griqualand West, 1872–1875" (MA, University of Cape Town, 1973).

Purkis, A. J., "The Politics, Capital and Labour of Railway-Building in the Cape Colony, 1870–1885" (PhD, Oxford University, 1978).

Shillington, Kevin, "Economic Change among the Tlhaping" (MS, 1977).

Sieborger, Robert, "The Recruitment and Organization of African Labour for the Kimberley Diamond Mines, 1871–1888" (MA, Rhodes University, 1975).

Smalberger, John, "Mrs Help's Zulus and the Politics of Confederation: Southey, Barkly and the Colonial Office, 1872–1876" (MS, n. d.).

Sutton, I. B., "The 1878 Rebellion in Griqualand West and Adjacent Territories" (PhD, University of London, 1975).

Ticktin, David, "The Origins of the South African Labour Party, 1888–1910" (PhD, University of Cape Town, 1973).

Turrell, Robert, "Gonivas: Kimberley and Beaconsfield in the 1880s" (MS, n. d. [1978?]).

————, "Kimberley: Labour and Compounds, 1871–1888" (MS, n. d. [1979?]).

————, "Capital, Class, and Monopoly: The Kimberley Diamond Fields, 1871–1889" (PhD, London University, 1982).

Willan, Brian, "An African in Kimberley: Sol T. Plaatje, 1894–98" (MS, n. d. [1977?]).

Worger, William, "The Worker as Criminal: The Rule of Law in Early Kimberley" (seminar paper, Southern Africa Research Program, Yale University, 1979).

————, "White Mine Workers, Economic Struggle and Labour Consciousness in Kimberley, 1874–84" (seminar paper, Southern Africa Research Program, Yale University, 1980).

————, "White Mine Workers, Commercial Men, Monopoly Capitalists and Political Struggle, 1885–1888" (seminar paper, Southern Africa Research Program, Yale University, 1981).

————, "Kimberley: Company Town, 1888–95" (seminar paper, Southern Africa Research Program, Yale University, 1981).

————, "The Making of a Monopoly: Kimberley and the South African Diamond Industry, 1870–95" (PhD, Yale University, 1982).

# Index